American Church History

American Church History
A Reader

Henry Warner Bowden
and
P. C. Kemeny,
editors

Abingdon Press
Nashville

AMERICAN CHURCH HISTORY: A READER

Copyright © 1998 by Abingdon Press

This book is printed on elemental-chlorine–free paper.

Library of Congress Cataloging-in-Publication Data

American church history : a reader / Henry Warner Bowden and
    P.C. Kemeny, editors.
    p.   cm.
  Includes bibliographical references and index.
  ISBN 0-687-02544-3
    1. United States—Church history. I. Bowden, Henry Warner.
II. Kemeny, Paul Charles.
  BR515.A49 1998
  277.3—dc21   98-38367
                                                                     CIP

Scripture quotations noted KJV are from the King James Version of the Bible.

Scripture quotations noted RSV are from the Revised Standard Version of the Bible, copyright 1946, 1952, 1971 by the Division of Christian Education of the National Council of the Churches of Christ in the USA. Used by permission.

These essays appeared previously in unedited and unabridged form in the journal *Church History* and appear here with the kind permission of the American Society of Church History.

98 99 00 01 02 03 04 05 06 07—10 9 8 7 6 5 4 3 2 1

MANUFACTURED IN THE UNITED STATES OF AMERICA

To

Warner Hill Bowden

and

William Albert Kemeny

CONTENTS

GENERAL INTRODUCTION

Consideration of Essays in Historical Context and Current Scholarship

For more than a century the American Society of Church History has generated important religious scholarship in this country. It has advanced our knowledge of a variety of topics in all different time periods, but this has been especially true regarding studies of religion in American culture. This edited volume collects and presents some of the best essays that have appeared in this forum for the creative study of American themes.

Studies in American religion have gone through several stages, reflecting the intellectual climates of opinion during which they were written. The earliest publications were usually accounts of a single denomination, issued to reassure adherents that their church was the correct one and simultaneously to answer criticism from outsiders. Such apologetic literature was about all that existed in the early 1800s, showing that denominational rivalry and concern for legitimizing ecclesiastical preferences were strong factors in the early national period. In the second half of the nineteenth century a more ecumenical perspective replaced parochialism, at least among Protestants who dominated the religious scene. Denominational identity became less important as a more generalized pan-Protestantism presumed to define American culture, assuming to embody common values in opposition to an increasing number of immigrant Catholics and Jews.

By the early decades of the twentieth century another major development occurred in American church history: it became professionalized. Some denominational champions continued to write self-centered narratives, as did those who wanted to dominate American culture according to their own standards. But alongside those religiously oriented publications the ideal of writing factual, objective history began to emerge. Scholars in universities and seminaries aspired to write "scientific" history, unaffected by prior assumptions, unbiased by personal interests, and unafraid to let the facts speak for themselves. By the late 1920s this pervasive intellectual outlook had moved serious religion studies from ecclesiastical circles to academic circles.

Scientific history was a magnificent ideal, but it remained only that, a vision impossible to attain. Scholars soon admitted that they could not eliminate all preconceptions from their investigations and that their conclusions were influenced to some degree by subjective elements. Historians of American religion, as well as colleagues interested in more secular topics, recognized that their work was a blend of personal insights and procedures of strictest accuracy regarding past events. When the American Society of Church History published the first issue of its journal, *Church History*, in March of 1932, American religion studies had reached a plateau of sophisticated self-understanding and impressive attainments. From there, historians have developed a variety of perspectives which will enliven the readings in this book.

One of the themes that has attracted scholarly attention over the decades is the importance of religion in American life. Explorers, missionaries, and colonists brought strong religious convictions with them, and they molded societies with their faiths. National independence and territorial expansion saw no diminution of religion interacting with other cultural elements. Sydney Ahlstrom starts our consideration of this theme in part 1, probing for relationships between religious impulses and nationalist perceptions. Highlighting Puritan influences more than others, he traces ideas about this country as God's chosen nation to that theological tradition. Sidney Mead agrees that religious influences made Americans think of themselves as special, but he locates the primary cause in a different source. In his view the Enlightenment was more central than Puritanism. He also mentions ethnic diversity and the wilderness frontier as additional interpretive themes in national development. Neither historical view celebrates spread-eagle chauvinism but suggests rather a humble sense of destiny under divine judgment. We do not have to choose between Puritans and Rationalists as a single source of national character. What we should do is take each argument seriously and then reach our own conclusions after careful thought.

Robert Handy introduces a third topic that organizes religious history under a broad category: the manifold efforts to Christianize America. Citizens have long felt that our country has received supernatural blessings, and so they have tried to make general culture conform to that exalted status. The irony is that, as Handy points out, secular concerns have affected religious standards more than evangelism has transformed larger cultural priorities. Immigration is another perennial theme in American history. Jay Dolan argues effectively for its importance and demonstrates the fascination we find in learning about where people came from, how they fared in the new land, and what roles their faiths played in those experiences. Five hundred years have not ended the relevance of this interpretive theme in American life.

Though immigrants continued to arrive, most colonies had settled into comfortable routines by the eighteenth century. A fairly homogenous agrarian-capitalist economy and an Anglo-Saxon population constituted most settlements, no matter how they differed in coinage, weights and measures, or legal practices. Frank Lambert presents a theme that touches on the beginnings of colonial solidarity and eventual national union. This basic theme is revivalism, and it too furnishes a common denominator that covers much American religious experience through the generations. Lambert concentrates on George Whitefield, the first truly famous international evangelist. And while showing how Whitefield united colonists from different regions by emphasizing shared spiritual concerns, he also shows how revivalism slowly became a constant as Americans used religious elements to bolster united efforts in other walks of life. Leigh Schmidt brings an important but often neglected theme to our attention. Quite often people choose to belong to churches, prefer beliefs, or act according to different codes because of factors that have little to do with theology or the Bible. Matters of personal etiquette and cultural taste often determine religious identities, and Schmidt takes us through an informative survey of a way in which this happens.

Part 2 offers us a more focused set of readings, one that concentrates on something absolutely basic to American life: the great diversity of peoples who make up our country. Martin Marty starts off by showing the different ways in which groups have regarded their ethnicity. Sometimes embarrassed, sometimes proud, minority group identity remains a significant factor in American religious life, whatever the current attitude regarding it. Timothy Smith demonstrates this with a survey of different groups in Ohio during the early national period. His inclusive coverage of ethnic and denominational groups shows how pluralism produced mutual acceptance among diverse associations. C. C. Goen reminds us that regionalism is another kind of group differentiation. The American population has segmented into regions according to varying geographical, economic, and social conditions. Alienation between North and South has been the most intransigent of all such internal divisions, and Goen shows how religion served to justify and perpetuate this pervasive separatism.

African Americans were one of the ethnic groups caught in that regional conflict which finally resulted in civil war. Drained of native identity by forced importation and slavery, they sought their own self-understanding, especially during the late nineteenth century. Laurie Maffly-Kipp highlights several of the leading thinkers of that day and shows how they constructed group self-awareness with sacred and secular materials. Warren Platt furnishes a similar study by tracing the emergence of a new church based on ethnic consciousness. Of all the many kinds of Roman Catholics stemming from European origins, only one group has used ethnic identity to justify separating from the parent organization. Some Polish immigrants set up a rival social-ecclesial-theological platform for independent existence, and Platt clarifies the process. Finally, instead of treating large cultural forces, Mary Brown looks at one priest in a single parish to tell us about America. She simply takes for granted that people associate with their own kind; then she informs us about life in an Italian neighborhood and how religion permeated day to day activities there.

Part 3 brings us to intellectual history. Here we can study what people thought rather than how they associated together—though the two categories are often connected. Conrad Cherry begins with an analysis of an important concept in Puritan thought, giving us only a glimpse of the enormous mental energy in that formidable religious tradition. Sydney Ahlstrom provides a useful introduction to the school of thought called Scottish Realism and then shows how it remained important during several epochs of American thought. On a less expansive scale Timothy Smith chronicles the emergence of African American ideas regarding Christian redemption and human slavery. He uncovers and articulates the theological essentials which these little-known thinkers have used in their religious expressions for more than a century. Jacob Dorn informs us about intellectual ferment regarding another set of questions. When urban problems caused many clergy to seek social reforms, it became necessary to distinguish between secular impulses and those derived from biblical sources. Dorn's discussion of three eminent Social Gospel leaders clarifies matters along those lines.

Scott Appleby turns our attention to a more enduring problem, in this case, how one can reconcile traditional religious ideas with new ones generated by modern science. His account of one such episode is as instructive as it is sad. David Lindberg and Ronald Numbers pair up to lead us through centuries of such controversies. They are most useful in disproving the old chestnut that talks about religion and science as if they have always been enemies. They also shed light on scientific thought among church leaders at significant moments of intellectual change, thus affording us the most valuable product of any historical study: a combination of insight and perspective. Margaret Bendroth refers to ideas of yet another sort, pointing to an interplay between vaguely defined prejudice and the clear-cut ideas used to counteract it. Her exposé of religious convictions that reinforce male chauvinism is informative.

Part 4 honors the notion that several features of American religious life are actually more representative than others. There is a dominant pattern that has characterized the great bulk of this country's citizens during our history. Sidney Mead reminds us that religious liberty has become one such distinguishing feature in American life, and his important survey helps us understand the early formation of this pervasive cultural pattern. Catherine Albanese takes a different tack by questioning what has been called "mainstream" religion and how future emphases might transform previous ones. Ann White looks at the traditional American commitment to missionary activity and at equally wide-spread convictions about the secondary status of women. The combination of those powerful forces educates us further about the general emphases that have affected most people.

Nathan Hatch challenges us to think of a denomination more representative in American culture than Methodism. He shows how it has embodied central cultural traits found among most citizens over the past two hundred years. Methodists could very well serve, he argues, as the epitome of what is most basic and wholesome about religion in this country. James Moorhead focuses on a single idea, or perspective, that was shared by a large segment of the population for centuries. Millennialism was a powerful ingredient in forging an identity that gave cosmic significance to the entire nation, and Moorhead's careful definitions help explain the force behind such widespread convictions. Thomas Tweed, on the other hand, uses a small setting rather than a large one to illustrate how "mainstream" religion tries to set the standards in a geographical locale. His chronicle of changes in early Miami is a test tube demonstration of American religious evolution. Finally, Bill Leonard points out how mainstream religious mentality emerges without becoming conscious of it. His acute observations on sectarian activity enable us to watch outsiders as they become part of the power structure, even when they do not recognize it themselves.

Part 5 explores the notion that there have always been important religious expressions in American life not represented by the majority. This section examines some of the *old* New Religious Movements. One of the most brilliant dissident voices in one of the most authoritarian settings was Anne Hutchinson, and Marilyn Westerkamp provides us with a scintillating exhibit of what was at stake in that early colonial confrontation. Norman Murdoch looks at another female leader whose quiet determination and steady example helped legitimize the growing conviction that women have equal rights in religious matters. Mario DePillis introduces us to Mormons, a distinctive and self-contained fixture in the kaleidoscope of American religions. His treatment of the group's nurturing forces shows how it survived, grew, and yet remained apart from mainstream denominationalism. Jonathan Butler describes the Adventist movement, a part of millennialist expectations with different emphases that constitute a significant alternative to everyday church participation. Catherine Albanese touches on marginal groups which have sought unconventional answers to conventional questions. She explores several perspectives and brings us to the threshold of Christian Science. Finally, Joel Carpenter's essay performs much the same function here as did Bill Leonard's in the previous section. He furnishes us with the essential details of fundamentalism survival. By explaining how this minority viewpoint is gathering institutional strength, his summary leaves us wondering what is an alternative religious position and what really is in the mainstream.

The following essays represent a rich variety of topics and interpretive perspectives for the study of religion in American history. They have been edited with the intention of retaining the gist of each presentation while keeping them short in order to include as many as possible. For those who wish to read the full text of any article as it was originally published, references are cited at the end of each introductory statement.

FOR FURTHER READING

General Survey Textbooks

Ahlstrom, Sydney E. *A Religious History of the American People*, New Haven, 1972.

Albanese, Catherine L. *America: Religions and Religion*, Belmont, CA, 1992.

Bednarowski, Mary Farrell. *American Religion: A Cultural Perspective*. Englewood Cliffs, NJ, 1984.

Carmody, Denise Lardner, and John Tully Carmody. *Exploring American Religion*, Mountain View, CA, 1990.

Corbett, Julia Mitchell. *Religion in America*, 3d ed. Englewood Cliffs, NJ, 1997.

Dolan, Jay P. *The American Catholic Experience*, Garden City, NY, 1985.

Handy, Robert T. *A Christian America: Protestant Hopes and Historical Realities*, 2d ed., New York, 1984.

————. *A History of the Churches in the United States and Canada*, New York, 1976.

Gaustad, Edwin Scott. *A Religious History of America*, 2d ed., San Francisco, 1990.

Glazer, Nathan. *American Judaism*, rev. ed., Chicago, 1972.

Hennesey, James T. *American Catholics: A History of the Roman Catholic Community in the United States*, New York, 1981.

Hudson, Winthrop S., and John Corrigan, *Religion in America*, 5th ed., New York, 1992.

Lincoln, C. Eric, and Lawrence H. Mamiya, *The Black Church in the African-American Experience*, Durham, NC, 1990.

Marsden, George M. *Religion and American Culture*, San Diego, 1990.

Marty, Martin E. *Pilgrims in Their Own Land: Five Hundred Years of Religion in America*, Boston, 1984.

————. *Protestantism in the United States: Righteous Empire*, 2d ed., New York, 1986.

Noll, Mark A. *A History of Christianity in the United States and Canada*, Grand Rapids, MI, 1992.

Sarna, Jonathan, ed. *The American Jewish Experience*, New York, 1986.

Tweed, Thomas A., ed. *Retelling U. S. Religious History*, Berkeley, 1997.

Wentz, Richard E. *Religion in the New World: The Shaping of Religious Traditions in the United States*, Minneapolis, 1990.

William, Peter, W. *America's Religions: Traditions and Cultures*, New York, 1990.

————. *Popular Religion in America: Symbolic Change and the Modernization Process in Historical Perspective*, Urbana, IL, 1989.

Primary Sources

Carey, Patrick W., ed. *American Catholic Religious Thought*. New York, 1987.

Ellis, John Tracy, ed. *Documents of American Catholic History*, Milwaukee, 1962.

Gaustad, Edwin Scott, ed. *A Documentary History of Religion in America*, 2 vols. Grand Rapids, MI, 1982–1983.

Hardman, Keith J., ed. *Issues in American Christianity: Primary Sources with Introductions*, Grand Rapids, MI, 1993.

Ruether, Rosemary Radford, and Rosemary Skinner Keller, eds. *Women and Religion in America*, 3 vols., San Francisco, 1981–1986.

Sermett, Milton C., ed. *Afro-American Religious History: A Documentary Witness*, Durham, NC, 1985.

Smith, H. Shelton, Robert T. Handy, and Lefferts Loetscher, eds. *American Christianity: An Historical Interpretation with Representative Documents*. 2 vols., New York, 1960.

Wilson, John F., and Donald L. Drakeman, eds. *Church and State in American History*, 2d ed. Boston, 1987.

Reference Works

Gaustad, Edwin Scott, and Philip L. Barlow, eds. *Historical Atlas of Religion in America*, 3d ed., New York, 1998.

Glazier, Michael, and Thomas J. Shelley, eds. *Encyclopedia of American Catholic History*, Collegeville, MN, 1997.

Lippy, Charles H., and Peter W. Williams, eds., *Encyclopedia of the American Religious Experience*, 3 vols., New York, 1988.

Melton, J. Gordon. *Encyclopedia of American Religions*, 5th ed., Detroit, 1996.

Reid, Daniel G., Robert D. Linder, Bruce L. Shelley, and Harry S. Stout, eds. *Dictionary of Christianity in America*, Downers Grove, IL, 1990.

Wilson, John F., ed. *Church and State in America: A Bibliographical Guide*, 2 vols., New York, 1986–1987.

Periodicals

The most efficient guide to access scholarly articles and chapters in multiauthor works are *Religion Index One: Periodicals; A Subject Index to Periodical Literature, Including an Author Index with Abstracts, and a Book*

Review Index, Evanston, IL: American Theological Library Association, 1949– ; and *Religion Index Two: Multi-Author Works*, Evanston, IL: American Theological Library Association, 1976– . *Religion Index One* is published semiannually with biennial cumulation and *Religion Index Two* is published annually. The databases for Religion Index One and Two are available for online computer search and on CD-ROM.

In addition, James E. Bradley and Richard A. Muller, *Church History: An Introduction to Research, Reference Works, and Methods*, Grand Rapids, 1995, provides an exhaustive bibliography of reference works, research tools, online, and computer databases on CD-ROM.

Web Sites

Several web sites provide links to a wealth of information on the history of Christianity in America in particular and American religious history in general.

Boston University School of Theology, Christian Resources,
<http://www.bu.edu/STH/Library/christian.html>

Center for the Study of American Religion, Princeton University,
<http://www.princeton.edu/~nadelman/csar/csar.html>

Institute for the Study of American Evangelicals, Wheaton College,
<http://www.wheaton.edu/bgc/isae>

Vanderbilt University Divinity School Library,
<http://divinity.lib.vanderbilt.edu/HomePage>

West Virginia University, American Religion Links,
<http://www.ece.wvu.edu/~bkt/link.htm>

PART I

Religion and Culture

INTRODUCTION TO ESSAY 1

During the 1950s there was considerable debate over the question of "American character": what it was and what had made it so. Many thought that American culture was distinctive in its basic traits, separate from and superior to all derivative sources. Ahlstrom plays with that theme and pays due attention to influences of lasting significance in national development. Like many historians before him, he notes impulses emanating from many colonies, but the ones he values most derived from New England Puritanism. Puritans had developed a line of thought from John Calvin, their theological fountainhead, whose ideas about Protestantism led them to see their efforts as nothing less than building God's new Israel. With Protestant America as the place that would consummate God's redemptive process, the new nation took on an aura of special status, chosen first to embody righteousness and then to expand divine purposes to a wider circle of national culture. As Ahlstrom shows, this vision made for heady self-congratulation and optimism, traits that have also inspired varieties of American imperialism both at home and abroad.

But being chosen meant being judged as well. God's elect nation had a duty to carry out transcendent purposes, and it faced divine judgment in view of success or failure. Using the biblical metaphor of prophetic lament, the Jeremiad, Ahlstrom stresses the burdens of national duty and responsibility alongside potential narcissism. At a time of bicentennial celebration he called for recognizing the nation's shortcomings as well as its accomplishments. Evaluating different aspects of American culture is possible, he argues, because religious influences have always been essential features of this country's development. They nurture the good and should condemn the evil.

Original source—CH 44 (1975): 492-522.

1

Religion, Revolution, and the Rise of Modern Nationalism

Reflections on the American Experience

Sydney E. Ahlstrom

In 1789, two months after the inauguration of George Washington as president of the "first new nation," the foundering regime of Louis XVI, in the 802d year of Capetian rule in France, was forced to convene the Estates General. As the French crisis deepened, all of Europe was deeply stirred. A threat of foreign intervention awakened the French nation and brought the revolution to a new pitch of excitement. Paris soon heard for the first time the thrilling strains of *La Marseillaise*. While a citizens army marched off against the forces of Reaction, the newly elected delegates to a constitutional convention made their way to Paris. Then on 20 September 1792, the very day on which the Convention proclaimed the Year One of the French Republic, the Prussian march on Paris was gloriously halted at the battle of Valmy in the Argonne near Belgium.

By a strange happenstance Johann Wolfgang von Goethe witnessed this famous cannonade while serving with a regiment of the Duke of Sachsen-Weimar; and that night, when queried on the significance of this defeat, he made his celebrated evaluation: "From this place and from this day a new epoch of world history is begun, and you can say that you were there." Hegel too kept alive the sense of a new day's dawn that had stirred him in Tübingen, and he continued to speak of the revolution as a "glorious sunrise." Victor Cousin reported him as declaring the French Revolution was "the greatest stride in the history of mankind since Christianity." In a letter to Schelling, he spoke of their common good fortune to be alive in times that were beholding the coming of the Kingdom of God. And in that most romantic of his major works, *The Phenomenology of the Spirit* (1807), he detailed the profound philosophical implications of these times of rebirth.

It is difficult to fault either of these two great thinkers for their perceptions of fundamental political and spiritual change. Indeed, it may not be too much to say that in the years between Goethe's oracular utterance at Valmy and Hegel's vision of spiritual rebirth, Europe did experience the advent of the modern. Interpreters as diverse as Karl Marx and Joseph de Maistre would agree that nothing of equal magnitude had occurred since the emergence of feudalism. And from a still longer perspective we can discern how that brief span of time between 1792 and 1807 experienced an outpouring of innovative genius that rivals any moment in Western history.

What we are less likely to discern, however, is the profound influence on Europe during this long revolutionary awakening of America's democratic colonies and their successful War for Independence. In France an idealized view of freedom, prosperity and felicity in the New World became a powerful instrument of social criticism. Among many German thinkers this leavening influence was also felt. In *Dichtung und Wahrheit*, Goethe tells how "the names of Franklin and Washington had begun to shimmer and sparkle in the political heaven." America, he said, was "the Eldorado of all who found themselves restricted in present circumstances." Hegel, too, in his later years (he was only six years old in 1776) almost repeated the Goethean vision of America:

America is . . . the land of the future, where, in the ages that lie before us, the burden of the world's history shall reveal itself. . . . It is a land of desire for all those who are weary of the historical lumber-room of old Europe.

When we move from the turmoil of the Old World to the new nation in the West, however, we are struck by the fact that the spiritual ethos of America during these very years was almost totally different. Perhaps most anomalous was the fact that in the United States the turn-of-century decades, despite many harsh political debates, were not a time of social trauma but of fulfillment. The death of George Washington in 1799 occasioned reverential celebration and thanksgiving for a democratic success story. And in

1801, the year of Thomas Jefferson's inauguration, the twenty-fifth anniversary of American independence was observed. The Revolution was fast becoming a legend. John Adams and many others, moreover, would remind the younger generation that the "real revolution" had in fact been accomplished in American hearts long before 1776.[1]

The second anomaly stems from the apparent non-existence of a spiritual and intellectual revolution similar to that which was being experienced in Europe. When one searches the American scene for a corollary to Europe's Romantic flowering at the century's turn, one can find little more than the birth dates of a gifted generation of thinkers and writers who would usher in "the golden day" of American Romanticism over thirty years later![2] In these unusual circumstances we seem to confront a vindication of Hegel's judgment that "it is for Americans to abandon the ground on which the history of the world had developed itself." In any case these anomalies were a major provocation for the present essay. And the basic guidelines to their resolution are in fact suggested by the observations of John Adams quoted just above.

The American revolution came so early and the rise of Romantic modernism came so late because the United States was the chief legatee of the Puritan revolution in both its political and its spiritual implications. As proclaimed all through the nineteenth century in thousands of Thanksgiving Day sermons, this "land of the pilgrim's pride" owed its liberties and prosperity as well as its chief religious commitments to its seventeenth-century founders, from Governor Bradford to William Penn. On this one point at least, popular tradition and historical scholarship seem to converge and agree. America in 1776 was not overthrowing the old regime and repudiating Rococo civilization; it was carrying out the implications of an English upheaval that had thrown two kings from their thrones. Without the encumbrances of aristocratic leadership it had been shaping a new kind of social order for over 150 years.

As to the delay of Romanticism, which has so often been attributed to cultural lag or to an inclination of Americans to provide a graveyard for European philosophies, it too is explained by the vitality of the Puritan religious tradition, which during these turn-of-century years was rejoicing in the outbreak of a Second Great Awakening of revivalistic religion. All across the country from Kentucky to Connecticut this evangelical surge was advancing, and it would march from victory to victory right down to the Civil War. Ralph Henry Gabriel, to be sure, proposed to rename this powerful current of antebellum Protestantism, calling it "Romantic Christianity,"[3] but this seems to be a needless confusion of traditional terminology that leaves no label for the critical efforts of later thinkers such as Emerson and Bushnell.

It is more useful to call attention to the one great area where Americans *did* in fact do some Romantic pioneering—that is, in the shaping of nationalism. In this realm a proper appreciation of American developments would modify the conventional wisdom. It is very often said that "Nationalism is a doctrine invented in Europe at the beginning of the nineteenth century."[4] But is this true? Had not the American republic by that time been committed to this "doctrine" for a full quarter-century? Indeed, is not "the first new nation" the birthplace of modern nationalism? An elaboration of an affirmative reply may be said to constitute the substance of the remainder of this essay. Far from being a celebrationist account, however, this essay is written in full consciousness of the many malignant consequences of modern nationalism, in American history and in the world.

It behooves us, nevertheless, to recognize that one of the most consequential social and ideological processes in modern history was moving to its crowning achievement in these American colonies during the years after the Treaty of Paris of 1763. American Whigs were moving toward a revolutionary result that would provide a major stimulus to the revolution in Europe, and through these events to the rise of "Romantic nationalism" as an historic reality. The advanced thinking and bold actions which created the new American republic marked the appearance in world history of religio-political nationalism in a new and highly contagious form.

• • •

Nationalism, of course, is not what a Cartesian would consider a clear and simple idea. It is in fact one of the most nebulous concepts in Western history. Carlton J. H. Hayes, Hans Kohn, and many others have devised long and heavily qualified definitions, while Boyd Shafer, despairing of that effort, attempted to rehabilitate the term by listing ten fundamental beliefs and conditions. Simply to indicate what I have in mind when using the term, let me draw together the main points expressed in these various efforts by suggesting that nationalism is, first of all, "a state of mind" that began to gain quasi-religious fervency only in the later eighteenth century. More specifically, it is an attitude which arises among ethnic or other groups whose sense of common peoplehood differentiates them from other peoples. These attitudes are justified and collectively maintained by an appeal to traditions, myths, rituals, songs, and national scriptures which usually are implicitly or explicitly religious in character. The aim of nationalistic endeavors is to legitimate the self-consciousness of a people, to deliver them from oppression and to provide them with the possibilities for autonomous expression and development.

The first place where nationalism took definitive shape, with full ideological, political, social, and religious accompaniments was in America. July 4th is the day on which Americans, albeit with declining fervor, celebrate this accomplishment.

In seeking an explanation for these developments, however, one must go to the root of the matter. And this means that we must seek the origins of the most decisive ingredient of the civilization in which nationalism arose, and then trace the tradition that gave birth to "God's New Israel" in America. This will lead us to see that the peculiar dynamics of Western society in general and American society in particular stem from that ancient Semitic matrix out of which Judaism arose. We see this characteristic Hebrew outlook already in that song of Jahweh the storm god, which is generally considered to be the oldest passage in the Hebrew Scriptures:

> O Yahweh, when thou camest forth from Seir,
> When thou marchedst from the steppes of Edom,
> The earth quaked, the heavens also shook,
> The clouds too dripped water,

> The mountains rocked at the presence of Yahweh,
> At the presence of Yahweh, the God of Israel.[5]

What gradually gained form and force in this tradition was an uncompromising type of prophetic monotheism and, with it, a severe conception of orthodoxy and right worship of Almighty God. A basic corollary was its firm opposition to polytheism, syncretism and the idea of multiple solutions to man's moral and religious problems. It also conveyed a linear conception of history which made the mighty acts of God, from Creation to the coming of the Messianic Kingdom, decisive for the understanding of all human events. History became relentlessly meaningful. J. J. Finkelstein does not exaggerate, therefore, when he declares that "the most revolutionary" statement in the entire Bible is the word of the Lord given to his Chosen People in the book of Exodus [19:6 RSV]: "You shall be to me a kingdom of priests and a holy nation." This statement contains an immensely important insight, though it is imperative that we fill in some vital elements of Finkelstein's drastically foreshortened account.

Certainly of most massive importance for the West is the fact that the early Christian church made the Hebrew Scriptures its own, and quite explicitly appropriated the momentous idea which Finkelstein isolated. In a famous passage of 1 Peter, the writer first quotes the words of Isaiah [28:16], "Behold, I am laying in Zion... a cornerstone chosen and precious," and then applies the Deuteronomic declaration to the Christian church: "You are a chosen race, a royal priesthood, a holy nation, God's own people" [1 Peter 2:6, 9 RSV].

As understood by a small and persecuted Christian church, this passage was utterly lacking in specifically national implications and took on essentially spiritual meanings. The "Holy Nation" was a community under the Cross. During the long era from the Emperor Theodosius to the Reformation, moreover, even this idea of Christians as a pilgrim people gradually lost its force. The Reformation, on the other hand, commonly understood itself to be a reassertion of Judaic themes. Primary in this effort, strongest in the Reformed or "Calvinistic" tradition, was a revival of the notion of the Christian church as a community called out from the world, an Elect Nation, a Holy People. But as the Protestant movement on the continent was caught up in the swirling forces of the Counter-Reformation, it came to pass that separate political jurisdictions, some united by inner ties of blood and language and some not, were declared also to be confessional communities. Of these various states and nations, none stood out as so singular as England's insular kingdom. Especially after the accession of Queen Elizabeth, militant Protestants of Reformed and Puritan persuasion came increasingly to see England itself as the elect nation. This belief that England was chosen for a special role became even stronger during the days of Cromwell. But, of course, as all Americans are very early taught, a new and more sharply defined British Zion was being set upon the North Atlantic's eastern shore even before the Puritan Revolution in England had resulted in civil war.

The earliest of these English plantations in the New World was not founded primarily out of Puritanic zeal; but it is well to remember that the first sermon preached to the stockholders of the Virginia Company was by the Reverend William Symonds, a well-known eschatologist, who took his text (almost inevitably) from the word of the Lord that had come to Abram: "Get thee out of thy Countree and from thy kindred and from thy father's house, unto the land that I will shew thee. And I will make of thee a great nation, and will bless thee and make thy name great and thou shalt be a blessing . . . and in thee shall all families of the earth be blessed" [Gen. 12:1-3 KJV].

Yet it was not Virginia that was to become the primary shaper of America's conception of its millennial role in history. That was chiefly the work of those far more theologically minded leaders of New England's colonies. Believing that England had failed to answer its holy calling, they translated the elect nation to American shores and there with great deliberation established virtually autonomous commonwealths, with carefully organized towns and churches. They also established a system of public education, a university, and an active printing press, all of which were designed to produce a literate, Bible-reading people that was pious, industrious and dedicated to the public well-being.

All of this was done, moreover, on the basis of a firmly held interpretation of scripture. In the famous and familiar words of Governor Winthrop aboard the *Arabella* in 1630, this commonwealth was to become a very "Model of Christian Charity." And he was sure that God was supporting them in this cause: "Wee must Consider that wee shall be as a City upon a Hill, the eyes of all people are upon us." William Stoughton was but reaffirming an established tradition when in 1668 he clinched his call for pious revival: "This we must know, that the Lord's promises and expectations of great things, have singled out New England, and all sorts and ranks of men amongst us, above any nation or people in the world."[6] So it was that Puritanism, the quintessential form of Judaic Christianity, became a dominant influence in the religious, moral, social, and political life of New England.

These Puritan commonwealths, moreover, were among the largest and most populous in America and provided a very large number of outwandering migrants to other colonies. They were not, however, the only institutionalized form of the Puritan impulse. Rhode Island's radicalism poured another vital stream into American life, especially if we give it a kind of symbolic credit for the large and constantly growing number of Baptist radicals, who soon made their presence felt in every colony and later became the chief bearers of the Puritan legacy in the New World. Then there is that last great flowering of Puritan statecraft in the Keystone State, where William Penn's great notions of the benevolent commonwealth were set in motion, and not only for Englishmen but for the Welsh, the Scotch Irish, and Germans of very diverse types. Even more than Rhode Island, Pennsylvania is the paradigm of American pluralism and of those idealistic immigration policies that by 1930 had led over fifty million Europeans to these shores and then out across this whole vast land.

The initial, almost apocalyptic fervor of the first American settlers would, of course, be routinized, and the Jeremiad would become an important literary genre during the later seventeenth and early eighteenth centuries. Yet before many decades had passed, spiritual awakenings began to occur. Then in the early eighteenth century a "great and general revival" with several points of origin swept through all of the colonies and revitalized almost every chief element of the Puritan revolution. The Great Awakening was thus not only a tumultuous religious event, but also a popular movement with powerful political and ideological implications.

Out of scattered colonies and peoples something approaching an "American nation" was now becoming conscious of itself, and within it there also arose a revived community of Puritanic evangelicals who were joined by many Anglicans, Presbyterians and Dutch Reformed of equally pietistic persuasion. And these various groups soon came to see themselves as jointly commissioned to awaken the nation and hasten the Kingdom's coming. Experiential religion and millennialism became more important than ever before. The groundwork for emotionally charged and future-oriented forms of American nationalism was securely laid.[7]

Yet America in the later eighteenth century was by no means unanimously Puritan in any strict doctrinal sense. Even though the overwhelming majority of those who declared their independence in 1776 did, in Winthrop Hudson's phrase, bear "the stamp of Geneva," one would have to admit that the enlightened philosophers who played so large a role as founders and theoreticians of the new republic were of another spirit, even though they were as committed to Puritan virtues as their more evangelical contemporaries. The Puritan ethic revealed an almost miraculous capacity for undergoing secularization without losing its ethical force. Due to its essential harmony with the new democratic and capitalistic culture, it continued to offer functional moral guidelines even after modern ways of thought had led many to regard the cardinal tenets of Puritan theology as untenable. In 1750, for example, the outspokenly rationalistic Jonathan Mayhew would celebrate the execution of Charles I with a strenuous defense of the Puritan Revolution. The remarkable scholarship of Bernard Bailyn, Edmund Morgan, and Wesley Frank Craven has also shown the great power of the Puritan ideology in the shaping of the revolutionary spirit.[8]

Neither Puritan nor Philosophe, as it happened, could prevent either the Declaration of 1776 or the Constitution of 1787 from a compromise with slavery, so the way was left open for William Lloyd Garrison's later words, "that the Union is not of heaven," but a covenant with Death and Hell. One must go on to say, nevertheless, that in an age of ideological confusion and imperial conflict the Founding Fathers did provide a rationale for democratic constitutionalism that is one of the great intellectual accomplishments of modern history. Speaking in the advanced philosophic idiom of the day with clarity and feeling, they formulated national ideals of great profundity and universal relevance. In the moral climate which they provided, slavery, too, would in fact be undone, and with it the Old Federal Union itself. Given their achievement, it is easy to understand why in later years Americans ascribed the accomplishments of the Founding Fathers to the providence of a benevolent deity, thereby revealing the persistence of the idea that Americans were, somehow and after all, God's Chosen People and that their republic was "a new order for the ages." There is a contradiction lying at the center of American nationalism, however, and it is to this circumstance that certain concluding reflections must be directed.

• • •

The nation which entered world history with the inauguration of George Washington was the product of two traditions: one, particularist, providential, supernaturalistic, Puritan, and Judaic; the other, universalist, rational, naturalistic, and cosmopolitan. In the evangelical resurgence of the antebellum decades, Enlightened attitudes lost their vitality and the "modern Puritanism" of the Protestant mainstream became oppressively strong. Convictions as to America's elect nationhood were also revived and set forth in hymns and sermons with a new kind of millennial fervor. In the resultant atmosphere new and more militant forms of expansionism flourished. America's manifest destiny became an article of religious belief.

Yet the prophetic and critical strain by no means expired, and especially after 1830 many evangelicals in their desire to shape the United States as beacon to the world, became leaders in the antislavery crusade and other reform movements. Despite the waning of rationalism, therefore, the great ideological contribution of the

Founding Fathers of 1776 endured. It provided ethical and political norms that over-arched parties, sects, and creeds. It made the federal union an inspiration for reformers, idealists, and dreamers, as well as for millions of immigrants who came with new visions of a land of promise.

Taken together and fused, as they were in most American hearts and minds, these two conflicting traditions created a mystique of the Union as a transcendent object of reverence and an almost divine source of strength, hope, and moral guidance. The fervent nationalism which it inspired in an increasingly heterogeneous people became a wonder of the world. Many atrocities would be committed in its name; and "self-evident" truths of egalitarianism were persistently subordinated to the claims of liberty and property. Yet the inherent ethical dimension of American nationhood would also provide grounds for bringing domestic and international injustices under judgment.

Despite a legacy of noble ideals, however, the nation's Bicentennial celebrations, like the Centennial observances of 1876, find the American people deep in compromise, morally confused and desperately in need of ideological reconstruction. One explanation of this widespread sense of ideological crisis is the fact that the Puritan tradition, which undergirded so many American attitudes, has lost its hold as a system of religious belief. The Puritan ethic, meanwhile, with its accent on work, exploitation, and productivity, is coming to be seen as anachronistic and counterproductive. Almost equally serious is the degree to which the optimistic confidence of the Enlightenment has faded away, leaving that epoch as a kind of "lost world" in the American mind.

Thus Americans of the 1970s have been living in the midst of a "modern revolution" into which their social, economic and technological development has hurried them ahead of all other nations. This very fact, moreover, has pitched them into a spiritual predicament for which they are ill prepared. The truly fundamental shift in Western thinking which Hegel announced, and to which the bolder American Transcendentalists had given an American application, is still far from being generally appropriated despite the radical provocations of the pre-Bicentennial decade.

No one can be confident, therefore, as to how Americans will respond to the need for innovative thinking in almost every area of human concern. Yet there are grounds for believing, or at least for hoping, that, given luck, leadership and intellectual boldness, the nation's inner confidence and its vast store of idealism can be refined and invigorated. The omens are, nevertheless, that only profoundly renovated conceptions of the Union can restore the country's sense of purpose.

ENDNOTES

1. John Adams to Hezekiah Niles, 13 February 1818. In the same letter he also declares that "its effects and consequences have already been awful over a great part of the globe. And when and where are they to cease?" *The Selected Writing of John and John Quincy Adams*, ed. Adrienne Koch and William Peden (New York, 1946), 203.
2. George Bancroft was born in 1800, Bushnell in 1801, George Ripley in 1802, Brownson and Nevin in 1803, Hedge in 1805, Whittier and Longfellow in 1807, Parker, Margaret Fuller, J. F. Clarke, and W. H. Channing in 1810, and so forth.
3. Ralph Henry Gabriel, *The Course American Democratic Thought* (New York, 1940), 38.
4. Elie Kedourie, *Nationalism* (New York, 1961), 9. The opening sentence of this well-received book is only cited as an example of the commonly accepted view.
5. Judges 5:4-5. For the version used and supporting comment see Theophile J. Meek, *Hebrew Origins* (New York, 1960), 99-100 et passim.
6. Perry Miller and T. H. Johnson, eds., *The Puritans*, 2 vols. (New York, 1963), 1:197, 210, 244.
7. It is on this point that my own thinking owes most to Sidney Mead's interpretations of the Lively Experiment and the ways in which the United States is "a nation with the soul of a church." Yet it is here, too, where I also differ with his emphasis; I would place much less weight on the continuing impact of Enlightened thought far more on the wide popular appeal of Puritanic evangelicalism. Among intellectuals and the general public alike Enlightened rationalism rapidly faded from view after the Second Great Awakening and the influx of Romantic modes of thought.
8. Bernard Bailyn, *The Ideological Origins of the American Revolution* (Cambridge, MA, 1967); Edmund S. Morgan, "The Puritan Ethic and

the American Revolution," *William and Mary Quarterly*, 3d ser., 24 (1967): 3-43; Wesley F. Craven, *The Legend of the Founding Fathers* (New York, 1956).

FOR FURTHER READING

Albanese, Catherine L. *Sons of the Fathers: The Civil Religion of the American Revolution*, Philadelphia, 1976.

Bercovitch, Sacvan. *The American Jeremiad*, Madison, WI, 1972.

Bonomi, Patricia U. *Under the Cope of Heaven: Religion, Society, and Politics in Colonial America*, New York, 1986.

Bozeman, Theodore Dwight. *To Live Ancient Lives: The Primitivist Dimension in Puritanism*, Chapel Hill, NC, 1988.

Bremer, Francis J. *The Puritan Experiment: New England Society from Bradford to Edwards*, rev. ed., Hanover, NH, 1995.

Gura, Philip F. *A Glimpse of Sion's Glory: Puritan Radicalism in New England, 1620–1660*, Middleton, CT, 1984.

Hatch, Nathan O. *The Sacred Cause of Liberty: Republican Thought and the Millennium in Revolutionary New England*, New Haven, 1977.

Hudson, Winthrop S., ed. *Nationalism and Religion in America: Concepts of American Identity and Mission*, New York, 1970.

McGiffert, Michael, ed. *Puritanism and the American Experiment*, Reading, MA, 1969.

Miller, Perry. *Errand into the Wilderness*, Cambridge, MA, 1956.

Morgan, Edmund, ed. *Puritan Political Ideals, 1558–1794*, Indianapolis, 1965.

Stout, Cushing. *The New Heavens and New Earth: Political Religion in America*, New York, 1973.

INTRODUCTION TO ESSAY 2

In searching for the roots of American character, Ahlstrom tended to favor impulses usually associated with Romanticism, but Mead emphatically declares the Enlightenment to be more important. In his attempts to rescue Enlightenment religion from the smear tactics of nineteenth-century evangelists, Mead insists that there were sound theological premises in the rationalist perspective. Foremost among them was a genuine, deep-seated belief in God. The cosmic deity of reason ruled both the natural order and the crucial sphere of human morality. Rational religionists hoped to fashion an environment where people, after being freed from superstitions based on claims about special revelation, could think for themselves and find untrammeled truth regarding personal virtue and social harmony. So they gave high priority to free speech in addition to belief in God. They were convinced that, if people were free to pursue it, truth would eventually prevail. Freedom to seek the truth, to speak openly of one's findings along the way, was thus seen as a basic right in the liberated American republic.

Abraham Lincoln embodied similar ideas during the Civil War, and Mead holds that they perpetuated the eighteenth-century precepts so fundamental to this nation's existence. Lincoln's private correspondence and formal addresses disclose a renewed sense of America in covenant with a God of justice, populated by citizens who were not essentially good but ones who might achieve virtue with divine guidance. At the end of this exposition, where Lincoln validates Enlightenment categories and bequeaths them for modern America, Mead points out a lesson for his contemporary audiences: democracy runs the risk of becoming tyrannical, but if Americans are careful to protect freedom as a means as well as an end, the republican experiment is worth risking. There is no better alternative.

Original source - CH 23 (1954): 3-16.

2

Abraham Lincoln's "Last, Best Hope of Earth"
The American Dream of Destiny and Democracy

Sidney E. Mead

Abraham Lincoln, in a real sense the spiritual center of American history, entering into the office of the presidency when sectional differences were rapidly moving into irrepressible conflict, spoke almost sadly in his First Inaugural of "our bonds of affection" and "the mystic chords of memory" that "will yet swell the chorus of the Union when again touched, as surely they will be, by the better angels of our nature." In the Second Inaugural he gave a definitely religious content to the "bonds of affection." "Both [North and South, he said] read the same Bible, and pray to the same God; and each invokes His aid against the other." Obviously "the prayers of both could not be answered—[and] that of neither has been answered fully." Why? Because in the movements of human history "the Almighty has his own purposes." This is to say that all the works of finite men stand always under the judgment of the infinite God—and, "the will of God prevails." Hence the most that finite men can do in all their striving is to stand "with firmness in the right as God [*now*] gives us to see the right"—the "right" being conformity with the ultimate purposes of the infinite God. But since man is finite he can never be absolutely sure that he rightly senses the will of the infinite God. Finally, then, he must bow in faith in humble acknowledgment that "if, after endeavoring to do my best in the light which he affords me, I find my efforts fail, I must believe that for some purpose unknown to me, he wills it otherwise."[1]

It is here suggested that for Americans the ideal was defined in terms of "destiny under God," and what Lincoln called "a constitutional republic or democracy—a government of the people by the same people."[2] America was to fulfill her destiny, under God, by working out in practice and demonstrating for all the world to see, the true possibilities of such government. The ideal and the way were inseparable; this is inherent in the idea of destiny. Hence the practice itself stood always under the judgment of God. Departure from the "way" was not only lamentable, it was insofar rebellion against God and hence always tinged with a sense of profound guilt. This is why, as Santayana put it so well, "To be an American is of itself almost a moral condition, an education, and a career." And here is suggested a way to get hold of the real religious roots and heart of America which it is the purpose of this paper to explore.

· · ·

A sense of destiny is of course not peculiar to Americans. Such a sense seems to be a necessary ingredient in the self-consciousness of every people; an element common to the mind of every Western nation that helps to define for its people their corporate sense of direction through the vast and misty labyrinth of history. This sense of destiny is deeply rooted in the formative experiences of a people. But the important thing is the interpretation of the experiences—that subtle combination of insight into and articulation of the meaning of the experiences that becomes so deeply persuasive and widely accepted that it becomes a part of the common consciousness and passes into the realm of motivational myths. The experience of the Hebrew people in breaking away from Egypt, crossing the Red Sea, and entering into a land of their own was striking enough to be celebrated in song and story. But the important thing was that this happened to a people who had it in them to translate the experience into "the exodus." This made the difference between merely a successful rebellion of an obscure people, and the myth of a chosen people that has remained a pillar of fire by night and of cloud by day throughout all subsequent history.

The outstanding peculiarity of the settlement of that part of the North American continent that became the United States was the mixture of peoples of many different traditions, and their outstanding experience was that of learning to live together side by side and eventually of launching out into independence and forming a new nation. "Here," said Crevecoeur, "individuals of all nations are melted into a new race of men." Here "from this promiscuous breed" has emerged "the American, this new man" who is "that strange mixture of blood" and traditions "which you will find in no other country."

What these emigrant people really shared was confrontation with the strangeness, the vastness, the challenges of the new country, and the consciousness of a new kind of freedom—the freedom offered by practically unlimited space with its untold opportunities. In this situation there emerged the sense of new beginnings— the sense that here was opportunity to begin all over again—to be in the new world a new man largely unfettered by tradition, custom, and law.

During the early formative years of English colonization the immigrants were overwhelmingly Protestants from the Christian nations of Europe, and hence when they came to think about the meaning of the new situation inevitably they thought within the context of their common background. While they shared the sense of new beginnings, they also shared a common Christian tradition and heritage ready to provide the molds into which their thinking about it, and their way of giving intellectual structure and meaning to it, necessarily ran. What they could think they were doing was determined by who they were at the time—and they were "Christians."

The principal human concern in colonization was "neither the rate of interest nor the discovery of gold, but the will of God." Within this climate of opinion every event, great and small, received meaning only as it was related to the purposes of God, and He did, of course, hold all the nations in the hollow of His hand, and He did use any and all men to effect his ultimate purposes in history. But Christians differed essentially from non-Christians in this matter in that they, guided by revelation and under grace, responded and consented consciously and willingly to God's calling. Christians, in brief, could know what it was all about. Here is one root of the doctrine of special calling, and the foundation of the idea of a "peculiar people."

Cotton Mather echoed a commonplace when he pointed to the parallel between the exodus of the Hebrews from Egypt and the flight of the Puritans to New England. John Cotton, on the eve of the departure of the Winthrop fleet in 1630, preached to the emigrants from 2 Samuel 7:10 [KJV]: "Moreover I will appoint a place for my people Israel, and will plant them, that they may dwell in a place of their own, and move no more."

He reminded them that "here is meant some special appointment, because God tells them it by his owne mouth . . . others take the land by his providence, but God's people take the land by promise." And John Rolph of Virginia was equally sure that the English migration to Virginia was a going forth of "a peculiar people, marked and chosen by the finger of God, to possess it, for undoubtedly he is with us."

In this view the Christian consciously sailed to the new land and planted colonies under a contract or covenant with God.[3] The purposes of God might not be seen clearly or in detail at the time, but it was known that God had a purpose which would be unfolded and thus revealed in the subsequent history, and in His own good time. Finite man stands always under the mercy and judgment of God, and knows God through blessings and through adversities. Man finally learns and reads the will and purpose of God in the unfolding of the history itself, guided by the Spirit and the light of His word.

Recognition of this place of providence in the thinking of the time obviates most of the complicated arguments about the primacy of religious, economic, political, or social motives behind the emigration and colonization. To many moderns it comes as a surprise that the contemporaries who wrote about the founding of New England or Virginia were just as aware of economic, social, and political motives, and just as hard-headed about them as the most blatant economic determinists of recent times. It is clear, for example, from John Winthrop's account of his reasons for emigrating, that he never thought for a moment that God spoke directly to him, telling him one day to pack up and go to America. Rather God in His infinite guiding wisdom created in England a situation no longer tolerable for a gentleman and true Christian, while at the same time he opened in America the opportunity to build the Church of Christ anew together with a Commonwealth suited thereto—and of course he made it somewhat profitable for commercially minded Christian gentlemen to do so.

Here is the basis for the American sense of destiny under God. The opportunity to begin all over again in the new land was seen as taking place under the infinite wisdom and providence of the Christian God of mercy and of judgment whose will was to be read in the events of the unfolding history itself. Thus the Americans, those new men, came to look upon themselves as a peculiar, a chosen people, set apart by God to serve a peculiar purpose in the history of mankind—a purpose that would be fully revealed in God's good time. This was their destiny which to be known had to be lived out.

• • •

Inherent in this conception of destiny under God, then, was the expectation that the way to its fulfillment would be revealed gradually through the ebb and flow of the daily life of these people. So they were prepared to work it out. And gradually during the complex give and take of the seventeenth and eighteenth centuries emerged the conviction that the way was that of democracy. This conviction was given its classic expression during the last quarter of the eighteenth century, and was then tried in the fires of revolution which burned it deeply into the spirit of the people.

No attempt to present the essence of the democratic way in schematic fashion can be universally satisfying to all, in large part because it was conceived as a way, a path, and not as a static system. But one may speak of certain fundamental beliefs upon which the whole structure of the experiment rests.

First, belief in God. "I [or we] believe in God . . ." is the first article of every Christian creed. And this means essentially that the believers presuppose in all their thinking that God exists. The God in whom they profess belief is a God of will and purpose, and hence the expression of belief is equivalent to the assertion that there is order and ultimate meaning in the universe which is discoverable at least in part by man. This was one of the central assertions and teachings of Christianity and a basic element in the matrix of all Western civilization.

Second, belief in "the people." "The people" is a complex concept, hard to describe and define. "The people" is the very stuff of history—the massive, unbroken stream of human life with its tremendous inertia and momentum—through which the Spirit of God works to the effecting of His infinite purposes. "The people" transcends all individuals and all groups, and even all their human conceptions of good and evil. "The people" is the bearer of the wisdom of God for the conduct and guidance of man. As Lincoln summed it up—"The will of God prevails . . . [and] the human instrumentalities, working just as they do, are of the best adaptation to effect his purpose."[4]

Third, belief that the will of the people, which is finally the surest clue to the will of God, can really be known only when all the channels of communication and expression are kept open. The profound Christian basis for this view is the idea that the Spirit of God cannot be fenced in, channeled through any human contrivances, or its working predicted. Lyman Beecher put his finger on the heart of the Republic when he spoke of "the powerful nation in the full enjoyment of civil and religious liberty, where all the energies of man might find full scope and excitement, on purpose to show the world by one great successful experiment of what man is capable."[5]

Fourth, belief, as Jefferson worded it in his "Act for Establishing Religious Freedom" in Virginia,

> that truth is great and will prevail if left to herself; that she is the proper and sufficient antagonist to error, and has nothing to fear from the conflict unless by human interposition disarmed of her natural weapons, free argument and debate; errors ceasing to be dangerous when it is permitted freely to contradict them.

These, then, are fundamental beliefs on which democracy rests: belief in God, belief in "the people," belief in the voice of the people as the surest clue to the voice of God, belief that truth emerges out of the conflict of opinions. Two comments may be made in enlarging upon some implications of these views.

(1) It is all too commonly supposed, even by ardent defenders of it, that the democratic way depends upon the essential goodness

and good will of the people—that is, that democracy will work only among men of goodness and good will. But in basic conception the democratic way rests not upon the view of the essential goodness of man, but upon a realistic view of the essential selfishness, evil, or depravity of all men which is deeply rooted in the Christian tradition. Lincoln, for example, was clear on this point. "Human nature," he said bluntly, "cannot be changed." And as for human nature, he once remarked that the Bible teaches us that all men are sinners, but he reckoned that we would have found that out merely by looking about us. Yet he could say nevertheless, that "the will of God prevails" and "the human instrumentalities, working just as they do, are of the best adaptation to effect his purpose." In brief, the man who by common consent most profoundly articulated the American democratic way had no illusions about the nature of man—held no utopian view of his essential goodness or of his ultimate perfectibility.

This realistic view of the nature of man is to be seen in connection with the idea of the emergence of the truth from the conflict of opinion itself. The democratic way is the way of open conflict between essentially selfish and biased individuals and groups, each contending for the truth as he sees it in his limited fashion, which may appear to others to be contention for his own selfish interests, under the general aegis of the freedom of each and all so to contend. It is based upon the faith that the maintenance of the give and take under such freedom for sinful men, is "the last, best hope of earth." This is a tough faith to hold—but it is the essence of the democratic tradition.

(2) Since both the ideal of destiny under God and the way of democracy were based upon a dynamic or experimental conception of human life under God, the primarily important thing is not where the society and government now are in the process of the great experiment, but the sureness of the people's sense of direction—the firmness of their belief in the essential rightness of the general tendency or movement. So long as there is widespread confidence among the people that the direction and way are essentially right, the system is sound and can function even in adversity.

If and when such confidence rooted in such faith is undermined, the people lose hope, lose a sense of direction, lose belief in the great common experiment itself. One of the most ominous things in the situation today is that increasingly the hope of the people is not based on belief in the great principles and hence on the general rightness of the movement, so much as on belief in a static system or "way of life," the primary defense of which is summed up in the phrase, "we never had it so good."

• • •

In actual practice the democratic way is the way of government by the consent of the governed. It is necessary, therefore, that the will of the governed be expressed and carried out according to established and generally accepted rules that are the result of long historical testing. These rules define the fundamental law under which the free people live, and to which they commonly consent.

Basic here is the majority principle, namely, that so far as the next step is concerned the will of the majority must be supreme. Hence the elaborate machinery for the correct and peaceful ascertainment of the will of the majority. All minorities must consent to this majority principle if the government by consent is to survive. Hence the government of the free people may, and indeed must, invoke its coercive power against any and all minorities that deny and flaunt the majority principle—for not to do so is to court anarchy and tyranny.

But if in practice the majority will must prevail step by step, yet the majority may be wrong at any one time, and a majority as well as a minority may be tyrannous.

The only safeguard against such trespass is the conviction that under God truth and right are not matters of majority vote. It is for this reason that "democracy" without faith in God is likely to sink into demagogic mobocracy. Only the belief that majority opinion does not determine truth, places the majority under the obligation and necessity to preserve the right of all minorities to free expression and open propagandization in order that the contention for the truth can go on. Hence the basic right of every minority in the democracy which must be protected is the right to become a majority if it can through free persuasion. This right is protected in the Bill of Rights, which is thus of the essence of the democratic way in practice. This is to say that in the democracy the *means* are as much of the essence as the *ends*. In this sense, indeed, the democratic faith is essentially a faith in certain means. The democracy cannot be defended with undemocratic means.

This way of government by the consent of the governed, hemmed in as it necessarily is by defined and commonly accepted means, is always subject to abuse for the simple reason that men have never been able to devise a system that would permit freedom to the good while as effectively curtailing the freedom of the evil. Even God, according to Christian tradition, could not devise a system that denied freedom to the devil. Further, government by consent which aims at equal freedom and justice for all, is always ponderous, cumbersome, and slow—or at least so it commonly appears in periods of threat and crisis.

The defenders of such government always have and of necessity must labor under the handicap of defending, not a sure thing, an accomplished fact, but a way of political life, an experiment worth trying in peace and even testing in adversity. The great defenders of the democratic way have not defended it in doctrinaire fashion, but when pressed have said in effect—where, judging from past human experience, are we to find a better alternative? Thus Lincoln in his First Inaugural, "Why should there not be a patient confidence in the ultimate justice of the people? Is there any better or equal hope in the world?" And later he added, making the meaning unmistakably clear—it is never a question of "Can any of us imagine better?" but "Can we all do better?" granted the nature of man and the present historical situation.[6]

Lincoln, even under the tremendous pressures of the Civil War, never gave a doctrinaire defense of the Union cause, but always presented the contest as part of the great experiment which "embraces more than the fate of these United States." At the beginning he saw that the contest was important because it forced men to ask, "Is there in all republics this inherent and fatal weakness? Must a government, of necessity, be too strong for the liberties of its own people, or too weak to maintain its own existence?"[7] And at Gettysburg in November 1863 he did not, as one of less rugged faith might well have done, celebrate the victory, but rather reminded the nation that the war was "testing whether that nation or any nation so conceived and so dedicated [i.e., dedicated to the proposition that all men are created equal], can long endure." We may suppose that he meant what he said—that he did not know with certainty—that he thought the struggle was real and that these people might indeed "nobly save or meanly lose the last, best hope of earth."

In "secular" language what these most profound defenders of government by the consent of the governed have always maintained is that there are risks involved in any way of life, and men must take chances for the simple reason that they cannot so rig human life as to assure themselves that they are betting on a sure thing. In traditional Christian language this is to say that finite men must live by faith.

ENDNOTES

1. "Reply to Mrs. Eliza P. Burney, Sept. [28?], 1862," in Philip Van Doren Stern, ed., *The Life and Writings of Abraham Lincoln* (New York, 1940), 728. Quotations from Lincoln below are from this collection, hereafter referred to as *ML.*
2. "Message to Congress in Special Session, July 4, 1861," in *ML,* 668.
3. See, for example, John Winthrop's "A Modell of Christian Charitie Written on Boarde the Arabela, on the Atlantic Ocean . . . 1630," conveniently found in abbreviated form in Perry Miller and Thomas H. Johnson, *The Puritans* (New York, 1938), 195-99.
4. "Meditation on the Divine Will, Sept. [30?], 1862," in *ML,* 728.
5. Quoted in Alice Felt Tyler, *Freedom's Ferment* (Minneapolis, 1944), 1.
6. "Annual Message to Congress," December 1, 1862, in *ML,* 745.
7. "Message to Congress in Special Session," July 4, 1961, in *ML,* 668.

FOR FURTHER READING

Cherry, Conrad, ed. *God's New Israel: Religious Interpretations of American Destiny,* Englewood Cliffs, NJ, 1971.
Hudson, Winthrop S., ed. *Nationalism and Religion in America: Concepts of American Identity and Mission,* New York, 1970.
Mead, Sidney E. *The Nation with the Soul of a Church,* San Francisco, 1975.
Oates, Stephen B. *With Malice Toward None: The Life of Abraham Lincoln,* New York, 1977.

Sandburg, Carl. *Abraham Lincoln*, 6 vols., New York, 1926-1939.
Smith, Elwyn A., ed. *The Religion of the Republic*, Philadelphia, 1971.
Stout, Cushing. *The New Heavens and New Earth: Political Religion in America*, New York, 1973.
Tuveson, Ernest Lee. *Redeemer Nation: The Idea of America's Millennial Role*, Chicago, 1968.
Wolf, William J. *The Almost Chosen People: A Study of the Religion of Abraham Lincoln*, Garden City, NY, 1959.

INTRODUCTION TO ESSAY 3

The concept of "Christian America," as either future objective or lost golden age, has played a part in almost every interpretation of American religion. In this essay, Handy, long known as one who looked for comprehensive themes in our country's experience, catches the dynamic undercurrent of aggressive evangelism that first emerged as a powerful force in the early national period. When Congress separated church and state as federal policy, it created a mixture of enthusiasm and anxiety that spurred all churches to try to win more converts. Success in such missionary outreach programs led to thoughts of converting and thus eventually Christianizing all of America. Handy's essay shows how a nation composed largely of white Protestants thus became the template for shaping the whole country. He exhibits this dominance of a homogenous majority while people still paid lip service to the ideals of individualism and religious liberty.

Perhaps Handy's most important contribution is to explain how religious forces could blend so easily and uncritically with prevailing social attitudes, how efforts to Christianize America became entangled in secular values and behavior. Culture could influence religion as well as vice versa, and as this acculturating process continued in the increasingly pluralistic and secular twentieth century, American religions became entrapped by secular standards. By 1900 denominations in this country had become supporters of popular attitudes on national questions. Their support gave theological backing to racial prejudice, polarization on capital and labor, and American jingoism in global politics. Would-be evangelical conquerors had to face the fact that, instead of shaping national life according to biblical tenets, their own values had become captive to secular standards.

Original source - CH 22 (1953): 8-20.

3

The Protestant Quest for a Christian America, 1830–1930

Robert T. Handy

A strange new world emerged as Lincoln's successors took up their duties, a strange new world that provided a changed and perplexing milieu for the Christian Church. The most expressive comment I have ever heard regarding the profound transformations of post–Civil War America was by Henry Adams:

> My country in 1900 is something totally different from my own country in 1860: I am wholly a stranger in it. Neither I, nor anyone else, understands it. The turning of a nebula into a star may somewhat resemble the change. All I can see is that it is one of compression, and consequent development of terrific energy, represented not by souls, but by coal and iron and steam.[1]

The difficulty of dealing with church history at such a time in any full-orbed way is evident: the difficulty is in some ways heightened by the very richness of source materials: books, sermons, periodicals, yearbooks, catalogs, pamphlets, tracts, newspapers, not to mention the archives of the denominations, the great societies, and the interdenominational agencies. But despite the difficulties, there is need for fresh and comprehensive overall view or themes of interpretation to guide and direct the study of recent American church history.

The Protestantism that faced post–Civil War America was far from being a static entity continually being challenged by external forces. Rather it was an aggressive, dynamic form of Christianity that set out confidently to confront American life at every level, to permeate, evangelize, and Christianize it. The results of this Protestant thrust were ambivalent: on the one hand there were some notable achievements, but on the other there was an entanglement and partial envelopment by an increasingly pluralistic and secularized culture.

Analyses of the national faith in democracy point to the decisive sway of Christian ideas; Professor Ralph H. Gabriel notes that "the foundation of this democratic faith was a frank supernaturalism derived from Christianity. The twentieth-century student is often astonished at the extent to which supernaturalism permeated American thought of the nineteenth century."[2] The cultural dominance of Protestantism was illustrated in the transition to a public tax-supported school system; this transition was palatable to Protestants because the schools were rather clearly Protestant in orientation, though "non-sectarian." Protestant cultural leadership was reflected in the realm of higher education also. As a reporter in 1857 stated it, "We might go through the whole list of American colleges, and show that, with here and there an exception, they were founded by religious men, and mainly with an eye to the interests of the Church." Historians whose major interests are not religious sometimes react with some surprise when they are forced to recognize how widespread Protestant influence was in the first part of the nineteenth century. Professor Whitney R. Cross, for example, in his useful work on *The Burned-over District* records how widespread was the circulation of religious journals in the first part of the nineteenth century and how avidly they were read. He comments, "Now that theology is a very nearly dead subject, one finds it extremely difficult to realize how such journals could have an extensive appeal. But appeal they did, in demonstrable fashion."[3]

The great revivals of 1857–59 provide further evidence of the power and prestige of evangelical Protestantism; a recent student of them has noted that "there was remarkable unanimity of approval among religious and secular observers alike, with scarcely a critical voice heard anywhere." There were of course Protestant groups whose interpretation of Christianity was not that of the conservative evangelicals, but they were small in comparison. The latter dominated the religious press, which had grown more than had the secular press in the twenty years before 1865 both in number of periodicals and in circulation. Protestantism was fully committed to the principle of religious liberty and the voluntary method in religion; it was profiting from them and anticipated continued progress under their sway. Finally, orthodox Protestantism had grown up with the individualism that characterized nineteenth century America, it had contributed to its rise and found it thoroughly congenial. In many ways, the middle third of the nineteenth century was more of a "Protestant Age" than was the colonial period with its established churches.

At the close of the Civil War there were approximately five million Protestant church members out of an estimated population of some thirty-two million. Protestantism's influence of course extended far beyond her actual membership; the vast majority of Americans were encompassed in "popular" if not in "ecclesiastical" Protestantism. The Protestants were an aggressive, self-confident, and surprisingly homogeneous group. To be sure, they were divided into denominations among which considerable tension could arise, yet there was a fundamental similarity. De Tocqueville stated that "they all differ in respect to the worship which is due to the Creator; but they all agree in respect to the duties which are due from man to man. Each sect adores the Deity in its own peculiar manner, but all sects preach the same moral law in the name of God."[4] As the denominations faced their country they saw no reason why their influence should not continue to grow and their numbers increase, and they set out to evangelize and Christianize every aspect of American life. This religious drive to Christianize the nation was a phase of the energy that characterized American life in general at that time, but the evangelical fervor of the Protestant denominations intensified it.

As Protestantism set about its task of permeating and Christianizing American life, the very seriousness of her effort magnified the tendency of churches to absorb the characteristics of those whom they serve. In the North and East particularly, the impact of evolutionary and historical thinking began to upset many, especially those of the educated classes. Their churches came to feel the obligation to understand the new conditions and mediate the gospel to such folk. Ministers who moved in the circles where such currents were flowing tried to stand between the new modes of thought and the old theology; it was from among the ardent evangelicals that the liberal pioneers came. The full secularity to which the new ways of thinking could run was not then clear, and the older theology was often expressed in intransigent and stylized forms that repelled Christians sensitive to the needs of their day. Hence "liberalism" arose not so much from outside as from within, as prominent evangelicals seeking to live out their faith moved among people troubled by new intellectual trends.[5] In the major denominations of the North particularly the liberal trend was evident in the late nineteenth century, at times painfully evident.

A great deal of Protestant America, of course, lived in rural and small town areas where the new winds blew faint. Hence the same post–Civil War years that are marked by the leftward trend are also characterized by the rightward movement of a counter-reformation which was rooted in the conservative, evangelical, revivalistic Protestantism of the earlier nineteenth century but showing a hardening and a narrowing of that tradition. Again, we see Protestant zeal at work; we see the Protestant churches identifying themselves with the concerns of the people, matching themselves to their level. The conservative reaction was of course by no means limited to the small town and rural areas; it swept into the great urban centers where city conditions were severing people from their cultural roots and where many of the city masses had a longing for the religious securities of their rural youth. Yet even in those stormy years the contending parties were far more alike than unlike. Though their definitions of Christianity differed, still they were one in their effort to Christianize a nation, and this essentially missionary task was perhaps what held the denominations together. To permeate society with the leaven of the Christian religion—this was the focus of Protestant energy and a source of Protestant unity despite diversity and tension.

The Christian social movements which arose in the years after the Civil War shared in the Protestant quest for a Christian America. Some within the church, particularly where liberalism had paved the way, were prepared to move more swiftly and go more deeply into this field than others. Yet the Christian social movement was not limited to the social gospel of the evangelical liberals—there was also an American Christian Commission, a Salvation Army, a rescue mission movement. In these movements both evangelical fervor and the drive to Christianize social relations are evident. There were crucial differences in theology and social philosophy between social gospel and conservative Protestants, but both groups strove to make America Christian. The Christian social movement was not only a response to external pressure, it was also a redirection, varied and often slow and cautious, of the inner vitality of Protestantism.

• • •

Despite its zeal and energy, Protestantism's dominance in culture and education so evident at the mid-nineteenth-century mark, had ebbed by the 1920s; many who had come from Protestant backgrounds had become estranged from the church or grown indifferent to it; secularization was clearly on the increase. Protestant thought, especially in certain liberal circles, was showing the effect of culture on it, more than the reverse.[6] The racial, sectional, and class lines that were still drawn within Protestantism suggest rather disturbingly that the Protestant effort to permeate and Christianize society had not had too profound an effect even on her own social fabric. The tide, flowing strongly in Protestant favor in mid-nineteenth century, had clearly turned by the third decade of the twentieth century. But consideration of the weaknesses of Protestantism and her difficulties in an associative culture must not blind us to her major institutional achievements in the years since Appomattox. The percentage of Protestant church membership in the total population more than doubled, and in a time when the general population had tripled—no small achievement. Protestantism slightly more than kept pace with the remarkable rise in the level of wealth, and though this brought certain dangers, it testifies to denominational energy. With somewhat diminishing force, this pattern continued throughout the 1920s. Protestant organizations grew steadily more extensive and complex as they dealt with the problems of the new age—to be sure the rise of denominational bureaucracy was an ambiguous blessing, but it reveals inner vitality. Though denominations were strained by theological tension and schisms resulted, major disruptions were avoided and unitive tendencies within denominations and denominational families operated ever more strongly as the years passed.

Since the Civil War an aggressive Protestantism hoped to strengthen further the position she had won in the middle third of the nineteenth century and further permeate American life. The result was remarkable achievement and yet an entanglement and partial envelopment by a culture increasingly associative in nature. Consider also the history of Roman Catholicism in the same period. Roman Catholicism in 1865 claimed three million adherents—already by far the largest single religious group. It had been the church of the lower class, the immigrant, the city worker, and formed a religious enclave in Protestant America, a despised minority group for the most part. In the post–Civil War years a new spirit began to sweep through Catholicism. Henceforth it was to be less apologetic, less concerned with mere survival and more with consolidation and naturalization. It began to dream of permeating American life and remaking it in its image.

These new motifs were evident at the meeting of the Second Plenary Council at Baltimore in 1866, where it was noted with enthusiasm that the number of churches and clergy had doubled since the First Plenary fourteen years before. The convert Father Hecker gave clear expression to the new hope of Catholics when in 1868 he suggested that, perhaps by 1900 the majority of Americans would be Catholic. He announced as his avowed purpose not only to "Catholicize America" but also to "Americanize Catholicism." In 1868 also James Gibbons was consecrated bishop, and he is so much the symbol of the Roman Catholicism of his time—he died in 1921—that those years can be styled "the age of Gibbons." His desire was to make the church at home in America, to naturalize the church, to identify her more closely with the life of America. Archbishop John Ireland was another prelate who expressed a dominant mood of the American Catholicism of the half-century after the Civil War. He once said preaching before a Catholic conference:

It will not do to understand the thirteenth century better than the nineteenth. . . . We should speak to our age; we should be in it, and of it, if we would have its ear. For the same reason there is needed a thorough sympathy with the country. The Church of America must be, of course, as Catholic as even in Jerusalem or Rome; but as far as her garments assume colour from the local landscape, she must be American.[7]

Here is evident the operation of the desire to permeate society and to this end to identify the Church with it to a certain extent, the same concern we have seen in operation in Protestantism. In the case of Catholicism with her authoritarian structure, the counter-tendencies could act more swiftly. The decision of the Third Plenary Council of 1884 to develop a parochial school system on a large scale is one evidence of this. The resistance from Europe to "Americanization," symbolized by Leo XIII's Apostolic Letter, *Testem Benevolentiae,* to Cardinal Gibbons in 1899, checked the drift to a yet more distinctive American Catholicism and pointed to the end of the era of fraternization. Through all of this half-century, to be sure, the church had to struggle hard against the disruptive tendencies of particular national groups in her membership; in some areas the church was so identified with the interests of particular enclaves of immigrants that there was serious, inner conflict. In Cahenslyism (1891) the disruptive tendencies of our associative, pluralistic culture had their impact in Catholicism, but they were resisted, and the foundation of present Catholic strength was cemented.

• • •

In conclusion, I want to underline the importance of this period for the Protestant church historian. It was then that the churches came face to face with the confused, troubled, fragmented, pluralistic, unstable new world of science and technology. The lessons learned from this first period of engagement with the kind of problems American churches are likely to be faced with for some time to come are important in their positive as well as their negative aspects. The achievements of that period provide much of the religious capital on which we still draw. The tensions that arose in that period have not entirely been resolved; historical study of them can help us to keep them from becoming destructive again. Many of the patterns of secularization that today keep men from a vital relationship to the Christian faith were developed and applied in this period. A profound knowledge of the religious history of the years since the Civil War can be useful in approaching such people, some of whom can be guided to see that the values they treasure are products of the Christian faith, and cannot be maintained long apart from positive Christianity. Finally, in many important respects the Church was carrying out its redemptive work on several frontiers, geographical, social, ecumenical—and as it appears that in the discernible future the Church will sojourn in an alien world, surely the history of the work of the Churches of Christ in that time of frontiers is highly significant.

ENDNOTES

1. *Letters, 1896–1918*, p. 279, quoted in Henry Steele Commager, *The American Mind: An Interpretation of American Thought and Character Since the 1880's* (New Haven, 1950), 134.
2. *The Course of American Democratic Thought: An Intellectual History Since 1815* (New York, 1940), 14.
3. *The Burned-Over District: The Social and Intellectual History of Enthusiastic Religion in Western New York, 1800–1850* (Ithaca, 1950), 108.
4. Alexis De Tocqueville, *Democracy in America*, 2 vols. (New York, 1945), 1:303.
5. Daniel Day Williams, *The Andover Liberals: A Study in American Theology* (New York, 1941).
6. Arnold Nash, ed., *Protestant Thought in the Twentieth Century* (New York, 1951).
7. Theodore Maynard, *The Story of American Catholicism* (New York, 1941), 550 and Willard L. Sperry, *Religion in America* (New York, 1946), 219.

FOR FURTHER READING

Bercovitch, Sacvan. *The American Jeremiad*, Madison, WI, 1972.

Cherry, Conrad, ed. *God's New Israel: Religious Interpretations of American Destiny*, Englewood Cliffs, NJ, 1971.

Handy, Robert T. *A Christian America: Protestant Hopes and Historical Realities*, 2d ed., New York, 1984.

———. *Undermined Establishment: Church-State Relations in America, 1880–1920*, Princeton, 1991.

Hudson, Winthrop S., ed. *Nationalism and Religion in America: Concepts of American Identity and Mission*, New York, 1970.

Hutchison, William R., ed. *Between the Times: The Travail of the Protestant Establishment in America, 1900–1960*, New York, 1989.

Marty, Martin E. *Righteous Empire: The Protestant Experience in America*, New York, 1970.

Niebuhr, H. Richard. *The Kingdom of God in America*, New York, 1937.

Noll, Mark A., Nathan O. Hatch, and George M. Marsden, *The Search for Christian America*, Westchester, IL, 1983.

Richey, Russell E., and Donald G. Jones, eds. *American Civil Religion*, New York, 1974.

Smith, Elwyn A. ed. *The Religion of the Republic*, Philadelphia, 1971.

Tuveson, Ernest Lee. *Redeemer Nation: The Idea of America's Millennial Role*, Chicago, 1968.

INTRODUCTION TO ESSAY 4

The previous two essays offer familiar perspectives on religion and American culture. This essay challenges such traditional ideas by offering a new vista, beginning with the observation that American history is the history of immigration. All of us are either immigrants ourselves or descendants from those in a previous generation who came to these shores. So, when trying to understand patterns in American life, it is important to realize who arrived here and when, how they treated those who came later, and what different cultural expressions resulted from that interaction. Initial paragraphs of this essay show Dolan's great desire to legitimize the field of immigration studies alongside other avenues of historical inquiry. In mentioning old standbys such as Puritan studies and new topics such as women in religion, he orients himself and then focuses on immigration as a theme that sheds light on an otherwise bewildering jumble of evidence.

Dolan reports on work he has recently completed, providing us with the benefit of several years reading in rich new archives that contain letters written by immigrants to those back home. This exercise is one of the most exciting adventures a reader can encounter: enjoying a summary of evidence put together for the very first time, learning something that nobody else has ever known before. It is intriguing to learn, for instance, that Irish and Jewish immigrants wrote seldom of God, while Norwegians and Dutch did so frequently and at length. One is immediately led to ask why. Further, what does one make of so few references to Jesus and Mary among Catholics? This type of essay tells us some of the facts about new Americans as they made their Atlantic (or Pacific) passage. Perhaps the next level of studies is to ask why it was so and what difference it made as people put down new roots on welcoming soil.

Original source - CH 57 (1988): 61-72.

4

The Immigrants and Their Gods
A New Perspective in American Religious History

Jay P. Dolan

In the past twenty years an explosion of historical information has taken place. So many articles and books have been published that it has become virtually impossible for any one person to keep up with this information explosion. The positive side of this development is that we know a great deal more about the history of religion in the United States than we did twenty years ago. Moreover, historians have developed new approaches to the study of religious history which have challenged our assumptions and provided new models for doing history. New questions are being asked about the past and new trends in the study of religious history are evident. This situation is as true of the historical study of religion in Europe as it is of American religious history, perhaps even more so. But there is also a dark side to this explosion of historical information. Because of this explosion any hope for synthesis or coherence has vanished. Thus, a central problem for historians is how to organize and integrate all this new information with the canon of American religious history.

This problem of the whole and its parts, or the one and the many, is common to all areas of history and has been discussed by many historians. Bernard Bailyn summed up one aspect of the problem in the following manner. "Modern historiography in general," he wrote, "seems to be in a stage of enormous elaboration. Historical inquiries are ramifying in a hundred directions at once, and there's no coordination among them. Even if one reduces the mass of new writings in the early modern period to the American field, and still further to the publications of card-carrying historians, the sheer amount of the writing now available is overwhelming." He then went on to note that "the one thing above all else that this outpouring of historical writings lacks is coherence."[1] For Bailyn and numerous others, defining the relationship between the whole and its parts is a major issue for historians. How then can we achieve coherence in the writing of history?

One way that historians of American religion can move toward a more coherent synthesis is to avoid a narrow, parochial approach to history. This faulty approach is found in all areas of history when such issues as nationalism and religious sectarianism motivate historians. The myopic vision of sectarian church history was commonplace not too long ago. It was divisive, narrow, and unappealing except to the zealot. Though it has not disappeared entirely, such an understanding of history is much less common today.

Denominational history is still very much in vogue and will remain so as long as the need exists for a more complete understanding of a specific religious tradition. Such histories are the building blocks from which any future synthesis will be constructed. But denominational history does not have to be parochial, and above all it should not be sectarian and apologetical. One way to avoid the intrinsically narrow nature of denominational history is to integrate such studies into the larger framework of American history in such a manner that they become central to the American experience.

To move toward more coherence in the writing of American religious history requires more than just avoiding narrow denominational history and sectarian myopia. It requires the grand vision. Historians must use a wide-angle lens when they look back at the past and seek to discover the dominant themes that shaped historical development. Such grand themes by their very nature clear away the debris of history and bring clarity and coherence to the past. They also transcend denominational boundaries and for this reason become more central to the American experience and thus more important to historians in search of a usable past.

Puritanism has become one of the grand themes of American colonial history. This theme served to organize that period of history, and the more Puritan studies progressed, the more understandable the past became. In fact, the theme of Puritanism unified colonial historiography to such an extent that it eventually dominated the field. At about the same time, however, historians began to look beyond Puritanism and the region of New England in order to understand colonial history more fully. Nonetheless, the study of Puritanism continues to have a unifying effect on the writing of colonial religious history.

More recently, the theme of evangelicalism has emerged as a grand theme in the study of nineteenth-century America. Books and articles on American evangelicalism continue to drop off the press in heaps. Like the grand theme of Puritanism, evangelicalism cuts across denominational boundaries and tends to unify the mass of historical information pertaining to the nineteenth century.[2] The study of evangelicalism, like the study of Puritanism, concentrates on the Protestant expression of this religious tradition. But this exclusive focus on Protestantism does not have to be. The evangelical tradition also found a home among Roman Catholics, and Puritanism was rooted in Augustine as well as Calvin.

The popularity of Puritan studies and evangelical studies reflects the dominance of intellectual history among historians of American religion. One reason for this is the long-standing bond between church history and theology; in fact, in some institutions church history really translates into the history of theology. Another reason is the intrinsic appeal of intellectual history and the ability it affords scholars to limit their focus to the thought of prominent clergy or laypersons. Such a focus, however, necessarily restricts the value of these studies since it excludes the vast numbers of laypeople who make up the religious population of the United States. In recent years scholars have sought to move beyond the pulpit to the pew in order to probe more thoroughly the rich complexities of American religious history. The major reason for this trend has been the emergence of social history.

In the past quarter century, social history has bulled its way in the marketplace and now occupies a very prominent position in the historical academy. Its influence is seen especially in colonial history, where community studies and other types of social histories of colonial religion have enhanced our understanding of the role of religion in American life. Social history also has made its mark in nineteenth-century historiography in such areas as the study of revivalism. The new history of American Catholicism also mirrors the influence of social history. Another major development in recent years has been the emergence of women's studies. Though significant cultural changes help to account for this development, the inclusive nature of social history has encouraged historians to examine the place of women and the role of gender in American society. Historians of American religion have not been as quick to follow this development, but every indication is that the issue of women and religion is moving from the periphery to the center in American religious historiography.[3]

• • •

Another area that has benefited from the renaissance in social history is immigration history. In the past quarter century immigration history has come into its own, and in the United States it now has its own journal and professional organization, as well as several research centers that concentrate on immigration studies. The number of published works in this area is most impressive, and the implications of these studies for American religious history cannot be overlooked.

Immigration has never attracted very much attention from American religious historians. In fact, until recently the historical study of immigration attracted the attention of only a handful of scholars. Even with this renewed interest in the study of the immigrants, historians of American religion have remained reluctant to turn their attention in this direction. Immigration was an important aspect of colonial history and remains very much a part of contemporary American life. I want to focus on the nineteenth century, pointing out how the study of the immigrant experience not only will enrich our understanding of that era of American religious history, but also will bring greater coherence to the study of religion in the nineteenth century. Puritanism, evangelicalism, and fundamentalism are intellectual or theological principles, systems of belief, and for this reason they are able to provide coherence or synthesis for a particular period of study. As a theme or organizing principle of study, immigration can function in a similar manner and provides historians with a perspective through which they can view the development of American religion.

First, immigration was a phenomenon that cut across denominational boundaries. It was not limited to Italian Catholics, Russian Jews, or Norwegian Lutherans. It was a typically American experience. The 1916 census of religious bodies points this out very clearly. Of the 200 denominations studied, 132 reported a part or all of their congregations using a foreign language. Equally striking is the revelation that forty-two languages were in use in these churches. Among Roman Catholics, twenty-eight foreign languages were spoken; the Methodists reported twenty-two different languages in use. Clearly, immigration affected all religious traditions in nineteenth-century America.[4] Because it transcends denominational boundaries, the theme of immigration provides historians with a perspective that enables them to examine issues that are common to many religious traditions. For this reason it brings greater coherence and synthesis to the historical study of American religion.

Second, studying the immigrant experience in the United States will force historians to acquire a comparative perspective. Religion is such a distinguishing feature of American life, and yet rarely is it studied comparatively. Immigration can provide that comparative perspective for the nineteenth century and force historians to look beyond the American scene and ask if what happened in America may have differed from what went on in the Old World. Did the establishment of the Dutch Reformed tradition in the United States differ significantly from developments in the Netherlands, and if so, why? Did the American environment alter the folk religion of Italian Catholics, and if so, how? Only through such a comparative perspective will we find out how distinctive the American religious experience was. And in discovering this distinctiveness, historians will better understand the development of religion in the United States.

By studying the immigrant experience American religious historians also will be able to draw on the vast amount of published material produced by immigration historians in the past twenty years. Not only will this lead church historians beyond the confines of their own field, but it also will provide them with a rich source of historical information pertinent to the study of religion in American life. Historians of immigration have examined the old-world background of the newcomers, their patterns of settlement in the United States, and their efforts to adjust to American society and the stresses and strains this adjustment caused. The issues of language and Americanization also have attracted the attention of immigration historians.

All of these issues have relevance for religious history. Realizing this, many historians of immigration have incorporated the theme of religion into their work. Some historians have focused on the issue of conflict in the immigrant community. Not surprisingly, a good deal of attention in such studies centers on religious conflict. In recent years historians have begun to examine the persistence of old-world cultures in the New World. One of the major keepers of culture was the church; this role was manifested in architecture, theology, and devotional practices. The relationship between religion and politics in the immigrant community also has attracted the attention of scholars, and their work has demonstrated how influential religion was in shaping politics in the immigrant community. These are just some of the issues pertinent to American religious history which historians of immigration have studied. A survey of these studies clearly reveals that religion was central to the immigrant experience. It was especially important in rural areas where community was essential to the survival of immigrant culture. If there was no church, there was no colony; and without a colony, the culture of the immigrants would have disappeared.

Because the issues immigration historians study transcend denominational boundaries, they have a unifying influence on religious history. The persistence of religion in the New World is not something unique to Polish or Italian Catholics. Norwegian Lutherans and English Methodists experienced it as well. By examining this issue within various denominations, historians will be able to study an experience common to all immigrant communities. In this manner historians can bring more unity to a field that of its nature tends to be very splintered. This is what I have tried to do in my own work in American Catholic history. Not only have I relied on the writings of historians of immigration, but I have used immigration as an organizing theme in my work. This method has enabled me to bring a greater measure of synthesis and coherence to the history of nineteenth-century American Catholicism.[5] I believe that if a similar approach is used in the study of nineteenth-century American religious history, scholars will gain a richer understanding of the field and religion will become more central to the study of American history.

• • •

For the past two years I have been reading immigrant letters, both published and unpublished, in an effort to understand the religious world of the immigrants. Though still in the midst of this research, I have read enough letters from a variety of people that I can make some observations about the immigrants and their gods.

God-talk was an integral part of the immigrant letter. The God of the immigrants was always present, watching over the people, and many letters refer to God in this manner. Some groups were more inclined to God-talk than others. Irish Catholics and Jews were reticent when it came to God-talk. Norwegian Lutherans, Dutch Reformed, and English Methodists liked to talk about God in their letters. Among the Irish, God-talk was more a decorative feature of their letters, with "thanks be to God" often being about as effusive as they could get. Among Norwegian Lutherans, however, it was common for a letter writer to speak about God in a lengthy sentence or two. Only rarely does a letter writer discourse at length about God or religion; those so inclined tended to be individuals of an evangelical persuasion who often would write at length about a conversion experience.

The God of the immigrants was very busy. The divinity watched over the people at all times, protecting them from all types of adversity. A Dutch Reformed traveler recounted his experience on board a sailing vessel and the fear that gripped him and his wife as the ship began to roll on its side during a storm. Then, he wrote, "most likely, in answer to the prayer of one or other pious passenger, the Lord God spared us and caused the storm to abate." For a Norwegian Lutheran in Texas, God was always arranging "everything so well."[6] In a letter to his family in Ireland a young Irish immigrant, Denis Harley, noted the historic importance of the new year of 1876 and then wrote the following prayerful remark: "May Almighty God be equally propitious to us with his favors in the

New as He has been in the old. May he preserve us from family broils, bitterness and contention, and enable us to live in unity, peace and harmony to the end of our lives."[7] At first glance Harley's remarks appear innocuous, the pious thoughts of a lonely young man. Nonetheless, they paint a portrait of the divinity that was common among all the people whose letters I have read. The God of nineteenth-century immigrants was a personal God who was in close touch with the people. The divinity was not remote, but was a constant companion, guide, and savior in whom the immigrants learned to trust "for everything." The God of the immigrants was not a stern Calvinist who stirred up fear in the people, nor did the divinity resemble the Roman Catholic God of judgment who was ready to pounce on people because of their sins.

The immigrants were not immune to suffering and hardship. Disillusionment with the New World, loss of the harvest, sickness, and death itself were frequent themes in their letters. Despite the harshness of these experiences, the immigrants put such suffering in a religious context. A Dutch Catholic writing from Wisconsin to his mother, brothers, and sisters talked about the misfortunes that had struck his family. "Of the four children which we brought from Holland," he wrote, "Johanna is the only one left." He continued, "misfortunes in our family have been too many and too severe. But it is God's will, and we must carry our Cross no matter how heavy it is." A Norwegian woman spoke of the suffering she had to endure and then stated that "God often sends us sufferings and tribulations to test our faith if we have patience both in good fortune and adversity."[8] The immigrants shared a common understanding of suffering and it was obvious that they had learned this teaching very well. In the good times they thanked God for many blessings; in the bad times they also saw the hand of God at work.

Another common concern reflected in these letters is the immigrants' belief in the afterlife. Moreover, they had a distinctive understanding of what life would be like beyond the grave; the most frequent comparison was to a place of reunion. An Irish letter writer who held a strong belief in the afterlife as well as in God's providence assured his mother that they would meet again in heaven. A Norwegian immigrant ended his letter with greetings to his mother, daughter, and "all my relatives, acquaintances, and friends." He then prayed that "we sometime with gladness may assemble with God in the eternal mansions where there will be no more partings, sorrows, no more trials, but everlasting joy and gladness." This understanding of the afterlife as a place of reunion mirrored the social experience of the immigrants and the sense of separation inherent in the immigrant experience.

One of the most striking features in these letters is the absence of Jesus. For the vast majority of letter writers he seemed not to exist and thus he was rarely mentioned. The letter writers did not talk about sin either. Another striking omission is the absence among Catholic writers of any reference to Mary or individual saints or any devotions thought to be so central to Catholic belief. In fact, in many instances it would be difficult to determine the religious affiliation of the letter writers based on their references to religion. Denominational distinctiveness seldom appears, and because of this absence the belief systems of these people appear to be remarkably similar. They are spartan in their simplicity, with God, suffering, and the afterlife forming the major religious themes. The immigrants manifested a strong belief in a personal God who was very involved in their lives.

The one noticeable denominational difference that does appear in the letters that I read was the preoccupation of some writers from the more hierarchically structured churches (the Episcopal and Roman Catholic in particular) with clergy, ritual, and church. Irish Catholics frequently talked about the clergy, and in very positive terms. On occasion they also mentioned some Catholic rituals, mostly the mass and the parish mission. Both Episcopalians and Roman Catholics talked about the absence of church and clergy. When they did so, however, it was not in a religious or spiritual manner. It was more a statement of fact than an expression of belief. Methodists seldom commented on church and clergy. Good evangelicals that they were, Methodist letter writers were more inclined to talk about revivals and conversion. They met God at revivals and in a conversion experience, whereas Roman Catholics and Lutherans met God when they encountered suffering and the providential hand of the divinity.[9]

One striking observation that emerges from this study is the difference between the religion of Roman Catholic immigrants articulated in prayer books and rituals, and that found in their letters. The letters reveal a very plain religion centered around a God who cares about people. The prayer books and rituals reveal what I have called the Catholic ethos: a belief system grounded in sin, authority, ritual, and the miraculous. These four marks of the Catholic ethos are found in prayer books and rituals developed by the clergy, whereas the letters of the people articulated a more plain religion or ethos. In the people's writings the emphasis was on simplicity, and especially on the miraculous or transcendent aspect of religion. They were not preoccupied with sin in their letters, whereas the clergy emphasized conversion from sin. This striking difference leads to at least two conclusions: as valuable as they are, immigrant letters cannot be the only resource used in searching for the religious world of people; and, as revealing as it might be, the behavior of people at church-sponsored rituals does not completely express the religion of the people. They practiced their religion in other settings, and oftentimes the beliefs professed on these occasions, in this case, in the course of reflection and writing, were more plain and uncomplicated.

• • •

For too long historians of American religion have neglected the study of the immigrant experience. There is no reason to continue this neglect. Now is the time for the recovery of immigration as a theme and organizing principle in the writing of American religious history. Social historians of immigration have provided us with a substantial amount of historical information pertinent to the study of American religious history, and we cannot afford to overlook this work. Moreover, historians of American religion are desirous of writing a more representative history, one that incorporates the laity as well as the clergy. The study of immigration encourages this development by focusing the attention of historians on the religious world of the people. Such a perspective will enable scholars to understand more completely the uniqueness and complexity of religion in American life. Finally, the use of immigration as an organizing theme of study can bring greater coherence to a field which, because of its denominational traditions, is inclined to splinter into disconnected phenomena.

ENDNOTES

1. Bernard Bailyn, "The Challenge of Modern Historiography," *American Historical Review* 87 (1982): 2-3; see also Carl N. Degler, "In Pursuit of an American History," *American Historical Review* 92 (1987): 1-12.
2. Leonard I. Sweet, "The Evangelical Tradition in America" in *The Evangelical Tradition in America*, ed. Leonard I. Sweet (Macon, GA, 1984), 1-84.
3. Rosemary Radford Ruether and Rosemary Skinner Keller, eds., *Women and Religion in America*, 3 vols. (San Francisco, 1982–1986).
4. *Religious Bodies 1916* (Washington, D.C., 1919), pt. 1, 76, 85, and pt. 2, 457.
5. Jay P. Dolan, *The American Catholic Experience: A History From Colonial Times to the Present* (New York, 1985).
6. Henry S. Lucas, ed., *Dutch Immigrant Memoirs and Related Writings*, 2 vols. (Seattle, 1955), 2:89; Theodore C. Blegen, ed., *Land of Their Choice: The Immigrants Write Home* (St. Paul, MN, 1955), 348.
7. Correspondence of Denis and Michael Harley, Carson, NV, to parents in Clonakilty, Ireland, 6 January 1876, Archives of City of Cork, Ireland.
8. Lucas, *Dutch Immigrant Memoirs*, 2:168; Blegen, *Land of Their Choice*, 187.
9. See Charlotte Erickson, *Invisible Immigrants: The Adaptation of English and Scottish Immigrants in Nineteenth-Century America* (Coral Gables, FL, 1972), 87-92, 127-28.

FOR FURTHER READING

Archdeacon, Thomas J. *Becoming American: An Ethnic History*, New York, 1983.

Balmer, Randall H. *A Perfect Babel of Confusion: Dutch Religion and English Culture in the Middle Colonies*, New York, 1989.

Bratt, James D. *Dutch Calvinism in Modern America: A History of a Conservative Subculture*, Grand Rapids, MI, 1984.

Bodner, John, *The Transplanted: A History of Immigrants in Urban America*, Bloomington, IN, 1985.

Dolan, Jay P. *The Immigrant Church: New York's Irish and German Catholics, 1815–1865*, Baltimore, 1975.

————. *Catholic Revivalism: The American Experience, 1830–1900*, Notre Dame, 1978.

Greeley, Andrew M. *The Catholic Myth: The Behavior and Beliefs of American Catholics*, New York, 1990.

Moynihan, Daniel Patrick, and Nathan Glazer, *Beyond the Melting Pot: The Negroes, Puerto Ricans, Jews, Italians, and Irish of New York City*, Cambridge, MA, 1963.

Liptak, Dolores. *Immigrants and Their Church*, New York, 1989.

Olson, James Stuart. *Catholic Immigrants in America*, Chicago, 1987.

Sarna, Jonathan, ed. *The American Jewish Experience*, New York, 1986.

INTRODUCTION TO ESSAY 5

Many historians hold that the First Great Awakening was the earliest phenomenon in this country that bound the colonies together in a shared interest. Revivals all along the eastern seaboard made citizens who lived as far away as Georgia aware that they had the same concerns as people in Massachusetts. Lambert demonstrates the validity of this theme without pressing it as his main interest. His primary concern is with the most outstanding individual of that entire era, a magnetic, complex, and ultimately enigmatic prototype of American evangelism. Indeed, if the words "television" and "films" were substituted for "journal" and "newspaper," then we can as easily discern the ways of Billy Graham in our own day as we learn about George Whitefield, who dominated eighteenth-century colonial revivalism.

In a few deft paragraphs Lambert sketches Whitefield's origins, training, and his feeling that God had called him to an aggressive preaching ministry. Exploiting the relatively new medium of print, especially newspapers and inexpensive books, Whitefield created an image of himself as God's chosen instrument of salvation. Widespread consumption of such items confirmed that forceful image among the citizenry. Sermons, journals, and letters—all written with an eye toward publicity—enhanced Whitefield's reputation as an evangelist. One might argue that Whitefield used the press more to draw attention to himself than to warn sinners of their need for spiritual rebirth. Lambert makes plain, however, that Whitefield's innovative advertising techniques expanded awareness of spiritual awakenings, making something public and national out of what had previously been only private and local.

Original source - CH 60 (1991): 223-46.

5

The Great Awakening as Artifact
George Whitefield and the Construction of Intercolonial Revival, 1739–1745

Frank Lambert

Throughout the 1720s and 1730s evangelical preachers sparked revivals from New England to New Jersey. George Whitefield's arrival in October 1739 changed the scope and character of colonial evangelical revivals. The Anglican itinerant connected the local awakenings, fashioning them into an intercolonial movement crafting a national event before the existence of a nation. He propagated the message of the new birth in every colony through the spoken and printed word. And he lifted the revivals out of narrow denominational boundaries by helping to create a "religious public sphere" in which supporters and opponents of revivalism debated the Great Awakening before a literate, rational, and independent audience. Whitefield's transformation of revivals into a national, public event took place in the press, especially in newspapers. Indeed, the network of colonial newspapers represents a necessary if not sufficient explanation for the Great Awakening.

Historians have generally overlooked the press in Whitefield's transformation of evangelical revivalism. Through the widespread distribution of newspapers, broadsides, pamphlets, sermons, and journals, Whitefield constructed the Great Awakening, crafting a common message, fashioning an intercolonial context, and creating a religious public discourse. Whitefield's exploitation of the press to promote his services distinguished him from his evangelical predecessors.[1]

While Jonathan Edwards wrote an account of the Connecticut Valley revival of 1734 and 1735, he did not publish his account until 1736, months after the awakening had subsided, and only then at the urging of the Boston minister Benjamin Colman.[2] By contrast, Whitefield publicized his itinerancy through a "print and

preach" strategy that flooded the colonies with his printed sermons, journals, and letters. Whitefield also exploited the expanding network of colonial newspapers, inserting third-person
accounts of his revival services, including reports written by the
revivalist himself. Having developed a bold, innovative press campaign in England from 1737 to 1739, the Grand Itinerant arrived in
America as a well-publicized success with advance publicity
designed to attract large crowds to his services. As a result,
Whitefield crafted a new religion out-of-doors, beyond parish
boundaries and clerical authority. Through the expanding press,
Whitefield discovered a more efficient means of delivering his
message of the new birth to a mass audience.

• • •

Whitefield's message of the necessity of a spiritual new birth
echoed the central themes preached by Edwards and Tennent.
More borrowed than created, Whitefield's version of the gospel
contained language familiar to Puritan descendants on both sides
of the Atlantic. Restricting true conversion to the "indwelling of
Christ," Whitefield charged that too many church members were
"destitute of a true and living faith in Jesus Christ," possessing
only "head-knowledge without that of the heart." The industrious
revivalist lamented what he considered the flaccid quality of
Anglican religion which practiced a monotonous round of "good
works" as if those empty deeds could lead to justification.
Whitefield admonished his followers to engage in rigorous spiritual exercises, "watch[ing] against all temptations to sloth . . .
liv[ing] every day as holily as [possible], be[ing] frequent in self-
examination morning and evening, and wrestl[ing] with God,
beg[ging] him to hasten the new birth." Although salvation came
only through divine election, the seeker should "never leave off
watching, reading, praying, striving, till [he or she] experimentally
find[s] Christ Jesus formed within."

Although Whitefield did not invent the concept of the new birth,
he constructed his own meaning of the conversion process.
Proclaiming that salvation transcended traditional church boundaries, the revivalist delivered his message to a mass audience. He
warned that too many church members "deceive[d] themselves

with false Hopes of Salvation . . . flatter[ing] themselves that they [were] really born again" simply because they attended services and performed good works. But he also offered the hope of a spiritual new birth to men and women who professed no church affiliation, to "those who [were] dead in Trespasses and Sins." He warned that instead of "overcoming the world [many were] immersed in it." He urged them to make the attainment of salvation "the one business of [their] Lives."

Whitefield based his qualifications for proclaiming the necessity of the new birth on his acquaintance with "experimental religion" not his mastery of prescribed theology. He linked his message to the personal experience of the messenger, filtering the message of the new birth through his own intense conversion. As a nineteen-year-old student at Pembroke College, Oxford, Whitefield sought salvation through a series of personal efforts including extreme asceticism, a period of fasting which resulted in such a weakened physical condition that in 1735 he withdrew from school for six months to regain his strength. Upon returning, at John Wesley's encouragement, he read deeply in the devotional works of the Puritans.[3] He discovered that "true religion was [nothing less than] union of the soul with God, and Christ formed within" men and women. Whitefield testified that upon reading those words, "a ray of Divine light . . . instantaneously darted upon my soul, and from that moment, but not till then, did I know that I must be a new creature." Through his own personal alteration, Whitefield fashioned his interpretation of the new birth.[4]

In his spiritual autobiography, Whitefield made bold claims about his divine calling. The revivalist saw God's hand in every aspect of his life, including the circumstances of his birth. He pointed out that his nativity occurred in an inn, following "the example of [his] dear Saviour, who was born in a manger belonging to an inn."[5] The Boston antirevivalist Charles Chauncy objected to Whitefield's claims and to his giving "publick Notice" of parallels to Christ's birth. Whitefield defended his autobiography by insisting that "the circumstance of my being born in an Inn has often been of Service to me" in introducing men and women to the new birth. In 1756, long after establishing his transatlantic popularity, Whitefield deleted all comparisons with Christ's birth, confessing that the original version contained "too much [of his] own Spirit when [he] thought [he] was writing and speaking entirely by the assistance and Spirit of God."

Crafting his spiritual autobiography for a mass audience, Whitefield disseminated the volume throughout the Atlantic world. Publishing the work in 1740 in both America and Britain, he authorized ten editions: four in London, one in Edinburgh, three in Boston, and two in Philadelphia. Printers directed the book toward the widest audience, releasing it in three different sizes including one in sextodecimo that even the lower sorts could afford. American readers eagerly purchased Whitefield's *Life*. The Boston printer and bookseller Daniel Henchman published two different runs of fifteen hundred volumes each—a large number for an age when "the more successful writing sold 1500" in the print capital of London. Through wide circulation of his account that God called him to preach the necessity of the new birth, Whitefield sought to strengthen the bond between message and messenger.

Although other evangelicals within the Church of England also sought to convey the necessity of the new birth, Whitefield fashioned a negative view of the Anglican Establishment. Alarmed by the decline in religion, morality, and manners, some clergy such as Thomas Bray developed a number of voluntary organizations to educate people in the principles of Protestant faith. Early in the eighteenth century, English subscribers raised capital to form the Society for the Promotion of Christian Knowledge (SPCK) and the Society for the Propagation of the Gospel in Foreign Parts (SPG). When Whitefield arrived in America in 1739, scores of SPG missionaries were preaching from Maine to the Carolinas. By the Revolution, 309 Anglican missionaries had served in the colonies with many sparking local spiritual awakenings that saw hundreds brought into the Christian faith.[6]

However, Whitefield discounted the SPG accomplishments, viewing the Anglican missionaries more as competitors who delivered a dangerous message than as colleagues in propagating the gospel. He publicized his assessment of the Anglican missionaries in his *Journals* and elsewhere, claiming that he would "rather that people had no minister than such as are generally sent over." In fashioning his own view of the state of religion, Whitefield employed an array of negative adjectives to describe the condition of Anglicanism: dead, decayed, declining, dry, formal, empty, and cold, to name a few. By contrast, he depicted pietism as alive, vital, growing, spontaneous, fulfilling, and quickening.

As Whitefield's popularity increased on the eve of his departure for America, the revivalist made his success a central theme of his message. Whitefield attributed his success to both invisible, inward manifestations of God's special calling and to visible, outward signs evidenced by numerous listeners. Throughout his *Journals*, Whitefield noted the "uncommon manifestations granted [him] from above." He claimed that he was "overpowered with a sense of God's Infinite Majesty" and stirred by the Divine "to prepare [men and women] for the coming of the Son of Man." Whitefield demonstrated to others that his ministry was the work of God by providing evidence of "the outward visible Effects of his Preaching, viz. the Crowds that attended it, and the Numbers proselytized to his Doctrine." In a typical report on the success of his itinerancy, Whitefield published a statistical account of his activities in the spring of 1740, indicating he had traveled for thirty-three days, traversed over eight hundred miles, preached fifty-eight sermons, attracted crowds of up to twenty thousand, and collected "near 500 pounds sterling" for the orphanage he founded in Georgia. He concluded that particular report with an assessment of the revival's spiritual results: "Great and visible effects followed his preaching. There was never such a general awakening, and concern for the things of God known in America before."

When Whitefield arrived in the colonies on 30 October 1739, he had already shaped public perception through the press. He had fashioned a message that placed him in the Reformation tradition in opposition to the Church of England whom he depicted as betraying Reformed theology. Whitefield had carefully crafted a view of himself as a special instrument selected by God to proclaim the necessity of the new birth. Writing in promotional language as well as in theological discourse, Whitefield presented himself as a well-publicized success "recently arrived from

England." Just as colonists read about the expanding choice of consumer goods imported from Britain, they read about one who arrived offering them a new religious experience. And by promoting his revivals in all the colonies, Whitefield prepared the way for a national event with men and women from disparate regions bound together by shared experiences.

• • •

In addition to providing a powerful means of conveying his message of the new birth, the colonial press, especially newspapers, enabled Whitefield to construct an intercolonial revival. Preaching imposed obvious restrictions on the itinerant: at any given time he could appear at only one place. Print allowed him to extend both the spiritual and temporal dimensions of his mission. While Whitefield preached in one location, men and women throughout the colonies participated in the revivals by reading newspaper accounts of his progress, scanning advertisements for his printed works, following pamphlet debates between Whitefield's supporters and opponents, or reading one of his sermons. Whitefield's exploitation of the press was central to his making the Great Awakening a national event.

Through his printed sermons, journals, and letters, Whitefield extended the revival into remote areas where he was unable to deliver the spoken word. Through the distribution of printed sermons in sparsely populated settlements, Whitefield expanded the spatial scope of his ministry. Intercolonial newspaper coverage also represented a temporal extension of Whitefield's ministry, enabling evangelicals to participate in the revivals long before and after the itinerant's actual visit. Jonathan Edwards wrote to Whitefield that "the Success of your Labours in other places [aroused my] desire to see and hear you in this Place." Edwards and other New Englanders followed with anticipation Whitefield's progress as he moved through the Chesapeake and middle colonies before his arrival in Rhode Island in the fall of 1740. The pastor at Lyme, Connecticut, Jonathan Parsons observed that the "frequent Accounts of the Success [Whitefield] had in many Places were serviceable among us." And the Boston evangelical minister Thomas Prince noted the cumulative impact of

Whitefield's advance publicity on New Englanders. Prince observed that printed "Accounts of the Reverend Mr. Whitefield as they *successively* arrived before his appearance here . . . prepar'd the Way for his Entertainment and successful Labours among us."

In addition to enabling men and women to anticipate Whitefield's preaching, his intercolonial newspaper coverage allowed evangelicals to continue following the revival's progress after his departure. Subsequent to Whitefield's second trip to New England in 1744 and 1745, New Englanders read of his activities as he traveled toward Bethesda, his orphan house near Savannah, Georgia. Whitefield forwarded to the *Boston Gazette* and other newspapers accounts of his successes in New York, Pennsylvania, Maryland, Virginia, and Carolina en route to Bethesda. Through the press, men and women participated in a national event that extended far beyond the boundaries of their local parishes.

Whitefield forged an intercolonial evangelical news exchange that united men and women from disparate regions and created an imaginary evangelical community. Through printed works revivalists participated in awakenings throughout the Atlantic world. Even when Whitefield was absent from the colonies he kept American evangelicals informed of the revival's progress. For example, he forwarded his writings to Edwards and others to "shew you what the Lord is about to do in Europe." Whitefield's opponents noted that through print the evangelist had indeed forged a national community. Edward Wigglesworth identified Whitefield as the leader and "blameable Cause" of the religious disorders spread throughout the colonies. When Whitefield claimed that he did not know many of the itinerants Wigglesworth cited as disseminating confusion among the churches, Wigglesworth retorted, "nor will it much alter the Case, tho' some who may have had a Hand in [the disorders], are Men whom you never knew. For tho' you are unacquainted with them, yet they are but too well acquainted with your Writings and Bad Example."

By printing and preaching throughout the colonies Whitefield standardized evangelicalism. He created a common language of the new birth that evangelicals employed everywhere to distinguish themselves from those who had not undergone a spiritual conversion. Through publicizing testimonials of the new birth, Whitefield provided a model that tended toward encouraging a uniform response to his message. Such uniformity extended to publicity itself. As Whitefield approached Charleston, local evangelicals wondered how they should publicize his coming. They decided that their welcome should be similar to that extended in other places. Submitting an announcement to the *South Carolina Gazette*, Josiah Smith indicated that "the Publick will naturally expect some Account of Mr. WHITEFIELD, in imitation of other Places where he has preached."

• • •

While enabling Whitefield to construct a national evangelical revival, the press also provided a new public discourse for revivalists and antirevivalists alike to debate the "Great Awakening." By addressing a mass audience through newspapers, Whitefield shifted religious discussion from a private sphere defined in denominational terms to a public arena in which literate men and women employed their rational powers to judge among contending views. However, the same public context Whitefield helped shape constrained him, forcing him to fashion arguments based on evidence rather than mere assertion.

Whitefield recognized that in the religious public sphere readers would exercise their independent judgment. In the preface to his *Journals* he acknowledged that readers shaped common sense. Admitting to the limitations of his own reasoned appeal to persuade people of the necessity of a new birth, Whitefield wrote, "What reasons I can urge for this persuasion is needless to mention, because few in this case would judge impartially; and what seems a reason to me, may not be deemed so by another."[7] One of Whitefield's most ardent supporters, Josiah Smith of Charleston, also appealed to rational, impartial readers. In a testimonial for the Grand Itinerant, Smith penned, "My design in writing this is to shew my impartial opinion." He noted that Whitefield's doctrines were "agreeable to the dictates of reason; evidently formed upon scripture; exactly correspondent with the articles of the establishment." He argued that Whitefield presented truths no unprejudiced inquirer should miss. Having presented his reasonable defense of Whitefield, Smith invited others to show their opinions with the same impartiality.

Although the debate over the evangelical revivals was highly partisan, writers on both sides learned that the reading public demanded reasoned argumentation supported by evidence. His opponents frequently charged Whitefield with enthusiasm, claiming that he relied on direct divine revelation rather than on scripture. Whitefield denied such charges, warning against those "who claimed to have power to work miracles such as restoring sight to blind eyes." Whitefield recognized the importance of reason in discerning religious truth, subscribing to the view that "reason seems to be the faculty given us by God to direct our enquiries in all things." Unconvinced, Whitefield's opponents claimed that proponents of revivalism could not be trusted. John Caldwell charged that the evangelicals had insulted public reason "from Pulpit and Press" and thereby offended common sense. Caldwell warned, "Let us be careful of such Teachers as are leading us blindfold to their Opinions . . . and also such who are for confining us to the hearing or reading only their Side of the Question in Controversies." Caldwell argued that the revivalists' tendentious strategy "is intended to bypass our judgments, to prepossess us in Favour of their Doctrines, and a tacit Acknowledgment of their Fear least the contrary Opinion would appear probable and better supported than theirs, if Men give them a fair hearing." He finished by insisting that "if readers were to reach reasoned conclusions, they needed 'evidence,' not partisan assertion."[8]

Whitefield and his opponents triggered newspaper wars as they disputed evangelical revivalism. In some instances, Whitefield and his detractors debated their opposing position within the same newspaper. One-third of the issues of the *South Carolina Gazette* published between the summers of 1740 and 1741 carried as the front page story a debate between Whitefield's supporters and opponents. Prorevivalists submitted partisan accounts of Whitefield's ministry in the name of "Publick Service." They presented his theology as consistent with the Articles of the Church of England, claiming that Whitefield "guarded against a licentious abuse . . . of doctrine." In other words, Whitefield preached a reasonable theology. However, opponents assailed him as one who "composes not sermons like a man of letters," implying that his discourses did not conform to sound reason. The newspaper's printer Peter Timothy was more than willing to provide a forum for the debate which enabled him to sell special editions to satisfy public demand.

Thus through his vigorous use of the press Whitefield participated in creating a new religious public sphere that extended throughout the American colonies. Indeed, by exploiting the expanding print market of the mid-eighteenth century Whitefield had redefined popular religion, fashioning something public and national out of what had been private and local. In the process he had empowered men and women. Far from being passive consumers of religious notions shaped by the clergy, including Whitefield himself, ordinary men and women exercised their independent reason to construct their own meanings of the revivals. While Whitefield and others established the terms of the public debate, readers forced writers to provide evidence in support of their claims. Whitefield employed a range of authorial strategies aimed at rendering his intercolonial message authoritative, commonsensical, and impartial. Nevertheless the final judgment of Whitefield's construction rested with the religious public he had helped create.

ENDNOTES

1. George Whitefield, *Sermons on Important Subjects* (London, 1828), 242-48.
2. Perry Miller, *Jonathan Edwards* (New York, 1949), 136-37.
3. Charles E. Hambrick-Stowe, *The Practice of Piety: Puritan Devotional Discipline in Seventeenth-Century New England* (Chapel Hill, NC, 1982), 54-90.
4. George Whitefield, *Journals* (London, 1960), 47.
5. Ibid., 37.
6. For SPG efforts in eighteenth-century America, see Jon Butler, *Awash in a Sea of Faith: Christianizing the American People* (Cambridge, MA, 1990), 164-76; Sydney Ahlstrom, *A Religious History of the American People* (New Haven, 1972). 221.
7. Whitefield, *Journals*, 97.

8. Richard Bushman, ed., *The Great Awakening Documents on the Revival of Religion, 1740–1745* (Chapel Hill, NC, 1969), 159.

FOR FURTHER READING

Balmer, Randall H., and Edith W. Blumhofer, eds. *Modern Christian Revivals*, Urbana, IL, 1993.

Goen, C. C. *Revivalism and Separatism in New England: Strict Congregationalists and Separate Baptists in the Great Awakening, 1740–1800*, New Haven, 1962.

Hall, David D. *Worlds of Wonder, Days of Judgment: Popular Religious Beliefs in Early New England*, Cambridge, MA, 1990.

Heimert, Alan. *Religion and the American Mind: From the Great Awakening to the Revolution*, Cambridge, MA, 1966.

Heimert, Alan, and Perry Miller, eds. *The Great Awakening: Documents Illustrating the Crisis and Its Consequences*, Indianapolis, 1967.

Lambert, Frank. *"Pedlar in Divinity": George Whitefield and the Transatlantic Revivals, 1737–1770*, Princeton, 1994.

McLoughlin, William G. *Revivals, Awakenings, and Reform: An Essay on Religion and Social Change in America, 1607–1977*, Chicago, 1978.

Schmidt, Leigh E. *Holy Fairs: Scottish Communions and American Revivals in the Early Modern Period*, Princeton, 1989.

Smith, Timothy L. *Revivalism and Social Reform: American Protestantism on the Eve of the Civil War*, rev. ed., Baltimore, 1980.

Stout, Harry S. *The Divine Dramatist: George Whitefield and the Rise of Modern Evangelicalism*, Grand Rapids, 1991.

———. *The New England Soul: Preaching and Religious Culture in Colonial New England*, New York, 1986.

INTRODUCTION TO ESSAY 6

In recent years historians have begun to move beyond grand interpretive schemes to explore religion "from below." In this essay Schmidt focuses not on ideologies or rituals but on the dynamic interplay between religious ideas and the tactile or material dimensions of life. Most religion studies concentrate on theology, rituals, personal ethics, or public action. In this essay Schmidt focuses not on traditional ideologies but on questions of personal taste. He begins by noting that religious and social values are intertwined and interactive. Religious principles do affect other spheres, but secular standards help shape religious attitudes, too. Schmidt asks new questions here, all based on the provocative idea that social status and economic interests have a strong impact on religious identity. Here we see Puritans, Anglicans, and Methodists in light of a new and illuminating consideration: how religion affected the way they thought about clothing and at the same time how social tastes shaped the contours of their spiritual lives.

When someone chooses to attend a particular church, transfers to a different one across town, or moves to another denomination altogether, the reasons often have as much to do with social sensibilities as with religious principle. People do not usually determine their actions by theological or biblical precepts alone; they also make decisions according to what they think is beautiful (or ugly), dignified (or unseemly), and important (or far-fetched and ridiculous). Religious activity is always a mixture of impulses drawn from doctrine and popular tastes drawn from the surrounding culture. With this important insight Schmidt helps explain religious behavior in the past, and in our own day as well.

Original source - CH 58 (1989): 36-51.

6

"A Church-Going People Are a Dress-Loving People"

Clothes, Communication, and Religious Culture in Early America

Leigh Eric Schmidt

Protestant cultures are almost proverbially cultures dominated by spoken and printed words, above all by the preached Word. In her recent book *Image as Insight*, Margaret R. Miles has reminded scholars anew of Luther's telling words: "The ears are the only organs of a Christian."[1] Religious understanding for Protestants, so the wisdom goes, was to come primarily through the hearing of the Word. Christianity in its purest form was a faith of the preached Word, unencumbered by external rites and corrupt accretions. Thus have Protestant cultures often been characterized, and no doubt with some truth. In enshrining the preached Word Protestants denigrated traditional images and rituals and attempted to turn their spiritual pilgrimages away from Catholic forms.

Since the religious culture of early America shared to a large degree in this Protestant ethos, historians not surprisingly have generally followed this common line in their treatment of religion in the British colonies. Two recent, far-ranging, and excellent studies of early American religious history reveal the prevalence of this guiding view. Harry S. Stout probes the centrality of the sermon in the religious culture of colonial New England. According to Stout, the sermon was the consummate "medium of communications" in New England, for the Puritans were above all else a "people of the Word." Patricia U. Bonomi adopts a similar view for the colonies more generally. For Bonomi, as for others, spoken and printed words were the "quintessential" forms of religious expression in the colonies. Thus have the modes of communication in the religious culture of early America been considered to be primarily aural and textual, not ocular and visual. Preached words and read ones have been taken to be the preeminent, almost exclusive, way that people made sense of their religious world.[2]

Though attending closely to words, early Americans nonetheless did not close off other avenues of communication but instead kept them open and traveled them extensively. As Rhys Isaac and Dell Upton have averred and substantiated in their recent studies of colonial Virginia, early Americans had complex repertoires for communication at their disposal, and the various Protestants among them—whether Anglicans or Baptists—hardly constituted exceptions. In concentrating on verbalization, historians of American religion have tended to neglect the many other ways in which religious people communicated with one another in the colonial and early national periods. Gesture, deportment, posture, and procession, as well as architectural settings, objects, and emblems—all these and more were employed to carry religious messages. Nonverbal communication was a full and rich part of the religious culture of early America; these media that aimed at the eyes instead of the ears were indeed intricate, highly expressive, and often-used forms of communication. In sum, while historians know a great deal about what religious people heard and read in early America, they have wondered far less about what they saw.[3]

Clothing was one aspect of visual communication that was particularly vital in early America. Though only a handful of historians have considered its significance, dress was clearly instrumental in defining age, social status, gender relations, and political authority. More than socially instrumental, dress was also highly expressive, for clothes were often invested with religious meanings and thus carried significance for the spirituality of those who wore them. Interpreting this important but little-studied channel of communication within the religious culture of early America should help us to understand better the way people constructed and experienced their religious world. In thus interpreting dress, this essay is not intended as a history of costume but instead as a small attempt at cultural history or historical anthropology.[4] More suggestive, illustrative, and propositional than definitive, this article probes various layers of meaning that were contained in clothes in the religious culture of early America.

• • •

Perhaps the first and most obvious point to be made is that dress and hierarchy were inextricably interrelated in the colonies. It was axiomatic, as Cotton Mather said, that "the *Ranks* of People should be discerned by their *Clothes*." Sumptuary laws, though in practice hard to enforce, were probably the clearest embodiment of this wisdom, as such legislation attempted to regulate the dress that people of different stations and ranks were permitted to wear. Fines were instituted for violators who were "judge[d] to exceed their ranks & ability in the costlynes or fashion of their apparel in any respect." Thus were modes of dress understood as being critical to the definition of the social order and to the construction and maintenance of social hierarchy.

The experiences of an eighteenth-century Anglican rector, Devereux Jarratt, give specificity to the interrelationship of dress and social status in early America. Born into a simple farming family, Jarratt noted the great social distance between his kind and what he dubbed "the *richer sort*." "To such people I had no access," he related. "We were accustomed to look upon, what were called *gentle folks*, as beings of a superior order. For my part I was quite shy of *them*, and kept off at a humble distance." As Jarratt advanced in social status from poor farm boy to esteemed parson, clothes clearly marked out his elevation. At the first stage he obtained "an old wig" so that he might "appear something more than common, . . . and be counted somebody." Advancing in both education and the social circles in which he traveled, he procured "a tolerable suit of cloaths" and was then able "to think more highly of myself" than formerly. Finally, upon his ordination, he was given "a new suit of the best black broad cloth" that clearly marked his attainment of a new social and religious status, his hierarchical elevation above the simple and the common.[5] Jarratt's repeated experience of social distinction and his sense of its clear embodiment in dress were basic parts of the mentality of many colonial Americans. Perhaps this awareness found clearest and simplest expression in the title of a pamphlet published anonymously in Philadelphia in 1772: *The Miraculous Power of Clothes, and Dignity of the Taylors: Being an Essay on the Words, Clothes Make Men.* As this tract suggested and Jarratt's experiences confirmed, social status, station, and power were displayed, articulated, and sustained through dress.

The interrelatedness of dress and hierarchy in colonial society invested clothes with considerable symbolic power—a power that dissenters were quick to tap. For various groups—Quakers, pietists, and evangelicals—plain dress became a central expression of social and religious protest. For those disaffected by the fineries of the genteel, religious groups that invested simplicity with virtue and identified plainness with godliness clearly trumpeted an appealing and subversive message. Often not having the same access to the printed word as did the elites, evangelicals and other dissenters took up the medium of dress and exploited this form of communication as a vehicle of religious and social protest. Wherever there was dissent from the hierarchical religious traditions of colonial America, dress became a pivotal form for expressing discontent with the existing order and for fostering a more egalitarian religious culture. The plain dress of Quakers, pietists, and evangelicals carried, in sum, significant social, economic, and religious messages in early America. It was invariably in tension with the pageantry of hierarchy.

Forms of plain dress contributed to more than an expression of egalitarianism; they were also a way to define a community and to identify a people. Of the English groups in the colonies the Quakers were the most persistent in trying to preserve their identity as a people through distinctive modes of plain dress. With a vision of themselves as a holy people, the Quakers strove to construct clear boundaries that would distinguish the devout from the worldly. Very specific rules for proper clothes had to be maintained if the Quakers were to remain identifiable as "a plain People."

If whole religious communities could be defined in part through dress, the specific pastors, priests, and prophets who led them could be as well. Clerical roles were given partial definition through clerical garb. To don the black gown of the Congregational minister or the white surplice of the Anglican priest was to clothe oneself with moral and spiritual authority. An example of the interconnectedness of ministerial authority and proper forms of dress can be seen in the eighteenth-century pastor John Rodgers, who spent most of his career as a Presbyterian minister in New York City. Rodgers, it was said, carried himself with "a peculiar, apostolical dignity" that quelled any "frivolity, impiety, and profaneness" in those who saw him. This dignity stemmed in part from his solemn manner and in part from his being "always attentive to his dress." "Like his manners and his morals," his early biographer Samuel Miller related, "[his dress] was invariable neat, elegant, and spotless." All ministers, Miller said, should follow Rodgers's example and neither be "a clerical fop" nor "a clerical sloven." Instead, dressing like Rodgers, pastors were to clothe themselves in such a way as "to inspire respect," thus giving added weight to their verbal instructions. With Rodgers as a case in point, Miller suggested that the very authority of any minister over parishioners or within a community was bound up with his dignified dress. Finding considerable corroboration in gowns, bands, vestments, and other distinguishing marks of ministerial dress, this assumption carried substantial credence in the religious culture of early America.[6]

This sort of clerical authority, which was founded on elite notions of decorum and gentlemanly manner, was hardly a model throughout early America. Evangelical itinerants and lay preachers worried little about garnering traditional ministerial authority which they associated with an untoward clericalism. Certain itinerants during the Great Awakening in New England such as Samuel Buell, Andrew Croswell, and James Davenport were actually reported to have stripped off a fair portion of their attire when preaching in some of the more effervescent assemblies, thus doing without a distinctive clerical badge and thus leveling one of the social distinctions that separated them from their auditors. Indeed, itinerants throughout the colonies showed little interest in the sort of clerical authority that Rodgers embodied. Their own forms of dress became in turn an expression of their revolt from sacerdotalism and their solidarity with the common people.

Clothes were fundamental as well in drawing the boundaries that delimited the spheres of women. Proper forms of dress reified the virtues and dispositions that were considered essential for a pious woman. Instructed to avoid "the smallest appearance of immodesty" in their apparel, godly women were to dress in such a way that their very appearance communicated orderliness, humility, and devotion. "Their outward Garb" was to express such inward virtues as meekness, submissiveness, and modesty. Female dress was even seen to be constitutive of "this meek and quiet" disposition that was "so necessary a part of the female character." Taking their lead from scriptural warnings—especially 1 Timothy 2:9-10 and 1 Peter 3:3-4—and from the early church fathers—especially Tertullian and Chrysostom—zealous advocates of modesty in apparel aimed their strongest efforts at chastening the sensuality of women and at instilling in them a piety of meekness and shamefaced obedience.

Such pious ideals for the dress of women were not easily achieved by those ministers, moralists, or magistrates who promoted them. Struggle, as much as submission, was evident in debates over the clothes of women. Though ministers regularly sought to prescribe rules for dress and fashion, they often found that women paid little attention. That women embraced such fashions over ministerial injunction suggested a challenge to male authority—to the prerogative to prescribe not simply female fashions, but women's roles. In this context dress could embody both a male assertion of hegemony and a female struggle for autonomous self-expression.[7]

• • •

Clothes in early America clearly helped order religion and society: they contributed to notions of authority, hierarchy, community, and gender. At the same time, dress evoked significant spiritual and theological meanings within the religious culture of early America. Images of the Sabbath, of ritual, of sin, of good works, of purity, of eschatology, of redemption—all were made vivid through the medium of dress.

Hallowed in a variety of ways, the Sabbath was at the center of the religious culture of early America, and dress in particular helped mark the sacrality of the day. People were concerned on the Sabbath to dress themselves in their best clothes; "Sunday best" was already proverbial. Even pietists and evangelicals who insisted on plain dress nonetheless made sure that their bodies were gravely and decently clothed. They made certain that pride and show were avoided and that instead earnestness and devotedness were clearly displayed in their modestly adorned bodies.[8]

The expanse of ritualism in the religious culture of early America is highlighted in the regulations surrounding dress. Extending beyond patterns of worship, this ritualism informed as well the diurnal routines of many of the faithful. Numerous rubrics guided the way the pious lived, and rules about dress were often among the most important. Thus the Quakers, for example, held to rules not only about clothes—though plain dress was a principal concern—but also about household furnishings, diet, speech, and recreations. Religion in early America was seen and acted out in a myriad of ways; it was embodied in various rituals and rubrics, of which rules about dress were but one revealing indication.

Besides its importance to ritualism, dress contained doctrinal significance. Clothes were regularly connected with notions of sin and pride; indeed, they were regularly seen as tangible embodiments of such ideas. Beyond symbolizing the sin of pride and even more grandly the Fall itself, the wearing of certain clothes could also embody the sins of lust and sensuality. Women in particular (and not surprisingly, given that much of the literature focused on their immodesty) were charged with exciting hellish fires in the hearts of "Male Spectators" by exposing, as Cotton Mather said, "unto *Common View* those parts of [the] Body, which there can be no Good *End* or *Use* for the *Exposing* of"—notably, the back, shoulders, and breasts. In such sights the eyes betrayed the heart, for, as one British pamphlet entitled *Just and Seasonable Reprehension of Naked Breasts and Shoulders* declared, "the *Devil* makes use of the windowes of our bodies, for Death by Sin to enter into our Souls." The seeing of such provocatively dressed bodies was especially dangerous on religious occasions as it distracted people from

91

devotion and gave rise instead to lustful thoughts. For the pious this danger of sexual distraction made modesty in apparel all the more needful. Thus did dress intertwine with sensuality and with religion. As potential symbols and embodiments of *"Lust,"* clothes had to be carefully monitored by the faithful.

For those Puritans, pietists, or evangelicals who saw sin in fine dress, the issue was founded upon more than repressive fears of worldliness, sensuality, and distraction. To all those who made so much of plain dress it was a pressing ethical issue; to many it even became an issue of compassion versus hypocrisy, of good works versus negligent frivolity. Few made this point more eloquently or urgently than did John Wesley:

> The wearing [of] costly array is directly opposite to the being adorned with good works. Nothing can be more evident than this; for the more you lay out on your own apparel, the less you have left to clothe the naked, to feed the hungry, to lodge the strangers, to relieve those that are sick and in prison, and to lessen the number-less afflictions to which we are exposed in this vale of tears. . . . [W]hat you put upon yourself, you are, in effect, tearing from the back of the naked; as the costly and delicate food which you eat, you are snatching from the mouth of the hungry. For mercy, for pity, for Christ's sake, for the honour of his gospel, stay your hand! Do not throw this money away! Do not lay out on nothing, yea, worse than nothing, what may clothe your poor, naked, shivering fellow-creature!

Wesley's prophetic thoughts on dress were keenly felt in the American context. Not only did his reflections serve as a basis for early American Methodist pronouncements on the matter, but Wesley himself, in one of his few successes in his brief sojourn in Georgia, carried out a reform of dress along this prophetic line. Plain dress, in Savannah as elsewhere, was linked to prophetic witness.[9]

The visual, richly symbolic medium of dress was capable of communicating a multiplicity of meanings. Thus could clothes point not only to sin, pride, selfishness, and sensuality but also to purity, redemption, and heaven. Saintliness as much as sinfulness might be communicated through clothes. White raiment, for example, was the covering of the saints, of angels, and of the transfigured Christ. Baptists, when they processed down to the river to immerse new believers, dressed those to be baptized in white linen, clearly pointing to the purity and righteousness of the saints and suggesting initiation into that communion. Among the Seventh-Day Baptists at Ephrata, members were required to clothe themselves in white year-round. "In summer-time," one observer reported, "the clothes are of linen or cotton, and entirely white; in the winter-time they are white woollen cloth." Dressing themselves "white as snow" for worship, members of this Protestant cloister expressed through clothing their union with the saints in heaven and their readiness and longing to meet with Christ. A revealing pictorial image produced at Ephrata showed heaven crowded with saints dressed in this distinctive white garb—a graphic illustration of how this earthly community connected itself through dress with the heavenly communion of saints. The religious meanings of dress, far from stopping with notions of sin and pride, spread outward and upward to signify saintly purity and heavenly attainment.[10]

Clothes could intertwine as well with ideas, and even experiences, of repentance and awakening. Methodist itinerant Peter Cartwright told of a gentleman of fashion at a camp meeting in 1810 who, though "much engaged" at the mourners' bench, still seemed impeded from accepting Christ. "I was praying by his side, and talking to him," Cartwright related, "when all [of] a sudden he stood erect on his knees, and with his hands he deliberately opened his shirt bosom, took hold of his ruffles, tore them off, and threw them down in the straw; and in less than two minutes God blessed his soul, and he sprang to his feet, loudly praising God." Thus did clothes become caught up in the process of repentance and conversion. A way of concretizing and externalizing the abstract, interior notion of sin, dress became interwoven in such spiritual relations with transformation.[11]

• • •

The symbolic meanings that early Americans could fathom and express through the medium of dress were manifold. Clothes, to play upon an anthropological trope, were good to think with. They helped people express ideas about hierarchy, equality, gender, clerical authority, community, ritual, purity, repentance, redemption, sin, pride, shame, and last things. They offered a powerful channel of communication through which people—whether literate or illiterate, lay or clerical—conveyed various messages to one another. An examination of the importance and versatility of this medium of communication suggests that historians have allowed the preached Word to monopolize unduly their understanding of the forms of religious expression in early America. Verbal texts were critical, indeed, essential parts of the religious culture of early America, but they were hardly the sum of the culture. The religious culture of early America was thicker than that. Resources for communication went well beyond words, and these resources were used fully and creatively. Understanding the religious culture of early America in something approaching its fullness requires probing the various ways people found to give meaning, order, and shape to their lives. It requires seeing how people constituted their religious world through more than words; how they used their eyes as well as their ears to understand themselves, their neighbors, and their God.

ENDNOTES

1. Margaret R. Miles, *Image as Insight: Visual Understanding in Western Christianity and Secular Culture* (Boston, 1985), 95.
2. Harry S. Stout, *The New England Soul: Preaching and Religious Culture in Colonial New England* (New York, 1986), 3, 7; Patricia U. Bonomi, *Under the Cope of Heaven: Religion, Society, and Politics in Colonial America* (New York, 1986), 3-4.
3. Rhys Isaac, *The Transformation of Virginia, 1740–1790* (Chapel Hill, NC, 1982), esp. 43-44, 323-57; Dell Upton, *Holy Things and Profane: Anglican Parish Churches in Colonial Virginia* (Cambridge, MA, 1986); Allan I. Ludwig, *Graven Images: New England Stonecarving and Its Symbols, 1650–1815* (Middletown, CT, 1966).
4. For standard reference works on the history of early American costume, see Alice Morse Earle, *Two Centuries of Costume in America, 1620–1820*, 2 vols. (New York, 1910); Elisabeth McClellan, *History of American Costume, 1607–1870* (New York, 1942); Edward Warwick,

Henry G. Pitz, and Alexander Wyckoff, *Early American Dress: The Colonial and Revolutionary Periods* (New York, 1965); Peter F. Copeland, *Working Dress in Colonial and Revolutionary America* (Westport, CT, 1977).

5. Devereux Jarratt, *The Life of the Reverend Devereux Jarratt, Rector of Bath Parish, Dinwiddie County, Virginia* (Baltimore, 1806), 14, 26-27, 41-42, 78.

6. Samuel Miller, *Memoirs of the Rev. John Rodgers, D.D.* (New York, 1813), 340-42. For a study of clerical costume, mostly in Britain but still useful in places for the American side, see Janet Mayo, *A History of Ecclesiastical Dress* (London, 1984).

7. *Englands Vanity: Or the Voice of God Against the Monstrous Sin of Pride in Dress and Apparel* (London, 1683), 62-65. For further discussion of gender and dress, see Alison Lurie, *The Language of Clothes* (New York, 1981), 212-29.

8. John Demos, *A Little Commonwealth: Family Life in Plymouth Colony* (New York, 1970), 53-54.

9. John Wesley, *The Works of John Wesley, A.M.*, 14 vols. (London, 1872), 7:20-21, 11:474. See also *The Nature, Design, and General Rules of the Methodist Societies* (New York, 1809), 7-16; *Advice to the People Called Methodists with Regard to Dress* (Baltimore, 1808); *On Dress* (Boston 1811); Peter Cartwright, *Autobiography of Peter Cartwright*, ed. Charles L. Wallis (New York, 1956), 61-63, 73, 334.

10. Peter C. Erb, ed., *Johann Conrad Beissel and the Ephrata Community: Mystical and Historical Texts* (Lewiston, NY, 1985), 96, Felix Reichmann and Eugene E. Doll, eds., *Ephrata as Seen by Contemporaries* (Allentown, PA, 1953), 44, 48, 53, 61, 77, 98, 115, 136, 147, 156, 159.

11. Charles G. Finney, *Memoirs* (New York, 1876), 173-74; Cartwright, *Autobiography*, 63.

FOR FURTHER READING

Chidester, David, and Edward T. Linenthal, eds. *American Sacred Space*, Bloomington, IN, 1995.

Hudnut-Beumler, James P. *Looking for God in the Suburbs: The Religion of the American Dream and Its Critics, 1945–1965*, New Brunswick, NJ, 1994.

McDannell, Colleen, *Material Christianity: Religion and Popular Culture in America*, New Haven, 1995.

Moore, R. Laurence. *Selling God: American Religion in the Marketplace of Culture*, New York, 1994.

Morgan, David. ed. *Icons of American Protestantism: The Art of Warner Sallman*, New Haven, 1996.

Schmidt, Leigh Eric. *Consumer Rites: The Buying and Selling of American Holidays*, Princeton, 1995.

PART II

Religion and Ethnicity

INTRODUCTION TO ESSAY 7

For much of the twentieth century a single social image dominated American culture: the melting pot. This conveyed the idea that people of different origins lost their old characteristics after arriving in this country and blended into an overwhelmingly WASP culture. In this essay Marty considers the recent challenge that "unmeltable ethnics" have made to that old model, and he weighs the alternatives of whether it is better to be absorbed into the sameness of a single cultural norm or to resist homogenization by remaining loyal to smaller cultural units. Marty refers initially to ethnicity as a skeleton in the closet, indicating that people are occasionally ashamed to admit that some of their distinctive traits still define them as an ethnic group. Then, noting the "new particularization" of recent times, he describes ethnic self-consciousness as a skeleton that provides a basic framework on which various groups can flesh out images of themselves. After he discusses several ways of saying what "ethnicity" can mean, he turns to the benefits such a category can provide in studying American religions.

Previously many religious historians used their own melting pots, rendering particularities down to a common denominator of sameness. Marty explores five ways in which American religions have been treated in this manner, concluding that such an essentially Protestant, academic exercise has tried to avoid the shame of the closet skeleton. But making something positive out of the fact that diversities persist in religious and group identification, he urges us to think instead of the skeleton in terms of a framework. Minority groups resist amalgamation, and their particularities should be valued, not violated by being subjected to Procrustean categories. Distinctive cultural, racial entities retain confessional, liturgical expressions of noteworthy singularity. These neglected themes can enrich our understanding of American life—past, present, and future.

Original source - CH 41 (1972): 5-21.

7

Ethnicity
The Skeleton of Religion in America

Martin E. Marty

"The story of the peopling of America has not yet been written. We do not understand ourselves," complained Frederick Jackson Turner in 1891.[1] Subsequent immigration history contributed to national self-understanding. Eighty years later historians have turned their attention to a second chapter in the half-told tale of the peopling of America. They have begun to concentrate on the story of the regrouping of citizens along racial, ethnic religious lines, and of their relations to one another in movements of what have come to be called "peoplehood."

First, the realities of black power, black religion, black theology, and black churchmanship inspired historians of religion in the 1960s to explore hitherto neglected elements in the makeup of spiritual America. The murder of integrationist leader Martin Luther King Jr. and the publication of separationist Albert Cleage Jr.'s *The Black Messiah* in 1968 were signs of a developing sense of "peoplehood" among blacks as well as of what Cleage called the "religio-cification" of a black revolution.

The black revolution triggered or was concurrent with other expressions of peoplehood. The American Indian frequently stated his case in religious terms and even provided a metaphor for understanding all the movements; people came to speak of the presence of "a new tribalism." Meanwhile, many Jews resisted being blended into the American mixture. They reinterpreted their community around two particular historical events, the Holocaust and the formation of modern Israel; their new self-consciousness resulted in "the retribalization of the Jew."

"Peoplehood" movements brought to view the 9.2 million Americans of Spanish descent, including the newly assertive Chicanos, chiefly in the Southwest. Americans of Eastern

Orthodox descent made moves to recover their heritages. Chinese and Japanese all across the country became subjects of curiosity by their non-Oriental contemporaries who showed interest in Eastern religion, in Yoga, or Zen. Nationalist separatist groups in Quebec gathered around French culture and Catholic faith in neighboring Canada and provided local examples of a worldwide neo-nationalism.

The racial and ethnic self-consciousness of what had been called minority groups led to a new sense of peoplehood among those which together made up the American majority. Austrians, Baltics, Czechoslovakians, German Catholics, Hungarians, Italians, Poles, and other heirs of earlier immigration from Europe were often led to see a common destiny despite their past histories of separation and often of mutual suspicion or hostility. Finally, there is "one of America's greatest and most colorful minority groups," the "White Anglo-Saxon Protestant," further qualified today as "native-born of native parentage." The acronym and designation WASP in the 1960s represented only about 30 percent of the population. It was divided into 60 percent urban and 40 percent rural, 35 percent southern and 65 percent non-southern communities and included great inner variety. But its critics tended to lump all WASPs together, and increasing numbers of Americans accepted membership in this "people." Among them are large numbers "who happen to be both Anglo-Saxon and white, but whom none would think to describe in terms of WASP power structures. Despite internal variety, at least as late as the 1960s, "the White, Anglo-Saxon Protestant remains the typical American, the model to which other Americans are expected and encouraged to conform."[2] One of the most significant events in the recent study of the peopling of America has been the growing sense, however, that WASPs are a minority themselves. They have at least lost statistical bases for providing a national norm for ethnic self-understanding.

These good years for peoplehood have given rise to whole new historical and social inquiries concerning "ethnicity." Today it is coming to refer to participation in "an ethnic group—racial, religious, or national in origin."[3] In this essay, "racial" is a species of the genus "ethnic." People may have authentic or only imaginary ties to a common place of origin. The new movements of peoplehood and the expressions of ethnic and racial consciousness have led them to neglect, gloss over, or deliberately obscure the durable sense of peoplehood in the larger American community. This also left many members of the fraternity ill-prepared to tell the stories of those who shared new styles of ethnic consciousness. If that argument can be established, we may properly speak of ethnicity as the skeleton of religion in America.

In a plea for historically informed ethnic studies and in an account of the history of the neglect of ethnic groups, Rudolph J. Vacoli says: "Ethnicity in American historiography has remained something of a family scandal, to be kept a dark secret or explained away."[4] This suggests two dictionary images. One is that of "a skeleton in the closet," which is "a secret source of shame or pain to a family or person." The other is that of "a skeleton at the banquet," a "reminder of serious or saddening things in the midst of enjoyment." Equally serious, ethnicity is the skeleton of religion in America because it provides "the supporting framework," "the bare outlines or main features," of American religion.

When the new particularism was first asserted in the 1960s, students had been enjoying their realization that consensus-minded America no longer seemed to be "tribal." In the midst of the enjoyment, tribalism reappeared. Black messiahs, black madonnas, the black Jesus, "the Great Spirit," the Jewish identification with the land and soil of Israel and charges that white Gentile America had been worshiping a localized self-created deity suddenly disturbed the peace. The issues of ethnicity and racism began to serve as the new occasions for a re-examination of the assumptions and often hidden biases of students of American religion.

For the sake of convenience, these students can be divided into two broadly defined schools. Members of the first seek some sort of spiritual "sameness," if not for the whole family of man, then at least for the whole American people. In the course of time that vision had to be enlarged so that it could accommodate other Americans though many of these others have regularly complained ever since that Protestant views of "sameness" and "essentially one religion, and one common soul" were superimposed on non-Protestants. Many Roman Catholics, on a somewhat different set of terms, also affirmed a religious nationalism that transcended their particular creed. Frederick Jackson Turner, the historian who had wanted the "peopling of America" to be studied for the purposes of national self-understanding, chose to concentrate on the frontier. He argued that "in the crucible of the frontier the immigrants were Americanized, liberated, and fused into a mixed race, English in neither nationality or characteristics."[5] His successors came to expect that a spiritual fusion would accompany the amalgamation of peoples.

Through the years the seekers of spiritual sameness or oneness and ethnic fusion or assimilation had to include the physical presence and spiritual striving of ever more varied peoples. Those who advocated what John Dewey in 1934 had called *A Common Faith* made little secret of their desire to overcome particularisms of religion, race, and class. For some this desire may have been born of weariness over all tribal-religious warfare; for others, it grew out of conscious philosophical choices about reality, religion, and nation. J. Paul Williams spoke of a "societal religion," and criticized men like Walter Lippmann for having been content to describe it merely as a "public philosophy" when it ought to have been termed a religion, and called moreover for "spiritual integration."

The dean of American church historians throughout this period, Sidney E. Mead, gave a generally positive interpretation of "the religion of the democratic society and nation" (over against "the religion of the denominations"). While he clearly retained a Lincolnian sense of judgment over against idolization of the nation, he was critical of those who stressed religious and theological particularity at the expense of the idea of the nation's "spiritual core."[6]

The defenses of the common vision as against the particular contention were based on historical observations of good moments in past American expressions of religious "sameness." They also revealed philosophical commitments toward the high unity. Most of the defenders overlooked ethnic and racial factors because these usually reinforced senses of difference. Regularly throughout

American history, those who failed to be assimilated or who stressed separate racial, ethnic, or religious identities were embarrassments. Ethnicity became the skeleton in the closet and had to be prematurely pushed aside and hidden from view.

The other line of interpretation has been dedicated to the love of what the philosopher Leibnitz and the historian Marc Bloch spoke of as "singular things." The historians and analysts who dealt more critically with "sameness," "oneness," and "common" religion in America after midcentury ordinarily devoted themselves to the religious shape of this pluralism. Only as the result of the racial upheavals and the new ethnic consciousness, which were manifested during the 1960s, have some of them begun to perceive again that ethnicity has been the skeleton, "the supporting framework," of American religion. These historians and other observers have seen that racial, ethnic, class, partisan, religious, and ideological conflicts in America have countered or qualified the homogenizing ideals that earlier held together the "consensus" schools of history.

• • •

The two general approaches just described can be best studied by reference to several prevailing models which are regularly used for historical explorations and contemporary analyses of the shape of American religion. First, some advocates of "sameness" have chosen a *secular* interpretation of American religious life. In this view the belief is expressed that there will be progressively less religion in society. Secular men will unite on the basis of some sort of emergent godless, homogenizing, technological, and political scheme. The result will be a global village marked by non-religious synthesis for world integration.[7]

A second line of interpretation is close to the secular one. It simply says that a man's beliefs are *private* affairs and that these have little common or civic consequence. Ideological support for this view is deep in the American tradition. While Thomas Jefferson supported the idea that those moral precepts "in which all religions agree" could be supportive of civil order, he believed differing private religions to be a luxury: "It does me no injury for my neighbor to say that there are twenty gods, or no God." One could be for sameness and for a common faith independent of private religious opinions.

The third model for religion in America, the *pluralist*, moves the discussion to the center of the debate over "sameness" versus "unlikeness" on national *versus* ethnic-racial and religious lines. The religious pluralist interpretation was born in the face of the problem of identity and power which increased as ethnic origins of Americans became progressively more remote and vague. In a sense, it served to push the skeleton of ethnicity into the closet. Ethnic and racial pluralism, however, did not go away just because religious pluralism was able to serve some social purposes during the religious revival of the 1950s. The religious revival eventually waned, and many people in a new generation no longer found it possible or desirable to define themselves in terms of Protestantism, Catholicism, or Judaism. Most of all, ethnic and racial reassertion did provide identification and community for the "different," who were dissenters against a common faith for all Americans.

The fourth interpretation has to be taken more seriously because of its obvious appropriateness on so many levels. This is an application to the whole of American Christianity by others of Sidney E. Mead's classic statement that *denominationalism* is the shape of Protestantism in America.[8] Catholicism is also regarded as a denomination by historians. Judaism, too, is formally denominationalized. But it would be easy to overstress the importance of denominational pluralism.

For one thing, the denominations are divided down the center in a kind of two-party system. The differences on vital issues (such as racial and ethnic matters) are expressed within and not between denominations. What is more, on matters of deepest significance, even where denominational names have been useful, denominational designations reveal little. Black, Indian, Chicano, white ethnic, and other movements of peoplehood found neither the denominational shape nor the nation's soul to be as effective for promoting identity and power as they found race or ethnicity, which was still—or again—the skeleton or supporting framework for their religion.

The fifth major line of interpretation has been implied throughout. In it "sameness," "oneness," and a "common faith" found their home in a societal or civil religion that informed, infused, and inspired virtually the whole population. How does it fare in a time of new peoplehood or "new tribalism"? Its expression is complicated and compromised. The black child in the ghetto or the Amerindian youngster may engage in ceremonies of civil religion. But they may think of something quite different from the world of the white child's pilgrims or founders when they sing of a "land where my fathers died." This is the land where their fathers were enslaved or killed. Most of the movements of racial and ethnic consciousness have found it important to oppose militantly the symbols of civil religion. The delineations of civil religion themselves are never universal in origin, content, ethos, or scope; they are informed by the experience of the delineators' own ethnic subcommunities. It is precisely this feature that has led to attempts at rejection of civil religion and "common faith" on the part of so many ethnic and racial groups.

In summary, it would appear that the five main models for interpreting American religious "sameness"—the secular, the private, the pluralist, the denominational, and the common-religious— apply appropriately only to the white and largely generalized Protestant academic circles where they originated. Other ethnic-racial-religious complexes can be only occasionally and partially interpreted through these.

• • •

To suggest that ethnic and racial themes have to be reintegrated into the schemes for posing historians' questions is *not* to say that these should displace the others. The secular tendencies in America will probably not be successfully countered by the new religious practices of minority groups. Many people can find identity in the private sphere without explicit reference to ethnic and racial religious motifs. Protestantism, Catholicism, Judaism may long serve to identify practitioners of a common American religion. Denominationalism may indeed be the shape, and civil religion the soul, of American religion—just as ethnicity is its skeleton or supporting framework. But as the most neglected theme until recently, racial and ethnic particularity deserves compensatory interest and inquiry.

Numerous benefits could result from such an effort. Concentration on religious dimensions of peoplehood could lead to a more accurate portraying of the way things have been—that is always the first goal of the historian. Historians in the once-majority traditions, WASP and white ethnic combined, can re-explore their own assumptions and may be able to discern the ethnic aspects in what they had earlier regarded as their universal points of view. The theories seeking "sameness" and "oneness" tended to be based on a kind of optimistic and voluntaristic spirit. Ethnic-racial recovery should help historians deal more adequately with the fated, predestined, tragic, and even violent elements in religion in America.

Even though the future is not the historian's province, it is sometimes asked whether it is worth scholars' efforts to re-tool so that they can henceforth include the ethnic and racial questions. The assimilating, blending, melting processes do remain and are accelerating. There are few new immigrants. The children of old ones intermarry and expose themselves to common value systems in education and through the media or by travel; they move out of vestigial ghettos. Perhaps the attention to the quest for identity through ethnic and racial communities will pass again as soon as certain needs have been met. The political and psychological use of WASP terms such as "white ethnics" and "WASPs" may soon be exposed as inauthentic, and the new and artificial ethnic coalitions may break apart. Maybe the focus on peoplehood has been only a fashion, a passing fancy, one which can be a partial setback in the quest for expressions of a common humanity.

If the ethnic factor remains strong, certainly there will be times of crisis when a sort of "tribal confederation" will be instinctively and informally convoked so various peoples can get together and affirm their common, not their separate, symbols. The historians can then stand ready to interpret both the past interplay between conflicting particularities and homogenizing concordant elements in national life and the considerable assets and liabilities of each.

Whatever happens, however, it seems clear that not all of a

person's needs can be met by secular interpretation and private faith, by tri-faith or conventional denominational life, or by a common national religion. New particularisms will no doubt continue to arise, to embody the hopes of this "people of peoples." Meanwhile, when spokesmen for the oldest of American peoples, the American Indian, assert that they wish to Americanize the rest of the nation and that they would like to teach their fellow citizens the merits of life in tribes, these other citizens could appropriately reply: "In some senses, we never left home."

ENDNOTES

1. Quoted in Lee Benson, *Turner and Beard: American Historical Writing Reconsidered* (Glencoe, IL, 1960), 82.
2. Lewis M. Killian, *The Impossible Revolution* (New York, 1968), 18.
3. Charles H. Anderson, *White Protestant Americans: From National Origins to Religious Group* (Englewood Cliffs, NJ, 1971), viii. "Every American, as we shall use the term, is a member or potential member of an ethnic group—racial, religious, or national in origin."
4. Rudolph J. Vecoli, "Ethnicity: A Neglected Dimension of American History" in Herbert J. Bass, *The State of American History* (Chicago, 1970).
5. Quoted by Vecoli, "Ethnicity," 75.
6. J. Paul Williams, *What Americans Believe and How They Worship* (New York, 1962), 477-592; Sidney E. Mead, "The Post-Protestant Concept and America's Two Religions," in Robert L. Ferm, *Issues in American Protestantism: A Documentary History from the Puritans to the Present* (Garden City, NY, 1969).
7. Bryan Wilson, *Religion in Secular Society: A Sociological Comment* (Baltimore, 1966), 40 and 121.
8. Sidney E. Mead, *The Lively Experiment: The Shaping of Christianity in America* (New York, 1975).

FOR FURTHER READING

Abramson, Harold J. *Ethnic Diversity in Catholic America*, New York, 1973.
Batzell, E. Digby. *The Protestant Establishment: Aristocracy and Caste in America*, New York, 1964.
Bratt, James D. *Dutch Calvinism in Modern America: A History of a Conservative Subculture*, Grand Rapids, MI, 1984.

Dolan, Jay P., and Allan Figueroa Deck, eds. *Hispanic Catholic Culture in the U.S.: Issues and Concerns*, Notre Dame, 1994.

Dolan, Jay P., and Gilberto M. Hinojosa, eds. *Mexican Americans and the Catholic Church, 1900–1965*, Notre Dame, 1994.

Dolan, Jay P., and Jamie R. Vidal, eds. *Puerto Rican and Cuban Catholics in the U.S., 1900–1965*, Notre Dame, 1994.

Glazer, Nathan. *American Judaism*, 2d ed., Chicago, 1972.

Gleason, Philip. *Keeping the Faith: American Catholicism, Past and Present*, Notre Dame, 1987.

Greeley, Andrew M. *Ethnicity in the United States*, New York, 1974.

Herberg, Will. *Protestant-Catholic-Jew*, Garden City, NY, 1955.

Marzik, Thomas D, and Randall M. Miller, eds. *Immigrants and Religion in Urban America*, Philadelphia, 1977.

INTRODUCTION TO ESSAY 8

Using the early Midwest as a microcosm of Marty's previous macrocosmic notions about ethnicity, Smith surveys people in one geographical area as a way of learning how groups interact with one another. He also conveys another standard theme in contemporary American religious scholarship: separation of church and state works well in this country because the plurality of religions here prevents any of them from gaining too much political power or social influence. To set the stage for such beneficial interaction within a regional framework, he introduces six basic groups that furthered the cause of religious freedom by perpetuating their respective denominational differences.

Settings in other parts of America may at times have contained as many groups as Ohio had in the early 1800s, but Smith was shrewd to choose a particularly diversified place to study. In a few deft paragraphs he gives us enough information about pioneering denominations to make us want to know a great deal more. His references to Methodists, Episcopalians, Congregationalists, Presbyterians, Quakers, Amish, Baptists, Catholics, Jews, and Eastern Orthodox embrace many of the groups that have figured prominently in this country's religious kaleidoscope. Beyond informing us of these groups' existence in early Ohio, his larger point shows how their intermingling was an early example of mutual recognition and respect. As these churches accepted the validity of one another, they helped maintain harmonious relations, and through this mutual deference they learned the higher value of liberty for all forms of worship.

Original source - CH 60 (1991): 461-79.

8

The Ohio Valley
Testing Ground for America's Experiment in Religious Pluralism

Timothy L. Smith

The most extensive early test of the American dogma of the separation of church and state seems to me to have taken place in pioneer Ohio, where a complete range of the plurality of America's religious associations first confronted public consciousness. Virtually every sect whose members helped launch the settlement of Ohio was one of a family of related religious communities. Beyond this emergence of several ethnic and religious "families" in Ohio, six other factors encouraged growing public acceptance of religious pluralism there: (1) the coming of a self-conscious "evangelical" unity among several old-line Protestant denominations; (2) the early expansion of Methodism, partly because many Pennsylvanian Germans were adopting Wesleyan doctrines and evangelistic methods and partly because of a surprising interplay between America's Methodists and evangelical Episcopalians; (3) the scattering of a strong German-speaking minority among the population; (4) a large immigration of Baptists from both northern and southern states; (5) the founding of numerous settlements by members of both German and English-speaking pacifist denominations—the Friends, Mennonites, Amish, and Church of the Brethren; and (6) the appearance of three sharply differing kinds of non-Protestant minorities, the Roman Catholics, Jews, and Eastern Orthodox Christians.

All the major American Protestant denominations, then, came early to share the broad "evangelical united front" that has ever since characterized the Ohio Valley. These circumstances help us to understand better how and why Methodists came to dominate the religious life of the Buckeye State, though historians have continued to think of Wesley's followers as a strenuously sectarian movement. One factor in their dominance was Bishop Francis Asbury's long relationship with the Protestant Episcopal Church, whose first settlement in Ohio began when a Connecticut clergyman established a colony in the Scioto valley, just north of the great river. Episcopalian congregations thereafter spread slowly through the state's heartland towards Columbus and eventually into the Western Reserve.[1] Their arrival sheds much light on the rise of evangelical Episcopalianism in America. The story of Charles McIvaine's work after he was named bishop of the Ohio diocese in 1834 is most enlightening. Already a noted evangelical, McIvaine had gained prominence among the Episcopalian settlers of Hudson Valley, where he served for a time as chaplain of the military academy at West Point. Once in Ohio, he realized that many of his followers had professed conversion under Methodist influence in their home states. He no doubt had long since discovered that the first two Methodist bishops in America, Francis Asbury and Thomas Coke, had dreamed of bringing all former Anglicans into their denomination and so replacing the parent church. Among Bishop McIvaine's Ohio followers, then, were many who remained both Episcopalian and evangelical. Under his leadership they established Kenyon College in the village of Gambier, near Columbus, and helped him make Ohio a center of Episcopalian spirituality.[2]

The strategy of cultivating former Episcopalians and German pietists and of making clear the evangelical appeal of Arminianism and Christian perfectionism to poor people, blacks, and Native Americans helps explain more fully why Methodism became the strongest religious party in the Midwest by the middle of the nineteenth century. The preoccupation of scholars with the emotional character of early camp meetings in Kentucky has, I think, obscured this important fact, though the availability of Asbury's *Journal and Letters* after 1958 has made the frontier interpretation of Methodist history obsolete. A more broadly national perspective, that relies first of all upon events in the former Anglican parishes and the early Methodist circuits of the eastern seaboard, brings us closer to what happened.[3]

In addition to this general triumph of American evangelicalism along early Ohio's Congregationalist and Presbyterian axis and its Methodist and Episcopal one, scholars should consider as of equal importance the influx of German-speaking peoples between 1795 and 1845. The multiplication of Pennsylvania-German denominations both large and small became so complex as years passed that simple generalizations about the tripartite character of Lutheranism, repeated above, are far from adequate. They do not cover the extensive migration to Ohio of German Reformed settlers, to say nothing of the Moravians, the Mennonites, the German Wesleyans, or the company of plain farmers sometimes called "Dunkers" or "German Baptists" who made up the Church of the Brethren. True, the eighteenth-century Moravian quest for order through the ostensibly ecumenical "Congregation of God in the Spirit" testifies to a powerful sentiment of national unity; but it did not reveal a specifically German passion for organization in the New World.[4] On the contrary, opposition to any specific recipe for order was endemic in both the larger and smaller German denominations. This opposition obstructed for seventy-five years the consolidation of Lutheran Synods both old and new, separating them into suspicious and sometimes warring factions and extending the earlier divisions among the Mennonites, United Brethren, Schwenkfelders, and Amish.

The contributions of Catholics and Jews to Ohio's pluralism was not to invent but to enrich what became the American system of religious order. The Roman Catholic population in the pioneer state was divided between German and Irish. German Catholics had to endure much Protestant antipathy that was rooted in religious rivalry that flourished among their homeland cities and provinces both before and after 1870. The Irish parishes, however, were remarkably urban and felt themselves increasingly part of an American nationality that they thought of in terms of the pre-eminence of fellow Irishmen in the politics of Pittsburgh, South Bend, and Chicago, or the more distant cities of New York and Boston.[5]

German Jews, by contrast, dominated the whole of their religious culture for many decades. Among their leading rabbis was a group who could and did help them identify with the high intellectual achievements of Jews in German cities and universities. This eventually encouraged Jews in the early Ohio Valley towns to recruit outstanding intellectuals like Isaac Mayer Wise to become their rabbis. Wise, whose roots had been in German reformed, or "neolog" Judaism, for two decades made his "Union of American Hebrew Congregations" well known among all America's educated Jews through his widely circulated lectures and essays and his conviction that Mosaic law was fundamental to both Christian and Hebrew civilization. Many of his more radical admirers, especially those who lived in towns with too small a Jewish population to support a viable community, joined, or at least attended, a Unitarian Church. This was simply a sign, however, of their awareness of the advantages Jews might gain by living among Yankees where anti-Semitism seemed rare. Michael A. Meyer's rich chapters on the deeply religious ideas that flourished among liberal Jews on the European continent and around Wise and his fellows in America, has helped religious historians of all backgrounds to understand the notions that nineteenth-century American Jews widely embraced.[6]

• • •

This story of how American pluralism profited from the varied experiences of all of early Ohio's religious groups cannot be complete, of course. Much of the essential tendency of that pluralism was to revise traditions and to search for new ways to organize religious beliefs. Such ideas helped not only Ohio's residents (whose sojourn in that state was, from the perspective of our nation's development, always temporary) but the people of the whole nation to seek the paths of mutual recognition and mutual respect that we believe democracy demands. And we have not down to the present day, I believe, deserted seeking those paths, despite many obstructions along the way.

ENDNOTES

1. James M. Miller, *The Genesis of Western Culture: The Upper Ohio Valley, 1800–1825* (Columbus, OH, 1938).
2. Wilbur Carus, ed., *Memorials of the Rt. Reverend Charles P. McIvaine*, 2d ed. (London, 1882); Daniel Alexander Payne, *Recollections of Seventy Years* (Nashville, 1888; reprint New York, 1968) 93-94, 102-08, 112-13,

121, 225-27; Charles Pettit McIvaine, *Bishop McIvaine on the Revival of Religion* (Philadelphia, 1858), 4, 11, 22; and William W. Manross, *A History of the American Episcopal Church*, 2d ed. (New York, 1956).

3. Francis Asbury, *Journal and Letters, vol. 2, 1794–1816* (Nashville, 1958) recounts his visits from New England to Georgia, and from Delaware to Western Kentucky. See also Henry M. Baird, *The Life of the Rev. Robert Baird, D.D.* (New York, 1867) recounting Baird's story. Educated at Washington College, near Wheeling, W. Virginia, then a missionary in Ohio, Baird began his career in rural Ohio and New Jersey before going, with Methodist blessing, to promote the Evangelical Alliance in Britain.

4. John Frantz, "The Awakening of Religion Among the German Settlers in the Middle Colonies," *William and Mary Quarterly* 33 (1976): 266-88; Donald F. Durnbaugh, ed. *The Church of the Brethren, Past and Present* (Elgin, IL, 1971), 21; Roy B. Leedy, *The Evangelical Church in Ohio: Being a History of the Ohio Conference and Merged Conferences, 1816–1951* (n.p. [Ohio?], 1959).

5. Timothy J. Meagher, ed., *Urban American Catholicism: The Culture and Identity of the American Catholic People* (New York, 1988). Harry S. Stout, "Ethnicity: The Vital Center of Religion in America," *Ethnicity* 3 (1975): 204-24.

6. Michael A. Meyer, *Response to Modernity: A History of the Reform Movement in Judaism* (New York, 1988); Marc Lee Raphael, *Jews and Judaism in a Midwestern Community: Columbus Ohio, 1841–1975* (Columbus, OH, 1979).

FOR FURTHER READING

Axtell, James. *The Invasion Within: The Contest of Cultures in Colonial North America*, New York, 1985.

Bowden, Henry Warner. *American Indians and Christian Missions: Studies in Cultural Conflict*, Chicago, 1981.

Frankel, Sandra Sizer. *California's Spiritual Frontiers: Religious Alternatives in Anglo-Protestantism, 1850–1910*, Berkeley, 1988.

Greene, Jack. *Pursuits of Happiness: The Social Development of Early Modern British Colonies and the Formation of American Culture*, Chapel Hill, NC, 1988.

Hatch, Nathan O. *The Democratization of American Christianity*, New Haven, 1989.

Hood, Fred J. *Reformed America: The Middle and Southern States, 1783–1837*, Tuscaloosa, AL, 1980.

Maffly-Kipp, Laurie F. *Religion and Society in Frontier California*, New Haven, 1994.

Pointer, Richard W. *Protestant Pluralism and the New York Experience: A Study of Eighteenth-Century Religious Diversity*, Bloomington, IN, 1988.

Szasz, Ferenc Morton. *The Protestant Clergy in the Great Plains and Mountain West, 1865–1915*, Albuquerque, 1988.

Walsh, H. H. *The Church in the French Era: From Colonization to the British Conquest*, Toronto, 1966.

INTRODUCTION TO ESSAY 9

If struggles between various social groups have characterized the American experience since colonial times, none have become more entrenched than those created during the era of the Civil War. Goen acquaints us with distinctive regional practices and shows their importance in national life. By 1840 human slavery had existed in this country for more than two centuries, but at that time several major denominations split over the question of what to do about the institution. Goen's main concern, however, is to show that when churches in southern states seceded from national church bodies, they provided examples of peaceable separation, ones which many erroneously thought could be transferred to the political sphere as well. Religious factors often influence larger cultural patterns, and here we see churches playing a crucial role in shaping a widespread mind-set in favor of secession.

On more tightly focused topics, Goen shows how southern religious groups rationalized their actions, often masking their proslavery attitudes behind appeals for freedom. He supplies details about the major denominational struggles over slavery and uses the resultant structural realignments to illustrate how churches proliferate and maintain separate existences in American history. The slavery controversy indicates a more pervasive reality too: different churches in one part of the country often resemble one another more than their denominational counterparts far away. Goen's depiction of this instance of "sectionalism" is especially striking as he lets proponents speak for themselves. Here he chronicles the enmity and bitterness that became diehard convictions during armed conflict. Succeeding generations perpetuated those feelings in separate churches and unreconciled sectional prejudice, some of them still affecting churches today.

Original source - CH 52 (1983): 21-35.

9

Broken Churches, Broken Nation
Regional Religion and North-South Alienation in Antebellum America

C. C. Goen

Evangelical Protestantism was a major bond of unity for the United States during the first part of the nineteenth century. The chief institutional forms of this faith were the large popular denominations—Methodist, Baptist, Presbyterian, each with nationwide constituencies; these denominations, increasingly agitated by disputes over slavery, sundered into northern and southern factions long before political rupture, thus opening the first major cleavage between slaveholding and free states; and the denominational schisms portended and to some extent provoked the crisis of the Union in 1861. Presbyterians divided in 1837 and again in 1857, after a series of quarrels in which sharp differences over slavery figured significantly if not decisively. The Methodist Episcopal Church sundered in 1844 and the national Baptist societies in 1845, explicitly because of unyielding postures in the same dispute. In each instance participants and observers alike expressed many dire forebodings about the effect the divisions would have on political unity. After 1845 every cumulating portent of national breakdown became an occasion for recalling how the denominational schisms had weakened the Union, and it now appears that the church controversies were rehearsing in ecclesiastical context the same bitter conflict that would soon rend the Union.

• • •

The South's religious leaders, like most of its political theorists, customarily thought of the United States as a confederacy, and they regarded the Constitution as a compact among sovereign states. Many of them had drunk deeply from John C. Calhoun's doctrines designed to protect southern interests from northern encroachment. Calhoun had proposed, for example, a dual executive for the United States, that is, a president for the South and one for the North. That idea appeared in ecclesiastical garb in the Methodist General Conference of 1844 immediately after Bishop James O. Andrew was ordered to desist from all episcopal functions as long as he remained a slave owner. Southern Methodists had reason to fear a "tyranny of the majority." At the beginning of denominational life in 1784, 90 percent of Methodist church members lived below the Mason-Dixon line, mostly in Maryland and Virginia. By 1812, however, the North had overtaken the South, so that in the General Conference of that year there were forty-two northern delegates and thirty-five southern. Four years later General Conference seated sixty northern delegates and forty-five southern. By 1844 the sectional representation of elected delegates was 118 to 58 in favor of the North, causing a frustrated Mississippian to sigh, "We can out-speak them, but they will always be able to out-vote us."[1] Such imbalance is precisely what Calhoun had foreseen in the political sphere, and he hoped to prevent the disadvantage to the South by his concept of the concurrent majority. Southern Methodists were acting out of Calhoun's perspective when in 1845 they rejected "the *proscription and disability* under which the Southern portion of the Church must of necessity labour, . . . unless some measures are adopted to free the minority of the South from the oppressive jurisdiction of the North."[2]

Virginia Baptists were thinking along the same lines in March 1845 as they issued their call for the "consultation" that would result in the formation of the Southern Baptist Convention. The Virginians declared that Baptists of the South "indignantly refuse to co-operate with [the General Convention] on any terms implying their inferiority."[3] Failing to win adequate concessions from the northern majority, the Southerners withdrew.

Whoever would understand the secession crisis must take account of the fact that it was in the churches that Southerners first acted to free themselves from "the oppressive jurisdiction of the majority of the North" by the simple expedient of seceding. As the crisis drew on, there was a striking congruence between earlier arguments for splitting the churches and those for breaking the federal Union. This should not be surprising, since the same divisive forces that had torn the churches apart were also tearing at the nation. The religious covenant dissolved earlier than the political compact, not only because the bonds of political union were diffused over a broader cultural spectrum, but also because in the churches the moral issue was focused more sharply and absolutes were affirmed more dogmatically. But the same passions were at work in both arenas, and in each case the seceders thought it more important to preserve slavery than to maintain unity. At the close of the 1844 Methodist General Conference the separating Southerners justified their withdrawal. "The opinions and purposes of the Church in the north on the subject of slavery, are in direct conflict with those of the south, and unless the south will submit to the dictation and interference of the north . . . there is no hope of any thing like union or harmony."[4] At the same time a southern Baptist, distracted by the slavery controversy in his own denomination, was advising an identical course of action. "Depend on it, brethren, if we desire peace, and quietness, we should separate from these Northern societies."[5]

Thus the *Sumter Banner* was simply echoing the earlier arguments of seceding churchmen when it shouted in 1849, "The only remedy which will free . . . [the South] from Northern oppression . . . is the SECESSION OF THE SLAVEHOLDING STATES IN A BODY FROM THE UNION AND THEIR FORMATION INTO A SEPARATE REPUBLIC." The following year, in his last major speech (4 March 1850), Senator Calhoun stated flatly that "the South will be forced to choose between abolition and secession." As the choice drew nearer, Mississippi newspapers urged, "Let every Southern man insist on his rights IN the Union, or let him seek them OUT of it." William Gilmore Simms, romantic novelist of South Carolina, asked, "Of what . . . value to a Christian man is that sort of union which persists in keeping men in the same household, who hate and blaspheme each other?" Throughout the region southern nationalists argued forcefully, as their church leaders had earlier, that the strife over slavery could be ended only by withdrawing to pursue an independent course free from northern interference.

Southerners were not the only ones speaking of separation as the most appropriate solution of the sectional conflict. The number of Northerners willing to let the South go its own way was far more than a noisy band of radical abolitionists. After 1845, if anyone asked how the South could survive outside the Union, the question could be answered by pointing to the southern denominations. They had been demonstrating for several years that they could be viable as sectional independents. Schism had stilled internecine strife; and their institutional life, to all outward appearances, was healthy.

The division of the national church bodies had been easy—deceptively so—and the reasons for this reach far back into history. Sectarian Protestantism long ago had breached the barriers to fundamental schism, so that a sense of continuity with the historic Christian tradition rested very lightly, if at all, on their shoulders. Antichurchly bias, aroused in the Reformation, and more especially in left-wing Puritanism, had been reinforced by migration to the New World. After a long development which is exceedingly significant for understanding the character of religion in America, some of the erstwhile sects had become mainline denominations while remaining notoriously contemptuous of tradition and authority. More than a century of experience in America had given them a high regard for individualism, experimentation, and local autonomy, which further eroded their sense of history. Their formal religious authority was still the Bible—the *sola scriptura* of the Reformers—though unlike the Reformers they interpreted it less according to the norms of classical Christianity than through the presumed competence of private reason and individual experience. Such a mood comported easily with the ahistorical temper of revivalism, confirming the popular churches in a reductionist ecclesiology that accorded less importance to the church than to the experience of salvation. The church, in this perspective, was simply a place to gather the converts of the revivals. In fact, the word "church" itself more often than not signified a local congregation, not the whole company of the faithful, and congregations might be multiplied or divided easily according to shifting local needs and preferences. This easygoing ecclesiology suggested a simple way for people influenced by such churches to dissolve their political compact, for the belief that converted people create the church is exactly parallel to the idea that consenting people create the state.

The peaceable division of the churches was not only easy; it was also deceptive. Those who tried to transpose the tactic to the political arena rarely stopped to consider that even though the national government was formed originally "by consent," as an ongoing polity for a whole people, it was inescapably an organic unity; and breaking it apart would be terribly more traumatic than dividing the churches. The churches were already disunited denominationally and even within denominational families; their "unity in diversity" rested on the intangible ground of common feeling and experience, and such subjectivities were hard to absolutize. The nation, on the other hand, had long been gathering to itself more of the traditional "churchly" attributes than the various denominations could ever display. Nationalism flourished as a profoundly religious *faith* in the period of the Revolution and afterwards. Abraham Lincoln, member of no church and yet deeply religious, has been described accurately enough as revering the Union with a sense of awe approaching religious mysticism.[6] Nor was he alone. If there was any "high-church" sense of visible unity, catholicity, mission, and destiny in antebellum America, it plainly attached to the nation itself more than to any of its various churches. Thus the churches might agree to "multiply by dividing," but that option was not open to the nation without wrenching trauma.

The rhetoric of secession sometimes outdid that of the earlier denominational schisms, even in turgid biblical allusions. Listen to Governor John J. Pettus of Mississippi preaching his state into the Confederacy:

> Mississippi must go down into Egypt [Join the Confederacy] while Herod rules in Judea [Lincoln in Washington]. . . . And when in after years it shall be told you that they [Republicans] who sought the life of this Prince of Peace [slavery] . . . are dead, you may come up out of Egypt [rejoin the Union] and realize all the fond hopes of . . . peace on earth and good will among men.[7]

Southern church folk could respond "Amen!" because they had already fled to their ecclesiastical Egypt. Living as they did in tight symbiosis with southern culture, they found their attitudes and those of their region resonating easily together. Many of them, especially in the lower South, advocated secession before it came, applauded when it did, and in the resulting war gave unqualified support to the southern cause. Having already broken church fellowship with northern Christians, they felt few restraints against political cleavage; indeed, the heady experience of having taken the initiative in crossing that Rubicon added to the stridency of their regionalism. Withdrawing from the Union would vindicate their church schisms, and they could then regard total separation from the North as a surpassing moral victory.

According to a growing consensus among Civil War scholars, a major factor in the nation's breakdown was a deepening sense of alienation, even isolation, that distanced North and South from one another in the 1850s. David Potter described it:

> As they became isolated, instead of reacting to each other as they were in actuality, each [section] reacted to a distorted mental image of the other—the North to an image of a southern world of lascivious and sadistic slave drivers; the South to the image of a northern world of cunning Yankee traders and of rabid abolitionists plotting slave insurrections.[8]

My point is simply that the divided churches played a crucial role in creating and sustaining those distorted images and psychological attitudes. After the popular denominations split, each side of what was formerly a far-flung network of relationships was left to nurture its grievances against the other with far fewer opportunities to check its deepening suspicions by fraternal encounter. And so it came to pass. Estranged churches North and South regarded their sectional counterparts as apostate and assiduously reinforced their respective region's twisted perceptions of the other. From both sides came repeated accusations of malevolence which widened the gap of alienation, provoked some to extreme positions, and thrust the strained nation closer to an open break.[9]

An obvious way in which regional religion hardened the lines of sectional conflict was the sharp divergence in religious perspectives that grew out of the bitter dispute over slavery. Many northern clergy thought that connivance with slavery corrupted both the gospel and the preachers who claimed to represent it. Southern theologians insisted that slavery was an ordinance of God fully sanctioned in scripture: Abraham and the patriarchs held slaves, apparently with God's approval; Jesus lived in a world where slavery was rampant and never condemned it; Paul wrote explicit instructions for the duties of masters and servants and even sent a fugitive slave back to his master. Sectional partisans in other denominations were equally bitter. Southern Baptists condemned the "lawless reign of terror" in the North which threatened "to wage upon the South a warfare of savage barbarity, to devastate our homes and hearths with hosts of ruffians and felons, burning with lust and rapine." Northern preachers hurled comparable vituperations against Southerners as moral degenerates and apostates, "traitors, rebels, thieves, plunderers, cowards."

Thus the denominational schisms not only severed a bond of national union and set a deceptive example for the states to follow; they also cast the sectional churches in an adversarial relationship that actively furthered the alienation of North and South until sectional differences were felt to be irreconcilable. As early as 1868 Jesse T. Peck noted in his *History of the Great Republic* that "the feeling of difference [was] always stronger than the reality."[10] This is highly significant, for feelings were preeminently the springs of action for evangelicals. Their stress on the personal response of deep moral feeling equipped them to make a crusade out of abolitionism or slaveholding with equal ease. Both sides portrayed the controversy in cosmic terms—eternal right against eternal wrong, God against Satan, the "conflict of the ages"—until mutual recriminations drove the estranged factions beyond the possibility of reconciliation.

The bitterness of estrangement among those who had once regarded themselves as one in the family of God and in the Union of God's own making may be gauged by the belligerence of a Louisiana minister who defied northern ministers to set foot in the South.

I am one of five ministers, of three different denominations, in a single company [of the Confederate army], armed for the defence of our rights and liberties, three of whom are between 50 and 60 years old. And I tell you in candor, and in the fear of God, that if you or any of the *brethren* who have urged on this diabolical war, come on with the invading army, I would slay you with as hearty a good will, and with as clear a conscience, as I would the midnight assassin. . . . You are my enemy, and I am yours.

One Mr. Black, a northern Methodist minister in Newport, Kentucky (opposite Cincinnati), reciprocated the hostility.

He prayed that the Union may be preserved, "even though blood may come out of the wine-press even unto the horses' bridles . . ." [Rev. 14:20]. In the course of his sermon he said: "I trust our troops will rally and wipe out the disgrace of Manassas, though it cost the life of every rebel under arms. Let Davis and Beauregard be captured to meet the fate of Haman [Esther 7]. Hang them up on Mason and Dixon's Line, that traitors . . . may be warned. Let them hang until the vultures shall eat their rotten flesh from their bones; let them hang until the crows shall build their filthy nests in their skeletons; let them hang until the rope rots, and let their dismembered bones fall *so deep into the earth that God Almighty can't find them on the day of resurrection.*[11]

● ● ●

It must not be forgotten that the all-transcending provocation of the denominational schisms, as of the Civil War itself, was slavery and the giant contradiction it presented to the most basic of American values. It was the consuming controversy over slavery that rent much of the Christian community, and it was a sectional Christianity that exacerbated the national struggle over slavery. The churches were critical agents in a reciprocal process of cumulating alienation. In the onrushing tragedy it became evident that the Christian religion, a powerful cultural force in both sections, had been turned to the purposes of regional identity and defense, that equally earnest expositors could draw from the same scriptures diametrically opposite conclusions about the most distinctive feature of the southern way of life, and that the common faith that had once undergirded national unity had itself become an instrument of division. And after six hundred thousand American men had died by their brothers' hands, in the stillness at Appomattox, there was little contrition in the broken churches that had prefigured the broken nation.

ENDNOTES

1. William Winans, quoted in the *Christian Advocate and Journal* (New York), 21 May 1845, 162.
2. Proposal for a separate denomination, signed by 51 southern Methodist ministers, in R. Sutton, *The Methodist Church Property Case* (Richmond, 1851), 90.
3. *Religious Herald* (Richmond), 13 March 1845.
4. Document in Charles Elliott, *History of the Great Secession from the Methodist Episcopal Church* (Cincinnati, 1855), 1045.
5. *A Calm Appeal to Southern Baptists in Advocacy of Separation from the North in All the Works of Christian Benevolence* (n.p., [1845?]), 7.
6. The observation was made by Alexander H. Stephens, vice president of the Confederacy. See Edmund Wilson, *Patriotic Gore: Studies in the Literature of the American Civil War* (New York, 1961), 97, 422.
7. Quoted in David Potter, *Lincoln and His Party in the Secession Crisis* (New Haven, 1942), 226.
8. Ibid., 43; see also David Potter, *The South and the Sectional Conflict* (Baton Rouge, 1968), 94-95; and Don E. Fehrenbacher, "Disunion and Reunion," in *The Reconstruction of American History*, ed. John Higham (New York, 1962), 117.
9. James H. Moorhead, *American Apocalypse: Yankee Protestants and the Civil War, 1860–1869* (New Haven, 1978), 29-32.
10. Jesse T. Peck, *History of the Great Republic, Considered from a Christian Stand-Point* (New York, 1868), 693.
11. Frank Moore, ed., *Rebellion Record: A Diary of American Events*, 12 vols. (New York, 1861–1868), 3:P-13, 4:P-22.

FOR FURTHER READING

Bailey, Kenneth. *Southern White Protestantism in the Twentieth Century*, New York, 1964.

Farmer, James Oscar, Jr. *The Metaphysical Confederacy: James Henley Thornwell and the Synthesis of Southern Values*, Macon, GA, 1986.

Goen, C. C. *Broken Churches, Broken Nation*, Macon, GA, 1985.

Hill, Samuel S., Jr., *Religion in the Southern States: A Historical Study*, Macon, GA, 1983.

———. *The South and the North in American Religion*, Athens, GA, 1980.

———. *Southern Churches in Crisis*, New York, 1966.

Loveland, Anne C. *Southern Evangelicals and the Social Order*, Baton Rouge, 1980.

Matthew, Donald G. *Religion in the Old South*, Chicago, 1977.

Shattuck, Gardiner H., Jr. *A Shield and Hiding Place: The Religious Life of the Civil War Armies*, Macon, GA, 1987.

Wilson, Charles Reagan. *Baptized in Blood: The Religion of the Lost Cause, 1865–1920*, Athens, GA, 1980.

———. *Religion in the South*, Jackson, MS, 1985.

INTRODUCTION TO ESSAY 10

Another group involved in sectional squabbles was African Americans, slaves and free, who eventually formed their own religious groups and compounded the pluralistic character of national religious life. In the following essay Maffly-Kipp explores materials in several new fields. She begins by explaining that history is an important tool for self-perception. As a group perceives its previous experience, it defines its present situation and maps out future possibilities. Here the author focuses on a generation of African American historians who flourished in the four decades preceding World War I, showing how these writers used memory, imagination, and narratives of a constructed past to bolster pride in their race.

Using broad categories, this essay chronicles the maturation of an ethnic group's self-understanding through management of its past. On a more specific level, Maffly-Kipp introduces us to dynamic figures of the African American intelligentsia. We see how they used emancipation and enfranchisement as benchmarks of racial progress. Struggling against prejudices in their own day, these historians told of a past where good triumphed over evil, and they pointed to a future where blacks could reach higher achievements through education, determined effort, and moral purity. These authors differed among themselves in thinking about African origins, slave spirituality, and early abolitionists. But such independent expressions combined to create an image of African Americans who deserved the gains they had made in this country. Their religious affiliations, also products of this sense of historical development, helped strengthen and perpetuate their distinctive, integral place in national life and in American religious history.

Original source - CH 64 (1995): 610-26.

10

Mapping the World, Mapping the Race
The Negro Race History, 1874–1915

Laurie F. Maffly-Kipp

In 1883, the African American Baptist preacher George Washington Williams published his *History of the Negro Race in America, 1619–1880*. The book, a fundamentally optimistic account of the black presence in the New World, represented an attempt by the well-educated, northern divine to balance his commitments to an American evangelical tradition with an awareness of the ongoing oppression of his fellow African Americans at the hands of whites. "I commit this work to the public, white and black," he noted in the preface, "to the friends and foes of the Negro in the hope that the obsolete antagonisms which grew out of the relation of master and slave may speedily sink as storms beneath the horizon; and that the day will hasten when there shall be no North, no South, no Black, no White—but all be American citizens, with equal duties and equal rights."[1] The work revealed much about Williams: his upbringing in antebellum Pennsylvania as the child of an interracial union, his training at Howard University and Newton Theological Seminary, and his work experiences at Baptist churches in New England and Ohio. But this particular passage highlights the motivating force behind the book: it reveals, in anticipation of a historical narrative of over two hundred years of African enslavement, Williams's desire to recast much of the American past. Williams's historical account was, at heart, an attempt to impart more meaning to the present by reconstructing the historical consciousness of both blacks and whites. In this desire, Williams fit precisely Friedrich Nietzsche's characterization of "historical men," those who "believe that ever more light is shed on the meaning of existence in the course of its *process*, and they look back to consider that process only to understand the present better and learn to desire the future more vehemently."[2]

In this quest for comprehension and desire he found himself in good company. Although African Americans had been writing both personal and communal narratives for several decades before the Civil War, it was not until after the emancipation of the slaves that the genre of "race history" emerged as an increasingly popular form of black literary expression. Between 1874 and 1915, several dozen writers authored studies of the Negro past, present, and future in an effort, as Edward Johnson put it, to record "the many brave deeds and noble characteristics" of the race. These histories also had deep religious impact. Writing in the years prior to the professionalization of history as a "scientific" mode of discourse, many early race historians were ordained ministers; some had theological training. All were interested in the prospective possibilities of history, the potential for narrative to shape the future of the free community. As blacks and as Protestants, these writers imbued the past, present, and future of the Negro with moral and spiritual significance. These histories are important, then, not simply for what they reflect about the history of African Americans. They are even more significant for what they reveal about the wide-ranging public discourse among post-Reconstruction black leaders regarding representations of the race—representations that served both to counter white racial images and to reimagine the African American community itself on different terms. For these Protestant leaders, Reconstruction and its aftermath encompassed more than social and institutional reconstitution: it also included the reconfiguration of time itself.[3]

• • •

The social production of race histories was part and parcel of the ongoing mission to ex-slaves in the late nineteenth century. As northern missionaries moved into the southern states in the years following emancipation, they brought with them an emphasis on education as the key to moral behavior and middle-class respectability. As Evelyn Brooks Higginbotham has argued, literacy and rational discourse allowed Protestant clergy and laity to control access to correct religious doctrine, and thus to systematically shape the beliefs and ritual lives of the ex-slaves. Literacy rose quickly in the freed population in the 1880s and 1890s, and church-sponsored presses stood ready with journals, newspapers, and books to fill the new demand for printed materials.[4]

Equipped with this newly available "technology of power," black Protestant leaders hoped to influence the development of southern freedmen in a typically Protestant way: through conversion of the head and heart. Their various approaches reflected the contentiousness of Protestant roots as well; authors interpreted the "facts" of history in divergent ways. Race historians may have been similarly motivated by historical circumstances to create historical narratives, but they differed greatly in their diagnoses of past ills and their prognoses for future improvement.

Race historians may have disagreed about whether slave spirituality was something that needed to be rooted out or whether it could provide a necessary basis for the growth of "true" Christianity. These differences of opinion reflected, in part, their position as self-appointed mediators between whites and southern blacks. Like many middle-class black religious leaders in the late nineteenth century, race historians had an ambivalent relationship to the black masses for whom they wished to speak. Most were, in fact, relative outsiders to the dilemmas faced by ex-slaves: many had been educated or had lived in the North. Separated from their northern Protestant colleagues by race, black Protestant leaders were thus distinguishable from southern blacks along class-based and often regional lines. Ironically, Williams's popular appellation as the "Negro Bancroft," while intended as a compliment, symbolized his distance from both other blacks and other Protestant divines. Race histories provided African American leaders with a means of rhetorically uniting the various religious, social, and racial loyalties that constituted their singular stations in life. But in doing so, ironically, their narratives often revealed division more than unity, distancing them from the people they sought to "improve."

William Hannibal Thomas, born in 1843, was a mixed-blood lawyer with seminary training. While growing up in Pickaway County, Ohio, Thomas witnessed his parents' service as conductors on the Underground Railroad. After a brief preparatory school education, Thomas tried to enlist as a Union Army volunteer in

1860, but was turned away because of his color. Eventually he found his way into the war, fought to the end, and, after professional training at a Presbyterian seminary, headed south in 1871 to organize schools for freed blacks. In 1876 he was elected to the legislature of South Carolina. In *The American Negro*, a highly contentious work published in 1901, Thomas expressed unmitigated anger toward southern blacks. True religion, Thomas asserted, is characterized by "clearness of spiritual perception" and "purity of ideal." The "mass of Negro religionists" do not have this perception of the principles of truth, but are instead irrational, and worship a God of "personal characteristics and human idiosyncrasies."[5] Other authors agreed with the substance of Thomas's judgment, but expressed less vitriol and more optimism about the ability of ex-slaves to rise from the "extreme fanaticism" of slave spirituality to religious rationalism.

George Washington Williams was another mixed-blood Civil War veteran who had fled his native Pennsylvania to enlist. He later graduated from Howard University (1871) and was the first black graduate from Newton Theological Seminary (1874). Williams, a parish minister who had served Baptist churches in both New England and Cincinnati, saw more to encourage him in the growth of Protestant institutions among ex-slaves. Black churches, as he saw it, were "the best proof of the Negro's ability to maintain himself in an advanced state of civilization." The progress of the race would come about as blacks learned to do for themselves.

Race historians used familiar tools to construct their historical narratives, but they organized them in ways that diverged from Euro-American sacred and national histories. A number of writers began their works by outlining the glorious and mighty culture of the Negro race in ancient Egypt. The Baptist minister L. T. Smith, born in Virginia, employed as a teacher by the Freedmen's Relief Association of Pennsylvania, and later educated at Hampton Institute in the 1870s, advised readers of his 1883 history *A Great Truth in a Nutshell* to "Wake up! Arise from the bed of dead lethargy . . . and, as I shall draw back the curtains of time, look! if you please, twenty-five hundred years back into the grim face of antiquity and see! O! see the elevated and lofty positions of honor, integrity, and so forth, your race once occupied in the scientifical world."[6]

The recovery of ancient Egypt also signaled more than the placement of African figures in a previously white classical landscape. Smith and the Baptist journalist J. Max Barber argued that Europeans and Americans had actively distorted the past by conspiring to prevent African Americans from recognizing their contributions to it. "We are taught to believe that the history of the race began with slavery," Barber began. "The white man has tried to rob us of Egypt because Egypt is the mother of modern civilization." Perry asserted that during slavery, "the white man wrote for white men; and now the black man must write for black men." Nonetheless, none of these authors recommended dispensing with the Christian tradition because of its associations with the evils of a Euro-American culture and the subsequent "regression" of Africans to a condition of "barbarism and heathenism." All saw the hand of providence working even in the dimmest light. "God has a purpose in all of this," concluded Barber, "and He will bring it to pass that all men shall have their turn at the wheel." Smith similarly asserted that "its purpose for good is yet veiled from our eager eyes."[7]

As prominent as the culture of ancient Egypt was in several of these accounts, and in spite of its growing importance as a symbol of cultural nationalism in the Pan-African movement, race historians generally used it as a foundation and stepping stone to link the biblical origins of the Cushites to the Christian era. Most of the survey histories briefly mentioned Africans in the ancient world in order to establish firmly the monogenetic account of human origins. However, they concentrated on the Euro-American tradition, and particularly on American history. In doing so, race historians did not depict the era of African enslavement, for all its moral complexities, as a period of unmitigated suffering. By restructuring American history through their narratives, Protestant leaders both lauded human heroism and simultaneously rejected the Anglo-Saxon triumphalism of white accounts. What is perhaps most fascinating about these revisions is the extent to which the narratives both sacralized the history of slavery, and revised sacred history to highlight the current spiritual dilemma of the Negro. Put another way, race historians used elements of the Christian paradigm to explain the significance of black emancipation and, significantly, to indicate the dawn of a new spiritual era in the late nineteenth century.

By setting Emancipation as the axis around which the rest of history turned, race historians also identified a host of antislavery activists and other friends of the cause of abolition as prophets of the coming new order. American history thus became a sacred drama of black activism. The chronicling of these prophets sometimes differed radically from white accounts of important American heroes, religious or otherwise. The most popular object of affection and reverence, for writers, was John Brown. Stanford hailed the leader of the Harper's Ferry revolt as a "Puritan hero, Christian philosopher," and "martyr for the slaves." In George Washington Williams's account, Brown was a martyr who "ranks among the world's greatest heroes"; "his ethics and religion were as broad as the universe, and beneficent in their wide ramification."[8]

Nat Turner also occupied a prominent place in many race histories. Edward Johnson's *School History of the Negro Race in America* called him a prophet, and mused that "he was, undoubtedly, a wonderful character." Williams was more guarded in his praise, owing, perhaps, to his awareness of white ambivalence toward a rebel slave who had murdered scores of women and children. Nonetheless, he too compared Turner to Moses and John the Baptist: the abolitionist was a remarkable prophet who "preached with great authority," and his early years were rendered in romantic terms as a steady stream of divinely inspired visions and spiritual growth. Perhaps trying to appeal to whites and blacks alike, Williams carefully avoided the subject of the massacre itself; in addition, he placed both the word "prophet," when referring to Turner, and the word "tragedy," when referring to the slave revolt, in parentheses, as if to buffer against criticism from either side. But his meaning was clear: he concluded by remarking that although no stone marked Turner's grave, his image was "carved on the fleshy tablets of four million hearts."

Despite the generous space accorded to Turner, Brown, the slave rebel Gabriel Prosser, Denmark Vesey, and other heroes of the abolitionist cause, race authors did not simply write a black-centered history of America. Most also accorded space to white harbingers of liberty. Race historians thus claimed selected events in Euro-American history as part of their own sacred heritage, but subordinated them to the unfolding drama of race emancipation. Rather than assimilating African Americans into "white" history, these narratives incorporated the tragedies and triumphs of American life into a lengthier account of moral and spiritual struggle. Previous battles, from the Reformation to the American Revolution, served as prophetic preludes to the central drama of the black jubilee.

Peter Thomas Stanford captured well the twists of thought that many contemporary observers have dismissed as simple capitulation to white values. Stanford was born a slave in Hampton, Virginia, lived briefly in a home for black orphans, and was subsequently sent to the family of Perry L. Stanford in Boston. After running away to New York City at age twelve, he was converted to Christianity during a revival conducted by evangelist Dwight Moody and was assisted educationally through the largesse of Harriet Beecher Stowe, Henry Ward Beecher, and Henry Highland Garnet. From then on, his life reflected both an indebtedness to white Protestant support and a commitment to the unity of African Americans. In *The Tragedy of the Negro in America*, Stanford insisted on understanding the history of slavery, the "record of iniquity," not on the temporal plane of human history, but within the realm of "God's record," in which all human history was subordinated to a recognition of the clarity of divine justice. This view compelled Stanford, he declared, to be mindful of "fairness to both black and white" in his narrative; although he condemned specific social ills such as the convict lease system and the scourge of lynching, he interpreted the evil of slavery as one of many human failings throughout sacred history: "the outrages of to-day are merely repetitions of previous outrages, the bad, poisonous fruit of seed sown in the distant and near past."[9]

Although differing in detail, these stories provided blacks with a new sacred narrative, one that extended beyond the bounds of God's dealings with his people in a land of bondage. To varying degrees, they incorporated some of the more salient features of recent Christian and American history into the account of the African American journey to freedom. They held up new saints and martyrs, and some even incorporated new documents, such as the Emancipation Proclamation, into the sacred canon. These were histories for a new community, one that had moved beyond the need for supernatural deliverance from the world's woes. Race authors, motivated by their own understandings of the progressive nature of sacred history, stressed the dawning of a distinctive era, one in which blacks would take their rightful places as equals among the races of the world.

These works reveal a great deal about their authors' attempts to place themselves and their own "maps of the world" at the center of debate over African American identity and destiny. Despite their many disagreements over the specific interpretation of racial history, race historians were more alike than not. Heirs to an ongoing debate in the United States about race, and newly armed with technologies and institutional networks that facilitated the ability to speak on behalf of a community, these religious leaders fashioned a novel form of historical narrative aimed at the representation of a renewed African American collectivity in the years after emancipation. Much of their art, as they themselves knew, sprang from wishful thinking. Late-nineteenth-century blacks were far from united in their views on nationality, race, or religion. Race historians hoped that their accounts would be both self-fulfilling prophecies of racial unity and prophetic indictments of contemporary racial and religious practices.

In the rush toward objectivity and scientific racialism, twentieth-century historians have forgotten the worldview that motivated early race authors. Indeed, their self-understanding has long eluded description by even the most careful historians. The key to the puzzle provided by a generation of race historians in the four decades preceding World War I is grounded in a historical consciousness that was at once thoroughly Protestant and thoroughly African American. Synthesized in a new way by a new generation of middle-class black Christians, this consciousness took into account a temporal sweep measured in centuries rather than decades, evaluated by providential rather than human means. This sweep frequently allowed for both the acknowledgment of universal human strengths and weaknesses and for ultimate forgiveness, and also for an unyielding commitment to a historically specific collective destiny embodied in the suffering and future triumphs of the Negro race. Neither assimilationist nor separatist, inspired by Euro-American philosophy and African American cultural unity, this worldview was articulated in the only form that could fully represent its dependence on a linear and progressive notion of time: chronological narrative. If contemporary observers have difficulty identifying the moving force behind these self-understandings, it is perhaps attributable to the racial dichotomies through which we ourselves view these histories, as well as to the failings of our own dichotomous discourse about race that conceives of choices, both metaphorically and literally, as being either "black" or "white."

ENDNOTES

1. George Washington Williams, *History of the Negro Race in America, 1619–1880: Negroes as Slaves, As Soldiers, and As Citizens* (1883; repr. New York, 1968), x.
2. On Williams's life, see John Hope Franklin, *George Washington Williams: A Biography* (Chicago, 1985).
3. In 1915 W. E. B. DuBois, the first black history Ph.D., published *The Negro*, a study of the race in both Africa and America; and Carter Woodson published his first work, *The Education of the Negro Prior to 1861*. See August Meier and Elliott Rudwick, *Black History and the Historical Profession, 1915–1980* (Urbana, IL, 1986) and Alfred A. Moss, Jr., *The American Negro Academy: Voice of the Talented Tenth* (Baton Rouge, 1981).
4. From just 5 percent of the black adult population in 1860, black literacy rose dramatically to 70 percent by 1910. Higginbotham, *Righteous Discontent: The Women's Movement in the Black Baptist Church, 1880–1920* (Cambridge, MA, 1993), 11, 44. See also Eric Foner, *Reconstruction: America's Unfinished Revolution, 1863–1877* (New York, 1988), 88-102; Leon Litwack, *Been in the Storm So Long: the Aftermath of Slavery* (New York, 1979); and William E. Montgomery, *Under Their*

    Own Vine and Fig Tree: The African-American Church in the South, 1865–1900 (Baton Rouge, 1993).

5. William Hannibal Thomas, *The American Negro: What He Was, What He Is, and What He May Become* (New York, 1901), 146-48.

6. L. T. Smith, *A Great Truth in a Nutshell. A Few Ancient and Modern Facts of the Colored People, by One of Their Number* (n.p., 1883), i-ii, 9.

7. J. Max Barber, *The Negro of the Earlier World: An Excursus into Ancient Negro History* (Philadelphia, n.d.) 6, 16.

8. Williams, *History of the Negro Race*, 2:214, 223.

9. Peter Thomas Stanford, *The Tragedy of the Negro in America* (Boston, 1898), iii, 9.

FOR FURTHER READING

DuBois, W. E. B. *The Soul of Black Folk*, Chicago, 1903.

Frazier, E. Franklin. *The Negro Church in America*/C. Eric Lincoln, *The Black Church Since Frazier*, New York, 1974.

Frederickson, George. *The Black Image in the White Mind: The Debate on Afro-American Character and Destiny, 1817–1914*, New York, 1971.

Johnson, Paul E., ed. *African American Christianity: Essays in History*, Berkeley, 1994.

Levine, Lawrence W. *Black Culture and Black Consciousness: Afro-American Folk Thought From Slavery to Freedom*, New York, 1977.

Lincoln, C. Eric. *The Black Muslims in America*, 3d ed., Grand Rapids, MI, 1994.

———. *Race, Religion, and the Continuing American Dilemma*, New York, 1984.

Lincoln, C. Eric, and Lawrence H. Mamiya. *The Black Church in the African American Experience*, Durham, NC, 1990.

Moses, Wilson. *The Golden Age of Black Nationalism, 1850–1925*, New York, 1978.

Raboteau, Albert J. *Slave Religion: The "Invisible Institution" in the Antebellum South*, New York, 1978.

Smith, H. Shelton. *In His Image, . . . Racism in Southern Religion, 1870–1910*, Durham, NC, 1972.

Wilmore, Gayraud S. *Black Religion and Black Radicalism: An Interpretation of the Religious History of Afro-American People*, 2d ed., Maryknoll, NY, 1983.

INTRODUCTION TO ESSAY 11

The Roman Catholic Church mirrors the pluralistic nature of this country's population better than any other denomination in America. For over four hundred years it has accommodated every ethnic group living here, doing so within a single framework that is based on shared hierarchical and liturgical patterns. Of course various immigrant communities have clustered together to form separate congregations, and clergy of compatible culture served those people faithfully. But such groups did not become separate forms of Catholicism. The idea of erecting separate churches, a theory called Cahenslyism in the nineteenth century, was firmly opposed by those who wanted to retain different cultural expressions under one overarching structure. There is one exception, and Platt takes us through the basic antagonisms and the specific circumstances wherein the Polish National Catholic Church became the only group to break away from Catholic solidarity.

Casting a wide net to record Polish dissatisfaction around the country, Platt settles on Francis Hodur as the real leader of this separatist movement based on ethnicity. At the same time he also demonstrates the effects of American culture on the new church, noting its acceptance of denominationalism and its favorable attitude regarding more lay participation. After explaining origins, the author also provides a glimpse of teachings as Hodur shaped them in the fledgling church. It is illuminating to compare PNCC doctrine with that of other churches on such topics as salvation, ecclesiastical authority, Christology, heaven, and hell. It is also interesting to speculate with the writer about the future of a group that tries to perpetuate a quasi-separatist national attitude in America's ethnically diverse and religiously pluralistic culture.

Original source - CH 46 (1977): 474-89.

11

The Polish National Catholic Church
An Inquiry into Its Origins

Warren C. Platt

The last decade of the nineteenth century witnessed a number of trends in the American Catholic religious scene with special reference to new immigrants:

1) The immigrants developed a cohesion and identity based on language that tended to obscure provincial loyalties and to transcend village patriotism.

2) This new sense of identity, a product of nationalist ideology and the influence of the American experience, received its primary expression in the ethnic church. This institution, founded primarily on linguistic lines, encompassed those who spoke the same tongue and resided within the same ghetto or patch.

3) The ethnic parish, an expression of immigrant identity and a matrix for social activities, retained the close association of society and religion that the immigrants knew in the peasant village and which the American reality was starting to dichotomize.

4) In attempting to construct ethnic parishes that would meet their religio-social needs, the immigrants within the Roman Communion faced the dual problem of attaining a significant degree of power in the American hierarchy and of mitigating the frequent hostility of the local bishop toward the establishment of a national parish.

It was in this atmosphere of immigrant demands and ethnic rivalry that there emerged a number of simultaneous, but unrelated, schismatic uprisings among Polish immigrants in this country. The

Polish immigrants found the Catholic church in this country, at least as they came into contact with it, practically an institution of the Irish and, in the Middle West, of the Germans. The tension on the parochial level was reflected on the national level where the Poles demanded a place in the hierarchy, a seat of power by which the right of Poles to organize ethnic parishes and select their own priests would be guaranteed and protected.

This and similar demands were met by resistance from the American hierarchy. The inability of the Poles to quickly secure a place in the episcopate seemed to threaten their establishment of more national parishes and their control of the existing ones. It was the ethnic parish that symbolized the unity of the immigrants and was itself based upon those very values which the new environment threatened: language and tradition. For the Polish immigrant, the parish was necessary as a means for worship and as an instrument for the unification, organization, and solidarity of the Polish-speaking community. But the efforts to found and to operate national parishes were handicapped by a number of controversies, chiefly:

1) disputes between Polish immigrants and the local bishop on the right to establish a Polish-speaking parish,

2) disputes between Polish immigrants in a Polish parish and the rector of the same parish who is of a different nationality,

3) disputes between Polish immigrants in a Polish national parish and the Polish priest of the same centering on lay control over parish finances and the accountability of the priest on fiscal matters, and

4) disputes between Polish immigrants in a Polish-language parish and the local bishop on the right of the congregation to choose or dismiss its priest and to exercise lay control over parish life.

As can be seen, these controversies often centered on the suitability of the priest and the right of the individual congregation to choose him. The Americanist wing advocated the naturalization of the ethnic clergy who would then return to their parishes as agents of acculturation. The Pole viewed such requests as threats to his very survival and, in the disruptive atmosphere of the American religious scene with its emphases on voluntarism and lay initiative, there emerged a number of revolts in various Polish settlements in the northeastern United States.

The Reverend Anton Kozlowski, a curate at St. Jadwiga's Polish Roman Catholic parish in Chicago, capitalized on parochial dissatisfaction with the unpopular rector and organized the independent parish of All Saints' in January 1895. Other parishes joined and, in order to legitimatize his movement and assert its authority as a Catholic body, Kozlowski sought and gained consecration at the hands of the Old Catholic bishops of Europe. The Polish Old Catholic Church, as the new body was called, encompassed twenty-three parishes; its creed conformed to the principles of the Old Catholic movement and the movement won the approval of Bishop Grafton of the Episcopal church.[1]

Another major revolt was to happen at St. Mary's Polish Roman Catholic parish in Scranton, Pennsylvania. The Polish coal miners and factory workers at the parish had contributed toward the building of a new church and requested Father Richard Aust, the German-speaking rector of the parish, for some representation in parochial affairs. The request was denied and the anti-Aust faction, a majority in the parish, founded the independent parish of St. Stanislaus one-half block away. The Reverend Francis Hodur, the pastor of a Polish parish in a neighboring village, was called to be the rector of the new parish; the reforms he enunciated as necessary were to be the basis for deciding on a permanent and definitive schism and the principle of the church he regarded as fundamental provided the raison d'être for the denomination.

Hodur attempted a final reconciliation and visited Rome in 1898 to plead his case. Here he insisted on four imperative reforms:

First, that a Polish bishop be sent to America; secondly, self-government among the Polish people, and new rules in the managing of church funds be adopted; thirdly, that church properties be in the name of the congregation, and not deeded to the bishop of the diocese, and the last, that the Polish people select their pastor.[2]

But Hodur received no encouragement, and the rejection of his ideas was soon followed by his own excommunication. On December 16, 1900, the Parish Assembly at St. Stanislaus made the final break with Rome. In 1904 delegates from various independent parishes in the northeast met in Synod and organized the Polish National Catholic Church, employing the basic principles enunciated by Hodur and ordering the Latin Missal to be translated into Polish. The Synod chose Hodur as bishop and adopted a constitution that provided for a congregational system slightly modified by a hierarchical structure. The Polish National Catholic Church expanded and, upon the death of Bishop Kozlowski (who left no successor), absorbed the Polish Old Catholic Church in 1907. Because of the death of Kozlowski, the Old Catholics in Europe were willing to consecrate Hodur to the episcopate and thus give him the opportunity to claim the legitimacy of the apostolic succession.[3]

The Polish National Catholic Church spread through the Polish communities of the northeast and its congregational structure appeared to new communicants to provide not only a religious life but also those opportunities for leadership not found in a typical parish or in secular life. The movement spread to Polish settlements that lacked an ethnic parish and to those parishes that experienced altercations between the laity and their clerical leadership. Thus the American religious strains of voluntarism and lay control allowed the discontent of the immigrants and their desire for self-government and its corresponding amenities to come to fulfillment. The synod of 1904, while attempting to create a Polish church in this country, actually established a Polish-American church that employed a sense of national identity as the fundamental principle of religious organization, thereby responding to American culture in the manner most easily understood by that society and in the way the immigrants themselves had been shaped by it and made cognizant of self-identification. The structure of congregational government with its lay control and explicit parochialism were obvious influences of the culture's religious traditions of disestablishment and decentralization. The synod's use of the word "denomination" to describe itself and other religious bodies shows the penetrating influence of American pluralism to the point where universal religious truth was recognized and the claim to exclusive revelation denied; it also manifests the degree to which religious self-identification had changed from a universal basis to a particularist one that defined itself on national origins while seeking harmony and cooperation with other religious bodies. The de-emphasis on doctrine correlative to the last point only reflected the increasing latitudinarianism in American Protestantism, the tolerance of varying doctrinal views in the American scene, and the need to unify Poles in America on the broadest possible basis without insisting on rigid doctrinal formularies that might hinder union or cause controversy within the independent movement.

The formation of the Polish National Catholic Church must be considered in relation to the total sociological situation of its adherents; it appears that there existed a psychological and sociological context of unadaptability and marginality that favored the accession of the new denomination. The shock of immigration and the disappointments of a new social condition made the Pole aware of his insecurity, unadaptability, and anomie. All led to a hunger for identification in the face of a hostile society and an alien culture. The opportunities to found his own parish and administer it to his own liking, two opportunities permitted by the associative nature of American society, were not lost to him. In this context he would meet his fellow countrymen, pray with them, and be understood—his craving for affiliation would be answered. The Polish parish offered him fraternity, participation in familiar and satisfying rites, and immediate relationship with religious symbols with which he identified himself.

The Polish National Catholic Church must be seen as a religious form of protest against social exclusion and discrimination, a religious expression of the resentment that flowed from disappointment and humiliation, and a pattern of compensation destined to restore social status and a sense of internal worth. For an independent parish and an autonomous Polish Catholic denomination, being lay-oriented and decentralized, provided not only the identity, solace, and assurance found in a Polish Roman Catholic parish, but also the self-assertion and self-respect to be found only in a church controlled and administered by immigrant laymen and under a hierarchy composed of members of their own race.

Francis Hodur was born in a small village outside Cracow (in what was then Austrian Poland) in 1866. Educated in government schools, he found religion, art, and literature to be attractive vocations; his personality led him to seek the priesthood as a vocation and he was ordained in 1892 upon completion of his studies at the Catholic Seminary at Cracow. He was sympathetic to the Polish nationalist movement that had developed among the intellectuals in that divided country; influenced by the thinking of Mickiewicz and Konopnicka, he found himself in agreement with the spirit of messianism and nationalism developed by the former and with the idealization of the poor enunciated by the latter.

For a religion to have vitality and effectiveness it must be rooted in the soul of the people professing it, Hodur believed, and, for this reason, selection of a nation's religious teachers could not be a matter of indifference.

> Shall only we Poles form an exception and allow ourselves to be forced to follow a line laid down by others? Shall we renounce our God-given right, the freedom of our Polish soul, the Polish national character with which God has endowed us, just because higher ecclesiastical authorities order it so? If our nation has any mission in humanity's reach toward higher goals, then it must also have a "faith" bearing an imprint of the Polish character and a free National church as all creative national bodies have. Our Polish National Catholic Church in America, a country of the free, must be free. Ecclesiastical autocracy in a democracy is an anomaly, a contradiction.[4]

Hodur's theory of "national religions," in which religious leaders worked primarily for their own people framing for them religious systems suited to their native character, and only secondarily influenced other national groups, did not create the new national-linguistic identity of the recent immigrants; this was a response to and an imitation of American reality. Rather it helped to articulate the new loyalty, to foster the burgeoning sense of religio-cultural-national values and expressions, and to provide a defense for the Polish National Catholic Church, which was as much a racial and cultural institution as a religious one. Hodur believed that the Poles, under their own leaders, should develop a Polish-Christian faith and that this national faith would be exemplified in the Polish National Catholic Church, the Poles' first step toward religious freedom and national independence. In conjunction with this he advocated a mission to Poland though political circumstances there and economic circumstances here prevented its realization until 1923. In this way Hodur resembled that small group of secular nationalist emigres from Poland who sought to make the Poles in America the fourth part of Poland. To this extent Hodur and other bishops authorized the establishment of parochial schools; the intent was the same as that of other ethnic denominations where schools were "fostered not only that the children might receive instruction in religion but also that they might learn the mother-tongue and with it the attitudes and social-ideals of the old homeland." In these Polish schools church teaching and religious education were combined with Polish history and literature; church hymns alternated with Polish folk songs and patriotic music; Polish saints were emulated as well as Polish heroes such as Krasinski and Konopnicka.

Through the Synod of 1904 and the formation of the Polish National Catholic Church, the Polish Catholics banded together under the leadership and thinking of Hodur, conformed to a standard of ethnic denominationalism. The irony that they had gone from a universalist position to a particularist one did not concern them; but even greater than this was the irony of establishing a church whose fundamental principle was Polish nationalism. This principle could not really survive the first generation; and the subtle changes in the nationalist ideology of the church from a Polish to a Polish-American nationalism reflected the gradual acculturation of the Polish immigrants and the development of an ethnic community neither truly Polish nor truly American but a fusion of the two.

• • •

In discussing the doctrines of the church and their formulation in the first two decades of the church's life, it is essential to remember that the cause of the schism was an ethnic and social one, and not doctrinal. For this reason the preparation of a basis of faith was "in fact, an afterthought." The Synod of 1904 agreed on a few simple points originally devised for the schismatic Polish parish in Scranton: these stressed the unity of the church with the primitive, undivided church, the rejection of Roman additions, and the essential value and goodness of man "as a child of God redeemed by Jesus Christ and sanctified through the manifold gifts of the Holy Spirit."[5]

Owing to the influence of Bishop Hodur, there appeared early in the history of the church and its doctrinal writings teachings at variance with both Roman and Old Church beliefs. Hodur was influenced by rationalism, reductionist liberalism, and certain aspects of Protestantism. For Hodur, a man's salvation depended solely on a living faith: man is saved by the grace of God and "gives evidence of his saved condition by good works flowing from his living faith. Good works are not means of salvation, but the fruit of it." In accord with the Old Catholics of Europe, papal authority in matters of faith and morals was explicitly rejected. Of the seven ecumenical councils, only the first four were formally accepted; the remaining three were also admitted but held to be nonessential. Beyond these, only the General Synods of the Polish National Catholic Church were recognized as authoritative. The teaching on the nature of God was orthodox. However, the Christology, as revealed in the Creed and Our Way of Life, was somewhat "low." Christ was described as the

Saviour and the Spiritual Regenerator of the World ... the Messenger of God ... this Nazarene Master made known his divine Mission on earth through his life: a perfect ideal of goodness, wisdom, and self-consecration for others' sake, especially for sinful and disinherited people; that through his work, his teaching, and his death of suffering, he became the spark enkindling a new life of humanity.[6]

Hodur avoided mention of the traditional christological concerns of Incarnation, Atonement, and Resurrection; Jesus was primarily an example of high ethical concerns rather than a revelation or manifestation of the nature of God.

The ecclesiology was also at variance with traditional Catholic understanding. Not only did Hodur recognize, in accord with American denominationalism, that no one Christian church is the exclusive exponent of the Christian faith, but he also adhered to the liberal Unitarian position on the universality of religious truth. The doctrine of the sacraments also failed to conform to Roman standards: baptism and confirmation were united as one sacrament and the Word of God, read, expounded, or listened to, formed yet another sacrament; the remaining five were the same as those observed in Rome. In the liturgy of the Mass, there was a certain emphasis on the Eucharist as a spiritual food rather than as a sacrifice.

Finally, the doctrine on the last things varied significantly from Catholic teaching. Hodur was unconcerned with the problem of Hell and eternal damnation. All men would eventually attain the goal of heavenly union with God, the degree of this union and bliss determined by the state of one's life and faith at death.

Corresponding to this optimistic view on judgment and universal salvation was Hodur's view on man and sin; he made no mention of original sin and the stress of the church's doctrine on the dignity of man and his longing for perfection ruled out any emphasis on man's depravity and his life away from God.

In summary, the doctrines of the Polish National Catholic Church as enunciated by Bishop Hodur reflected many aspects of American religious and social thinking of the time: the dignity of man, the emphasis on progress and man's capability of attaining his goals, the worthiness of all religions, the utility of religion for social control and the forming of right customs, and the distaste for pessimistic views of many and their accompanying religious imagery of original sin, depravity, judgment, and propitiatory sacrifice. Organizationally, the emphasis on decentralization and congregationalism coupled with a weak hierarchical control reflected the influence of the fluid and disruptive American scene. The body of theology and liturgy, especially Hodur's views on national religion and ideals of the church, was pervaded by a strong nationalistic attitude that has tended to force the church into a sectarian and isolationist position, emphasizing its Polish character at the expense of fellowship with other Christian communities.

• • •

The Polish immigrant was of peasant stock, and in the United States he found himself divested of his former work, trade, and style of life. The industrial economy had displaced the agricultural world, and the Pole, deprived of his old social institutions, found himself drawn into larger spheres of activity. But, as his numbers increased, the Pole acquired the capacity to satisfy his religious and social particularity. Schisms resulted and parochial life was recognized as an instrument of social cohesion and religious tradition.

Bishop Hodur, like other Polish priests, was influenced by nationalist feeling in his native land, and he encouraged a sense of national cohesiveness among his followers. This nationalism was encouraged by the immigrants' isolation in American society and their conflicts with Yankees and others on matters ranging from ecclesiastical control to labor problems.

True to these concerns, the Polish National Catholic Church focused on ethnic nationalism, a force defined by language which would outline the Polish character of the affiliated, and the nationalism propagated by Hodur that accentuated Polish liberation and its coupling with a theology of national religions. Under his leadership an early synod of the church dedicated itself to "work resolutely and with all determination to win the Polish nation to the idea of a free church for a free people" and "to fight for the freedom of the Polish soul against a settled policy of alien despotic domination." But this second nationalism, lacking the mass appeal of ethnic nationalism, became a secondary element in the church's appeal; the nationalism of the Polish National Catholic Church thus became an ethnic nationalism with limited political interest.

The emergence of the Polish National Catholic Church is a testament to the ethnic parish as an effective voluntary association for the preservation of linguistic, cultural, and religious traditions; at the same time, it was a product of the American experience whose traditions of voluntarism and free association allowed its creation and whose religious structure of denominationalism provided the necessary organizational framework.

ENDNOTES

1. Charles Grafton, *A Journey Godward* (Milwaukee, 1910), 281.
2. Martina Hammill, *Expansion of the Catholic Church in Pennsylvania* (Pittsburgh, 1960), 127.
3. Father Hodur was consecrated Bishop at the Old Catholic Cathedral in Utrecht on 29 September 1907 by Gerald Gul, the archbishop of Haarlem, and Nicolaus Spit, the bishop of Deventer.
4. Paul Fox, *The Polish National Catholic Church* (Scranton, PA, 1957), 115-16.
5. Theodore Andrews, *The Polish National Catholic Church* (London, 1953), 40.
6. Ibid., Article 2 of the Creed (author's translation).

FOR FURTHER READING

Colman, Barry. *Catholic Church and the German Americans*, Milwaukee, 1953.

Dolan, Jay P., ed. *The American Catholic Parish: A History from 1850 to the Present*, Volume 1, *The Northeast, Southeast and South Central States*; Volume 2, *The Pacific, Intermountain West and Midwest States*, Mahwah, NJ, 1987.

Janowski, Robert. *Growth of a Church*, Scranton, 1965.

Kuzniewski, Anthony J. *Faith and Fatherland: The Polish Church War in Wisconsin, 1896–1918*, Notre Dame, 1980.

Orton, Lawrence. *Polish Detroit and the Kolasinski Affair*, Detroit, 1981.

INTRODUCTION TO ESSAY 12

Instead of the far-ranging generalizations made by Marty and Smith, this essay contains a comfortably narrow focus on one priest in one parish. After making a few comparisons between Italian Catholics and those of other cultures, Brown concentrates on the day-to-day activities in a representative ethnic church at the peak of twentieth-century immigration to this country. Instead of giving us theories and broad patterns, Brown provides a wealth of detail about how people shared problems, achieved mutual support, and relied on their pastor to reach workable solutions. Through a report on the efforts of one selfless cleric Brown gives us the realistic feel of what life was like on New York's Lower East Side.

By all standards, Antonio Demo was a remarkable historical figure. He did not affect national events or enlarge the shelf of theological literature. What he did was serve his people for decades—demonstrating in concrete terms how religion has given ethnic enclaves spiritual solace and social guidance as ways of helping immigrants cope with events in their adopted homeland. Brown lists Demo's many efforts to help his parishioners: social welfare, charitable organizations, education, relief work in wartime, and pastoral care amid local tragedies. Moreover, she places such activities in a larger interpretive context of various immigrant parishes. But the lasting impression we have of this giving parish priest is that Father Demo was the salt of the earth.

Original source - CH 62 (1993): 41-59.

12

Italian Immigrant Catholic Clergy and an Exception to the Rule

The Reverend Antonio Demo, Our Lady of Pompei, Greenwich Village, 1899–1933

Mary Elizabeth Brown

Italians have long been the exception to generalizations about ethnic American Catholicism. Nineteenth-century observers and twentieth-century scholars offered two interpretations of Italian lay-clergy relationships. Some noted that pervasiveness of anti-clericalism among Italian men. Others cited the poor quality of the Italian clergy. In either case, there was a greater distance between Italian clergy and laity than between the clergy and laity of other ethnic groups. Reverend Antonio Demo, P.S.S.C., is a significant exception to this judgment because he was an active leader who presided over a community which considered its parish an important institution; and yet he belonged to the one ethnic Catholic group widely regarded as lacking strong parishes and clerical leadership.

Antonio Demo was himself an immigrant. He was born 23 April 1870 in Lazzaretto di Bassano, Vincenza, Italy. He joined the Pious Society of Saint Charles, more often called the Scalabrinians after founder Bishop Giovanni Battista Scalabrini. The Scalabrinians were dedicated to ministering to Italian immigrants on their journeys and in their new settlements. After ordination at Bishop Scalabrini's own hands in 1896, he departed for the mission field of Boston's North End. He may have learned some English in Italy, or he may have learned on the job in America; his English, while always clear, occasionally included an odd word or construction. He was appointed Pompei's pastor 19 July 1899.

Pompei had been founded in 1892. Unlike the southern Italians who made up the majority of immigrants and who reproduced their distinctive outdoor *feste* in America, Pompei's parishioners hailed from around the city of Genoa, a northern Italian area the religious traditions of which more closely matched those of other parts of Europe. Parishioners divided into two classes. A small group of men were heads of households and owners of businesses who interested themselves in parish management. A larger group in the parish were unskilled laborers and the chief recipients of Demo's care. Pompei's parishioners remember Demo partly for his record in parish construction. When he became pastor, Pompei occupied a church at 210 Bleecker Street. Demo renovated the rectory there, turned the basement into an auditorium, and opened a "kindergarten," or day care center, in 1915. When Sixth Avenue's extension demolished the church, he purchased land on the corner between Bleecker, Carmine, and Leroy Streets, where in 1928 he opened the church which Pompei still uses. A school followed in 1930.[1]

One can think of Demo as conducting his ministry within a series of concentric circles, at the center of which was the parish itself. The parish was surrounded by a circle of sister Italian Catholic parishes. Beyond that was a circle of social service institutions run by and for members of the ethnoreligious group. Beyond that was a circle of non-Italian but Catholic institutions which parishioners could also utilize for assistance in family crises. Beyond that was a circle of public welfare institutions and private philanthropies. This last was territory into which the Catholic laity were warned against venturing; one reason for the Catholic benevolent institutions was to keep Catholics out of Protestant and public institutions. It was in his contact with this larger universe, outside the stereotypical world of the narrow ethnic Catholic ghetto, that Demo was most unusual.

• • •

Under Demo, Pompei touched its parishioners' lives from cradle to grave. At that time, there were no diocesan-sponsored workshops or retreats for engaged couples. The affianced made arrangements with the parish a few weeks before their wedding. When children were born, there were no baptism classes for parents or godparents: Pompei baptized weekly, after the last Sunday Mass. Until the school was built, the children had their catechism classes in the church, different grades occupying different sections of pews. One of Pompei's claims to fame is that Mother Frances Xavier Cabrini, later a canonized saint, taught at Pompei, and came to Demo for confession. During most of Demo's tenure, the Christian Brothers organized the Sunday school, and directed Pompei's young lay women in teaching some of the grades. During the week the kindergarten saw up to ninety preschoolers a day. After 1930, children attended parochial school from kindergarten through eighth grade. Adolescents met for sodalities, rehearsals for fund-raising dramatic performances, and sports. Adults also had sodalities for their spiritual life, and from 1899 to 1923 the men of the Saint Joseph Society met monthly to assist the pastor with financial affairs.

Around Pompei was a network of other New York Italian Catholic parishes. By the time the Works Progress Administration counted them for one of their projects, there were forty-one parishes in the city and archdiocese of New York (the boroughs of Manhattan, the Bronx, and Staten Island) which used Italian for at least one Sunday sermon. These parishes' pastors attended one another's cornerstone ceremonies and anniversary celebrations, and, at least until Pompei began its move to Carmine Street, Demo contributed to some of the other parishes' fund-raising drives.

There were other Catholic institutions for Italians besides parishes. From 1912 to 1927 Demo served on an archdiocesan Italian Bureau, which supervised Italian parishes and priests. Until 1923, the Scalabrinians staffed the New York branch of the Saint Raphael Society for the Protection of Italian Immigrants, and after that year, the Italian Auxiliary, a joint project of the archdiocese and an Italian agency, cared for travelers. Mother Cabrini and the Missionaries of the Sacred Heart came to New York in 1889 to open an Italian Catholic girls' orphanage. Mother Cabrini also took over the Scalabrinians' Columbus Hospital. Several parishes besides Pompei had parochial schools and day care centers, and a couple of parishes ran summer camps where city children went for country vacations. Demo patronized Italian Catholic charities, sending Pompei's youngsters to summer camp, and donating money to other Italian day care centers. He supplied Columbus Hospital with a priest to give spiritual talks to the staff, and recommended its fund-raisers to his parishioners.

Beyond this circle of Italian Catholic parishes and agencies lay a larger circle of over two hundred "American" (English-speaking) Catholic benevolent agencies. Some provided institutional care. Others assisted people in their homes. Most parishes (Pompei was an exception) had Saint Vincent de Paul Societies which distributed charity, and there were Catholic foster home and parole-work societies. Beyond these Catholic institutions lay a larger circle of similar institutions run by the city or state government. Demo served as his parishioners' intermediary in their encounters with New York bureaucracy. His most regular contacts with non-Catholic public and private agencies were with those that had offices in Greenwich Village.

The founding of New York City's public school system was the direct result of antagonism between non-Catholics and Catholics.[2] Until 1842, the city allocated public funds to a private Public School Society for the purposes of educating the poor. As the numbers of poor Catholic Irish increased, so did tension between the native Protestant middle-class Public School Society and its clients. Thus New York's Roman Catholic bishop John Joseph Hughes (Archbishop Hughes after 1851) requested that Catholics be allowed a share of the tax money. When the city government refused, Hughes organized a slate of pro-Catholic candidates for the fall election. He was defeated, but he taught the state a lesson in Catholic voting power. In an effort to satisfy Hughes and the Catholics, New York established a truly public school system which did not involve itself in catechesis. The lack of religious education was equally unacceptable to Hughes. He became a leader in the movement to erect a parochial school in every parish. Demo's own experience with New York's public schools contrasted with Hughes's. Several teachers and principals in Greenwich Village public schools were Catholic. Like modern workers who attend churches near their place of work for daily Mass or prayers, Catholic public school personnel were quasi parishioners at Pompei. They took an interest in their pupils' religious education, and notified Demo if they encountered children they thought needed catechetical instruction. Demo did his part to ensure professional relationships with village educators.

The Children's Aid Society (CAS), founded in 1853, was one of the oldest philanthropies in New York. Like the public schools, CAS had a history of troubled relations with the Catholic church, especially where Italians were concerned.[3]

Protestant and Catholic leaders differed on how best to help the poor, but when Demo saw a source of aid for his parishioners, he took advantage of it. He supported CAS, and once offered to assist in its fund-raising campaign. He referred parishioners to the CAS district office at 27 Morton Street. Since CAS did not give money, it sometimes referred Demo's parishioners back to him to fund until CAS could complete the paperwork necessary for referral. CAS paid the rent for people who were waiting for their applications to be processed, and there are numerous letters indicating that when the applicants were parishioners, CAS and Demo, the latter using Pompei's funds, each paid half the rent. The reference checks CAS conducted were supposed to see if the poor were the "worthy poor." Judging from the correspondence, CAS and Demo agreed on standards for worthiness, with the predictable exception of Catholics' attitude toward divorce and remarriage which CAS social workers found frustrating.

Progressive philanthropists developed a new social service institution, the settlement house. American-born, college-educated young men and women "settled" among the urban, working-class, immigrant poor, studying their needs and offering them assistance. Catholics believed settlements were a new method of pursuing the old goal of "assimilating" immigrants away from their faith. When Mary Kingsbury Simkhovitch founded Greenwich House in 1901, she reassured New York Catholics by asking prominent members of the faith to serve on Greenwich House's board of directors. Demo had extensive and varied contacts with Greenwich House. A moving example of cooperation between Pompei and Greenwich House came as a result of the Triangle Shirtwaist Factory fire in 1911. The Triangle Shirtwaist Factory was located on the eighth, ninth, and tenth floors of a loft building within walking distance of both Greenwich House and Pompei. The fire broke out at about

5:30 on a Saturday afternoon. The building itself was fireproof, but the blouse factory was not. It had wooden work tables and benches, greasy oiled sewing machines, dangling electric wires, and paper patterns and thin cotton material everywhere. The fire escape was so decrepit it pulled away from the building with a full load of passengers on it, and the regular exits were kept locked to prevent employee theft. Employees tried to jump to safety, but the fire nets of the day were not strong enough to handle even a light young woman hurtling from a ten story height. The fire killed 146 people, 18 of them Pompei parishioners.

On 26 April 1911, Pompei held a month's mind, a memorial Mass for all those who died in the fire. Demo sent out English-language black-bordered announcements to people beyond the immediate parish community. He sang the Solemn High Requiem Mass, and Ernesto Coppo, a Salesian missionary who was pastor of the Church of the Transfiguration on Mott Street, gave the sermon. The church was crowded with Italian women mourning their friends and kin, and at some points the distraught congregation's weeping brought Coppo's sermon to a halt. One woman wrote to let Demo know how much she appreciated his attention to pastoral care for the bereaved: "I was eye-witness to this awful tragedy and can never forget its horrors." There was an unusual conclusion to the Mass. Simkhovitch was a member of the Women's Trade Union League, which brought together upper-class ladies and working-class women to improve working conditions for the latter. She and her colleagues, with what she called Demo's "cordial permission," stood outside the church after Mass distributing English, Italian, and Yiddish circulars calling for a campaign to enforce existing fire safety laws.

• • •

Two events accelerated Demo's contact with the world beyond Pompei. The first was World War I. On 1 August 1914, the chancery sent a circular requesting that archdiocesan congregations say special prayers to ward off the coming of war. But it was too late. At the outbreak of war, New York's Italian Catholics mobilized to help the Italians back home. When World War I ended, Italian Americans still had their responsibilities to those who suffered during the war. Pompei honored veterans with free admission to one of its fund-raising programs for anyone in military uniform. The Italian Red Cross and others continued to raise money on behalf of Italian civilian and military casualties. In 1921, Demo participated in a New York service held simultaneously with Roman obsequies for Italy's Unknown Soldier.

A second event which altered the concentric rings of organization in which Pompei moved occurred three years after World War I ended. Before the war, Cardinal Farley had begun bringing together New York's Catholic charities under an umbrella organization called United Catholic Works. The war and then Farley's death interrupted the plans. After the war, the organizational process started again, and in 1922 Catholic Charities was incorporated. According to public relations articles Catholic Charities was supposed to coordinate New York Catholics' efforts to do good. Rather than have two hundred separate agencies raise their own funds, Catholic Charities conducted one annual campaign, and from this collection gave funds to the separate agencies. Also, rather than have the agencies conduct their own public relations, and depend on hundreds of pastors to channel their parishioners toward the best sources of help, Catholic Charities had its own intake workers to make referrals.

Catholic Charities made two changes in Pompei's service to the poor. Like the other parishes, Pompei participated in the annual Catholic Charities fund drive. Second, once Catholic Charities opened its referral service, Demo's role as intake social worker changed. Instead of referring parishioners to a welfare agency himself, he referred them to Catholic Charities, explained what the problem was, and Catholic Charities was supposed to take care of the rest. There is nothing from Demo's own hand about his reasons for his extensive work beyond his parish. One can guess absolute necessity was among them. The early Italian immigrants' poverty meant Pompei had more people to care for, and fewer resources available for their care. Pompei had at least as many services and programs as other Italian Catholic parishes, and this was not enough. More people required assistance than the parish, or even the Catholic church, could provide.

Caroline Ware, a Greenwich House social scientist, offered a second reason for Demo's neighborhood involvement.[4] "Italian" Pompei really served two populations: Italian immigrants and their Americanized offspring. The former preferred to practice their faith as they had done in Italy. This presented the danger that the latter would reject their parents' faith along with their parents' customs as unsuitable for young Americans. As an Italian, Demo could sympathize with the older members of his congregation, and Pompei preserved many customs brought by the earliest parishioners. As a priest, though, Demo could not afford to lose the youths. He involved himself in the American life of Greenwich Village, so his young parishioners grew with their parish and not away from it.

• • •

There are three possible ways to use the work already done by other scholars to interpret Demo's experience. One way is to compare him with the Catholic immigrant clergy of other ethnic groups. Jay Dolan's pioneering work, *The Immigrant Church*, indicates that antebellum New York Irish and German priests combined expressions of pastoral care such as the administration of the sacraments with other such expressions, such as the establishment of parochial schools and other social service institutions.[5] John J. Bukowcyzk described Polish priests who shaped communities defined both by ethnicity and religiosity.[6] According to Myron B. Kuropas, Ukrainian clergy played a similar role in their community.[7] Stephen J. Shaw compared the German and Italian parishes of early twentieth-century Chicago, and found similarities between the clergy of the two groups.[8] Except for his willingness to use private and public secular philanthropies to meet his parishioners' needs, Demo seems like his clerical colleagues in other ethnic groups. Thus, Demo's activities challenge the notion of an Italian "problem," and make the Italians seem more like other ethnic groups than has been previously thought.

A second possible interpretation again involves books such as Dolan's *Immigrant Church*, which notes that the Irish and German immigrants arriving in antebellum America were not as thorough in their knowledge of their faith, nor as regular in their practice of it, as later generations of Irish and German Americans were. In her history of the Archdiocese of Detroit, Leslie Tentler Woodcock emphasizes that every ethnic Catholic group came to Michigan much less observant of Catholic practice than their descendants later became.[9] There is probably a relationship between recency of migration and the degrees to which the ethnic group's version of Catholic practice is acceptable to the host group. Again, the result of this research is to make Demo, and the Italians he helped to shepherd, seem less like exceptions to the rule and more like their immigrant colleagues, only with a later arrival date and therefore a delayed start in the generations-long process of assimilation.

There are few studies of people such as parish priests, who worked close to the grass roots, and few studies which concern family welfare. More work needs to be done in this area to flesh out the history of the relationship between Catholics and private and public secular social service institutions to find out if Demo was the exception to the rule of a wall of separation between Catholics and others in early twentieth-century American life, or if he was part of an unnoticed current leading toward greater cooperation between Catholic and public officials on behalf of those in need.

ENDNOTES

1. Robert A. Orsi, *The Madonna of 115th Street: Faith and Community in Italian Harlem, 1880–1930* (New Haven, 1987); Jay P. Dolan, *The American Catholic Experience: A History from Colonial Times to the Present* (Garden City, NY, 1985); Marco Caliaro and Mario Francesconi, *John Baptist Scalabrini, Apostle to Emigrants*, trans. Alba I. Zizzmia (New York, 1977).

2. Diane Ravitch, *The Great School Wars: New York City, 1803–1973: A History of the Public Schools as Battlefields of Social Change* (New York, 1974), 3-76.

3. Charles Loring Brace, *The Dangerous Classes of New York and Twenty Years' Work Among Them* (New York, 1880; reprint, Montclair, NJ, 1978), 198-99.

4. Caroline Ware, *Greenwich Village, 1920–1930: A Comment on American Civilization in the Post-War Years* (New York, 1935; reprint, New York, 1965), 312.

5. Jay P. Dolan, *The Immigrant Church: New York's Irish and German Catholics, 1815–1865* (Baltimore, 1975).

6. John J. Bukowczyk, *And My Children Did Not Know Me: A History of Polish-Americans* (Bloomington, IN, 1987).
7. Myron B. Kuropas, *The Ukrainian Americans: Roots and Aspirations, 1884–1954* (Toronto, 1991).
8. Stephen J. Shaw, *The Catholic Parish as a Way-Station of Ethnicity and Americanization: Chicago's Germans and Italians, 1903–1939* (New York, 1991).
9. Leslie Tentler Woodcock, *Seasons of Grace: A History of the Catholic Archdiocese of Detroit* (Detroit, 1990).

FOR FURTHER READING

Dolan, Jay P., ed. *The American Catholic Parish: A History from 1850 to the Present*, Volume 1, *The Northeast, Southeast and South Central States*; Volume 2, *The Pacific, Intermountain West and Midwest States*, Mahwah, NJ, 1987.

McGreevy, John T. *Parish Boundaries: The Catholic Encounter with Race in the Twentieth-Century Urban North*, Chicago, 1996.

Meagher, Timothy J., ed. *Urban American Catholicism: The Culture and Identity of the American Catholic People*, New York, 1988.

Olson, James Stuart. *Catholic Immigrants in America*, Chicago, 1987.

Orsi, Robert A. *Thank You, St. Jude: Women's Devotion to the Patron Saint of Hopeless Causes*, New Haven, 1996.

Taves, Ann. *The Household of Faith: Roman Catholic Devotions in Mid-Nineteenth-Century America*, Notre Dame, 1986.

PART III

*Exploring Dimensions in
Religious Thought*

INTRODUCTION TO ESSAY 13

Some interpreters argue that revivalistic emotionalism choked off all concern for rigorous thought in American religious history. Such an observation may apply in general, but New England Puritans were certainly an exception. In the seventeenth century they brought a strong intellectual tradition with them to these shores and continued it for several generations. In our own time this tradition has been brought to our attention once again, largely through the writings of one scholar, Perry Miller. His seminal publications refreshed our understanding of Puritan ideas, their origins, colonial applications, and influence on later thought patterns such as Transcendentalism.

The author of this essay presumes a thorough acquaintance with Miller's work and then proceeds to pick a quarrel with part of it. Cherry focuses here on an important category in Puritan thought: the covenant, which is a special relationship between God and believers who feel chosen for righteousness. Miller interpreted latter-day Puritan Jonathan Edwards and his covenantal theology in a certain way; Cherry challenges Miller's interpretation at its root. In what follows we see Cherry unfolding what he thinks the Puritans meant regarding standard Calvinistic categories like atonement, sovereign grace, predestination, faith, and mutual obligations between God and humanity. Some of this analysis might initially strike us as quibbling over unimportant distinctions, but Cherry's closely reasoned arguments are good examples of what comprises many exercises in doctrinal study.

Original source - CH 34 (1965): 328-41.

13

The Puritan Notion of the Covenant in Jonathan Edwards' Doctrine of Faith

C. Conrad Cherry

The immense importance of the idea of the covenant for the Puritans of England and New England has been thrown into sharp relief by recent Puritan studies. Many problems regarding the origin and function of the Puritan covenant idea still await the careful attention of the student of Puritanism, but this much is clear: the notion of the covenant was decidedly a pervasive idea in Puritan theology, and the idea was developed in a rather elaborate scheme by a host of Puritan theologians.

Perry Miller, to whom every contemporary student of Puritan history is profoundly indebted, was something of a pioneer in uncovering the crucial role which the covenant played for the Puritans. Yet at one point Miller's understanding of the covenant must be seriously questioned. The point appears quite clearly in his interpretation of the relation between the covenant theology and the thought of America's greatest Puritan theologian in the eighteenth century, Jonathan Edwards. Miller contends that Edwards "threw over the whole covenant scheme" and "declared God unfettered by any agreement or obligation."[1] Miller's understanding of the covenant underlying this contention has made a formative impact on Puritan studies. It will be the argument of this paper, however, that Miller errs in two critical respects. First, Edwards did not "throw over the whole covenant scheme" but definitely adhered to some of the basic features of his forefathers' Covenant Theology. Second, the "agreement" nature of the covenant did not bind the Almighty to a human contract, as Miller suggests, but expressed rather a characteristically Puritan way of construing the meaning of Christological revelation.

In its theological essence the Puritan doctrine of the covenant represented a history of the manner in which God dealt with his people. God entered into covenant with man from the beginning. There was first a "covenant of works": here God promised salvation and felicity to man on the condition that man stay within the boundaries of divine law. Adam's disobedience and fall into sin was a rejection of this first covenant. But God did not give man up. He instituted a second covenant, a "covenant of grace," which respected man's weakness in sin. The covenant of grace included Israel under the Old Testament as well as the Church under the New. God's grace and promise in Christ were the foundation and possibility of Israel's relation to God in faith, although that grace was hidden under the forms of Israel's historical existence, forms abandoned with the historical coming of Christ. The covenant of grace is similar to the covenant of works in that promises and the performance of conditions are still assumed by both God and man.

The covenant doctrine had for the Puritan a wider scope than its theological essence. Perry Miller has made abundantly clear how this was especially the case in the Massachusetts settlement: "in the migration to Massachusetts all entered into a covenant, among themselves and with the Lord. In the one compact the people were dedicated both to theological and to social duties."[2] The scope of the Puritan covenant-idea was narrowed for Jonathan Edwards in this sense: it did not assume for him the same importance for an understanding of the saints' social and political life as it had for his forefathers. Yet the Covenant Theology was still extremely valuable to Edwards for describing the nature of the saints' relation to God in faith. In the context of his doctrine of faith, Edwards' use of the categories of the covenant scheme comes clearly to light, for there we find him working with two recurrent motifs in the scheme: God's "debt" to man in the covenant of grace; and man's faith as the "condition" of the covenant with God.

• • •

Perry Miller appeals to Edwards' 1731 Boston sermon on man's absolute dependence on God, as a substantiating piece of evidence for the thesis that Edwards abandoned the entire covenant scheme which tied God to an agreement or obligation. In that particular sermon Edwards insists that man's redemption is by the free and sovereign grace of God; hence man may make no claims on, but must simply depend upon, the power of God for salvation. "The Federal [or Covenant] Theology is conspicuous in his sermon by its utter absence," says Miller.[3] But in a sermon of 1733, the Covenant Theology is anything but utterly absent from Edwards' thinking. There Edwards not only speaks of salvation within the context of a "Covenant of Grace" which has as its "certain condition" man's belief in "the L.J.X."; he also says, "Salvation is an absolute debt to the believer from God that he may in justice demand delivery. . . ." And in another, undated, sermon Edwards maintains that men may through Christ demand salvation from God "as a Debt."[4]

Edwards rejects all Pelagian and Arminian claims to salvation on the basis of what man is or does (including the act of belief). In this context "debt" is to be understood in a "non-covenantal" way. In his adoption of the debt idea, Edwards is taking seriously the meaning of the Incarnation as God's condescension to man in history. Here "debt" takes on a very restricted meaning within the context of the biblical representation of the covenant-relation between God and man. On the latter level, Edwards is reaffirming, according to his understanding of the nature of faith, what is at the center of the Puritan theology of the covenant.

It is of no avail for a man to complain that he has done more to deserve salvation than another and that hence God is more obligated to him for salvation than to the other man. God has absolute disposal over the dispensation of salvation. The "great God" cannot "be tied up" by the sinner's claims or high opinions of himself. In the salvation of man, God remains sovereign Lord even as he is merciful. In brief, Edwards' rejection of the debt idea is a rejection of works-righteousness, of the attempt of the sinner to make claims on God on the basis of ostensible human holiness, a rejection which is quite characteristic of the broader range of Edwards' thinking on the nature of faith. Edwards stresses here what is central to his 1734 sermons on the doctrine of justification by faith alone: God in Christ justifies the sinner as a *sinner* who has no case to plead on the basis of his own goodness or righteousness. God is in debt to none. No creature can, on the basis of his own inherent righteousness, "tie up" the bestower of salvation.

Nevertheless, in another sense, on another level, God is in debt to man; man may demand his salvation from God as a debt. Edwards avers, "Those who are in a state of salvation are to attribute it to sovereign grace alone, and to give all the praise to him, who maketh them to differ from others. Godliness is no cause for glorying, except it be in God." The possibility of the believer's demanding salvation on the basis of his own godliness is precluded. *Man does not "tie up" God, but God ties himself to man in the covenant.* Here is the meaning of the Incarnation: God binds himself in covenant with the sinner, and in so doing God freely limits his freedom for man. The sinner-believer demands salvation through Christ, on the basis of God's binding himself in Christ, and never through or on the basis of his own goodness or obedience.

In a statement such as this, of course, Edwards presupposes a "limited" or predestinarian doctrine of atonement: the atonement does not open salvation to all but only to those eternally elected to have faith. But for the elect believer God is no longer the distant, arbitrary ruler; He is the God who has drawn near in Christ and who has revealed His ways in his Word. Since the believer is united to Christ in faith, he may demand salvation through the intercessor with whom he is united. God has entered human history as God-for-man, and God has promised the believer his salvation which the believer may demand as God's part of the covenant. The concept of "debt" in the Puritans' Covenant Theology was one way of accentuating the Calvinist doctrine of Christological revelation by stressing the vital and luminous presence of God in human history: God enters history as the believer's covenant partner. The idea surrenders neither Calvin's warning that man has no claims *of himself* on the Creator nor Calvin's insistence that it is as *sovereign Lord* that God reveals himself and saves man. On the basis of the covenant founded by God in Christ, the man of faith may indeed, for the covenant theologian, demand salvation from God.

Edwards consciously adopts this Puritan spirit attached to the notion of God's indebtedness. Man demands salvation from God not because he as man deserves it but because God has promised it. The sinner does not bind God in the covenant, but God binds himself to man. It is of the essence of the grace of God that He "should condescend to become bound to us by covenant," that He "should cease to be merely arbitrary" so that we "can challenge salvation of this Sovereign."[5] But the challenge to the Sovereign *is* a challenge to a *sovereign*. It is hence nothing but a prayer to God to fulfill his promises. The covenantal description of salvation as a debt to man is, in fact—when conceived according to the second level of interpretations—an explication of one important dimension of Edwards' understanding of the nature of faith. In faith man demands from God, sues God for, the salvation promised in Christ. What God owes the man of faith, what that man sues for, is the fulfillment of the promise of salvation God himself makes when He condescends to bind himself in covenant with man. And the demanding act of faith is itself a possibility only as God continues to uphold the relation of faith.

• • •

The notion of faith as the condition of the covenant of grace was closely related to the Puritans' understanding of faith as an "instrument." The covenant of grace was for the Puritans a mutual bond. Faith was the condition on the human side of the bond, salvation the condition on the divine side. But faith, unlike the meritorious work, was a gift of God and was an empty vessel, the instrument, for the reception of God's performance of salvation in Christ. Edwards maintains that faith is the human condition of the covenant of grace; and the covenant is not consummated until we have performed that condition. Edwards places the same restrictions on the concept of faith as condition as did his theological antecedents: the condition is itself a divine gift; and, unlike the meritorious work, it takes man off his own foundation. God is the efficient cause of faith, of the human condition of the covenant.[6] And faith is the condition of the covenant of grace only to the extent that it is truly faith, i.e., to the extent that it allows Christ to perform the ultimate condition of the covenant.

During Edwards' "better moments," then—during those moments when he conceived the nature of the covenant in light of the full range of his understanding of faith—he was careful to designate faith as the "condition" of the covenant only in the sense that in faith the covenant and its blessings are concretely and actively *received*. Far from throwing over the Covenant Theology, Edwards was quite dependent upon it—in fact, there is every indication that he had difficulty freeing himself from its categories even at the points where he discerned their shortcomings. What is of more importance, however, is that in his doctrine of faith Edwards was clearly a covenant theologian. For Edwards, the relation of faith is a covenant-relation. Because God has drawn near in covenant, man is taken up through faith into a continuous relation of dependence on him. And the God of faith is the God of Covenant: a promise-making, promise-keeping God who may be "dealt with" in faith as a covenant partner; not the God of an inscrutable hinterland.

ENDNOTES

1. Perry Miller, *Errand into the Wilderness* (Cambridge, MA, 1956), 98.
2. Miller, *The New England Mind: The Seventeenth Century* (Boston, 1961), 415.
3. Miller, *Jonathan Edwards* (New York, 1959), 30.
4. Sermon notebook on Ephesians 3:10, dated March 1733, Yale MSS; printed, undated, "Displayed in Salvation," in *Works*, Dwight edition, 7:66-114.
5. Sermon on Romans 9:18, Yale MSS.
6. "An Humble Inquiry into the Qualifications for Full Communion in the Viable Church of Christ," *Works*, 4:321.

FOR FURTHER READING

Cherry, Conrad. *The Theology of Jonathan Edwards*, Garden City, NY, 1966.

Daniel, Stephen H. *The Philosophy of Jonathan Edwards: A Study in Divine Semiotics*, Bloomington, IN, 1994.

Delattre, Roland A. *Beauty and Sensibility in the Thought of Jonathan Edwards*, New Haven, 1968.

Fiering, Norman. *Jonathan Edwards's Moral Thought and Its British Context*, Chapel Hill, NC, 1981.

Hatch, Nathan O., and Harry S. Stout, eds. *Jonathan Edwards and the American Experience*, New York, 1988.

Jenson, Robert. *America's Theologian: A Recommendation of Jonathan Edwards*, New York, 1988.

Kuklick, Bruce. *Churchmen and Philosophers: From Jonathan Edwards to John Dewey*, New Haven, 1985.

McDermott, Gerald R. *One Holy and Happy Society: The Public Theology of Jonathan Edwards*, University Park, PA, 1992.

Morgan, Edmund S. *The Puritan Dilemma: The Story of John Winthrop*, Boston, 1958.

Smith, John E. *Jonathan Edwards: Puritan, Preacher, Philosopher*, Notre Dame, 1992.

Tracy, Patricia. *Jonathan Edwards, Pastor: Religion and Society in Eighteenth Century Northampton*, New York, 1980.

Winslow, Ola E. *Jonathan Edwards, 1703–1753*, New York, 1941.

INTRODUCTION TO ESSAY 14

In this essay Ahlstrom uses his typically wide-ranging grasp of intellectual trends to identify another important strain in American religious thought. In fact the work that follows began a rehabilitation of Scottish Philosophy in much the same fashion Perry Miller helped restore our appreciation of Puritan ideas. Ahlstrom affords information on two different levels: telling us about individual thinkers as well as general categories germane to intellectual history of any sort. The main topic here is epistemology, theories about how we know things, and it soon becomes clear that this philosophical position is primarily interested in showing that one can attain reliable knowledge of God and moral principles.

It is difficult to show causation and influence in intellectual history, but it seems clear in this case that immigrants like John Witherspoon were effective agents in transferring ideas from Reid and Stewart in Scotland to these shores. Ahlstrom then shows how this philosophical position permeated Unitarians at Harvard, mildly Calvinist thinkers such as Taylor at Yale, and outspokenly Calvinist ones like Hodge at Princeton. Beyond that, he explains how and why this approach to knowledge was so useful in religious contexts, giving old doctrines a new vigor and reassuring generations of believers that they could embrace theological ideas with certitude and confidence.

Original source - CH 24 (1955): 257-72.

14

Scottish Philosophy and American Theology

Sydney E. Ahlstrom

The Scottish Philosophy is no longer in good repute despite its proud reign in another day. Indeed, few, if any, schools of philosophy have been given such disdainful treatment by historians as Common Sense Realism; and few, if any, philosophers have had to suffer such ignominious re-evaluations as Thomas Reid and Dugald Stewart, who were once lionized as the founders of a great and enduring philosophical synthesis. Yet the very decisiveness of this reversal creates a problem. Why, when its ultimate rejection was so complete, did the Scottish Philosophy for over a century play such a large and variegated role in Western thought, being in its origins a forceful liberalizing religious movement, in France the near-official "middle-way" of the Restoration and July Monarchy, and in America the handmaiden of both Unitarianism and Orthodoxy? The account which follows is directed to this question as well as to the factors in Scottish and American intellectual history which demonstrate the importance of asking it.

• • •

That the "Scottish Renaissance" of the eighteenth and nineteenth centuries is not just a state of affairs imagined by professional Scotsmen, is being made abundantly clear as the subject receives closer and more sympathetic study. It was a genuine cultural efflorescence which placed the Scottish universities in the European forefront and made Edinburgh one of the literary capitals of the world. Nor is it simply a work of piety to point out that during the eighteenth century Churchmen and sons of Churchmen played a major role in that flowering.

In view of the controversy that such a result entailed, it is more accurate to see the Scottish philosophers as a liberal vanguard, even as theological revolutionaries, than to preserve the traditional picture of genteel conservatives bringing reason to the service of a decadent orthodoxy.

The archetypical Scottish Philosopher is Thomas Reid (1710–1796), regent at King's College, Aberdeen, and active member of the Aberdeen Philosophical Society from 1752 to 1763 and thereafter successor to Adam Smith in moral philosophy at Glasgow. While still a parish minister, Reid was awakened from his Berkeleian slumbers by Hume's *Treatise on Human Nature* (1738–40). His own *Inquiry into the Human Mind on the Principles of Common Sense* (1764) was an effort to trace Hume's "skepticism" back to the errors of "represenationalism" or what Reid called the "ideal theory," and to put in its stead a realistic theory of perception. In the full statement of his mature thought published two decades later, however, Reid was engaged, as well, on the wider front of refuting materialism, ethical relativism, and kindred errors. This led him into alliance with rationalists like Richard Price.[1]

Reid's philosophy can be summarized in terms of four major conclusions—and it might be added that these four points, or most of them, take central place in the thought of any typical proponent of the "Scottish Philosophy":

   I. Philosophy depends on scientific observation, with the primary object of such observation being self-consciousness and not the external behavior of men.

  II. The observation of consciousness establishes principles which are anterior to and independent of experience. Some principles, like that of substance or cause-and-effect, are *necessary*, others, like the existence of things perceived, are *contingent*, but all are in the very constitution of the mind and not the product of experience.

 III. Nothing can be an efficient cause in the proper sense but an intelligent being; matter cannot be the cause of anything but is only an instrument in the hands of a real cause.

 IV. The first principles of morals are self-evident intuitions; moral judgments, therefore, are not deduced from non-moral judgments, for they are not deductions at all.[2]

Of all the exponents of this system none was more important than Dugald Stewart (1753–1828) who in 1785 succeeded Adam

Ferguson in the chair of moral philosophy at Edinburgh. Stewart added little or nothing to his master's system; but his rhetorical gifts and great erudition attracted the cultivated circles of Edinburgh and his books won a wide international audience.

• • •

It would be futile to try to discover the first entrance of the Scottish Philosophy into America; but since Reid's *Inquiry*—the *sine qua non*—was not published until 1764, the honor of being the first real ambassador should probably be assigned to John Witherspoon, who after long and almost coercive supplications finally left his native land in 1768 to become president of the College of New Jersey in Princeton. Witherspoon was not an ideal emissary, however, even though some have credited him with anticipating Reid's "discoveries," because his Evangelical bias blinded him to the real genius of the movement. Yet before his term as president ended, the "French mania" and Deism were becoming dangerously popular. Believing as his whole generation seemed to, moreover, that the then regnant views of Locke and Berkeley led inexorably to the "skepticism" of Hume or, worse yet, to the materialism of Condillac and French *ideologues,* they saw no other recourse but to defend orthodox theology with weapons forged in the Scottish universities for quite another kind of battle.[3]

As a result of Witherspoon's powerful influence, Reid *did* supplant Berkeley at Princeton, and due to the powerful advocacy of Archibald Alexander, the first and for a year the only professor in the Princeton Theological Seminary, and Charles Hodge, his great colleague and successor, the Scottish Philosophy was carried by Princeton graduates to academies, colleges, seminaries, and churches all over the country.

To a consideration of Alexander and Hodge I will return in due course; but to illustrate the impact of Scottish Realism on American doctrinal developments, it is advantageous to shift to the other end of the theological spectrum and consider, in turn, a series of early theologians at Harvard, Yale, Andover, and Princeton, beginning with the liberal and proceeding progressively through various degrees of conservatism.[4]

By 1810 Harvard was for all practical purposes a Unitarian institution, and the Scottish Philosophy became almost official both in the college and the new divinity school. Under the Alford Professors, Levi Frisbie, Levi Hedge, James Walker, and Francis Bowen, there was an unbroken succession of emphatic Scottish advocacy down to 1889. Of this group James Walker is typical. He was called in 1839 to the Alford Chair of Natural Religion, Moral Philosophy, and Civil Polity, and from 1853 to 1860 he was president of Harvard University. In the antebellum period he was, after Channing, probably the most respected figure in the Unitarian movement. Walker published no systematic work, but his *Sermons* are, in substance, chapters in moral philosophy. The Scottish imprint is unmistakable as he brings his eloquence to bear on the subjects of virtue, conscience, natural theology, and the role of reason. For use in his religion and ethics classes he even prepared special editions of both Reid and Stewart. James Bowen, his successor, added other editions of Stewart and Hamilton. How Scottish views fitted in to the liberal Christian theology of early Unitarians is too apparent to require further elaboration here.

The Unitarian movement, however, was an extremely limited phenomenon. Although it had by 1833 wrested almost a hundred of the old Congregational parishes from Orthodox control, the old saying that its preaching was limited to the fatherhood of God, the brotherhood of man, and the neighborhood of Boston is substantially true in the geographical sense—though not in the theological. In New England as a whole the theology of Andover and Yale was far more influential; and in the great Yankee diaspora of the nineteenth century, Unitarianism was left behind. For the evangelical response to infidelity, the greatest spokesman was probably Timothy Dwight, the grandson of Jonathan Edwards who became president of Yale in 1795. Yet Dwight, too, was a transitional figure who moderated the "Consistent Calvinism" of the Edwardians. The impact of wide reading in the Scottish philosophers is clearly visible.[5] The implications of his deviations are made clear in the theology of his greatest pupil, Nathaniel William Taylor, who was called as the professor of theology in the new divinity school at Yale.

Taylor was dissatisfied with the character of the campaign

against Unitarianism being waged by the professors at Andover. He let it be known, indeed, that he thought Leonard Woods had set back the Orthodox cause by fifty years! Taylor became as convinced as ever was Channing of the need for *rational* theology; and to each of them the Scottish Philosophy came like manna from heaven. "Those who find fault with Metaphysics," Taylor stated in his lectures, "are generally those who know nothing about it, and here as everywhere else, we are not to wonder when dogs bark at strangers." But he adds a *caveat* that one would expect from one of the greatest revival preachers in Connecticut: No proposition in mental philosophy is of any value, unless its statements can be reduced to the simple language of life. "We must," he insisted, "identify it with the principles of common sense." Nor is this a mere common-sensical reference to "common sense." Taylor's mental and moral philosophy is steeped in Scottish thought—and is of the same dye.

There are two ways of stating the central thesis of Taylor's theology. Perhaps first is his classic assertion that God could not prevent sin in a moral system. Man was the author of sin, not God. Man's sinful deeds were willed, not caused by any created, physical attribute of human nature. Sin was in the sinning. The will, he said, was a self-originating power; man was a free agent. To prove it he invoked the arguments of Reid and Stewart who, like him, were at odds with any "doctrine of inability" whether sprung from deterministic philosophy or predestinarian theology. In this sense Reid is to Taylor what Locke was to Edwards. Yet Taylor was no Arminian: it was still certain that man would sin. "Certainty, with power to the contrary," then, is Taylor's other famous slogan.[6]

When the cry of heresy went up, as it did soon and often, Taylor replied that his was the *faith* of a Calvinist but that the distinguishing features of Taylorism were mere "philosophical theories" employed to *explain* those doctrines. He was right—but more so than he knew, for his critics were also right in insisting that these "explanations" constituted a new divinity.

Edwards Amasa Park was the last creative figure in the New England Theology. It is a tragedy that posterity has remembered him only as the lonely, isolated mossback fighting a losing battle against liberal changes at Andover itself. Park, too, was a Common Sense philosopher. "New England divinity has been marked by a strong, practical common sense," he declared. "Our later theologians . . . were adept in the philosophy of Reid, Oswald, Campbell, Beattie, Stewart; and this has been termed *the philosophy of common sense.*"[7] On the question of freedom of the will he took the position of Scottish introspectionist thought. He found what Reid had found: a free will that made man responsible for his acts and which ruled out any doctrine of man's passive sinfulness. The "theology of the feelings," he admitted, often spoke in violent paradoxes on this subject; but not the theology of the intellect, for it proclaims only the "certainty of wrong preference" not the "inability of right." Park stood with Taylor.

It was left for Charles Hodge of Princeton—the great theological arbiter of midcentury Presbyterianism—to condemn *all* of the foregoing thinkers and schools of thinkers as heretics. Hodge was a Professor of *Polemical* Theology, and that meant defending true doctrine from its perverters within the fold. Hodge stood firm on the Westminster Catechism which he had memorized as a child and on Turretin's systematic works which he studied as a seminarian at the feet of Archibald Alexander. "A new idea never originated in this [Princeton] seminary," he boasted; and to any theologian who did practice innovation he could justify his own confidence with the remark that "a man behind the walls of Gibraltar, or of Ehrenbreitstein, cannot, if he would, tremble at the sight of a single knight, however gallant or well-appointed he may be."[8]

Yet Hodge brought truly unique gifts to his task. Intensive studies in Germany and his awareness of the new critical historical studies gave an authority to his pronouncements that was scarcely equaled in America. His long experience in biblical exegesis and his Old School Presbyterian loyalties, meanwhile, strengthened him against the charms of romantic idealism in all its forms. Even in the thinking of his two close friends, Tholuck and Neander, he could only lament the visible influences of Schleiermacher. Pantheism, he insisted, was the worst form of Atheism.

Hodge might condemn the innovations of Edwards or fulminate

against the semi-Pelagianism of Taylor; he might castigate Park's memorable distinction between "The Theology of the Intellect and That of the Feelings" as a reduction to poetry of all doctrine; he might denounce all Unitarianism as a form of infidelity. Yet the irony remains: Hodge himself is caught up in the anthropocentrism of Scottish Philosophy. Safe in Ehrenbreitstein as he was, he did not at first try to establish a rationalized mediate position between divine sovereignty and human freedom as New England theologians had done. This double truth was to him a sacred mystery. But later his confidence in "philosophical speculation" seems to have grown, and in his *Systematic Theology* he ventured upon a full metaphysical reconciliation. His central thesis was that "a free act may be inevitably certain as to its occurrence." The foundations of his ethic and his conception of natural theology, moreover, are Scottish rather than Calvinistic. Hodge reveals the influence of Scottish anthropology with special clarity in his interpretation of the doctrine that man's nature, not just his acts, but his *nature*, is "truly and properly sin." Despite his reiterations of dogmatic formulae, the optimism of the Scottish Renaissance interposes itself and separates his theology from that of John Knox and John Calvin.

• • •

My theological cross-section is now sufficiently drawn. It remains to assay the meaning of the amazingly diverse philosophical conquest. The first and most obvious observation is that the leading thinkers of the American Calvinistic tradition experienced in acute terms the need for an apologetical philosophy. This was in no significant way akin to that felt by medieval scholastics who were more interested in proving the orthodoxy of Reason than the reasonableness of Orthodoxy. In America the need stemmed from a concrete situation: the religious decadence of the Revolutionary epoch and the fear, felt particularly in the post-war period, that French infidelity was engulfing the universities. That such "scares" stimulated the apologetical spirit in Harvard, Princeton, and Yale is a familiar matter of record.[9]

The second observation is that the Scottish Philosophy countered precisely those intellectual currents which the philosophy-reading and church-going public of the later eighteenth and earlier nineteenth century had reason to fear. It not only got around Hume's "skepticism" by a *reductio ad absurdum* but short-circuited all the major metaphysical heresies.

The Scottish Philosophy was an apologetical philosophy, *par excellence*. And the secret of its success, I think, lay in its dualism, epistemological, ontological, and cosmological. Its other advantages were auxiliary. Reid's theory of knowledge affirmed a clean subject-object distinction. The world which men perceived was in no sense constituted by consciousness. On the mind-matter problem dualism facilitated an all-out attack on both materialism and idealism, as well as the pantheism that either type of monistic analysis could lead to. Furthermore, by a firm separation of the Creator and His creation, the Scottish thinkers preserved the orthodox notion of God's transcendence, and made revelation necessary. Dualism also made possible a synchronous affirmation of science on one hand, and an identification of the human intellect and the Divine Mind on the other. Scottish philosophers could thus be monotonously consistent in their invocation of Bacon or Newton and at the same time certify those rational processes of man which lead toward natural theology and even contemplative piety and away from relativism and romantic excesses.

The Scottish Philosophy, in short, was a winning combination; and to American theologians, even if they felt the need for philosophic support only subconsciously, it was the answer to a prayer. It was, moreover, free enough from subtlety to be communicable in sermons and tracts. It came to exist in America, therefore, as a vast subterranean influence, a sort of water-table nourishing dogmatics in an age of increasing doubt.

Yet a price was paid for this philosophical sustenance and a consideration of the exaction constitutes my third observation. In the seminaries and universities their American Calvinist theology lost its Reformation bearings; "the Augustinian strain of piety" suffered. The belief that Christianity had a proclamation to declare lost its vitality. Park hemmed in the Scriptures with so many criteria of interpretation that they came to be only an external support to his theological system. And for Hodge doctrine became less a living language of piety than a complex burden to be borne.

The forces leading to this result were manifold—many of them not philosophical at all—but three contributions of the Scottish Philosophy are salient. The *first* is attributable to the humanistic orientation of the Hutcheson-Reid tradition. As this philosophy was adopted, the fervent theocentricity of Calvin, which Edwards had striven to reinstate, was sacrificed and a new principle of doctrinal interpretation was increasingly emphasized. Self-consciousness became the oracle of religious truth. Man's need rather than God's Word became the guide in doctrinal formulation. Flowing from this first reorientation was a *second*. The adoption of the benign and optimistic anthropology of the Scottish Moderates by American Calvinists veiled the very insights into human nature which were a chief strength of Calvin's theology. This revision, in turn, affected the whole complex of doctrine and infused the totality with a new spirit. In a *third* and more general way, Scottish Realism accelerated the long trend toward rational theology which had developed, especially in England, during and after the long Deistic controversy. Combined as it was with an all too facile dismissal of Hume's critique, Reid's influence on subsequent thinkers in the Scottish tradition served to reinforce the prestige of thinkers like Locke, Butler, and Paley, who were reinterpreted in accordance with the typical Scottish emphasis. There resulted a neo-rationalism which rendered the central Christian paradoxes into stark, logical contradictions that had either to be disguised or explained away. Reformed theology was thus emptied of its most dynamic element. A kind of rationalistic rigor mortis set in.

In conclusion we may say, therefore, that the profound commitment of orthodox theology to the apologetical keeping of the Scottish Philosophy made traditional doctrines so lifeless and static that a new theological turn was virtually inevitable. Certainly there is no mystery as to why end-of-century theology in America turned with such enthusiasm to evolutionary idealism, the social gospel, and the "religion of feeling." It was in search of the relevant and the dynamic.

ENDNOTES

1. A. Campbell Fraser, *Thomas Reid* (Edinburgh, 1898), esp. letter, Reid to Price, 110 sq.
2. Andrew Seth, *Scottish Philosophy: A Comparison of the Scottish and German Answers to Hume* (Edinburgh, 1899).
3. L. H. Butterfield, *John Witherspoon Comes to America* (Princeton, 1953); Varnum L. Collins, *President Witherspoon,* 2 vols. (Princeton, 1925); Leonard J. Trinterud, *The Forming of an American Tradition* (Philadelphia, 1949).
4. This is not Ivy League provincialism, but a consideration of four of the oldest centers of theological training in the country: the divinity schools are usually dated Andover, 1808; Harvard, 1811; Princeton, 1812, and Yale, 1822.
5. Charles R. Keller, *The Second Great Awakening in Connecticut* (New Haven, 1942); Charles E. Cunningham, *Timothy Dwight* (New York, 1942).
6. *Lectures on the Moral Government of God,* 2 vols. (New York, 1859), 2: chapter 7.
7. Frank H. Foster, *Life of Edwards Amasa Park* (New York, 1936); Daniel D. Williams, *The Andover Liberals* (New York, 1941); H. K. Rowe, *History of Andover Theological Seminary* (Newton, 1933).
8. A. A. Hodge, *Life of Charles Hodge* (New York, 1880), 521, 553; Charles Hodge, *Essays and Reviews* (New York, 1857), 584.
9. Herbert M. Morais, *Deism in Eighteenth-Century America* (New York, 1934) and G. Adolf Koch, *Republican Religion* (New York, 1933).

FOR FURTHER READING

Bozeman, Theodore Dwight. *Protestants in an Age of Science: The Baconian Ideal and Antebellum American Religious Thought,* Chapel Hill, NC, 1977.

Grave, S. A. *The Scottish Philosophy of Common Sense,* Oxford, 1960.

Hoeveler, J. David, Jr. *James McCosh and the Scottish Intellectual Tradition,* Princeton, 1981.

Holifield, E. Brooks. *The Gentlemen Theologians: American Theology in Southern Culture, 1795–1860,* Durham, NC, 1978.

Howe, Daniel Walker. *The Unitarian Conscience: Harvard Moral Philosophy, 1805–1861,* Cambridge, MA, 1970.

Kuklick, Bruce. *Churchmen and Philosophers: From Jonathan Edwards to John Dewey,* New Haven, 1985.

May, Henry F. *The Enlightenment in America,* New York, 1976.

Meyer, D. H. *The Instructed Conscience: The Shaping of the American National Ethic*, Philadelphia, 1972.

Noll, Mark A. *Princeton and the Republic, 1768–1822: A Search for a Christian Enlightenment in the Era of Samuel Stanhope Smith*, Princeton, 1989.

Sher, Richard B., and Jeffrey R. Smitten, eds. *Scotland and America in the Age of the Enlightenment*, Princeton, 1990.

Sloan, Douglas. *The Scottish Enlightenment and the American College Ideal*, New York, 1961.

Smith, Wilson. *Professors and Public Ethics: Studies of Northern Moral Philosophers Before the Civil War*, Ithaca, 1956.

INTRODUCTION TO ESSAY 15

Now we turn to ideas of a different sort: those that emerged directly from experiences in a specific time period rather than ones drawn from church or university traditions. Smith once again starts with a piece of commonplace wisdom regarding religion in America and then offers a revisionist interpretation. On the question of African American slaves and Christian ideas, some have held that slaves accepted WASP propaganda about black inferiority; others argued that slaves used Christianity to incite revolts; most thought that Christianity served only to make people acquiesce in bondage. Smith uses firsthand expressions from participants themselves to paint a different picture. He shows the stark dignity of African American voices which provide the rudiments of what has become more sophisticated black theology in our own time.

An additional lesson in this essay is insight into the basic processes of theologizing. As people suffered under slavery, they reflected on those experiences with the help of Christian emphases, and reached conclusions that enhanced religious understanding and witness. Experiencing slavery as moral evil led African Americans to endurance without acquiescence, articulating both a self-respect and hope for eventual deliverance while still victims of an oppressive institution. Experiencing forgiveness in spiritual terms led in turn to expressions of forgiveness in temporal surroundings. Echoing themes first raised in Maffly-Kipp's essay, Smith blends Christian understandings of human nature with those of divine judgment, present duty, and a destiny of richer cultural achievements in the future. African American Christian consciousness was neither servile nor vindictive in its earliest formulations. It grasped the core of gospel teachings and validated them because of, and in spite of, daunting physical hardships.

Original source - CH 41 (1972): 497-512.

15

Slavery and Theology

The Emergence of Black Christian Consciousness in Nineteenth-Century America

Timothy L. Smith

Extensive discussion of the origin and nature of black Christianity in America has in recent years linked together two issues which are logically distinct: the degree of uniqueness attributable to the beliefs of African Americans, and whether or to what extent their faith sustained resistance to the system of slavery. Abundant evidence that slaveowners hoped Christian instruction would persuade black people to acquiesce in their bondage has been readily taken for proof that acquiescence was in fact the usual result of their conversion. This questionable conclusion has sometimes led to another: that such religious notions as occasionally inspired resistance were brought from Africa and were uniquely the heritage of black men. According to this view, the biblical rationales for revolt such as Denmark Vesey and Nat Turner appear to have employed were merely a gloss upon ideas of freedom and justice which they and their people had long held.

The reading of a wide selection of the testimonies, sermons, summaries of sermons, autobiographies and accounts of spiritual experience left by men and women reared in slavery or converted while under its shadow has suggested the substantially different interpretation offered in this essay. I have concluded, first, that what was unique in the religious consciousness of Negroes in nineteenth-century America was their ready absorption of the radical views of man's duty and destiny which characterized primitive Christian thought. This circumstance may have owed much to their African heritage. But the fact that evangelical Protestantism became the folk religion of black people in the United States while they were yet slaves seems a sufficient explanation of the moral and rational depth their faith displayed.[1] My second and corollary conclusion is that the Christian beliefs they adopted enabled the African exiles to endure slavery precisely because these beliefs supported their moral revulsion toward it and promised eventual deliverance from it without demanding that they risk their lives in immediate resistance. Endurance without acquiescence, then, and submission, which, because of its religious character pronounced judgment upon oppression, became the bondsmen's moral ideal.

• • •

Accepting the challenge to repent and believe the Gospel while still under the shadow of bondage required hard thinking. Only so could black converts deal with the ironies and hypocrisies of a situation in which Christian slave owners taught them grace, mercy, and righteousness. Picking their way through the maze of contradictions between the teaching and the practice of those who oppressed them, the African Christians emerged with a deep sense of the paradox and mystery of God's dealings with men. Hence the pathos of their songs and prayers. This intertwining of emotion and perception in their religious awakening gave birth to a theology of hope. It owed less to tradition, whether of black Africa or white America, than to the experience of having learned through the acceptance of biblical faith how to cope with what would otherwise have been overwhelming tragedy.[2]

The touchstones of the personal religious experience of black Christians in nineteenth-century America, then, seem to me to have been first, forgiveness, awe and ecstasy, then self-respect, ethical earnestness, and hope. These became, not surprisingly, the cornerstones of their theology as well. The experience of forgiveness and the doctrine of reconciliation were primary, whether one sets their beliefs in logical or chronological sequence. Considering these first may help to make plain how erroneous it is to call either revolt or acquiescence the central theme of Negro faith in America.

Black converts knew they had a lot to forgive. A long stream of testimony and reminiscence records their outrage at the injustice and hypocrisy of Christians who held them in bondage. Possibly in some cases this sense of outrage was nurtured by memories of the life-affirming character of African religions. Modern survivals of most of these regard as profoundly wicked not only witches and sorcerers but spirits and men who reject the worth of human beings and exploit or frustrate the free use of their powers. Such memories may help explain why newly arrived Africans were so quick to equate conversion with the right to be free. No such conscious remembrance was necessary, however, to prompt their children and grandchildren to perceive that the Christian idea of forgiveness laid both slavery and racial discrimination under divine judgment.

The centrality of the idea and the practice of forgiveness among black Christians stemmed first, then, from the psychic necessity of finding means to resist inwardly injustices they could neither condone nor for the moment curb. It also served to ease the excessive burden of guilt which they believed oppression had laid upon their souls. "The vile habits often acquired in a state of servitude are not easily thrown off," Richard Allen, the founder of African Methodism, wrote. Whites were unreasonable to expect superior conduct from a race whom they had for generations wrongly stigmatized as people of such baseness that they might properly be held in slavery. Nevertheless, Allen continued, the God who knew man's passion for freedom had forbidden oppressed Jews to hate Egyptians, and Jesus had commanded his followers to love their enemies. People reared under the shadow of slavery, therefore, thought it "a great mercy to have all anger and bitterness" removed from their minds.[3]

The experience of such reconciling grace helped to nurture the sense of spiritual superiority over whites which some of the earliest declarations of black Christians displayed. A principal consequence of this questioning acceptance of the doctrine of reconciliation was to expand the capacity of the more sensitive Africans to experience awe. Theologically, the outcome was their persisting conviction that God's exercise of his sovereignty over human history was essentially mysterious, compounding judgment, forgiveness, and love. Little wonder, then, that slaves and freedmen celebrated their conversions in experiences of ecstasy which both comprehended and transcended their anguish. Those experiences, I think, were an important source of the black traits now labeled "soul." The theological consequence was that the

Africans leaned naturally toward what today would be called an existential understanding of Christian teachings, whereas the white men who first taught them held generally to a magisterial conception of God and a scholastic view of the Scriptures. How did this come about?

The planters and clergymen and their wives and daughters who first began to instruct African servants in the Christian faith told them Bible stories, as to children. They used the simplest words possible, for their hearers' knowledge of the English language was both new and skimpy. Their professed aim was to help slaves to understand the idea of God as creator, lawgiver, judge, and loving redeemer. Hence they told them of Eden and the Fall, of Moses and the law, of Mary and her baby, and of the cross and resurrection of Jesus. Arching over all of these was the description of the joys of heaven and the horrors of Milton's, if not the Bible's, hell.[4]

Listening blacks heard these stories in the light of their own encounters with despair and hope. The story of Adam and Eve seemed to them from the outset a declaration of human solidarity, not only in creation but also in sin. Moses became the deliverer of an enslaved people as well as the bearer of the Ten Commandments. Jonah's trembling denunciation of the sins of the Ninevites affirmed their suspicion that the rich and powerful were not necessarily God's chosen. Biblical accounts of the conduct of believing Jews during the Babylonian exile—of Daniel, of the three who would not bow down, and of Esther the Queen—seemed to Christian blacks, as to generations of Jews, to be allegories of promise to the oppressed. The baby Jesus, needing tenderness and care, revealed a God whose love made him somehow vulnerable and dependent, and whose incarnation in the humiliation and weakness of human flesh joined him forever with the meek who would inherit the earth. These and similar interpretations of biblical narratives have been central in black preaching and gospel singing from the eighteenth century to the present. The hope of heaven held a central place in that preaching and singing because by affirming an eternal order of justice and love it rebuked all unjust orders, and so helped to give each one of these stories its healing power over the minds of men whose earthly existence was steeped in indignity.

The only volume I have found which purports to be a formal exposition of Christian theology written by a Negro in the nineteenth century illuminates this kinship in black consciousness between ecstasy and ideology, suffering and mission. Bishop B. T. Tanner's lectures on the Bible, delivered at Wilberforce University in 1893, were presented in three sections labeled respectively: Chronology, Symbolism, and the Harmony of the Gospels. In the first section, Tanner noted that Hebrew texts never used the words "Egypt" or "Ethiopia" but, rather, Mizraim and Cush, the names of the two sons of Ham, supposedly the first black man. He reveled in the contributions "black" Egyptians had made to civilization and quoted with delight a modern poetic translation of Isaiah's summons to the Ethiopians, "our ancient ancestors," when they were serving "as auxiliaries to the Mizraimites in their struggle with the mighty Sennacherib." The three chapters of the second section focused upon the poetic significance of biblical symbolism, its imagery, lyricism, and emotional power. Tanner completely ignored the question of inerrancy and the arguments over plenary versus verbal inspiration which characterized white evangelical writing on the Bible in this decade. His exposition celebrated instead the openness of the black man's soul, his capacity for joy. The final section, a learned and unsentimental discussion of the Gospels as both literature and theology, stressed the anguish and the degradation which God's Son took upon himself. The message implicit in the unusual outline of the book then becomes clear. The glory of this African's imagined past, represented by Egypt and Ethiopia, and his awareness of the richness of his own and his people's emotional responses to Christian faith, freed him from a merely compensatory identification with Israel's bondage and enabled him to identify the black man's mission with that of Jesus, the Suffering Servant.[5]

From such healing uses of Scripture flowed the self-respect which shielded many black Christians from the temptation to accept the slavemaster's estimate of their worth. The theological result was a strong emphasis upon the biblical doctrine of man. Their expositions of it offer no support at all to the "good black Sambo" myth.

Negro protests against slavery from the outset described it, in the words of the earliest published one, as "an affront to Divine majesty who has given to man His own peculiar image." Richard Allen's "Address to Those Who Keep Slaves and Approve the Practice," written just before the Nat Turner revolt, argued that because slaves were oppressed men, and not brutes, they were subject to God's command forbidding them to hate or do any violence to their masters. Nevertheless, he declared, "the dreadful insurrections" they had mounted when opportunity afforded were "enough evidence to convince a reasonable man that great uneasiness and not contentment is the inhabitant of their hearts." Hartford pastor Hosea Easton declared that it was not color at all but slavery, which, by its vicious code of laws and the prejudice concerning color which it awakened, attempted to brutalize blacks and to destroy the intelligence "which alone enables man to stand forth preeminent in all the works of God."[6]

At the end of the century, Francis J. Grimké, a black Presbyterian pastor in Washington, D.C., reiterated this doctrine of man. Warning that the revival of lynch law was producing in Negroes everywhere a feeling of bitterness which was "bound, sooner or later, to have its harvest in blood," he declared that the race question must be settled in harmony with God's law, or there could be no peace. "The white people in the South, and the white people in the North," he warned, "had just as well understand, once for all, that the Negro . . . will never be satisfied until he is treated as a man, and as a full-fledged citizen." Grimké believed, however, that a more dangerous challenge than the rebirth of "southern barbarism" arose from the temptations to materialism, drunkenness, and sexual license to which blacks were falling prey in such cities as Washington. Both challenges required that African Americans certify their manhood in Christian character and that they root their determination to resist injustice in reconciling grace.[7]

Grimké's preaching helps also to clarify the theological significance of the moral earnestness which for decades had penetrated every aspect of the religious thinking of converted slaves and freedmen. White Americans have been slow to appreciate the immense achievements of Negro moralism because they have been entangled in the myths of black childishness and emotionalism.

The ethical convictions of black Christians were in fact powerful, and stemmed from their experience. Having been subject to persons who presumed to own their bodies and souls, they saw readily that acknowledgment of God's ownership not only certified their right to liberty from lesser masters but also brought dignity and hope to their struggle with the mysterious forces which threatened them with psychic or "spiritual" bondage.

Underlying all these theological insights of converted slaves and freedmen was their radically Christian view of man's earthly and eternal hopes. With a steadfastness which few white churchmen were called upon to display, the spiritual heirs of such preachers taught black Christians to place their hopes in a supreme being who had not turned his back upon mankind but sought in judgment and mercy to redeem the whole earth. Something more than the traditionally expansive rhetoric of the Negro pulpit was at work when former slaves proclaimed the coming millennium. They saw "ignorance and superstition and prejudice banished in the light of God's truth, and injustice and discriminations of all sorts done away." King Jesus was not simply restoring the lost innocence of Eden, Bishop J. P. Campbell declared; that innocence was gone forever. Rather, he was establishing a new heaven upon earth by enabling sinners saved by grace to commit their wills to the God who had joined himself to their hopes, as Christ had taken upon himself their sin.[8]

• • •

Africans were pressed up against the wall by American slavery's vast assault upon their humanity. This tragic circumstance compelled them to discover in the religion of their white oppressors a faith whose depths few of the latter had ever suspected, enabling the black Christians to reconcile suffering and hope, guilt and forgiveness, tyranny and spiritual freedom, self-hate and divine acceptance. In that faith some of them found the strength to throw off their bonds, and many others the dignity, when once emancipated, to stand up free. Remarkable numbers of their preachers have ever since displayed the grace and good sense to declare, when few white men listened, that perceptions of Christianity grasped by enslaved blacks were the heritage of all men, and their hope as well.

ENDNOTES

1. E. Franklin Frazier, *The Negro Church in America* (New York, 1966), 52, 54-63; Joseph R. Washington, *Black Religion: The Negro and Christianity in the United States* (Boston, 1964), 37-42; the same author's *The Politics of God* (Boston, 1967), 167-68, 209; and Hortense Powdermaker, *After Freedom: A Cultural Study in the Deep South* (New York, 1967), 230-34, 245.

2. See Frederick Douglass, *My Bondage and My Freedom* (New York, 1855), 71-72, 86, 148-49, 166-68, 228-30, 235, Carter G. Woodson, ed., *The Mind of the Negro as Reflected in Letters Written During the Crisis, 1800–1860* (Washington, D.C., 1926), 166.

3. Richard Allen, *The Life, Experience and Gospel Labors of the Rt. Rev. Richard Allen, To Which Is Annexed the Rise and Progress of the African Methodist Episcopal Church* . . . (New York, 1960), 69-71. Compare Douglass, *My Bondage*, 166-69.

4. Frazier, *Negro Church*, 17-18; Howard W. Odum, *Religious Folk-Songs of the Negroes*, reprinted from *American Journal of Religious Psychology and Education* 3 (1909): 256-365; "To the People of Color, by a Colored Lady," *The Liberator*, 27 August 1831, quoted in Woodson, ed., *Mind of the Negro*, 230-232; and Martin Luther King's last speech: "I've been on the mountaintop . . . and I've seen the promised land," discussed in William B. Miner, *Martin Luther King, Jr.: His Life, Martyrdom, and Meaning for the World* (New York, 1968), 287f.

5. Benjamin T. Tanner, *Theological Lectures* (Nashville, 1894), 59-60, and, generally, 84-107.

6. Allen, *Life*, 15-41. Compare Mary Agnes Lewis, "Slavery and Personality: A Further Comment," *American Quarterly* 19 (1967): 114-21.

7. Francis J. Grimké, *The Negro: His Right, and Wrongs, The Forces for Him and Against Him* (Washington, D.C., 1899), 22, 38-40; and the same author's *The Afro-American Pulpit in Relation to Race Elevation* (Washington, D.C., 1893), 2-6, 12.

8. Jabez P. Campbell, "A Scriptural View, or the Statement Concerning Paradise That Was Lost, Regained," *The African Methodist Episcopal Church Review* 1 (1884): 13-15; Irvine Garland Penn, *The United Negro: His Problems and His Progress Containing the Addresses and Proceedings, the Young People's Christian Educational Conference* . . . (Atlanta, 1908), 91.

FOR FURTHER READING

Blassingame, John. *The Slave Community: Plantation Life in the Antebellum South*, New York, 1972.

Cone, James H. *Black Theology and Black Power*, New York, 1979.

Frazier, E. Franklin. *The Negro Church in America*/C. Eric Lincoln, *The Black Church Since Frazier*, New York, 1974.

Genovese, Eugene D. *Roll, Jordan, Roll: The World the Slaves Made*, New York, 1972.

Johnson, Clifton H., ed. *God Struck Me Dead: Religious Conversion Experiences and Autobiography of Ex-Slaves*, Philadelphia, 1960.

Levine, Lawrence W. *Black Culture and Black Consciousness: Afro-American Folk Thought From Slavery to Freedom*, New York, 1977.

Lewis, David Levering. *W. E. B. DuBois: Biography of a Race, 1868–1919*, New York, 1993.

Lincoln, C. Eric. *Race, Religion and the Continuing American Dilemma*, New York, 1984.

Lincoln, C. Eric, and Lawrence H. Mamiya. *The Black Church in the African American Experience*, Durham, NC, 1990.

Raboteau, Albert J. *Slave Religion: The "Invisible Institution" in the Antebellum South*, New York, 1978.

Smith, Theophus. *Conjuring Culture: Biblical Formations in Black America*, New York, 1994.

Wilmore, Gayraud S. *Black Religion and Black Radicalism: An Interpretation of the Religious History of Afro-American People*, 2d ed., Maryknoll, NY, 1983.

INTRODUCTION TO ESSAY 16

Just as the previous essay explored the impact of race and new social conditions on African Americans, this reading examines the dynamic impact of socio-economic changes on Protestant priorities. When urban problems stimulated religious outreach into new areas, the resulting Social Gospel emphasized practical remedies more than intellectual rationale. American clergy in this movement had come to terms with Socialist thought because secular emphases precluded religious ones in that viewpoint. Here Dorn picks three of the most important figures who faced the issue in this country. Through them he shows how controversial the Social Gospel was in its early years, raising questions about priorities between other-worldly salvation and this-worldly welfare. Their positions help us see why some religious activists denounced all involvement in social problems and why others emphasized the public effectiveness of Christianity so much that they failed to mention heavenly rewards at all.

As Dorn makes clear, definitions of "socialism" or "communism" are ambiguous and varied, ranging from utopian schemes of socio-economic harmony to anarchistic plans for destroying present-day systems that oppress the poor. Some drew on sociological analysis while others emphasized ethical principles; some called for change in physical conditions while others sought reform in the human heart. Dorn exhibits here a spectrum of views, showing that nuances abounded. Judging from these central voices, we note how the Social Gospel in America remained disjointed and unsystematic as it groped for solutions to modern problems. It is a good example of how religion in this country formed responsive movements rather than schools of thought when challenges arose.

Original source - CH 62 (1993): 82-100.

16

The Social Gospel and Socialism

A Comparison of the Thought of Francis Greenwood Peabody, Washington Gladden, and Walter Rauschenbusch

Jacob H. Dorn

For American Protestants who were sensitive to the profound social disruptions associated with rapid industrialization and urbanization in the late nineteenth century, the twin discoveries of the "alienation" of the working class from Protestant churches and of a rising and vibrant socialist movement caused much consternation and anxious soul-searching. Socialism offered not only a radical critique of American political and economic institutions; it also offered the zeal, symbols, and sense of participation in a world-transforming cause often associated with Christianity itself. The religious alienation of the working class and the appeal of socialism were often causally linked in the minds of socially conscious Protestant leaders.

It is not surprising, therefore, that one of the pioneer historians of the Social Gospel, Charles Howard Hopkins, should call socialism "the midwife and nurse to the social gospel." "Beyond the catalytic effect of liberal theology itself," he wrote, "no single force so stung American Protestantism into social action as did this gadfly of capitalism." Though none made so bald an assertion as this, the other prominent historians of the pre–World War I Social Gospel gave serious attention to this movement's encounter with socialism.[1] Given the importance that these historians attributed to the nexus between Christian social thought and socialism, the subject deserves fresh examination.

• • •

"Socialism," like "Christianity," is susceptible of more than one meaning. In its loosest usage, it could mean little more than unselfishness, or social cooperation, the opposite of "individual-ism." More concretely, it could mean an organized political and economic movement and/or a formal ideology. It is important to recognize that these—and other—distinctions were not always observed in public discourse. Like many of their contemporaries both inside and outside the socialist movement itself, Peabody, Gladden, and Rauschenbusch often slid from one meaning to another without careful definition. The term might mean, at one time, an attitude or social spirit; at another, the "scientific social-ism" of Karl Marx or its summation in the platforms of socialist parties; and at still another, a surging, idealistic movement of industrial workers and their allies in other social groups. Orthodox Marxists, of course, had no use for such sloppiness: without the ideology, there could be no true socialism. Many socialists, how-ever, were drawn to the movement not by philosophical or even economic doctrine, but by its appeal to a sense of justice, its his-torical sweep, or a desire for human solidarity. It should not be remarkable, therefore, to find that Marx was not necessarily the touchstone of socialism for Social Gospel leaders.

A professor of ethics and theology at Harvard from 1880 until his retirement in 1913, the Unitarian Francis Greenwood Peabody (1847–1936) was one of the first American academicians to teach a course on social ethics. The field was new, and he groped even for a name for his course, which eventually became a separate depart-ment, before adopting William James's suggestion, "Social Ethics." Utilizing the case-study method to elucidate ethical principles for charity work and municipal reform, he soon became a noted spokesman for the Social Gospel. In the 1890s he appeared before the World's Parliament of Religions and at Chautauqua, and when his own denomination established a social-service department in 1908, he wrote and spoke for it. From first to last, Peabody was sus-picious of precipitate action—of what he considered the nostrums and cure-alls of cranks and propagandists. Blueprints for society only interested him as objects of criticism. His first major work was *Jesus Christ and the Social Question* (1900). Instantly popular, it was reprinted five times by 1903 and translated into several languages. Its principal themes reappeared virtually unchanged, and often in identical phrasing, in *Jesus Christ and the Christian Character* (1913) and *The Christian Life in the Modern World* (1914). It is not too much to say that socialism stands in polar opposition to Christianity in all three books, and that *Jesus Christ and the Social Question* is preoccupied with it.

Peabody opened this book by noting that agitation for social change had become a dominant feature of the age. This agitation was marked by "radical intention" (or "scope of reconstructive purpose") and "ethical passion" (or "sense of wrong"), and also by a seeming kinship with the spirit of Christianity. Yet "nothing [was] in fact more conspicuous" than its irreligion. Though the estrangement between church and social protest was widespread, socialists, influenced by German philosophical materialism, displayed a particular "antipathy to spiritual ideals." "It is not enough to say that the socialist programme is indifferent to religion," he wrote. "It undertakes to provide a substitute for religion . . . an alternative to the Christian religion." Peabody granted that the link between philosophical materialism and socialist economic analysis might have been fortuitous— "a perversion of its characteristic aim, which can have occurred only through an unfortunate historical accident"—but for him that link was nonetheless fatal.[2]

As for those who attempted to ground socialism in the Christian faith, Peabody viewed their effort as unhistorical and unbiblical. He dismissed attempts by Ernst Renan (*Life of Jesus*, 1863), Francesco Nitti (*Catholic Socialism*, 1890), and George D. Herron (*Between Caesar and Jesus*, 1899) to make Jesus a revolutionary figure and the primitive church a normative or successful model of collective ownership. For Peabody, Jesus was "not a reformer but a revealer," "not primarily an agitator with a plan, but an idealist with a vision." The mission of this Jesus had been "religious"— "the disclosure to the human soul of its relation to God"—and he refused to let social conditions divert him from it. Though Peabody believed that Christian faith had social consequences, one searches his books in vain for principles of social equity or an imperative of justice in the relationships of social groups. Jesus' social ideal centered on the idea of the Kingdom of God, which was both present within individuals and coming as "an unfolding process of social righteousness." Jesus' method, however, was to regenerate individuals, who would then advance the process: Jesus "approaches the social question from within; he deals with individuals; he makes men"— "first persons fit for the Kingdom, then the better world."[3]

Socialists started at the wrong end by proposing to erect a social system that required unselfishness and cooperation without providing any means for promoting such virtues. Peabody emphasized repeatedly that progress rested on "character." In personal life, character meant poise, simplicity, peace, and grace; applied by the individual to social life, it meant sacrifice, service, and idealism. Peabody was rather sanguine about industrial conditions in his own day. Industrial conflict was "at bottom not an economic antagonism at all," but rather an expression of "moral distrust" on the part of the working class, which businessmen could alleviate through careful experiments with industrial cooperation. Any economic system could be abused by bad people, while conversely, any system, including capitalism, might be "sufficiently effective and just." The system was secondary and really meant little; character was not only primary, but, in Peabody's view, virtually the whole of the matter.

Washington Gladden (1836–1918), pastor of the First Congregational Church of Columbus, Ohio, shared Peabody's beliefs that Christianity begins by transforming individuals and that socialism slighted "character." His view of the interplay between the individual and social forces, however, led him to argue that the regeneration of persons and structural change must be concurrent. Though he also rejected socialism, he saw it as more than mechanical tinkering and tried to identify its affinities with Christianity. His experiences as an urban pastor also informed his thinking in ways that Peabody's studies seem not to have done.

Gladden was an idealist who judged society by principles of harmony and fairness he considered constant. He was also a pragmatist who tested programs by their workability and emphasized the next steps to be taken. His ideas about labor relations, race, municipal reform, and poverty reveal great flexibility in the light of changing conditions and fresh information. Nothing illustrates this flexibility better than his remarkable shift from paternalistic criticisms of trade unions in the 1870s to a grudging acknowledgment in the mid-1880s that if conflict was to govern industrial relations, workers must be able to protect their interests. Social conflict was not ideal, but justice demanded that one side not tyrannize the other. Gladden's appraisals of socialism extended from the mid-1880s to the 1910s and appeared in unpublished sermons, numerous articles, and several of his books. Though many points of emphasis remained unchanged in these years, a growing understanding of social discontent and increasing impatience with American capitalists are discernible.[4]

Gladden never accepted Karl Marx's doctrines of economic determinism, surplus value, class conflict, and the historical mission of the proletariat. He often admitted, however, that the socialist indictment of capitalism was "substantially correct": workers' wages had grown less rapidly than the national wealth, frequent depressions made their lives insecure, and they saw few avenues of escape, while business concentration and "plutocracy" grew apace. In his view, it was not capitalism per se that was wrong but, rather, a false view of society, in which the sole motive power is self-interest. "Intelligent socialists" simply wanted a political economy that provided "equal opportunities for all and special privileges for none" and spread social burdens evenly. "Surely," Gladden wrote, "Christianity demands nothing less than this." The weakness of socialism was not in its complaint, but in its methods and remedy, and it was here that Christians took exception to it.[5] When Gladden turned to criticism, he did so at two levels: one involved his objections to structural features of a socialist society; the other involved what he considered a fundamental difference over the dynamics of social change.

"Character" was of special significance to Gladden as it was to Peabody. He did not, however, push his critique to total rejection of socialism. His concern was to balance collective action through government, on one hand, and personal freedom and responsibility, on the other. The proper analogy for society was neither the "sand-heap" (individualism) nor the "chemical compound" (socialism), but the human organism, each part of which "is one" but "finds its life in the life of the larger unity." Without substantial freedom to own and use property, individual identity and character development would be in jeopardy.

Gladden welcomed the growth of government, which in a democracy was only an agent of "the economic and social cooperation of all the people for the common good." He envisioned, in short, a mixed economy and objected not to significant increases in state power, but to the speed and scope of the socialist approach.

The second level on which Gladden criticized socialism involved the relative importance of individual regeneration and structural change. He displayed little concern over the antipathy of some socialists to religion; unlike Peabody, who saw in socialism only a "material, external rearrangement of possessions and facilities," he found a religious yearning for a better world akin to the Christian hope for the Kingdom of God. But he believed that socialists focused too much on environment and neglected the task of creating socialized individuals. Any conception of the individual as other than a social being who is related continually and inextricably to others through natural social groups and institutions, and by law, morals, and custom, was fallacious. Changes of form would not change the spirit, but neither could a change of spirit express itself without a change of form. New wine demanded new wineskins. The dual aims of Christianity were inseparable. To create a perfect society, Christianity must "produce perfect men"; to produce them, it must "construct a perfect society." Gladden's attempt to balance the individual and the social was at the heart of both his criticism of socialism and appreciation of its corrective value. That socialists thought they could create the better world out of the old human nature was his fundamental criticism. That their emphasis on the social environment and on the social nature of human life was morally superior to an atomistic individualism was what made him treat them with an even hand. Peabody agreed only with the criticism.

Though Walter Rauschenbusch (1861–1918) endorsed political

and economic reforms no more far-reaching than those that Gladden supported, his engagement with socialism was more intimate and passionate than Gladden's. He identified more fully with socialist ideals, spoke and wrote under party auspices, and contemplated party membership. He exemplifies the extent to which a social gospeler could embrace socialism while remaining critically detached. Rauschenbusch's interest in socialism began in the late 1880s. A graduate of the Rochester Theological Seminary, to which he would return as a professor in 1897, he was unprepared for the suffering he encountered as pastor of the Second German Baptist Church on Manhattan's West Side. When in 1889 a Society of Christian Socialists (SCS) came into being in Boston, Rauschenbusch associated himself with its position. During a sabbatical in Europe in 1891, in which he furthered his study of socialism, Rauschenbusch discovered the organizing theme for all his subsequent thinking: the centrality of the Kingdom of God in the teachings of Jesus. Upon his return, he helped found the Brotherhood of the Kingdom, a group of like-minded individuals who met annually to share papers and issue occasional publications for the next twenty years. Given often to discussions of socialism, the brotherhood provided an important setting for him to develop his ideas about the meanings of Christianity and socialism for each other—and about the place of socialism in the coming Kingdom of God.[6]

The Christian socialism that Rauschenbusch embraced stood aloof not only from Marxian doctrine, but also from any socialist party. He moved closer to the socialist political movement as the years went on, but throughout his life he voiced serious reservations, not unlike those expressed by Peabody and Gladden, about its aims and methods. He ordinarily placed these reservations in the context of more important convergences between Christianity and socialism. Yet socialism carried grave dangers: a loss of individual freedom; a tendency to weaken the family and love of country; a proclivity to expect sudden change through force; and a "practical materialism" that overemphasized "improved arrangements and facilities." Like Peabody and Gladden, Rauschenbusch reserved his strongest language for the socialist threat to freedom and over-reliance on structural change. These were dangers, however, not reasons for rejecting socialism, and Christians "ought to join in it exactly to avert" them.

What "join[ing] in it" might mean for Christians remained unclear in this and all of Rauschenbusch's subsequent pronouncements on socialism. His distaste for Marxism was acute, and when he called himself a socialist he was expressing at most a sympathetic outsider's support for the gradualistic program of political-actionists within the American socialist movement. The Socialist Party of America that was taking shape in 1901, partly in reaction to the doctrinaire character and ineffectiveness of the older Socialist Labor Party, was strongly oriented toward the kind of "practical socialism" that commended itself to Rauschenbusch. Nevertheless, even when identifying affinities between Christianity and socialism, he continued to articulate features of socialism that he found objectionable. For example, he focused on socialist antagonism to the church as an "alloy" that repelled Christians from socialism who otherwise saw in it "the most thorough and consistent economic elaboration of the Christian social ideal" and "the most powerful force for justice, democracy, and organized fraternity in the modern world." Noting the German origins of the antireligious animus, the Socialist Party's stated neutrality toward religion, and the involvement of many ministers in the party, he concluded that antagonism toward religion was "in no way essential to Socialist thought."[7] Still, hostility to religion among socialists obviously disturbed him.

Rauschenbusch agreed with Peabody that Jesus was not "a social reformer of the modern type" and insisted that he approached the problems of his day from a moral and religious point of view. Whereas Peabody's Jesus did not apply categories of wealth or poverty to individuals, Rauschenbusch's Jesus taught that riches were obstacles to the "revolutionary" Kingdom standards of justice, equality, and love. After establishing the church's "stake" in this crisis, Rauschenbusch turned finally to "What To Do." His answer was complex. Individuals and churches with a social faith could do much to promote fairness and justice. As a historian, however, Rauschenbusch emphasized the collective, communal aspects of human life. With a strong sense of class alignment and class conflict in history, he insisted that the working class must be raised *as a class* if ultimate justice—an end to the class system—were ever to be achieved. Socialism promised to do that, he noted, and "if such a solution is even approximately feasible, it should be hailed with joy by every patriot and Christian."

It is possible to read Rauschenbusch's sequel, *Christianizing the Social Order*, as a more complacent book. His judgment that, of all the major social institutions, only business was not already "Christianized" supports such a conclusion. But this work is also striking in its indictment of capitalism and sympathy for a practical socialism. One of several anticapitalist chapters provides a litany of contrasts between Christianity and capitalism, "a mammonistic organization with which Christianity can never be content." For all his criticism of socialist irreligion, he concluded: "Socialism is one of the chief powers of the coming age. Its fundamental aims are righteous . . . because they are human. They were part of the mission of Christianity before the name of Socialism had been spoken. God had to raise up Socialism because the organized Church was too blind, or too slow, to realize God's ends."[8]

• • •

The rise of the socialist movement claimed the attention of Social Gospel leaders. Though the intensity of the engagement varied, socialism was of more than peripheral interest to three of the Social Gospel's most representative figures. However unitive Social Gospel principles—such as the Kingdom of God, the "fatherhood of God" and "brotherhood of man," and social salvation—may seem on the surface, they led to no unanimity when it came to socialism. From Peabody's repugnance, through Gladden's attempt at evenhandedness, to Rauschenbusch's contemplation of party membership, differences in temperament, biblical hermeneutics, life experiences, perceptions of class interests, and closeness to socialist networks shaped social gospelers' judgments. That socialism, whether as rival or as parallel idealistic force, demanded a response from Christians, there could be no argument. As to what that response should be, the Social Gospel offered no common answer.

ENDNOTES

1. Charles Howard Hopkins, *The Rise of the Social Gospel in American Protestantism, 1865–1915* (New Haven, 1940), 244; James Dombrowski, *The Early Days of Christian Socialism in America* (New York, 1936); Henry F. May, *Protestant Churches and Industrial America* (New York, 1949, reprint, 1967); Robert T. Handy, "Christianity and Socialism in America, 1900–1920," *Church History* 21 (1952): 39-54.

2. Francis G. Peabody, *Jesus Christ and the Social Question: An Examination of the Teaching of Jesus in Its Relation to Some of the Problems of Modern Social Life* (New York, 1900), 5, 9, 13-15, 18-20; *Jesus Christ and the Christian Character: An Examination of the Teaching of Jesus in Its Relation to Some of the Moral Problems of Personal Life* (New York, 1913), 6, 198; *The Christian Life in the Modern World* (New York, 1914), 38-42.

3. Peabody, *Jesus Christ and the Social Question*, 102; *Jesus Christ and the Christian Character*, 16.

4. Jacob H. Dorn, *Washington Gladden: Prophet of the Social Gospel* (Columbus, OH, 1967).

5. Washington Gladden, *Applied Christianity: Moral Aspects of Social Questions* (Boston, 1886), 102-145; *Tools and the Man: Property and Industry Under the Christian Law* (Boston, 1893), 255; *Christianity and Socialism* (New York, 1905), 122.

6. Dores R. Sharpe, *Walter Rauschenbusch* (New York, 1942), 219; Paul Minus, *Walter Rauschenbusch: American Reformer* (New York, 1988), 60-65.

7. Walter Rauschenbusch, *Christianizing the Social Order* (New York, 1912), 397-403; see also *Christianity and the Social Crisis* (New York, 1907), xiii.

8. Rauschenbusch, *Christianity and the Social Crisis*, 405-8; *Christianizing the Social Order*, 321-22, 313, 405.

FOR FURTHER READING

Carter, Paul A. *The Decline and Revival of the Social Gospel: Social and Political Liberalism in American Protestant Churches, 1920–1940*, Ithaca, 1954.

Cruden, Robert M. *Ministers of Reform: The Progressives' Achievement in American Civilization, 1889–1920*, New York, 1982.

Curtis, Susan. *A Consuming Faith: The Social Gospel and Modern American Culture*, Baltimore, 1991.

Gorrell, Donald K. *The Age of Social Responsibility: The Social Gospel in the Progressive Era, 1900–1920*, Macon, GA, 1988.

Hutchison, William R. *The Modernist Impulse in American Protestantism*, Cambridge, MA, 1976.

Luker, Ralph E. *The Social Gospel in Black and White: American Racial Reform, 1885–1912*, Chapel Hill, NC, 1991.

Sizer, Sandra S. *Gospel Hymns and Social Religion: the Rhetoric of Nineteenth-Century Reform in Changing America*, Philadelphia, 1976.

White, Ronald C., Jr. *Liberty and Justice for All: Racial Reform and the Social Gospel*, San Francisco, 1990.

———. *The Social Gospel: Religion and Reform in Changing America*, Philadelphia, 1976.

INTRODUCTION TO ESSAY 17

If some intellectuals in the late decades of the nineteenth century concentrated on social questions, others were absorbed in the relationship between science and religion—more specifically between evolution and biblical precepts. In this essay Appleby broaches a theme familiar to both Catholics and Protestants: how can one reconcile open-ended humanistic search for knowledge with a religious tradition based on claims to revealed truth and an insistence on confessional uniformity? Through the experience of one who was both a natural scientist and a Roman Catholic priest we also learn about the common problem of intellectual honesty trying to survive in an authoritative system. Both categories are mixed here, but we also glimpse the polarity between "pure science" and the "dirty politics" of ecclesiastical infighting.

On another level, the author provides valuable information about the development of American Catholic education. He shows that some academic pioneers were willing to face contemporary questions on a host of topics. But evolution is the main focus here, and we learn about the intricate philosophical and theological implications of paleontology. The fate of Father Zahm as a liberal thinker helps somewhat to explain why Pope Leo XIII condemned unfettered free thought in 1907 in his encyclical, *Pascendi Gregis*. Appleby's treatment also shows why, during the half century that followed, there was little discussion in American Catholicism of free inquiry into any secular topic that impinged on the sacred.

Original source - CH 56 (1987): 474-90.

17

Between Americanism and Modernism
John Zahm and Theistic Evolution

R. Scott Appleby

During the final decade of the nineteenth century, religious periodicals and secular newspapers alike chronicled the growing fascination of the American Catholic community with the public debate over the latest theories regarding the evolution of species. One figure in particular, John Augustine Zahm, a Holy Cross priest and professor of chemistry and physics in the University of Notre Dame, captured many of the headlines and captivated Catholic audiences with his sophisticated, clear expositions of the various theories in the post-Darwinian controversies and with his repeated assurances that the *idea* of evolution, properly understood, posed no obstacle to the faith of the individual Catholic.

In this regard Zahm played an unprecedented role in the religious history of the United States, for he combined in his person the seemingly diverse perspectives of the American citizen, the Catholic priest, and the evolutionist. Among the few American priest-scientists at the turn of the century, Zahm was the most competent, articulate, accomplished, and publicly prominent. Thus he was uniquely situated to contribute significantly to the process by which the American Catholic community came to know the modern world, for it was in the ongoing and bitter debate over evolution, and Darwin's theory thereof, that many American Catholics first encountered a scientific worldview buttressed by historical consciousness and developmentalist thought. Zahm was the first well-known American Catholic scholar to respond to the emergent theories of evolution. As a prolific author, frequent lecturer before scientific congresses, and popular speaker on the Catholic summer school circuit, Zahm reached a relatively large audience, especially from 1892 to 1896. He affirmed in no uncertain terms the ultimate compatibility of an evolutionary worldview and the central tenets of Catholic teaching on human nature, creation, and divine providence.

This public prominence also brought Zahm to the attention of the Roman Catholic curia. Curial officials moved to silence him when, like American Protestant and European Catholic scientists before him, he suggested revisions in the interpretation of certain doctrines affected by an acceptance of the general theory of evolution. In many ways "the Zahm affair" epitomized the Roman Catholic crisis over evolution. It reinforced in the minds of conservative churchmen their abiding suspicion that the application of critical methods of scientific inquiry to matters of revealed truth would lead Catholics into a web of heresies. Zahm's ecclesiastical opponents perceived in his methodology the outlines of a new heresy, characterized by a reinterpretation of patristic and scholastic terms and categories, a decided preference for inductive reasoning, and a hope of attaining a synthesis of modern science and the ancient faith. The defining of this heresy, namely, modernism, would engage them well into the next decade.

• • •

Born in Ohio to immigrant parents in 1851, Zahm entered the seminary at Notre Dame at the age of fifteen. Gifted with a natural aptitude for science, he rose rapidly in the ranks of the Congregation of Holy Cross. By the age of twenty-three he was professor of chemistry and physics, co-director of the science department, director of the library, curator of the museum, and a member of the Board of Trustees of the fledgling university. From 1875 to 1883 Zahm concentrated on building the science department at Notre Dame into a first-rate facility. During sojourns to Europe for research and to procure equipment for Notre Dame's laboratories, he absorbed the details of the discussion among European naturalists concerning Darwin's revisions of *The Origin of Species* (1859), and especially his *Descent of Man* (1871), which focused the debate on natural selection and human evolution.[1] Over the next decade, from 1883 to 1892, his own publications on the topic reflected a gradual but finally complete conversion to the general theory of evolution as the most scientifically sound and theologically appropriate explanation of the origin and development of species.

From 1893 to 1896 Zahm worked at a feverish pace to educate the public on the methods, hypotheses, and discoveries of modern science. To Catholic and Protestant audiences he characterized Catholic dogma as congenial to the implications of the new findings of biology, paleontology, and anthropology. During these years he published four books, four pamphlets, and twenty-one articles in this cause. He created a sensation at Catholic Summer School lectures in Plattsburgh, New York, and Madison, Wisconsin, became the *cause célèbre* of the International Catholic Scientific Congress at Brussels in 1894, and culminated his performance by accepting an honorary doctorate in philosophy from Pope Leo XIII in 1895.[2]

In his book, *Evolution and Dogma*, Zahn adopted a form of hypothetico-deductive reasoning as a *via media* between an "inconceivable" empiricism that guaranteed final certitude and a dogmatism, an "ultra-conservatism" based exclusively on deduction from a priori principles, that leads to "a fanatical obstinacy in the assertion of traditional views which are demonstrably untenable."[3] Zahm allowed himself only one a priori principle: science would not, *could not*, overturn truths revealed by God in scripture and tradition, for God is one and truth is one. In rejecting dualism, Catholicism allowed the scientists to proceed in their own realm of investigation, accepting the explanation of the origin of species most credible on scientific grounds, confident that the procedure would lead inexorably to a profound affirmation of theism. This approach did not hide fallible human science from the light of revelation, Zahm insisted, but it did restrain metaphysics from imposing prematurely upon the course of rational inquiry. Ultimately compatible in their respective conclusions, natural science and metaphysics are nonetheless different disciplines, each with its own integrity:

> The Copernican theory was denounced as anti-Scriptural... Newton's discovery of universal gravitation was condemned as atheistic.... That the theory of evolution should be obliged to pass through the same ordeal is not surprising to those familiar with the history of science; but there are yet those among us who derive such little profit from the lessons of the past, and who still persist in their futile attempt to solve by metaphysics problems which, by their very nature, can be worked out only by methods of induction.

Opponents of evolution tended to ignore the axiom that science "discloses the method of the world, not its cause; religion, its cause and not its method."[4] In a misbegotten attempt to safeguard divine providence, Zahm charged, they accepted special creation of immutable species despite overwhelming evidence of transmutation. To preserve belief in human creation in the image of God, they excluded a priori the possibility of human descent from lower forms of animal life.

In Zahm's estimation, this attempt produced inferior theology as well as inferior science. Modern science had weakened irrevocably the foundation of the creationist's worldview. Against the spontaneous generation of life, for example, Redi and Pasteur had demonstrated that in every instance life originates from antecedent life. Geologists described in convincing detail the fluctuations of the earth and "the multifold extinct forms entombed in its crust." Thus one must reckon the age of the earth not at six thousand years but "by millions if not tens of millions of years." Again, paleontologists confirmed that "a hundred million species or more have appeared and died out." Zahm concluded from empirical demonstrations of this sort that "everything seems to point conclusively to a development from the simple to the complex, and to disclose, in Spencer's words, 'change from the homogeneous to the heterogeneous through continuous differentiations and integrations.'" The changes and developments are the result "not of so many separate creative acts, but rather of a single creation and of a subsequent uniform process of Evolution, according to certain definite and immutable laws."[5]

Consequently, Zahm argued, the older views regarding creation must be materially modified to harmonize with modern science: "Between the two theories, that of creation and that of Evolution the lines are drawn tautly, and the one or the other theory must be accepted. . . . No compromise, no *via media*, is possible. We must needs be either creationists or evolutionists. We cannot be both." For Zahm, the choice between the two was a question "of natural science, not of metaphysics, and hence one of evidence which is more or less tangible." In delineating the grounds for "the almost universal acceptance of the theory by contemporary scientists,"

Zahm followed a procedure which he believed to be at the heart of Catholic wisdom: seek truth wherever it may be found, separate it from error, and reconcile it with other truths.

In spite of Zahm's professed zeal for the independence of scientific inquiry from metaphysical deduction, dogmatic considerations did play a role in his assessments of various theories. This point is quite clear in Zahm's treatment of the origin and development of the human race, a topic especially delicate for a Catholic apologist. He endorsed the theory of human evolution explicated in Mivart's 1871 work, *On the Genesis of Species*, which subordinated natural selection to the role played by "special powers and tendencies existing in each organism." According to this English Catholic, these special powers were the divine instrument employed in directing organisms to produce those forms which God had preconceived. The human body was derived by this evolutionary process, while the soul, source of humanity's ethical and rational nature, appeared in each case by divine fiat. Zahm came to be known as "the American Mivart" for his endorsement of this theory.

In adopting this position Zahm made a first attempt at "a perfect synthesis between the inductions of science on the one hand and the deductions of metaphysics on the other." In a sense, Zahm compromised with himself: as a naturalist, he surrendered strict adherence to inductive method by positing a supernatural act of God in infusing the rational soul; as priest, he surrendered the traditional view of the direct creation of the body of Adam. As it turned out, he ended up satisfying neither scientific nor religious purists.

Zahm claimed a freedom of interpretation in matters not defined dogmatically by the church, including the question of human origins. He announced boldly that the church is not committed to a theory about the origin of the world or its inhabitants: "Hence as a Catholic I am bound to no theory of Evolution or special creation, except in so far as there may be positive evidence on behalf of such theory." And as one who seemed at times to thrive on controversy, Zahm could not resist taking a swipe at his ecclesiastical opponents in Rome and America. He was unambiguous, and undiplomatic, in pointing the finger at the integralists who, in support of creationism and the process of deduction from metaphysical principles, refused to acknowledge the high degree of probability resting with evolutionary theory. Instead, Zahm charged, "they love to descant on the dictum of the Scholastics, possibility is far from implying existence."[6]

Evolution and Dogma was not the first occasion upon which Zahm criticized the neo-scholastic obstruction of scientific inquiry. Nor was this Zahm's first call for revisions in the Roman Catholic interpretation of the biblical and traditional witness on creation, providence, and human nature. But it was the first to attract international attention. It was translated into Italian (1896), French (1897), and Spanish (1904) and was promoted with an advertising campaign by publisher D. H. McBride that played up the controversial aspects of the book. It is not surprising, therefore, that *Evolution and Dogma* soon incited the antagonisms of curial of officials whose worldview it seemed to subvert.

• • •

The time of Zahm's intense and highly publicized activity as an apologist for science coincided with a period of ferment in the confrontation of Roman Catholicism and the modern age. From 1894 to 1899 conservative Roman ecclesial officials mounted a fresh assault in the campaign against modernity which culminated in the papal condemnation of Americanism in 1899. Because the heresies of modernity appeared to infect culture in all of its diverse expressions, traditionalists perceived the presence of the disease everywhere: in the application of the higher criticism to sacred texts; in the separation of church and state; in the attempt to assimilate Catholicism to the local and national communities to which the churches belonged; and, invariably, in the advances of the natural sciences.

In this context, Zahm's unflinching advocacy of the general theory of evolution placed him at the center of the storm, in large part because he also was identified by conservatives as a prominent member of the group of American priests and bishops who were attempting to "Americanize" the church. Indeed, there is evidence supporting the view that Zahm understood his crusade for evolution to be a significant contribution to the self-conscious effort on the part of many liberals to assimilate Catholics into the mainstream of American political and intellectual life.

But the tide began to turn against Zahm as early as 1894. That year witnessed both the publication of his *Bible, Science and Faith* and, coincidentally, a swing of mood in Rome, where conservatives seemed to awaken to the threat evolutionism posed to the neo-scholastic worldview. Undaunted, Zahm published *Evolution and Dogma* in February of 1896 and lectured on it at the Catholic Winter School in New Orleans. However, upon his return from New Orleans he learned to his dismay that he had been transferred to Rome by Gilbert Francais, Superior-General of Holy Cross, to take the post of Procurator-General for the congregation. Critics in the Catholic press speculated that the transfer was designed to deter Zahm from further publication. "The evolution bacillus is a dangerous thing," chirped Arthur Preuss, editor of the conservative *Review*. He suggested that the pure air of Catholic orthodoxy would help Zahm recuperate.[7] "I have never been 'disciplined,' as they put it, and it is not likely that I shall be," Zahm replied bravely. "My views may be not looked upon with favor by all in Rome," he admitted, "but I know that every eminent man of science throughout Europe is in perfect sympathy with my opinions." Nonetheless, he rushed into print a slender volume, *Scientific Theory and Catholic Doctrine*, in which he repudiated Darwin and Huxley unequivocally.

On 10 September 1898 Zahm received word from Francais that an edict by the Roman Congregation of the Index had banned *Evolution and Dogma*. The edict read, in part: "the most reverend Cardinals in a general meeting on September 1, 1898, having heard the exposition and the vote of the consultors, after mature deliberation have decreed: The work of the Reverend Zahm is prohibited; the decree, however, is not to be published until . . . the author will be heard out by his Father General whether he is willing to submit to the decree and reprove his work. . . . The prohibition . . . extends to all translations made in any language."[8] For the next eight months Francais, Zahm, and friends worked assiduously to prevent publication of the decree. Zahm's mood fluctuated from bitter disappointment to outrage. He wrote Francais immediately, promising full submission to the decree. Yet he maneuvered to avoid any public retraction of his position and expressed frustration about the shadow cast on Holy Cross by the affair.

By the turn of the century, neo-scholastic philosophers and theologians in power at Rome began to perceive Americanism and evolutionism as aspects of a larger historical movement which challenged their positions of privilege in the church, in so far as it threatened to overturn the philosophical and theological assumptions upon which the institutional system of their era was founded. Zahm represented a threat of a different kind as well. As an evolutionist he adopted a methodology which seemed to reflect a new and dangerous way of thinking about church and world—a new "episteme." Zahm took as a starting point not deductions from revealed truth, but "unbiased" inductions from empirical data. He promised a "synthesis" of these inductions and the "authentic" teaching of the Catholic tradition. He interpreted scripture critically, assigning different levels of authority to different passages and scientific competence to very few. And he claimed that the defined teachings of the church on these matters were few in number, which allowed him to proceed liberally in most questions.

Of course neither Zahm nor his opponents followed the implications of this inductive, or hypothetico-deductive, method to its unforeseen ends. But in 1899 they jousted on the tip of an iceberg against which neo-scholasticism and the church it claimed to represent would crash in the first decade of the new century. By the time of the condemnation of modernism in 1907, Zahm long since had retired from independent research and apologetics for science and Catholic dogma. Zahm had been one of the first casualties in the war against the proposed syntheses of "the ancient faith and modern thought."[9]

ENDNOTES

1. Peter J. Bowler, *Evolution: The History of an Idea* (Los Angeles, 1984), 219.
2. Ralph Weber, *Notre Dame's John Zahm: American Catholic Apologist and Educator* (Notre Dame, 1961), 70-76.
3. John A. Zahm, *Evolution and Dogma* (reprint ed., New York, 1978), 435-38.

4. Ibid., xvii, 69-70, 433.
5. Ibid., 50-53, 83; note the similarity of approach in John Gmeiner, *Modern Scientific Views and Christian Doctrines Compared* (Milwaukee, 1884), 3-4.
6. Zahm, *Evolution and Dogma*, xiv. See also James R. Moore, *The Post-Darwinian Controversies: A Study of the Protestant Struggle to Come to Terms with Darwin in Great Britain and America, 1870–1900* (Cambridge, UK, 1979).
7. "Dr. Zahm," *The Review*, 23 April 1896.
8. Quoted in Weber, *Notre Dame's John Zahm*, 107.
9. Margaret Mary Reher, "Americanism and Modernism: Continuity or Discontinuity?" *U.S. Catholic Historian* 1 (1981): 87-103.

FOR FURTHER READING

Appleby, R. Scott. *Church and Age Unite: The Modernist Impulse in American Catholicism*, Notre Dame, 1992.

Daly, Gabriel. *Transcendence and Immanence: A Study in Catholic Modernism and Integralism*, Oxford, UK, 1980.

Durant, John, ed. *Darwinism and Divinity: Essays on Evolution and Religious Beliefs*, Oxford, United Kingdom, 1985.

Gillespie, Neal. *Charles Darwin and the Problem of Creation*, Chicago, 1979.

Kauffman, Christopher J. *Tradition and Transformation in Catholic Culture: The Priests of Saint Sulpice in the United States from 1791 to the Present*, New York, 1988.

Kurtz, Lester J. *The Politics of Heresy: The Modernist Crisis in Roman Catholicism*, Berkeley, 1986.

Lindberg, David C., and Ronald L. Numbers, eds. *God and Nature: Historical Essays on the Encounter Between Christianity and Science*, Berkeley, 1986.

O'Connell, Marvin R. *John Ireland and the American Catholic Church*, St. Paul, MN, 1988.

INTRODUCTION TO ESSAY 18

Once again we start with a cliché, a popular fabrication that shrinks in the light of historical reality. If we base our attitude on just the experiences portrayed in the previous essay, we will think of religion and science as having been bitter enemies throughout Christian history. The authors of the present essay explain why such tired old metaphors as "warfare" and "irreconcilable differences" are misleading. Beginning with the early church fathers, progressing through Copernicus and Galileo—and preparing us for today's wrangles over evolution and creationism—we gain here a broader perspective on what was really at issue in these cases. We see a complex interaction between ideas and personalities, another important factor to keep in mind when studying any segment of intellectual history.

On a broad level this essay nurtures a healthy regard for unprejudiced analysis and reasonable discussion. Once errors are identified and put aside, then a candid exchange of ideas can produce a better grasp of ideas and set the agenda for further search for the truth. In a more limited area, the authors show us here that many attacks on revealed religion are as shallow-minded as the target they seek to defame. When American publicists equate theology with dogmatism, and natural science with academic freedom, their simplistic categories bear little resemblance to what really occurred. Any continuation of such unrealistic cant will perpetuate confusion between today's religious leaders and their critics, just as it already has done many times.

Original source - CH 55 (1986): 338-54.

18

Beyond War and Peace
A Reappraisal of the Encounter Between Christianity and Science

David C. Lindberg and Ronald L. Numbers

On a December evening in 1869, with memories of civil war still fresh in their minds, a large audience gathered in the great hall of Cooper Union in New York City to hear about another conflict, still taking its toll— "with battles fiercer, with sieges more persistent, with strategy more vigorous than in any of the comparatively petty warfares of Alexander, or Caesar, or Napoleon." Although waged with pens rather than swords, and for minds rather than empires, this war, too, had destroyed lives and reputations. The combatants? Science and Religion.[1] The bearer of this unwelcome news was Andrew Dickson White, a thirty-seven-year-old, Episcopal-bred historian who had taught at the University of Michigan and served in the New York State Senate before becoming the first president of Cornell University at the age of thirty-three.

White's Cooper Union lecture appeared the next day as "The Battle-Fields of Science" in the *New-York Daily Tribune*. In the years following, White fleshed out his history of the conflict between science and religion with new illustrations, some drawn from contemporary hostilities between creationists and evolutionists. Along the way he also narrowed the focus of his attack: from "religion" in 1869, to "ecclesiasticism" in 1876, when he published a little book entitled *The Warfare of Science*, and finally to "dogmatic theology" in 1896, when he brought out his fully documented, two-volume *History of the Warfare of Science with Theology in Christendom*. In this last version of his thesis he distinguished sharply between theology, which made unprovable statements about the world and took the Bible as a scientific text, and religion, which consisted of recognizing "a Power in the inverse" and living by the Golden Rule. Religion, so defined, fostered science; theology smothered it.[2]

Such judgments, however appealing they may be to foes of "scientific creationism" and other contemporary threats to established science, fly in the face of mounting evidence that White read the past through battle-scarred glasses, and that he and his imitators have distorted history to serve ideological ends of their own. Although it is not difficult to find instances of conflict and controversy in the annals of Christianity and science, recent scholarship has shown the warfare metaphor to be neither useful nor tenable in describing the relationship between science and religion.[3] In the remainder of this paper, we wish to support this conclusion with a series of examples drawn from recent scholarly studies thereby giving White's thesis a more systematic critique than it has heretofore received.

• • •

White viewed the early centuries of the Christian era as an unmitigated disaster for science. By his account, the church fathers regarded all scientific effort as futile and required any crumbs of scientific knowledge acquired through patient observation and reasoning to yield to puerile opinions extracted by dogmatic church leaders from sacred writings. Such "theological views of science," he wrote, have "without exception . . . forced mankind away from the truth, and have caused Christendom to stumble for centuries into abysses of error and sorrow." The coming of Christianity thus "arrested the normal development of the physical sciences for over fifteen hundred years," imposing a tyranny of ignorance and superstition that perverted and crushed true science.[4]

White and other writers on science and religion have suggested that science would have progressed more rapidly in the early centuries of the Christian era if Christianity had not inhibited its growth. Counterfactual speculations about what might have occurred had circumstances been otherwise are of questionable value. But it is worth pointing out that the study of nature held a very precarious position in ancient society; with the exception of medicine and a little astronomy, it served no practical function and generally failed to win recognition as a socially useful activity. As a result, it received little patronage from either pagans or Christians.

The church fathers used Greek scientific knowledge in their defense of the faith against heresy and in the elucidation of Scripture, thereby preserving and transmitting it during the social and political turmoil of the first millennium of the Christian era. Science was thus the handmaiden of theology—a far cry from its modern status, characterized by autonomy and intellectual hegemony, but also far from the victim of Christian intolerance that White portrayed. Christianity was not the enemy, but a valued (if not entirely reliable) servant.

In addition to serving theology, Greek scientific knowledge occupied a prominent place in Christian worldviews, from the time of Basil of Caesarea and Augustine through the end of the Middle Ages and beyond. The notion that any serious Christian thinker would even have attempted to formulate a worldview from the Bible alone is ludicrous. For example, contrary to popular belief (which White's *Warfare* has helped to shape), the church did not insist on a flat earth; there was scarcely a Christian scholar of the Middle Ages who did not acknowledge its sphericity and even know its approximate circumference.

• • •

In 1543 Nicolaus Copernicus (1473–1543), a Catholic church administrator from northern Poland, announced a heliocentric astronomy that removed the earth from the center of the universe and led, ultimately, to the overturning of the medieval worldview. White's interpretation of these events is almost as wide of the mark as his understanding of the Middle Ages. White reports that Copernicus feared to publish his discoveries in Rome or Wittenberg, the centers, respectively, of Catholicism and Protestantism. Instead, the astronomer turned to Nuremberg, where his work was published with a "grovelling preface," and thus the apologetic lie. "The greatest and most ennobling, perhaps, of scientific truths" was "forced, in coming before the world, to sneak and crawl." Copernicus died within a few hours of receiving his first copy of the book and thus, in White's words, placed himself "beyond the reach of the conscientious men who would have blotted his reputation and perhaps destroyed his life."[5]

White's picture of unremitting religious hostility to heliocentrism is no longer defensible if, indeed, it ever was. If Copernicus had any genuine fear of publication, it was the reaction of scientists, not clerics, that worried him. Other churchmen before him had freely discussed the possible motion of the earth—Nicole Oresme (a bishop) in the fourteenth century and Nicholas of Cusa (a cardinal) in the fifteenth—and there was no reason to suppose that the reappearance of this idea in the sixteenth century would cause a religious stir. Indeed, various churchmen, including a bishop and a cardinal, urged Copernicus to publish his book, which appeared with a dedication to Pope Paul III. Had Copernicus lived beyond its publication in 1543, it is highly improbable that he would have felt any hostility or suffered any persecution. The church simply had more important things to worry about than a new astronomical or cosmological system. Although a few critics noticed and opposed the Copernican system, organized Catholic opposition did not appear until the seventeenth century.

Concerning the Protestant response to the ideas of Copernicus, White claims that "all branches of the Protestant Church . . . vied with one another in denouncing the Copernican doctrine as contrary to Scripture." He also maintains (and his account has been repeated endlessly) that the theologians Martin Luther, Philipp Melanchthon, and John Calvin all bitterly attacked the new theory. In fact, from Luther we have only a single off-the-cuff remark, made during a "table talk" in 1539 (four years *before* publication of Copernicus's book), in which he refers to "that fool who wants to overturn the whole art of astronomy." Melanchthon expressed early disapproval of heliocentrism as a description of reality but later softened his position. Calvin spoke out against heliocentrism in a sermon on 1 Corinthians 10 and 11 (dating from 1556), denouncing the propagators of such vain novelties for their contentious spirit, which undermines the quest for truth; but his interest in such matters was not deep, and cosmological issues never entered systematically into his theology.[6]

The seventeenth century, according to White, produced a "new champion" of heliocentrism, the young Galileo, equipped with a new scientific instrument, the telescope. "Against him," White writes, "the war was long and bitter. . . . Semi-scientific professors, endeavoring to curry favour with the Church, attacked him with sham science; earnest preachers attacked him with perverted Scripture; theologians, inquisitors, congregations of cardinals, and at last popes dealt with him, and, as was supposed, silenced his impious doctrine forever." This dramatic tale has come, for many, to symbolize the theological assault on science. The Catholic church assumed a firm stance on biblical interpretation at the Council of Trent (1545–1563), forbidding the interpretation of Scripture on any matter of faith or practice "contrary to the sense determined by the Holy Mother Church." The hermeneutic flexibility of the Middle Ages had become a thing of the past.

When Galileo burst on the scene in 1610, he came equipped not only with telescopic observations that could be used to support the heliocentric theory, but also with liberal arguments about how to interpret biblical passages that seemed to teach the fixity of the earth. Galileo argued that God spoke through both Scripture and the "book of nature," that the two could not truly conflict, and that in physical matters authority should rest with reason and sense. Challenged by demonstrative scientific proof, any scriptural passage to the contrary would have to be reinterpreted. Galileo was flirting with danger, not only by entering the domain of the theologians, but also by defending hermeneutic principles clearly at odds with the spirit of the Council of Trent. The trouble in which Galileo eventually found himself, and which led ultimately to his condemnation, then, resulted not from clear scientific evidence running afoul of biblical claims to the contrary (as White tells the story), but from ambiguous scientific evidence provoking an intramural dispute within Catholicism over the proper principles of scriptural interpretation—a dispute won by the conservatives at Galileo's expense. Galileo never questioned the authority of Scripture, merely the principles by which it was to be interpreted.

The details of Galileo's condemnation need not detain us long. Galileo's campaign on behalf of Copernicanism was halted abruptly in 1616, when the Holy Office declared the heliocentric doctrine heretical—though at the time Galileo faced no physical threat. Eight years later Galileo received permission from the new pope, the scholarly Urban VIII, to write about the Copernican system as long as he treated it as mere hypothesis. After many delays, Galileo's *Dialogue Concerning the Two Chief World Systems* appeared in 1623. In it, Galileo not only unambiguously defended the heliocentric system as physically true, but also made the tactical mistake of placing the pope's admonition about its hypothetical character in the mouth of the slow-witted Aristotelian, Simplicio. Although the official *imprimatur* of the church had been secured, Galileo's enemies, including the now angry Urban VIII, determined to bring him to trial. The inquisition ultimately condemned Galileo and forced him to recant. Although sentenced to house arrest for the rest of his life, he lived comfortably in a villa outside Florence. He was neither tortured nor imprisoned—simply silenced. [7]

The Galileo affair was a multifaceted event. Certainly it raised serious questions about the relationship between reason and revelation and the proper means of reconciling the teachings of nature with those of Scripture. Nonetheless, it was not a matter of Christianity waging war on science. All of the participants called themselves Christians, and all acknowledged biblical authority. This was a struggle between opposing theories of biblical interpretation: a conservative theory issuing from the Council of Trent versus Galileo's more liberal alternative. Both were well precedented in the history of the church. Personal and political factors also played a role, as Galileo demonstrated his flair for cultivating enemies in high places.

Throughout the nineteenth century, but especially after the publication in 1859 of Charles Darwin's *Origin of Species*, the hottest battles in White's warfare were fought over the biblical account of creation. These conflicts allegedly pitted the "great body of theologians" against a coalition of scientists drawn from the fields of astronomy, geology, biology, and anthropology who sought to substitute a dynamic, natural history of the world for the static, supernatural account found in Genesis. Each encounter, says White, followed a predictable pattern: theologians first marshaled biblical texts against the offending scientific doctrine, then sued for peace, after the development of a scientific consensus, by offering "far-fetched reconciliations of textual statements with ascertained fact."

The appearance of Darwin's controversial theory of organic evolution, which made humans animals and left God virtually unemployed, understandably stirred passionate debate. But White's polemical analysis confuses rather than clarifies the issues. According to White, Samuel Wilberforce, the Bishop of Oxford, launched the theological offensive against Darwin and set the tone of the debate by writing an essay for *The Quarterly Review* in which he condemned Darwinism for contradicting the Bible. Later, on 30 June 1860, in an address at Oxford before the British Association for the Advancement of Science, Wilberforce repeated his objections, this time congratulating himself "that he was not descended from a monkey." Upon hearing this remark, Darwin's friend the zoologist Thomas Huxley shot back: "If I had to choose, I would prefer to be a descendant of a humble monkey rather than of a man who employs his knowledge and eloquence in misrepresenting those who are wearing out their lives in the search for the truth" a shot, says White, that "reverberated through England" and indeed the world. To White's credit, he refrained from passing on an even more sensational (and apocryphal) version of the story, according to which the bishop impertinently asked Huxley whether it was "on your grandfather's or grandmother's side that you claim descent from the apes." Replied the irreverent zoologist: "I would rather be descended from an ape than a bishop." This is a dramatic and memorable story, but one, as J. R. Lucas and others have shown, that perpetuates many errors and places Wilberforce in a grossly unfair light.[8]

The Huxley-Wilberforce exchange, far from setting the tone of the Darwinian debate, went virtually unnoticed at the time. The botanist Joseph Hooker, who later endorsed the legend, reported to Darwin shortly after the meeting that he, not Huxley, had responded most effectively to the bishop. And a writer covering the meetings for *The Athenaeum* neglected even to mention Huxley's alleged riposte. Wilberforce and Huxley did, without doubt, exchange words, but the words became memorable only with the passage of time, as victorious Darwinians began reconstructing the history of their struggle for recognition. In their memories Huxley won the day at Oxford, but contemporary records indicate otherwise: Wilberforce's supporters included not only the majority of clerics and laypeople in attendance, but "the most eminent naturalists" as well.

In recent decades, the encounter between William Jennings Bryan and Clarence Darrow at the Scopes trial in 1925 has achieved similar legendary status as a major turning point in the war between science and religion. According to common opinion, the evolutionists, though defeated on legal grounds, scored a stunning public-relations victory, halted the anti-evolution crusade, and exposed the bumbling Bryan as an ignoramus. A more careful look suggests that they did nothing of the sort. Even liberal contemporaries, Paul M. Waggoner has shown, tended at first to view the trial as a disturbing fundamentalist victory, and the anti-evolution campaign continued to prosper for several years after the trial. By present standards, Bryan displayed remarkable open-mindedness for a creationist. Publicly, he not only accepted the testimony of geologists regarding the antiquity of the earth, but conceded that the "days" of Genesis represented long periods of time. Privately, he allowed to friends that he had no quarrel with "evolution before man."[9]

White's seeming compulsion to reduce every episode in the history of science and Christianity to a simple warlike confrontation blinded him to the possibility that Darwin's critics might have been motivated by honest scientific objections or that his supporters might have been attracted for theological reasons. Thus he tells us that Harvard's venerable Louis Agassiz rejected evolution because he could not escape "the atmosphere of the little Swiss parsonage in which he was born" and that the Canadian geologist Sir William Dawson opposed Darwinism for theological reasons ignoring in both cases their scientific complaints. Likewise, White overlooked the affinity between Darwinism and Calvinism that apparently encouraged such orthodox Christians as the botanist Asa Gray and the geologist-clergyman George Frederick Wright to accept natural selection. We are not suggesting that all was harmony—that serious conflict did not exist—only that it was not the simple bipolar warfare described by White.

• • •

This brief excursion into some of White's old battlefields has demonstrated that the historical relationship between science and Christianity—or, more properly, scientists and theologians—cannot be reduced simply to conflict or warfare. Additional examples would only strengthen this conclusion. However, discrediting the warfare thesis represents only the beginning of the historical task confronting us. We also must construct a satisfactory alternative, for until we do, it is likely that the military metaphor will continue to dominate historical analysis. We require a fresh history of science and religion, free (or as free as we can make it) of the distortion of malice and self-interest. Reinterpreting something as complex as the encounter between Christianity and science is a delicate and arduous task that can hardly be accomplished within the scope of one paper. Nevertheless, we wish to offer a few caveats and suggestions that may help to define a suitable program.

First, to insure that we will not be misunderstood, we wish to assert plainly that our displeasure with White's warfare thesis is matched by our aversion to its converse. That is, in denying that unremitting hostility and conflict have characterized the relationship between Christianity and science, we do not in any way mean to suggest that Christianity and science have been perennial allies. Such an interpretation, though widely held in some circles, particularly among Christian apologists, fails to pass historical muster.

Second, one of the great attractions of White's view is its simplicity; few qualifications and nuances detract from the clarity of his picture. The memorable imagery found in his writings helps to explain their remarkable longevity. Unfortunately, we will never find a satisfactory alternative of equal simplicity. Any interpretation that begins to do justice to the complexity of the interaction between Christianity and science must be heavily qualified and subtly nuanced—clearly a disadvantage in the quest for public recognition, but a necessity nonetheless.

Third, we are convinced that traditional categories—enemies versus allies, conflict versus consensus—are misleading, even pernicious, because they direct us toward the wrong questions. For more than a century historians of Christianity and science like White have wasted their time and dissipated their energies attempting to identify villains and victims, often with polemical or apologetic intent, and always within a framework heavily laden with values. They tacitly have assumed that science has been, and continues to be, one of Western civilization's most valuable cultural artifacts—so valuable, indeed, that nothing should be allowed to interfere with it. Then they have proceeded to inquire why the most perfect expression of scientific activity (namely, modern science) was so long in coming into existence, as if its creation were a simple and inevitable matter; they have leapt quickly to the conclusion that science has suffered various indignities at the hand of assorted enemies, of which Christianity was chief. Such scientism must not pass unchallenged.

In offering these criticisms, we do not mean to question the significance or value of the scientific enterprise. We mean only to suggest that to start with scientific assumptions is no way to understand the nature and genesis of science. If we only celebrate the rise of science, we are not apt to understand it. Besides, partisan historians of religion can play a similar game: by supposing religion to be the premier cultural property, to which everything else (including science) must be subordinate, they discover that science frequently has interfered with the progress of religion. Both games, though seductive for their apologetic function, are of little merit to the historian, because the outcome is, in very large measure, predetermined by the value-laden rules of the game being played. Sound scholarship requires a more neutral starting point.

In the future we must not ask "Who was the aggressor?" but "How were Christianity and science affected by their encounter?" We are confident that research will show that the encounter has been multiform, the range of effects enormous. We will discover shifting alignments and dual memberships. We will uncover as much struggle and competition within the Christian and scientific communities as between them. Most important, we will see that influence has flowed in both directions, that Christianity and science alike have been profoundly shaped by their relations with each other. If, however, we fail to escape the trap of assigning credit and blame, we will never properly appreciate the roles of science and Christianity in the shaping of Western culture; and that will deeply impoverish our understanding.

ENDNOTES

1. "First of the Course of Scientific Lectures Prof. White on 'The Battlefields of Science,'" *New York Daily Tribune*, 18 December 1869, 4.
2. Andrew Dickson White, *A History of the Warfare of Science with Theology in Christendom*, 2 vols. (New York, 1896), 1:vii-viii. On White, see Glenn C. Altschuler, *Andrew D. White—Educator, Historian, Diplomat* (Ithaca, 1979).
3. For a brilliant critique of the warfare metaphor, see James R. Moore, *The Post-Darwinian Controversies: A Study of the Protestant Struggle to Come to Terms with Darwin in Great Britain and America, 1870–1900* (Cambridge, U.K., 1979), 19-122; David C. Lindberg and Ronald L. Numbers, eds. *God and Nature: Historical Essays on the Encounter Between Christianity and Science* (Berkeley, 1986).
4. White, *A History of the Warfare*, 1:325. For a fuller account of science and the early church, see David C. Lindberg, "Science and the Early Church," in *God and Nature*, 19-58.
5. White, *A History of the Warfare*, 1:123-24, 375.
6. On Luther and Melanchthon see B. A. Gerrish, "The Reformation and the Rise of Modern Science," in *The Impact of the Church Upon Its Culture: Reappraisals of the History of Christianity*, ed. Jerald C. Brauer (Chicago, 1968), 231-65. For the latest word in the long debate over Calvin's position, see Robert White, "Calvin and Copernicus: The Problem Reconsidered," *Calvin Theological Journal* 15 (1980): 233-43.
7. White, *A History of the Warfare*, 1:49-63; Ronald L. Numbers and Ronald C. Sawyer, "Medicine and Christianity in the Modern World," in *Health/Medicine and the Faith Traditions*, ed. Martin E. Marty and Kenneth L. Vaux (Philadelphia, 1982), 134-36; James J. Walsh, *The Popes and Science* (New York, 1908).
8. Charles Coulston Gillispie, *Genesis and Geology: A Study in the Relations of Scientific Thought, Natural Theology, and Social Opinion in Great Britain, 1790–1850* (Cambridge, MA, 1951); White, *A History of the Warfare*, 1:70-71, 218, 234; J. R. Lucas, "Wilberforce and Huxley: A Legendary Encounter," *The Historical Journal* 22 (1979): 313-30.
9. Paul M. Waggoner, "The Historiography of the Scopes Trial: A Critical

Re-evaluation," *Trinity Journal* 5 (1984): 155-74; Ronald L. Numbers, "Creationism in 20th-Century America," *Science* 218 (1982): 538-44; Edward J. Larson, *Trial and Error: The American Controversy over Creation and Evolution* (New York, 1985).

FOR FURTHER READING

Banister, Robert C. *Social Darwinism: Science and Myth in Anglo-American Social Thought*, Philadelphia, 1979.

Boller, Paul F., Jr. *American Thought in Transition: The Impact of Evolutionary Naturalism, 1865–1900*, Chicago, 1969.

Cashdollar, Charles D. *The Transformation of Theology, 1830–1890: Positivism and Protestant Thought in Britain and America*, Princeton, 1989.

Desmond, Adrian, and James R. Moore. *Darwin: The Life of a Tormented Evolutionist*, New York, 1991.

Durant, John, ed. *Darwinism and Divinity: Essays on Evolution and Religious Beliefs*, Oxford, U.K., 1985.

Gillespie, Neal. *Charles Darwin and the Problem of Creation*, Chicago, 1979.

Livingstone, David N. *Darwin's Forgotten Defenders: The Encounter Between Evangelical Theology and Evolutionary Thought*, Grand Rapids, MI, 1987.

Moore, James R. *Post-Darwinian Controversies: A Study of the Protestant Struggle to Come to Terms with Darwin in Great Britain and America, 1870–1900*, Cambridge, U.K., 1979.

Numbers, Ronald L. *The Creationists: The Evolution of Scientific Creationism*, Berkeley, 1992.

Robert, Jon H. *Darwinism and the Divine in America: Protestant Intellectuals and Organic Evolution, 1859–1900*, Madison, WI, 1988.

Russett, Cynthia. *Darwin in America: The Intellectual Response, 1865–1912*, San Francisco, 1976.

Turner, James. *Without God, Without Creed: The Origins of Unbelief in America*, Baltimore, 1985.

INTRODUCTION TO ESSAY 19

Women have always been a significant part of church life in every age, despite general attitudes that assigned women inferior status. Reform movements in recent times have redressed this imbalance somewhat, but cultural patterns change slowly, especially when religious ideas bolster social prejudices. As a student of women's activities in twentieth-century America, author Bendroth focuses on missionary activities that found expression in missionary boards and auxiliary societies. There she uncovers for us a contemporary dilemma: women have been largely excluded from denominational leadership, yet they have participated actively in evangelical outreach. They have been suppressed, yet they are devoted to the cause.

It is a truism worth repeating that conservative religious thought changes more slowly than in circles where liberals constantly seek reformulation. In the context of conservative or fundamentalist attitudes regarding women, Bendroth finds the usual biases, this time with their own theological gloss. She gives us some of the basic facts about denominational struggles over this issue among conservatives in Presbyterian and Baptist churches. She allows fundamentalist voices to disclose themselves on the issue, showing paradoxes in some people who both need women's help and scorn it at the same time. Bendroth suggests that the attrition experienced in fundamentalist camps since the 1920s cannot sustain outworn attitudes that consign women to second place. Feminism is here to stay, and it will make its mark even in fundamentalist thought.

Original source - CH 61 (1992): 221-33.

19

Fundamentalism and Femininity
Points of Encounter Between Religious Conservatives and Women, 1919–1935

Margaret Lamberts Bendroth

Increasing uncertainty about women's role reflected a general unrest in the Protestant churches in the 1920s. The fundamentalist/modernist controversy of that decade ruptured denominational unity and left both clergy and laypeople confused and angry. And it appeared to resonate deeply with new questions about women's "place." In fact, according to a recent study on gender and fundamentalism, the seismic shift in gender roles in the early twentieth century virtually defined the fundamentalist movement's rising anxiety about the modern world.[1]

The diversity of fundamentalism, especially before the 1930s, defies a simple analysis of attitudes toward femininity. While this essay focuses first on public battles over women's ordination and theological orthodoxy, it does not present a panoramic conclusion. By 1920, fundamentalism was growing in Presbyterian and Baptist circles, as well as in a myriad of independent educational and missionary institutions. As this essay will show, attitudes toward the role of women were often influenced by circumstance; denominational insiders under stress voiced sentiments far different from Bible institutes eager for students. In this respect, it is important to bear in mind the shortcomings of different source material: fundamentalist periodicals, especially those tied to nascent institutions, rarely volunteered unduly strict interpretations of Saint Paul. Or, in other cases, the sexist rhetoric of fundamentalist leaders did not necessarily entail deliberately sexist practice. Unpublished sources, including sermons and correspondence, are a necessary balance to the more restricted public forum of a fundamentalist periodical.

Institutional politics helped shape fundamentalists' complicated attitudes toward women and the world itself. Certainly their world-denying premillennialist theology and biblical literalism made them inhospitable to the claims of feminism. Yet, as Betty DeBerg argues, the fundamentalist "impulse" was not primarily a theological one; a good deal of its energy also came from competition between the sexes. Fundamentalists encountered women as rivals and, at the same time, as important allies. Women were the keepers of religion in American society and, even more important, an active and powerful church constituency. In this sense, they were a symbol of the culture that fundamentalists were trying at once to win over and to escape. Using George Marsden's metaphors, America was both Jerusalem and Babylon, a prize to be captured for Christ, and an unredeemable pit of human depravity. This paradox also describes fundamentalist attitudes toward women. Contrary to their popular stereotype, these men did not despise women or things feminine, any more than they rejected the world itself; they viewed both with a similar mixture of disdain and baffled longing.[2]

Yet fundamentalism, a movement far too easy to explain in simple categories, defies both extremes. By no means a simplistic reaction to modernity or to issues of gender, fundamentalism, as it shook loose from established, denominational moorings, played in the open the confusion and frustration many Americans experienced in the hectic years of the early twentieth century. Increasingly a movement of "outsiders" not bound by the evolving social ethic of sexual equality, it provides an instructive parable of a conflict deeply rooted in an inescapable partnership.

● ● ●

The 1920s was a pivotal decade for fundamentalists and women in the leading Protestant denominations. During that time, mergers of women's missionary societies into denominational boards and token advances toward women's ordination coincided with the fundamentalists' loss of power and their unhappy exodus from Northern Baptist and Presbyterian seminaries and missionary agencies. Among Presbyterians it is possible to link their disaffection with the women of their denomination to their own sense of alienation from centers of influence.

After World War I liberal Presbyterian leaders seemed to be bending over backward to assuage feminine discontent as they battled more and more openly with conservatives. Twice during the 1920s, in 1920 and 1929, the denomination considered women's ordination. The second time it approved an overture for women elders. Those behind the move freely admitted its value in muting feminine anger over the merger of the independent women's mission boards into a single board with proportional (though permanently unequal) male and female representation.

Such events clearly soured leading Presbyterian conservatives on the "woman question." In 1920, when the overtures for female elders were first introduced, they occasioned a genteel debate in the *Presbyterian*, a leading conservative journal, over Greek translations and principles of hermeneutics. Although a lead article by B. B. Warfield rejected all forms of public female leadership, other contributors castigated him for literalistic prooftexting, and ignoring the "time, conditions, and circumstances" of Pauline proscriptions. Nearly all endorsed the denomination's stance of the past half-century, that "women's work" in the church was too valuable to ignore, and impossible to restrict. When the debate resumed in the *Presbyterian* ten years later, its tone was bitter. In the intervening years, the conservatives' brief success in silencing liberal Harry Emerson Fosdick had been followed by a series of devastating defeats. The loss of control over Princeton Theological Seminary in 1925 was the beginning of the exodus of J. Gresham Machen and an exclusivist faction. This group founded Westminster Seminary and, in 1936, the Orthodox Presbyterian Church. By 1929, most conservatives were convinced that the overture for female elders was the product of the "well-laid plans, schemes and designs" of an elite, hand-picked few.

The debate also unearthed a deeper pessimism about femininity itself. In 1929 Clarence Macartney noted that "When the apostle speaks of false teachers leading off 'silly women,' he has a very modern sound. From Eve down to Mrs. Eddy, women have played a sad part in the spread of anti-Christian doctrines, and that under the guise of Christian teachings." "The adversary is clever enough in his dealings with men to inject in their theology many dangerous errors," agreed a fellow Calvinist, "but he got his masterpiece through a woman's brain."[3]

Leading Baptist fundamentalists also resented women's apparent new role as denominational "insiders." Although Baptist women's missionary societies remained independent until 1955, the pressure began during the 1920s. In 1926 John Roach Straton denounced the Women's Missionary Society from his New York City pulpit. By accepting half a million dollars from John C. Rockefeller, he charged, this group of weak women "could not with any face at all resist the strength of the modernist." Straton was particularly irked with the apparent naivete of Helen Barrett Montgomery, leader of the missionary society elected the first woman president of the Northern Baptist Convention in 1921. In the midst of controversy over the orthodoxy of Baptist seminaries and missionary candidates, she publicly bestowed on them a "clean bill of health." Moreover, in her convention address she belittled the fundamentalist defense of the faith as a string of "petty accusations," "irresponsible statements," and "wild charges."[4]

Although in fundamentalist eyes women might be the naive tools of modernists, they were still not easily ignored. Two-thirds of the religious population, newly enfranchised and increasingly socially liberated, they were also a constituency to be wooed and won. Put simply, fundamentalists could not afford to ignore women any more than liberals could.

Most fundamentalists agreed that women's presence in church and society was a double-edged sword. To the sentimental myth of women's superior religiosity, they added an ominous corollary. "Since woman is the determining factor in social life," Baptist evangelist J. C. Massee warned, "woman must of necessity be religious or destroy the very society she creates." Even on a practical level, fundamentalists could not afford to alienate women. As Janette Hassey has shown, grassroots fundamentalism shared the general openness of evangelical Protestants toward female evangelists and preachers. Throughout the early 1920s, Bible institutes boasted large female enrollments, regularly graduating similar proportions of men and women. In 1921 *Moody Bible Institute*

Monthly—the conservative standard-bearer for similar schools around the country—printed an enrollment appeal specifically for women. "Yes, God Uses Women Workers," the headline ran; glossy photographs and résumés of three female graduates proclaimed the exciting opportunities open to Moody's women graduates.[5]

Fundamentalists were also literally indebted to women for the movement's support. This indebtedness might account for the relative lack of agreement among fundamentalists on biblical mandates for women's role. Presbyterian conservatives, fighting denominational initiatives to ordain women and with little to lose in terms of constituencies, had apparently closed ranks around the issue by 1929. Independent fundamentalists, who were more in control of their institutional destinies but indebted to their constituencies, more often maintained the traditional evangelical openness to female teachers and evangelists, and used what were by then standard biblical defenses for the practice.

The Conflict, a novel written in 1923 by Elizabeth Knauss, a popular lecturer on premillennialism, described the fundamentalists' predicament as a romantic intrigue. As the story opens, two young women are vying for the affections of Paul Hadley, a young, handsome, and orthodox country pastor. The more aggressive suitor is Alice Jordan, a scheming, thoroughly modern churchwoman who serves the poor as a "hobby." Her ally is the foppish liberal preacher Dr. Frahm, who "appealed to the frivolous set of young women." Not surprisingly Alice's shallow efforts to win Paul Hadley are in vain; the novel provides a modest, pious church secretary to set him on the right path of love and doctrinal purity. But the deepest relationship in the story is Hadley's with another young fundamentalist, Franklin Phillips, "a fine specimen of manhood, tall, built on generous lines, a man to make his presence realized anywhere." Theirs is the one relationship free of "conflict."

The novel's portrayal of the friendship between the two men as an escape from conflict was based in reality. During the 1920s and after, the fundamentalist movement increasingly closed its ranks against "feminized" religion and around a fortress of masculine rhetoric and exclusively masculine companionship. "Feminized" religion, a product of female dominance in nineteenth-century evangelical Protestantism, reflected both the organizational strength of women and their preference for a personal, empathetic Christ. As the lines of conflict formed in the early twentieth century, fundamentalists purposefully identified the true faith with masculine values and liberalism with weak, shallow femininity. The blunt masculine rhetoric of "muscular Christianity," which was a popular form of expression in the early twentieth century, ultimately became an identification of true Christianity with "self-mastery."[6]

In the increasingly militant ethos of the 1920s, fundamentalists found masculine imagery particularly effective. For one thing, the tactic prodded liberals in a vulnerable point, their own worry that modernism might become a thin, effeminate faith, devoid of honest emotion or true conviction. "Conservative critics are telling us that our modern theology, though intellectually clear, is emotionally weak," the *Christian Century* admitted ruefully. "Modern religion needs stronger, sane feelings—the convictions, sentiments and loyalties which give dynamic to ideals." A writer in the *Atlantic Monthly* challenged modernists to "find a way to say the word 'God' in a voice of conviction and command."

The masculine defense of Christian orthodoxy also served to protect the one vulnerability fundamentalist leaders shared—they were clergymen. As such they all fought the popular stereotype that men of the cloth were neither male nor female. As one layman described it, "Life is a football game, with the men fighting it out on the gridiron, while the minister is up in the grandstand, explaining the game to the ladies." Individual fundamentalist leaders strove to counter the popular image of the clergyman as meek and feminine. They projected an assertive masculinity that gloried in controversy, and shunned the easy popularity of the crowd-pleasing liberal. William Bell Riley's biographers took pains to emphasize his fondness for outdoor sports and rowdy male company. Presbyterian Mark Matthews, sometimes derided as "effeminate," prized his reputation as the "pistol-packing parson" of Seattle. John Roach Straton, fighting his reputation as a "dandy," regularly walked the streets of New York's "red light district." An admiring friend recalled him as "absolutely fearless. He never cringed; he never wavered; he never compromised."[7]

But the fundamentalist defense of the faith passed beyond the rhetoric of "muscular" Christian piety to an identification of the cause itself as essentially masculine. "It is manly to follow Christ," the Baptist *Bible Champion* snorted defiantly, declaring that "the Bible is virile literature" and Christ himself "the most manly of men." "Christianity has no place for pusillanimity or churlishness," Presbyterian David Kennedy agreed. "It makes bigger, stronger men in every way." Baptist fundamentalists blustered against their critics, defending their leaders as "manly, full-blooded," and "vigorous"—not a "soft, gushy and mushy group of men" to "shed briny tears" over heretics.[8]

Fundamentalists readily agreed that a materialistic faith was, at best, unmanly. Not surprisingly, they equated "worldliness" with peculiarly feminine temptations. American society in the 1920s held no more potent symbol of unrestrained "self-expression" than the receding hemlines of the liberated "flapper." But even Christian women could not be trusted. "If the professing Christian women in the churches had done their full duty and had not surrendered to Satan," wrote one scandalized critic, "there would have been firms manufacturing the kinds of dresses, etc., that they needed." Sensitive to such discontent, schools like Moody Bible Institute issued careful measures to insure modesty among female students. Before they even set foot on Moody's campus, young women received a detailed description of dress codes from the superintendent of women, followed by regular warnings and discussions. Failure to comply with the rules rendered students liable to discipline, and gross or continued failure, to dismissal.

Fundamentalist legalism was only one sign of a gradual but far more significant process of institutional, emotional, and spiritual separation from things feminine. For reasons no participant openly admitted, women played a marginal role in the fundamentalist controversy. In 1922 a critic of the Baptist Bible Union observed that not one woman numbered among the 135 signers of its "Call and Manifesto." Women were equally invisible in Presbyterian battles.

While liberal Protestant organizations inched toward sexual inclusivity, rising fundamentalist organizations segregated or excluded women. During the 1930s nearly all the older women's organizations were either merging with their parent boards or becoming involved in wider concerns for racial equality and world peace; but many denominations within the fundamentalist orbit relegated women to narrowly defined foreign missionary auxiliaries with far fewer social concerns than their Victorian predecessors.

Other fundamentalist organizations followed a similar pattern. In 1930, the World Christian Fundamentals Association, with only a handful of women in visible leadership, formally segregated its female members into a "woman's auxiliary." The convention that year had no female speakers, or even a separate women's meeting; it did, however, include several talks for "Busy Men" and laymen. Also in 1930, Gordon Divinity School, a leading fundamentalist institution, instituted a quota system to keep the number of women students below one third of its total enrollment. By 1936 the proportion of women students dropped from one half to one third; during the 1950s no women enrolled. Again in 1930 the Independent Fundamental Churches in America explicitly eliminated women from membership. From then on, as one adherent explained, "their role was rather minimal." The Independent Board of Presbyterian Foreign Missions, the alternative to the liberal denominational board, listed eight men and one woman, a high school history instructor, on its executive board. Presbyterian women, long dominant in missionary work, were already bitterly complaining of their stingy representation on the denominational mission boards, fifteen seats out of forty.[9]

• • •

The long-term significance of the fundamentalist/modernist controversy is not easy to estimate. It seems clear that what was at the time an internecine debate among seminary professors and clergymen would hold immense consequences for women in the religious traditions it affected. Indeed, in this "post-feminist" age the heirs of fundamentalism are still earnestly debating the biblical propriety of women's ordination. The "neo-evangelical" movement has yet to find a feminine "voice" or a generation of women in influential leadership. Although many fundamentalists and evangelicals frame the issue as one of biblical authority, the continuing debate is clearly rooted in recent history.

The experiences of the twenties helped create a simultaneous attraction and repulsion toward femininity, a reaction which mirrored the longing and regret characteristic of the fundamentalists' stance toward American culture. As George Marsden has argued, the movement's "fortress mentality" of the 1930s and 1940s was one way to deal with the pain of separation, and to develop a new "basis for solidarity" in a hostile world. The masculine image of a fortress is apt. In the new institutions fundamentalists created, women might be supporters but not rivals. It was a recourse that would prove to be painful, and ultimately, not possible.

ENDNOTES

1. Betty A. DeBerg, *Ungodly Women: Gender and the First Wave of American Fundamentalism* (Philadelphia, 1990).
2. George M. Marsden, *Fundamentalism and American Culture: The Shaping of Twentieth-Century Evangelicalism* (New York, 1980).
3. Clarence Macartney, "Shall We Ordain Women as Ministers and Elders?" *Presbyterian*, 7 November 1929, 7; Euclid Philips, "Woman's Place in the Church," *Presbyterian*, 16 September 1930, 10.
4. John Roach Straton, "Why I Am Cutting Loose from the Apostate Ecclesiastical Baptist Machine Though I Am a Better Baptist Than Ever Before," sermon preached at Calvary Baptist Church, 29 October 1926, 10, Straton Papers, American Baptist Historical Society, Rochester, NY.
5. Janette Hassey, *No Time for Silence: Evangelical Women in Public Ministry Around the Turn of the Century* (Grand Rapids, 1986); "Yes, God Uses Women Workers," *Moody Bible Institute Monthly* 21 (1921): 344. See also Michael S. Hamilton, "Women, Public Ministry, and American Fundamentalism, 1920–1950," *Religion and American Culture* 3 (1993): 171-96; Virginia Lieson Brereton, *Training God's Army: The American Bible School, 1880–1940* (Bloomington, 1990), 129-32.
6. Elizabeth Knauss, *The Conflict: A Narrative Based on the Fundamentalist Movement* (Los Angeles, 1923); Ann C. Douglas, *The Feminization of American Culture* (New York, 1977); Peter Filene, *Him/Her Self: Sex Roles in Modern America*, 2d ed. (Baltimore, 1986).

7. Quoted in Paul A. Carter, *Another Part of the Twenties* (New York, 1977), 53-54; Austen K. Dabbles, "John Roach Straton: An Appreciation," *The Baptist*, 30 November 1929, 1484.
8. A. William Lewis, "The Investment of Manhood," *Bible Champion* 34 (1929): 384; Kennedy, "Quit You Like Men, Be Strong," *Bible Champion* 30 (1924): 134 and "Notes and Comments," *Bible Champion:* 141.
9. Letha Scanzoni and Susan Setta, "Women in Evangelical, Holiness, and Pentecostal Traditions," in *Women and Religion in America, 1900–1968*, eds. Rosemary Radford Ruether and Rosemary Skinner Keller (San Francisco, 1986), 228; James O. Henry, *For Such a Time as This: A History of the Independent Fundamental Churches in America* (Westchester, IL, 1983), 42, 126-29.

FOR FURTHER READING

Bendroth, Margaret Lamberts. *Fundamentalism and Gender 1875 to the Present*, New Haven, 1993.

Boyd, Lois A., and R. Douglas Brackenridge, *Presbyterian Women in America: Two Centuries of a Quest for Status*, Westport, CT, 1983.

Boydston, Jeanne, Mary Kelly, and Anne Margolis. *The Limits of Sisterhood: The Beecher Sisters on Women's Rights and Woman's Sphere*, Chapel Hill, NC, 1988.

Carpenter, Joel A. *Revive Us Again: The Reawakening of American Fundamentalism*, New York, 1997.

Higginbotham, Evelyn Brooks. *Righteous Discontent: The Women's Movement in the Black Baptist Church, 1880–1920*, Cambridge, MA, 1993.

Longfield, Bradley J. *The Presbyterian Controversy: Fundamentalists, Modernists, and Moderates*, New York, 1991.

Marsden, George M. *Reforming Fundamentalism: Fuller Seminary and the New Evangelicalism*, Grand Rapids, MI, 1987.

McDannell, Colleen. *The Christian Home in Victorian America, 1840–1900*, Bloomington, IN, 1986.

Sweet, Leonard I. *The Minister's Wife: Her Role in Nineteenth-Century American Evangelicalism*, Philadelphia, 1983.

Trollinger, William Vance, Jr., *God's Empire: William Bell Riley and Midwestern Fundamentalism*, Madison, WI, 1990.

PART IV

"Mainstream" Religion

INTRODUCTION TO ESSAY 20

We now move to treatments of central themes in American religious history, and in this first essay we are able to read afresh one of the most influential interpretations ever written in this field. Perhaps the most outstanding theme in American religion is separation of church and state, and Mead begins by informing us that the practice was not a popular idea in colonial times. Most Protestants in power—Anglicans in the South, Puritans in New England—worked from within established churches to consolidate their authority and perpetuate religious uniformity. Religious liberty did not stem primarily from Puritan thought, Mead holds, but from minority groups who saw some promise in "the lively experiment." One such group were rationalists or Enlightenment thinkers who wanted government to have no religious responsibilities. Pro-revival pietists made up another group, this one wanting to protect religions from state interference. Others joined this coalition, even though they favored establishment in theory, because they wished to see no church favored if theirs could not be the one. Disestablishment had more strategic value than doctrinal rectitude.

Practical considerations and self-interest worked alongside high principles to achieve religious freedom in this country. In the early days there was toleration of religious differences because economic need dictated accepting nonconformists. Then, in what Mead calls a "strange rope of circumstances," rationalists, pietists, and pragmatists worked together to create a federal constitution that remained neutral on religious questions. As a result, private consciences could not be forced to accept alien doctrine; church traditions could flourish without statutory restraint; freedom for a few led to freedom for all. It was a tenuous achievement at first, unsettling to many because it was so unprecedented, but it soon became a distinguishing characteristic of the new nation.

Original source - CH 25 (1956): 317-37.

20

From Coercion to Persuasion
Another Look at the Rise of Religious Liberty and the Emergence of Denominationalism

Sidney E. Mead

So far as religious affairs are concerned, the colonial period of our history begins with the planting of the first permanent English colony in 1607, guided by the intention to perpetuate in the new land the religious patterns to which the mother country had grown accustomed. Chief of these for our purposes was uniformity enforced by the civil power. The period culminates just 180 years later with the complete rejection of this central intention in the provisions for national religious freedom in the Constitution (1787) and the First Amendment (1791).

Regarding these provisions Philip Schaff said, "Congress was shut up to this course by the previous history of the American colonies and the actual condition of things at the time of the formation of the national government."[1] In brief, it was recognized at the time that if there was to be a *United* States of America, there had to be religious freedom on the national scale. The following interpretation of developments during the colonial period is therefore guided by two questions: what was this "actual condition of things" and how had it come to be?

• • •

All the original ventures in settlement in the new world—including the English—were guided by the intention to establish for whatever reasons outposts of European empires where the general social, religious, and political patterns of the homelands would be perpetuated. By the time that English colonization got underway early in the seventeenth century, the Reformation movement had shattered the once tangible unity of European Christendom in one church. With differences unimportant at this point, these "right-wing" groups agreed with Roman Catholics on the necessity for religious uniformity in doctrine and practice within a civil state, and enforced by the civil power. This view of more than ten centuries' standing in Western Christendom they accepted as axiomatic.

Meanwhile in the social crevices created by universal upheaval certain "sects" or "left-wing" groups were emerging, as blades of grass soon thrust themselves up through the cracks once a cement sidewalk is broken. Throughout Europe both Catholics and Protestants universally tried to suppress these groups by force as heretics and schismatics who constituted a threat to the whole structure of Christianity and civilization as then conceived.

All the first settlements on that part of the continent that was to become English were made under the religious aegis of right-wing groups, with the exception of Plymouth where a handful of separatists made a small, bustling noise in an empty land. But Anglicans who were making a bigger noise on the James, as were the Dutch Reformed on the Hudson, Swedes on the Delaware, and Puritan Congregationalists on the Charles, all assumed that the pattern of religious uniformity would of necessity be transplanted and perpetuated in the colonies. And all took positive steps to insure this—even the Pilgrims. For as Plymouth colony prospered it made support of the church compulsory, demanded that voters be certified as "orthodox in the fundamentals of religion," and passed laws against Quakers and other heretics.[2]

With these beginnings, it is notable that in contrast to the success in this respect of Roman Catholics in New France and the Spanish settlements in South and Central America, the intention to perpetuate uniformity in the several Protestant colonies that were gathered under the broad wings and "salutary neglect" of mother England during the seventeenth and eighteenth centuries was everywhere frustrated, and the tradition of thirteen centuries' standing given up in the relatively brief time of 180 years. By around the middle of the eighteenth century "toleration" was universally, however reluctantly, accepted in all the colonies, and within fifty years complete religious freedom was declared to be the policy of the new nation.

There would seem to be fairly wide consensus on Professor

Schaff's view that "Congress was shut up to this course." In explaining why this was so two factors are to be weighed and balanced. The first is that of the positive thrust for such freedom represented for example by the Baptists and given voice by individual leaders in most of the other groups. The second factor is that represented by Perry Miller's thesis that "by and large Protestants did not [willingly] contribute to religious liberty, they stumbled into it, they were compelled into it, they accepted it at last because they had to, or because they saw its strategic value."[3]

It is my first impression that Protestant writers have commonly stressed the first factor. And if in this article I stress the second factor, it is primarily for the purpose of bringing into the discussion what I hope will be a salutary and corrective emphasis. This emphasis necessarily somewhat discounts the historical importance among Protestants of a positive, self-conscious, and articulated aspiration for religious freedom for all, such as gained a place in their popular folklore. It does not deny the existence of the important seminal ideas among "left-wingers" and other outcasts such as the Roman Catholics who established Maryland, or even among the respectable Puritans and Presbyterians. Nor does it underestimate the long-term symbolic value of the halting steps taken along this road by the Baltimores, and the surer steps of Roger Williams, William Coddington, and that motley collection of the banished in Providence, Portsmouth, and New Port, or those of William Penn and his Quakers in the Jerseys and Pennsylvania. But it should also be kept in mind that the freedom extended to all in early Maryland was connived in only so long as was necessary. Rhode Island was the scandal of respectable New England precisely because of its freedom, and was commonly referred to by the Bay dignitaries as the sewer and loathsome receptacle of the land, that was not cleansed because they could not. And by the time that Penn launched his holy experiment in Pennsylvania, coerced uniformity had already broken down in the neighboring colonies, and England herself, having experimented extensively with toleration between 1648 and 1660, and unable to forget it with Restoration, was trembling on the verge of toleration.

Accepting the view that the original intention of the dominant and powerful groups was to perpetuate the pattern of religious uniformity, the thesis here developed is that intention was frustrated primarily by the unusual problems posed by the fast pace with which the Planters had to deal in coming to the new land, by the complex web of self interest in which they were enmeshed, and the practical necessity which these imposed to "connive in some cases," and finally by effective pressures from the motherland.

Self-interest dictated in more or less subtle and devious ways a kind of connivance with religious diversity that helped to spell out toleration in the colonies, the efforts even of the most authoritarian groups to enforce uniformity on principle were dissipated in the vast spaces of the new land. There was of course another aspect of space—the distance from the motherland, which, relative to existing means of movement and communication, was immense. The Puritans began with the idea that

> . . . God hath provided this place to be a refuge for many whome he meanes to save out of the generall callamity, and seeinge the Church hath noe place to flie into but the wildernesse, what better worke can there be, then to goe and provide tabernacles and foode for her against she comes thither.[4]

They sensed early the protection inherent in the great distance, as is evidenced by their ingenious idea of taking the Charter and the Company bodily to New England. Thereafter they perfected a system of sanctified maneuvering within the time granted by distance that frustrated all attempts of English courts and crown to control them for about three generations.

By around 1720, then, the original intention to perpetuate religious uniformity had been almost universally frustrated in the colonies by the strange rope of circumstances woven from various kinds of self-interest and the problems growing out of the great space confronted. Effective interference from the motherland in the interests of broader toleration served only to hasten the process. But it is probably not to be wondered at that most of them adhered to the inherited standards and conceptions of the church with religious fervor sometimes bordering on desperation. It took the prolonged upheavals associated with the great revivals to break the hold of the old patterns, give the new an opportunity to grow, and inextricably to scramble both with others emerging out of the immediate situation.

Once it was seen that uniformity was impracticable, two possible paths lay open before the churches: toleration, with a favored or established church and dissenting sects—the path actually taken in England—or freedom, with complete equality of all religious groups before the civil law. In this situation it is important to note that transplanted offshoots of Europe's state churches were clearly dominant in all but two of the colonies, and indeed remained so until after the Revolution. Further, nine of the colonies actually maintained establishments—Congregationalism in New England, Anglicanism in the South and, nominally, in part of New York—while none of the other dominant churches as yet rejected the idea on principle, and indeed, as witness Presbyterians in the South and Anglicans in New England, were willing to acknowledge the prerogatives of establishments by assuming the role of dissenters. On the eve of the great revivals, then, the prevailing sentiment in these churches is probably best described as tolerationist based on necessary connivance.

Meanwhile, in Rhode Island and the stronger middle colonies, religious freedom prevailed—in New York practically, ambiguously, and largely because of necessity, in Rhode Island and Pennsylvania actually and more clearly on principle and experience. Further, as has been intimated, the factors that had confounded the uniformitarian intentions of the churches originally established in the new land, had also encouraged the numerical growth, geographical expansion, and bumptious self-confidence of the dissenting and the free groups in all the colonies. However, these were as yet largely unconscious of their real strength for facing the future, which lay in their necessary espousal of voluntaryism as the basis for a church, and their consequent experience with dependence upon persuasion alone for recruiting members and maintaining their institutions in competition with other groups. An entry in Henry M. Muhlenberg's *Journal*, November 28, 1742, suggests how rapidly a minister, transplanted from a European state church, might size up the realities of the new situation in America and come to terms with them. Sent over to bring some order into the scrambled Lutheran affairs, he immediately ran into a squabble in one of the churches, and recorded:

> The deacons and elders are unable to do anything about it, for in religious and church matters, each has the right to do what he pleases. The government has nothing to do with it and will not concern itself with such matters. Everything depends on the vote of the majority.[5]

Such espousal of voluntaryism by these American offspring of Europe's right-wing state churches meant, of course, that they accepted one aspect that of necessity had been common to the left-wing sectarian groups of Europe from their beginnings. But this was a triumph of a left-wing influence in America, as is sometimes held, only in a "guilt by association" sense.

Much more important for the future than left-wing influence was the movement called Pietism, which had originated in the European right-wing state churches during the last quarter of the seventeenth century under leaders who sought to provide more palatable spiritual food for the hungry souls of the common folk who were then languishing on Protestant scholasticism and formalism. Conceived and projected by its leaders as a movement *within* churches aimed at the revitalization of the personal religious life of the members and a restoration of Christian unity, Pietism did tend to develop its own patterns of doctrine and polity. While assuming the validity and continuance of traditional standards and practices, Pietists tended to make personal religious experience more important than assent to correctly formulated belief and the observance of ecclesiastical forms—which was to intimate that the essence of a church was the voluntary association of individuals who had had the experience. Stress on the intuitive religion of the heart "strangely warmed" by "faith in Christ," as John Wesley was later to put it, was of course a possible seedbed for the dreaded religious "enthusiasm." However, in Europe the movement was always somewhat constrained by the sheer existence and accepted forms of the powerful state churches.

But, sprouting indigenously in their American counterparts, or transplanted thereto by such leaders as Freylinghuysen, Muhlenberg, Zinzendorf, and the great Whitefield, where such constraining ecclesiastical forms were already weakened, Pietism, cross-fertilized by other movements, grew rankly and blossomed in the spectacular phenomena associated with the Great Awakenings that swept the colonies from the 1720s to the Revolution, transforming the religious complexion of the land.

In the context of our general interpretation it is important to note two things. The first is that the revivals took place largely within the entrenched and dominant churches of right-wing tradition. The second is that everywhere, whether among Dutch Reformed and Presbyterians in middle colonies, Congregationalists in New England or Anglicans in the South, they resulted in a head-on clash between the pietistic revivalists and the powerful defenders of the traditional authoritarian Protestant patterns of doctrine and polity. For the latter correctly sensed that the revivalists, in keeping with their pietistic sentiments, stressed religious experience and results—namely conversions—more than correctness of belief, adherence to creedal statements, and proper observance of inherited forms, and hence that their work in the churches tended to wash out all traditional standards.[6]

The revivalists defended themselves primarily on the basis of their sense of the importance of personal religious experience, which they thought the traditionalists neglected. Gilbert Tennent struck their key note in his sermon of March 8, 1740, which he called "The Danger of an Unconverted Ministry." Such ministers, he asserted, are "Pharisee-teachers, having no experience of a special work of the Holy Ghost, upon their souls." Of course, he added, "God, as an absolute Sovereign, may use what Means he pleases to accomplish his Work by," *but* "we only assert this, that Success by unconverted Ministers Preaching . . . very seldom happens, so far as we can gather."[7]

At this point it is worthwhile to note specifically that the battle was not one between tolerant "left-wing" sectarian revivalists riding the wave of the democratic future, and anachronistic "right-wing" churchmen stubbornly defending the past and their own present prerogatives. Actually all the outstanding revivalists belonged to churches of right-wing tradition, and it might cogently be argued that what growth accrued to left-wing groups as a result of the revivals came largely through their ability to reap where others had sown. Once this point is clear, we may note that during the clash between traditionalists and revivalists, the latter were thrown willy-nilly—but somewhat incidentally—on the side of greater toleration and freedom. It was not that they developed clearly formulated theories about religious freedom—in fact the striking thing about the whole pietistic movement, as A. N. Whitehead pointed out, was that it "was singularly devoid of new ideas," never appealed to any "great intellectual construction explanatory of its modes of understanding," and its sweep in the churches marks the point at which "the clergy of the Western races began to waver in their appeal to constructive reason."[8] What they appealed to was religious experience and feeling, and as John Wesley said of his Methodists, they spread "scriptural religion throughout the land, among people of every denomination; leaving every one to hold his own opinions, and to follow his own mode of worship."[9]

Hence such freedom as the revivalists came to represent during the controversies was not generated by a theoretical consideration of its ultimate desirability on principle, but by a practical desire for freedom from the immediate restraints and oppressions imposed by the dominant churchmen. What they fought for at the time was the freedom to publish their own point of view in their own way, unmolested by traditional civil and ecclesiastical customs and laws—which to their mind served primarily to prevent getting the show on the road. But here the revivalists *were* riding the wave of the future, and theirs was to become, in Protestant America, the most prevalent conception of the meaning of religious freedom.

Meanwhile the rationalist permeation of the intellectual world during the eighteenth century meant that any man or group that appeared to be fighting for wider toleration of religious differences would attract the sympathetic attention of "enlightened" men in positions of social and political leadership. Furthermore, these men *were* interested in giving such freedom rational theoretical justification. The rationalists' theoretical defense of freedom was based on the view that since religion is one's "opinion" about the "duty which we owe to our creator, and the manner of discharging it," and "the opinions of men" depend "only on the evidence contemplated in their own minds" and "cannot follow the dictates of other men," therefore, true uniformity is impossible except insofar as it can be achieved through persuasion alone. Coercion, in the interests of uniformity, said Jefferson, had served only "to make one half the world fools, and the other half hypocrites."[10]

Hence came that apparently strange coalition of rationalists with pietistic-revivalistic sectarians during the last quarter of the eighteenth century that provided so much of the power that lay behind the final thrust for national religious freedom that was written into the fundamental laws of the new nation. This coalition seems less strange if we keep in mind that at the time religious freedom was for both more a practical and legal problem than a theoretical one, and that they agreed on the practical goal.

● ● ●

Finally then, to hark back to Schaff's thesis, we have traced the "previous history of the American colonies" that is pertinent to our understanding of the consequent "condition of things at the time of the formation of the national government." This "condition of things" can now be briefly summarized.

First, the churches of right-wing background were still dominant in every area. But no one of them, and no possible combination of them, was in a position to make a bid for a national establishment plausible. Meanwhile, the sweep of pietistic sentiments through these churches during the revivals had undermined much of their desire for establishment. On the question of religious freedom for all, there were many shades of opinion in these churches, but all were practically unanimous on one point— each wanted freedom for itself. And by this time it had become clear that the only way to get it for themselves was to grant it to all others.

Second, the situation had actually made all previous distinctions between established churches and sects, between right- and left-wing groups, practically meaningless. Hence the true picture is not that of the "triumph" in America of right-wing or left-wing, of churches or sects, but rather a mingling through frustration, controversy, confusion, and compromise forced by necessity, of all the diverse ecclesiastical patterns transplanted from Europe, plus other patterns improvised on the spot, to form a complex pattern of religious thought and institutional life that was peculiarly "American," and is probably best described as "denominationalism."

Meanwhile, most of the effectively powerful intellectual, social, and political leaders were rationalists, and these men made sense theoretically out of the actual practical situation which demanded religious freedom, and gave it tangible form and legal structure. This the churches, each intent on its own freedom, accepted in practice but without reconciling themselves to it intellectually by developing theoretical defenses of it that were legitimately rooted in their professed theological positions. And they never have.

Meanwhile, by the time that the original intention to preserve religious uniformity was seen to be impossible of fulfillment in the new land, there had been incubated, largely within the dissenting groups (which were not necessarily "left-wing"), ideas, theories, practices that pointed the way toward a new kind of "church" in Christendom consistent with the practice of religious freedom. During the upheavals of the Great Awakenings in the colonies, these dissenters' patterns of thought and practice infiltrated the dominant churches, and through confusion and compromise there began that historical merging of the traditional patterns of "church" and "sect," "right" and "left" wings as known in Europe into the new kind of organization combining features of both plus features growing out of the immediate situation. The resulting organizational form was unlike anything that had preceded it in Christendom, and for purposes of distinctive clarity it is best known as the "denomination."

ENDNOTES

1. Philip Schaff, *Church and State in the United States* (New York, 1888), 23.
2. Evarts B. Greene, *Religion and the State: The Making and Testing of an American Tradition* (New York, 1941), 37; Joseph P. Thompson, *Church and State in the United States* (Boston, 1873), 55.
3. See the article, "The Contribution of the Protestant Churches to Religious Liberty in America," *Church History* 4 (1935): 57-66.
4. As quoted in Charles M. Andrews, *The Colonial Period of American History* (New Haven, 1934), 1:386.
5. *The Journals of Henry Melchior Muhlenberg*, trans. Theodore G. Tappert and John W. Doberstein (Philadelphia, 1942), 1:67.
6. See Wesley M. Gewehr, *The Great Awakening in Virginia, 1740–1790* (Durham, NC, 1930), 16, 65.
7. From Leonard J. Trinterud, *The Forming of an American Tradition: A Reexamination of Colonial Presbyterianism* (Philadelphia, 1944), 90-91.
8. Albert North Whitehead, *Adventures of Ideas* (New York, 1933), 27-28.
9. John Wesley, *Sermons on Several Occasions* (New York, 1851), 1:392.
10. James Madison, "A Memorial and Remonstrance on the Religious Rights of Man," as printed in Joseph L. Blau, ed., *Cornerstones of Religious Freedom in America* (Boston, 1949), 81; Saul K. Padover, ed., *The Complete Jefferson* (New York, 1943), 676.

FOR FURTHER READING

Curry, Thomas J. *The First Freedoms: Church and State in America to the Passage of the First Amendment*, New York, 1986.

Drakeman, Donald L. *Church-State Constitutional Issues: Making Sense of the Establishment Clause*, Westport, CT, 1991.

Finke, Roger, and Rodney Stark. *The Churching of America, 1776–1990: Winners and Losers in Our Religious Economy*. New Brunswick, NJ, 1992.

Howe, Mark DeWolfe. *The Garden and the Wilderness: Religion and Government in American Constitutional History*, Chicago, 1965.

Littell, Franklin H. *From State Church to Pluralism: A Protestant Interpretation of Religion in American History*, New York, 1971.

McLoughlin, William G. *New England Dissent, 1630–1833: The Baptists and the Separation of Church and State*, 2 vols., Cambridge, MA, 1971.

Mead, Sidney E. *The Nation with the Soul of a Church*, San Francisco, 1975.

Miller, William Lee. *The First Liberty: Religion and the American Republic*, New York, 1986.

Mullin, Robert Bruce, and Russell E. Richey, eds. *Reimagining Denominationalism: Interpretative Essays*, New York, 1994.

Noll, Mark A., ed. *Religion and American Politics*, New York, 1989.

Pfeffer, Leo. *Church, State, and Freedom*, rev. ed. Boston, 1967.

Sorauf, Frank. *The Wall of Separation: The Constitutional Politics of Church and State*, Princeton, 1976.

Wood, James E., Jr., ed. *The First Freedom: Religion and the Bill of Rights*, Waco, TX, 1990.

INTRODUCTION TO ESSAY 21

Taking the voluntary principles that Mead mentioned previously, Albanese brings them forward to today. In a centennial overview she leapfrogs denominational developments in colonial times through the Second Great Awakening, touches the Victorian era and World War II, and arrives at recent agitation over civil rights. She uses this background to introduce a "new voluntarism," considering religious affirmations that were previously deemed trivial but are now possibly the vanguard of a new mainstream. In doing so she finally settles on "mysticism" as a term for rudimentary religious experiences and thus uncovers the fundamental question of what, in the last analysis, is the basis for religion after all. She makes us wonder where religion comes from and why it endures, forming such a powerful influence in individual lives and in all of history.

Albanese has a special interest in New Age religious expressions. As a historian, she knows that there is nothing new about them at all, but she accepts today's jargon in order to focus on people unaffiliated with traditional churches. With striking ingenuity she compares Fundamentalists with New Agers and finds a surprising number of similarities. Those who seem to be pursuing alternative lifestyles turn out to have needs and goals that are, at bottom, much the same as believers linked with hidebound conservatism. Her penetrating observations about revelation, science, healing, and social change help us grasp how labels change while human emphases do not, how personal priorities can make even secular concerns really religious ones.

Original source - CH 57 (1988): 337-51.

21

Religion and the American Experience
A Century After

Catherine L. Albanese

In 1855 Philip Schaff wrote "America is the *grave of all European nationalities;* but a *Phenix grave,* from which they shall rise to new life and new activity." Beyond that he thought that America seemed "destined to be the Phenix grave not only of all European nationalities . . . but also of all European churches and sects, of Protestantism and Romanism." Schaff made it clear that the "Phenix grave" of nationalities would give rise to a new ethnos in an "essentially Anglo-Germanic form." More generally, his sight was Europe-centered; marked by the colonialist and racist views of his era. And his sight was also distinctly (and triumphantly) Christian, for what would arise from the grave of the churches was "the kingdom of Jesus Christ . . . favored by the most extensive emigration from all other countries, become more and more the receptacle of all the elements of the old world's good and evil, which will there wildly ferment together, and from the most fertile soil bring forth fruit for the weal or woe of generations to come."[1]

What is religion like in America, one century after Schaff's founding of the American Society of Church History? Should we speak of the "wild ferment" of its many expressions? Or can we find consistent fruit suggesting that "fermentation" in fertile soil has produced a specific plant? Is the crop, whether many or one, vigorous? Or do we find that a century after there is weakness? Schaff's near-mystical Hegelian vision of development almost demands that we ask these kinds of questions. The need for clarity by less romantic standards demands the same.

Writing in 1971 Martin E. Marty, then president of the American Society of Church History, called ethnicity the "skeleton of religion in America." Ethnicity was a skeleton in several ways: it was, like a skeleton at a banquet, something that evoked the serious or saddening at a time when people wanted to enjoy themselves. But as a skeleton it was finally a framework that supported religion in America and interpretive attempts to make sense of it. Marty noticed that some scholars chose to look away from the ethnic skeleton, either in the closet or, more visibly, at the banquet, and they did so by emphasizing religious or secular commonality. Other scholars, drawn to the theme of pluralism, found ethnicity an unavoidable structural presence. It is important to note too that in the America Marty was describing ethnos was not identical with nation. There were many ethnicities comprising the one nation that was the United States, and ethnics inhabited smaller cultural enclaves in which they were distinguished from other citizens.

But how long, we may well ask, does it take to create an ethnos? How many centuries are needed to turn the manyness of American immigrants into the oneness of a single people? It seems likely that it would begin to manifest itself gradually, that there would be stages along the way from inchoate beginnings to fully achieved form. If that is the case, then perhaps there is merit in asking if, even now, we can see the rough features of a distinctly American ethnos appearing. Perhaps there is value in looking again at what we have noticed before to see it in new ways. Moreover, perhaps there is value in looking in new places for what we have not noticed or have not noticed so well. It may be that we can read our discoveries as signs of an *ethnically* American religion. In the tradition of Philip Schaff we may begin to find an emergent organic growth produced by the nation's religious ferment.

• • •

In their study, *American Mainline Religion: Its Changing Shape and Future,* Wade Clark Roof and William McKinney tell us that the counterculture of the sixties and the evangelical revival of the later seventies unmistakably left their mark. "Far from being superficial or inconsequential," argue Roof and McKinney, both movements "unleashed new energies and cultivated psychoreligious cultures that are having, and are likely to continue having for sometime to come, a profound impact on the religious scene." Consequently, the mainline they identify looks decidedly different from what earlier scholars have seen. How, then, goes the reconstituted center, or the new mainline?

Taking their cue from Martin Marty's *Nation of Behavers*, Roof and McKinney privilege behavioral differences. In a still largely Protestant nation they find six religious "families" that share the center: liberal Protestants, moderate Protestants, black Protestants, conservative Protestants, Roman Catholics, and Jews. At the same time, the two note the steady decline of Protestant strength—from 67 percent of the nation's population in 1952 to 57 percent in 1985. Meanwhile, in the same period, they tell us, Catholics increased from 25 to 28 percent of the population, while Jews experienced a decline of 50 percent, from 4 to 2 percent of the total.

Where, we may well ask, have all the Protestants gone? Blacks and moderates have lost; liberals and conservatives, in hard numbers, have gained only slightly. Jews, relative to their population, have lost massively. Catholics, according to the survey data from recent years, have also suffered moderate (more than 5 percent) losses. Where, then, *have* the Protestants gone? "The big 'winner' in the switching game," say Roof and McKinney, "is the growing secular constituency." "Nonaffiliates," they claim, "are the greatest beneficiary of switching; all the groups lose more persons to this category than they receive from it."[2]

Even a glance at their statistical base suggests the weight of the evidence behind their words. While mainline groups gained or lost roughly between 2 and 10 percent of their members, the ranks of the unaffiliated increased by over 155 percent! Indeed, Roof and McKinney say that once nonaffiliates could be called a "marginal assortment of largely alienated and isolated Americans" but now they are "much more a part of the mainstream." They have acquired "significantly more education and higher occupational prestige than those who remain religiously affiliated." "Persons reporting they have no religious affiliation," they tell us, "are a diverse constituency, religiously as well as culturally. Many hold beliefs in the supernatural and the mystical and often show much interest in religious and quasi-religious phenomena. Few are actually militant secularists or committed atheists in their opposition to religion." Still, "affiliation with a congregation is not deemed essential to their spiritual quests." The nonaffiliated are "more committed to alternative life-styles, and oriented generally to an ethic of personal growth and self-fulfillment. Though we have no hard data on which to judge, these persons appear to be more 'new class' in outlook and ideology." Put another way, significant numbers of the unaffiliated may be drawn more or less in the direction of the New Age movement.

Thus far Roof and McKinney. Given the results of their study, what further sense can we make of the picture? Against the backdrop of Philip Schaff's more-than-century-old prophecy of ferment into new form, against the more recent skeleton of ethnic religion and the search for an American ethnos, what can we discover? I claimed earlier that we needed to look first at what we historians already know about the character of American religion to see if we might read it as the sign of an emerging ethnos. In this context, traits like the increasing voluntarism that Roof and McKinney identify—not to mention the activism and moralism (concern for the rules of action) that buttress it—appear in a different light. Perhaps to say that these traits are ethnic—that is, the national characteristics of Americans as Americans—is only to say what we could have said all along. Still, it bears naming them distinctly as *ethnic* traits if we are looking for an ethnos.

Moreover, if the "new voluntarism" supports and issues in a "new pluralism," the existence of voluntarism points us toward an ethnos that possesses a flexibility in its institutional commitments. It follows, therefore, that we need to search not only in institutions but also beyond and beneath and around them for signs of a national faith. I think that a key distinguishing characteristic of the emerging American ethnos is its mysticism. This mysticism ties together self, God, and nature in a religious expansionism that has refused to go away. And it provides as the bond of religious nationhood a rhetoric that links the extremes of the American religious spectrum and that, as the middle more and more loses definition, may find itself there as well.

From one perspective, to call the American ethnos mystical is only to particularize the work of Ernst Troeltsch. It is easy to forget that in his *Social Teaching of the Christian Churches* Troeltsch not only distinguished church from sect but also distinguished both from mysticism. Troeltsch believed that the growth of mysticism as a sociological form was tied to the rise of an "independent lay civilization" in the towns and cities of northern Europe. Predicated on the word made broadly available by the invention of the printing press, mysticism thrived on "a pure fellowship of thought." It came intertwined with the "autonomous individualism" of Protestantism; accompanied by the birth of the nation-state and a "growing national feeling among the peoples"; in league with the rise of early capitalism with its "civilization of the senses." "In the widest sense of the word," said Troeltsch, "mysticism is simply the insistence upon a direct inward and present religious experience." Indeed, in their own sociological study Roof and McKinney cite Ernst Troeltsch as they assess the American religious scene of the mid-1980s.

Certainly the "nexus between mysticism and modernity" refuses to go away; and no less a student of mysticism than the Jewish scholar Gershom Scholem found mysticism to be a third stage in the general evolution of religion. After the wonder world of the gods in a "mythical epoch," and after the more sober era of institutional religion with its cultus of the divine voice in revelation, the phenomenon of mysticism came into its own. Scholem linked its rise to "the romantic period of religion." Mysticism, he wrote, "strives . . . to bring back the old unity which [institutional] religion has destroyed, but on a new plane, where the world of mythology and that of revelation meet in the soul of man." For the mystic, revelation becomes continuous, and "instead of the one act of Revelation, there is a constant repetition of this act."[3]

In other words, mysticism recreates in a provisional way the diffused religion of the mythic age even as it incorporates the revelation of the institution through its appeal to a continuing inner voice. In so doing, mysticism, for want of a better word, "reprimitivizes" religion, conflates it with self and word and, therefore, in its amorphousness, also with society. Thus what can be read from one point of view as secularity may be seen from another as the diffuseness of a "reprimitivized" religious situation. In effect, mysticism can be the signal of an emerging modern ethnos. And if the

United States, which is less tied to the European past than the Europeans, could become the showcase of the modern, its embryonic national religion could come to exhibit an identifiable mystical quality. What remains is to locate the mysticism and, as much, to specify its American stamp.

• • •

Surely fundamentalists and representatives of the New Age make curious partners. They are openly hostile to each other: fundamentalists are decidedly more strident, but New Agers, for all their message of love and unity, are beginning to strike back. And the two groups preach strongly divergent religious messages not only in terms of doctrine but also as much in terms of enmity, at important places fundamentalists and New Agers converge. Looking to fundamentalists and New Agers for what they have in common may help us find what is rising from the "Phenix grave" of Europe and from much else.

Fundamentalism needs no introduction to readers, but it may be helpful to say a few introductory words about the metaphysical religion of the New Age. From one point of view this tradition is as old as Ralph Waldo Emerson, who disdained the "dry bones of the past" and wanted "a religion by revelation to us, and not the history of theirs [foregoing generations]." Beyond and after Emerson (and with a complex of causes), the birth of the New Age had been a standard millennial feature of the nineteenth-century metaphysical tradition. When it began its contemporary transmutation, first noticed in the 1970s, the New Age was born under the sign of the death of the Age of Pisces and the dawning of the Age of Aquarius— a time of peace, harmony, and universal brotherhood and sisterhood.[4]

Today, New Agers see a world in the midst of transformation and their great metaphor for religion is healing. In their way of thinking, healing includes but moves beyond the physical plane. It is forgiveness, a union between self and other and self and world, a reconciliation and binding up of wounds not unlike the healing of the Fisher King of Arthurian lore.[5] Thus, healing the self and healing the planet constitute the twofold agenda for the New Age movement. And if self and planet exist as one, so too, within the self, do body and mind. The continuity between matter and spirit insures a privileging of nature and environment and a preference for the feminine, the dimension of the human that is seen as most in touch with nature and with natural values. The sciences—the disciplines and data that deal with matter—are no enemy to the New Age: the movement welcomes what can transform both planet and private consciousness.

Meanwhile, in an eclecticism that is characteristic, New Agers pick and choose among beliefs that emerge from sources including spiritualism (like channeling) and the New Thought movement (like mental healing and prosperity consciousness), from Native American spirituality (like shamanism and sweat lodge rituals) and Eastern religions (like karma and reincarnation), and even, for a few, from evangelical Christianity. Not everyone holds all of these or related beliefs or engages in all of these or related practices. But they are widely diffused among those who claim a stake in the New Age.

What can such a movement have in common with fundamentalism? How can those who are mostly either secular humanists or, worse still, from the fundamentalist perspective followers of idols and demons, share religious ground with conservative Protestant Christianity? Let me suggest a series of convergences even as I point to differences between the two movements.

To begin, for both, personal transformation and direct spiritual experience are at the heart of one's life project, and, for both, private transformation must find its twin in the transformation of society. For fundamentalism, of course, personal transformation comes through the experience of conversion. For the New Age, it comes often more diffusely through one of a number of transformational events: meditation, bodywork, the discipline of the popular *Course in Miracles*, old-fashioned prayer, to name a few. For fundamentalism, societal transformation means conscious public effort to bring about an ordered world that harks back to an imputed era of wholesomeness and holiness. Such a world is a place where the family reigns supreme, with sexual ethic intact, and the God of Christianity is acknowledged in government and schools. For the New Age, societal transformation means an evolving planet in which green politics and eco-feminism are matched by a new economic distribution system and a politics of cooperation and peace. The planet is a place in which earth values are emphasized and creation is more important than redemption.

Both fundamentalists and New Agers hear voices more than see visions: their mysticism comes clad in a rhetoric of newness that is expressed as ongoing revelation. For fundamentalists, the word of the gospel continues in and through the private experience of the new birth. Conversations with Jesus are real and potent. Fundamentalists have them out loud, and preachers regularly report their content to congregations in rural churches or in television studios. New Agers hear the word in channeled messages or in the voice of intuition. They travel in body to places where heightened earth energy increases their ability to hear and answer. They travel in mind through hypnotic regressions that help them to recall past lives or through shamanic journeys that increase their sense of mastery.

Both fundamentalists and New Agers stress healing: fundamentalists notably in the deliverance tradition of their Holiness-Pentecostal sector; New Agers in their overriding concerns for holistic health and positive affirmation and thinking. In both fundamentalism and the New Age, a kind of ontological positivism predominates, linking both to the religious materialism they share. God is matter, they seem to say implicitly; embracing God means, however obliquely, embracing the world. For fundamentalists, the positivism is expressed in the exaltation of the literal in the Bible, so that literal reading becomes itself a symbolic test and quality. For New Agers, the positivism is expressed in a literalism of reincarnation and past lives, of lost continents in Atlantis and Lemuria, of channeled contact with spirit entities.

The "new voluntarism" of fundamentalism and the New Age is expressed in the popular, non-elite, do-it-yourself quality that characterizes both. Indeed, perhaps a major reason why they arouse the ire of professionals in the denominational middle is because they are sociological upstarts, untrained to ministry, untutored in the seminary tradition of most of the mainline. Clearly, both groups—fundamentalism and New Agers—are celebrators of spiritual democracy. Their mysticism is a mysticism discovered in action and deed, created by language and shaped by the rhetorical "falling forward" that Harold Bloom identified with Emerson. And for both the falling forward is fall into the millennium: for fundamentalists, in the end, in the premillennial voice of the returned Jesus; for New Agers, in their inheritance of postmillennial call.

• • •

My sketch must end, and I fear that it will please none. Surely fundamentalists who regard New Agers as messengers of the Devil cannot take delight in similarity. And surely New Agers, who see in fundamentalism a religion of fear, can hardly be glad. Meanwhile, from the ranks of the collapsed middle, representatives of the old mainline, disdaining the mystical and the metaphysical as well as the fundamentalists and the New Age, will not cheer. But fundamentalists and New Agers are not likely to disappear in the near future. Even given the difficulties of the interpretive and predictive tasks, seeing them together may tell us more about an emerging national ethnos than seeing either group alone.

Philip Schaff thought that the wild ferment of the American experiment would "bring forth fruit for the weal or woe of generations to come." "All is yet in a chaotic transition state," he wrote. "But organizing energies are already present, and the spirit of God broods over them, to speak in time the almighty word: 'Let there be light!' and to call forth the chaos a beautiful creation." It is appropriate to conclude with Schaff's words.

ENDNOTES

1. Philip Schaff, *America: A Sketch of Its Political, Social, and Religious Character,* ed. Perry Miller (Cambridge, MA, 1961), 51, 46, 71, 80-81.
2. Wade Clark Roof and William McKinney, *American Mainline Religion: Its Changing Shape and Future* (New Brunswick, NJ, 1987), 4, 168-70.
3. I borrow the phrase "nexus between mysticism and modernity" from David Biale, *Gershom Scholem: Kabbalah and Counter-History,* 2d ed. (Cambridge, MA, 1982), 146. Gershom G. Scholem, *Major Trends in Jewish Mysticism* (1954; reprint, New York, 1972), 7-9.

4. J. Gordon Melton, *Encyclopedic Handbook of Cults in America* (New York, 1986), 107-21; Marilyn Ferguson, *The Aquarian Conspiracy: Personal and Social Transformation in the 1980s* (Los Angeles, 1980).
5. Jessie L. Weston, *From Ritual to Romance* (1920; rprt., Garden City, NY, 1957), esp. 13-24.

FOR FURTHER READING

Albanese, Catherine L. *Corresponding Motion: Transcendental Religion and the New America*, Philadelphia, 1977.

Bednarowkski, Mary Farell. *Many Paths to Heaven's Gate: New Religions and the Theological Imagination in American Culture*, Bloomington, IN, 1989.

Bloom, Harold. *The American Religion: The Emergence of the Post-Christian Nation*, New York, 1992.

Butler, Jon. *Awash in a Sea of Faith: Christianizing the American People*, Cambridge, MA, 1990.

Ellwood, Robert S. *Alternative Alters*, Chicago, 1979.

———. *The Sixties Spiritual Awakening: American Religion Moving from Modern to Postmodern*, New Brunswick, NJ, 1994.

Flowers, Ronald B. *Religion in Strange Times: The 1960s and 1970s*, Macon, GA, 1984.

Frankiel, Sandra Sizer. *Spiritual Frontiers: Religious Alternatives in Anglo-Protestantism, 1850–1910*, Berkeley, 1988.

Kerr, Howard, and Charles L. Crow, eds. *The Occult in America: New Historical Perspectives*, Urbana, IL, 1983.

Roof, Wade Clark. *A Generation of Seekers: The Spiritual Journeys of the Baby Boom Generation*, San Francisco, 1993.

Stark, Rodney, and William Sims Bainbridge, *The Future of Religion: Secularization, Revival, and Cult Formation*, Berkeley, 1985.

Wuthnow, Robert. *The Restructuring of American Religion: Society and Faith Since World War II*, Princeton, 1988.

INTRODUCTION TO ESSAY 22

Missionary outreach has been a major theme in every decade of American religious history. And, as Bendroth has already made clear, women have figured heavily in these evangelical efforts. In the reading here we learn more about each of these important aspects of mainstream denominational activity. Foreign missions offered women opportunities still denied them at home, but as White discloses, prejudices still remained. Female devotion to duty in the face of such discrimination makes their selfless activities even more remarkable.

White shows us several basic patterns in missionary work: the special sense of vocation or calling which most envoys felt, the constant dilemma over whether cultural change should be part of Christianization, and the difficulty in deciding whether there were strains of imperialism alongside altruism in the motives behind such work. Beyond those constants, we are given many specifics about individuals who labored during the nineteenth century. We learn about efforts in China, Burma, and the Near East. Women with auxiliary status, doing the same work but receiving less compensation, formed the mainstay of missionary outposts. Their dedication to a cause forms a notable chapter in the chronicle of American churches and their impact on the world around them.

Original source - CH 57 (1988): 19-30.

22

Counting the Cost of Faith
America's Early Female Missionaries

Ann White

America's first unmarried female missionaries, women who went out to Asia and Africa in the early to middle nineteenth century, chose lives as intense and demanding as any man's. They chose the foreign mission vocation despite the belief, strong in their era, that women should accept the constraints and comforts of their "proper sphere," the home. To make their decision, these women struggled with two sets of ideas which coexisted in tension: equality of all persons before God, and the ideology of "woman's sphere." As persons of faith they could respond to God's commands in the same way as men without theological challenge, because equality of all persons before God was a major strand in their Christian tradition. As nineteenth-century women, however, they were asked to accept lowered status and protective restrictions, in keeping with woman's sphere ideology. These women chose to become missionaries, compromising on second-class status and protective restrictions. In their view, the missionary vocation was worth the cost of compromise.

The unmarried women missionaries were neither the first nor the only American women to go out to the mission field in the early nineteenth century. The American Board of Commissioners for Foreign Missions (ABCFM), the first American sending agency, sent married men from the beginning, believing that men should not be asked to go abroad without wives and that Christian family life was part of an effective missionary witness. Ann Hasseltine Judson, the most famous American woman missionary of the nineteenth century, was a missionary wife, a member of the very first group of five missionaries and three wives sent out by the infant ABCFM in 1812. Missionary wives confronted a difficult situation. They worked hard on the mission field but received no compensation and little recognition for their effort. This essay, however, focuses on unmarried women, who decided for themselves, apart from family commitments, to pursue the missionary vocation.

• • •

These women assumed their equality with all other persons before God, an idea which goes back from the Second Great Awakening through Puritan divines, Reformation leaders, and apostles, to Jesus himself. In Puritan New England, ministers gave their daughters the same spiritual counsel they offered to their sons; their sermons assumed the equality of women's and men's souls before God. Women of the Second Great Awakening, which brought religious renewal to New England, upstate New York, and the western frontier in the years 1790–1840, similarly assumed spiritual equality when they went to prayer meetings and joined congregations independently of their families.[1] The early female missionaries were daughters of the Second Great Awakening; the pivotal experience in their lives was the quickening of faith and its public profession when they joined a particular congregation. Most of the ABCFM's unmarried women missionaries were young when they professed their faith, in their teens or early twenties. In their youthfulness, in the quickening of their faith, and in their sense of urgency about preaching the Gospel in foreign lands, they paralleled exactly the experience of the young male Christians of their generation. It was, after all, four young male seminarians who prodded their elders in the church to found the ABCFM in 1810 out of their deeply felt conviction that foreign missions was a necessary task of the church. Eliza Gillette, who in 1820 made her public profession of faith in a New Haven Episcopal Church at the age of sixteen, wrote of having experienced spiritual surrender to God and of concluding that to be a missionary to the heathen was the "highest honor that can be conferred upon a Christian." She aspired to this honor for herself and nurtured her aspiration for twenty-two years while she worked to support her widowed mother. In 1843 she went to China as an Episcopal missionary. She did not consider that her religious experience and call to the missionary vocation were qualified in any way by her sex.

No early nineteenth-century churchman tried to say that a woman's religious experience or decision was less valid than a man's. On the other hand, "woman's sphere" ideology circumscribed women's opportunities to live out the practical implications of their faith. According to notions of woman's sphere, female moral powers and religious sensibilities were utilized best in the Christian home, where women's delicacy and refinement could be protected from the coarse "bank note world."[2] Thus women were completely closed out of the ordained ministry and also out of full "missionary" status on the foreign field, since this status belonged only to ordained ministers. Could women, however, hope to become "assistant missionaries" in the field, as were the printers, doctors, and missionaries' wives? No, said Rufus Anderson, who became Secretary of the ABCFM in 1823 and whose forty-three-year tenure in that position saw him emerge as the most significant strategist and administrator of an expanding American foreign mission movement. Anderson argued not on theological but on practical, "woman's sphere," grounds, stating that unmarried women should not live alone and unprotected in foreign lands. The only acceptable living arrangement was residence with another missionary family, which Anderson thought would be awkward unless they were relatives or intimate friends.

From its beginning in the second decade of the nineteenth century to the end of the century, the American foreign mission movement grew from a handful of missionaries sent by two agencies, the ABCFM and a Baptist society founded in 1814, to an enterprise incorporating hundreds of local and national societies with more than four thousand missionaries in the field. The great spurt in numbers of missionaries occurred in the last three decades of the century, but the organizational basis for this growth was laid in the pre–Civil War decades with the establishment of denominational organizations that were national in scope and that sent out gradually increasing numbers of missionaries. Unmarried female missionaries participated in this growth: at least ninety-three unmarried women were sent to Asia and Africa as missionaries by denominational agencies through 1870, thirty-eight before 1850, and fifty-five more in the next two decades. Baptists sent the very first, Charlotte White, who went to Burma in 1815. The ABCFM, which represented Congregationalist, Reformed, and Presbyterian churches, did not send out an unmarried woman until Cynthia Farrar went to India in 1827. After this beginning, however, it sent more unmarried women than the rest of the denominations combined: twenty-three before 1850 and thirty-three more by 1870. Baptists sent at least five single women in this period; the Methodists sent fifteen. Eight unmarried women were sent out by Presbyterian churches which supported their own board rather than the ABCFM. The Episcopalians sent at least three unmarried women before 1870. The size of this group has been dwarfed by the large number of missionary wives and of unmarried women who went out in the last three decades of the century. In comparison with these later numbers, the early unmarried women missionaries were only a handful of women, but a somewhat larger handful than has been supposed.[3]

Like their male counterparts, the early female missionaries wished to proclaim the Christian gospel. But they knew they would have no formal opportunity to do so. They were not ordained, and they were officially recognized on the mission field only in their role as teachers of native girls. With the burgeoning of the missionary movement in the post–Civil War years, however, enterprising women looked for and sometimes found opportunities to proclaim their faith in personal conversations or to informally assembled crowds in village streets.

Mary Andrews, who went out to the ABCFM's North China Mission in 1868, wrote that village work was the most arduous and also the most rewarding work she had ever done. It was physically arduous because the missionaries traveled from village to village by foot or on uncomfortable animals or carts. It was emotionally and intellectually arduous because they had to master a strange language and then use it to present Christian ideas. Sometimes they complained of the difficulties. Adelia Payson wrote in 1869 from Foochow, China, that she was studying four hours a day to learn Chinese (a "barbarous tongue"), and that she had to do so in "disagreeably noisy" quarters in the same building as the mission school. However, the bulk of these women's correspondence conveys an impression not of querulousness but of satisfaction with demanding and interesting work.

The women missionaries of course were expected to teach. As Rufus Anderson put it, "A good Protestant Christian [seeks] to give the Bible to the people." His mission strategy, which influenced the entire American missionary movement, saw schools as essential tools for teaching the Bible and the basics of the Christian faith. In missions to heathen civilizations, the missionaries dealt mostly with lower-class people, none of whom could read. In missions to Oriental Christian churches, such as the Nestorians, men might be able to read but women could not. Schools had to be founded to teach the people to read the Bible in their native languages.

American Protestant women, who were officially considered partners in this one aspect of mission life (though not in others), sought to accomplish their educational goal by bringing the female seminary to the Orient. Almost all of them had attended female academies in the United States; 10 percent had gone to Mount Holyoke, where headmistress Mary Lyon spoke daily of the importance of missions and posted missionary maps in her classrooms.[4] They adapted the institution to heathen lands, beginning in Asia with the Uduville School for Girls at the ABCFM mission in Ceylon, and in Africa with Methodist Ann Wilkins's Millsburgh Female Academy in Liberia. From the Eski Zagra School in European Turkey to Eliza Bridgman's school in Peking, female missionaries invited native parents to send their daughters to Christian schools. They taught in different languages and confronted differences in local customs, but they faced broadly similar problems. Persian parents, who customarily betrothed their daughters at age twelve, worried that an educated Christian girl would not get a husband. Chinese parents expressed the same fear, especially when missionary schoolmistresses suggested that they unbind their daughters' feet before sending them to school. Turkish parents begrudged the expense of a daughter's education. But perseverance brought a small growth in numbers of students. ABCFM missionary Fidelia Fiske reported a typical increase in enrollment when she wrote that the girls' school in Urumiah, Persia, which she had taken over in 1843 as a day school with three students, in 1853 as a boarding seminary enrolled forty-eight female students.

Why did the missionaries persevere in the face of such meager success? The answer lies in their image of Christian missions, shaped in the third and fourth decades of the nineteenth century by Rufus Anderson for the ABCFM but held also by Methodists and Baptists, and by male and female missionaries alike. In this view, which was based on the model of the apostle Paul, a missionary proclaims and teaches the Gospel, organizes small native churches, and then moves on, without expecting to "Christianize" or reform society. Devoid of cultural imperialism, this perspective trusted the power of Christian faith to transform individual lives and thus affect society.[5] Anderson argued very forcefully for the spiritual thrust of missions; he told the missionaries to focus on founding native churches and to eschew efforts to change native culture.

This view of missions shaped the organization of the girls' boarding schools, which were intended to equip native women to read the Bible, talk about it, and teach others to read it. The missionary headmistresses established "very simple plan[s] of study": reading, writing, arithmetic, grammar, and geography, taught in the native language. The girls were expected to keep "native habits of dress and modes of living," with a strong orientation toward neatness, order, and a sense of responsibility learned in the performance of daily chores. At the Uduville school, for example, older girls swept the mission house (under the supervision of missionary ladies) while the younger ones swept the schoolrooms and dormitories and "ground curry stuffs and coconuts for the day." Getting up at five and going to bed at eight were both accompanied by prayer, Bible reading and recitation, and the singing of hymns. Always the emphasis was on teaching the girls to read in their native language. Whether it was Arabic, Chinese, or Tamil, the missionaries learned it and used it, because they believed the vernacular was the best medium through which to establish native churches.

Both female and male missionaries agreed that girls' schools should serve the overall mission strategy, and both agreed that, as a male missionary in Syria put it, "there is the same capacity in the female mind of the country, that there is in the male." The object, then, was to enroll girls who showed promise of becoming valuable helpers in the missionary enterprise; daughters of Protestant parents often were considered the best candidates. The enrollment of large numbers of students was not the primary goal.

There was a difference of emphasis between this outlook and the literature which American churchwomen published, beginning in the 1860s, to solicit support for the commissioning of female missionaries. This literature announced that "woman's work for woman" on the mission field was intended to ennoble and uplift the degraded lives of women of the East. Women in the field, however, took a practical approach and rarely talked about ennobling womanhood. "Zenana work," talking to secluded Indian women, figured prominently in the promotional literature, so prominently that the Woman's Union Missionary Society was referred to as the "Zenana Missionary Society." Not all women missionaries in the field, however, considered Zenana work the best use of their resources; they believed that Indian women would never escape their husbands' domination and that it was better to focus attention on the daughters. The early women missionaries in China took a similarly pragmatic approach to foot binding. They discouraged parents from binding their daughters' feet and gave talks to young men explaining their opposition to the practice. But they declined to make a "rigid law" requiring every girl entering their schools to unbind her feet.[6] Their goal was to proclaim the Gospel in whatever ways seemed possible.

The women missionaries forsook the confines and the comforts of "woman's sphere" at home and pursued their vocation with energy, intelligence, and realism. But they paid the price of the compromises they had made to get to the mission field. Their "assistant" status allowed male missionaries and mission organization officials to devalue their work. Unmarried female assistant missionaries were paid less than married and unmarried men. The 1846 list of estimated expenses for the ABCFM's Nestorian Mission allowed $600 for each male missionary with a family, $400 for a single man, and $200 for a single woman. The

Methodists in 1847 paid a single male China missionary a $500 salary but sent sisters Beulah and Sarah Woolston to China in 1858 with salaries of $300 each. "Niggardliness" toward women missionaries is illustrated in the ABCFM's refusal to accept the request of widow Martha Wyman to be reappointed as a missionary in her own right at the Ceylon mission, where her husband had served until his fatal illness. Ignoring her experience and commitment, the board followed the mission secretary's recommendation that married women at the station (who were unpaid, of course) could run the school that Mrs. Wyman had been superintending before she left to accompany her sick husband back home. Willing to accept her unpaid labor, the board would not pay her for the same work when she no longer had a husband to support her.

Churchwomen back home thus had a clear agenda: provide adequate financial support for unmarried female missionaries. They began to do so with great success, through the Woman's Union Missionary Society and through the denominational women's societies, all of which published literature proclaiming the importance of "woman's work for woman." Such literature, though not always aligned with goals on the mission field, was right on target among American churchwomen, who opened their pocketbooks to send single women missionaries abroad. In some cases this money meant a real difference in comfort for the missionary women. The women's Foreign Missionary Society of the Methodist Church set salaries for their first two missionaries at a generous $750, much to the consternation of the male Methodist Board of Managers. However, Methodist women maintained a degree of control over their funds which other women's societies may not have been able to achieve. Presbyterian and ABCFM women missionaries continued to worry over who would pay for their outfit and equipment: their denomination's women's society or the male-directed denominational mission agency. They sometimes feared that money would be siphoned off from their girls' school for other expenses, and they complained that their salaries were not enough to live on when they came home for furlough or to recover from illness.[7]

• • •

Why did these women decide to become missionaries, when it meant low salaries and uncomfortably restrictive living conditions? Surely they went for the challenge and with a strong sense of purpose, for breadth and intensity of experience. Their decision to become missionaries was a decision for a lifetime vocation, not a brief tour of duty. Most of them would not go so far as Eliza Agnew, ABCFM missionary in Ceylon, who never took home furlough in forty years of missionary service, preferring to travel about the mission stations on her vacations. But as they gathered together their equipment ("saddle, bridle, and riding sticks, a stove, shovel, tongs, and bellows . . . writing-desk, portfolio, and large supply of stationery"), they knew that they were making a major and permanent change in their way of life. Increased organizational and financial support made it possible for post–Civil War missionaries to expect to come home from time to time on furlough. But even in this later period, and certainly in the earlier years, all the missionaries knew that hazards of travel and disease meant they might never see family and friends again.

The deeper element of the missionaries' sense of adventure was their belief that they were part of a larger Christian enterprise in which they were obedient servants of God. The early nineteenth-century emphasis on obedience, without thought of reward or result, gave way in the last three decades of the century to a concern with social improvement on the mission field. "Woman's work for woman" was part of this philosophy of social transformation, and it became as vulnerable as the rest of the American missionary enterprise to charges of cultural imperialism.[8] From the 1820s through the 1860s, male and female missionaries had seen themselves simply as communicators of the gospel who had come to found native churches among the heathen. Men did not see themselves as transformers of culture, nor did women see themselves as ennoblers of womanhood. As narrowly evangelical as this approach sounds to more modern ears, it had the advantage of being less patronizing to the native heathen than the social transformation approach. It also gave the female missionaries an equality of purpose which transcended their shabby treatment as "assistant" missionaries. No less than the men, they were obedient servants of the God who had commanded that the Gospel be preached throughout the world.

This understanding of the missionary as obedient servant gave the women freedom from taking themselves too seriously. They worked hard and hoped for results but were not disillusioned when their schools had few pupils, or girls' feet remained bound, or their own male colleagues treated them as inferior beings. Contrary to stereotypes based on later missionary attitudes, early nineteenth-century women missionaries were not earnest, humorless people. They were saved from excessively earnest seriousness about themselves by their focus on fidelity and obedience to God and their belief that God, and not they, would produce the results. In this larger view of things, they were completely equal to male missionaries, no matter in how many petty ways men might see to devalue their work.

America's earliest unmarried women missionaries paid the price which woman's sphere ideology exacted, even in distant lands. For them, the value of the missionary vocation exceeded the cost of demeaningly low status and salary and the discomforts of restricted living conditions. They understood the cost of their faith, paid it willingly, and, for them, "woman's sphere" became the world.

ENDNOTES

1. Mary P. Ryan, "A Women's Awakening: Evangelical Religion and the Families of Utica, New York, 1800–1840," in *Women in American Religion*, ed. Janet Wilson James (Philadelphia, 1980), 89-110.
2. The Phrase is Sarah Hale's in the *Ladies Magazine*. For a discussion of "women's sphere," especially Protestant ministers' views on it, see Nancy Cott, *The Bonds of Womanhood: Women's Sphere in New England, 1780–1835* (New Haven, 1977), 61-62, 157-59.
3. Past estimates have been as low as ten unmarried women before 1861. See Barbara Welter, "She Hath Done What She Could: Protestant Women's Missionary Careers in Nineteenth-Century America," in *Women in American Religion*, 114.
4. Edward Hitchcock, *The Power of Christian Benevolence Illustrated in the Life and Labors of Mary Lyon*, 3d ed. (Northampton, 1852), 358-62.

5. Wade Cawford Barclay, *History of the Methodist Missions,* 4 vols. (New York, 1948–1973), 3:160; Robert G. Torbet, *Venture of Faith: The Story of the American Baptist Foreign Mission Society and the Woman's American Baptist Foreign Mission Society, 1814–1953* (Philadelphia, 1955), 122-23.

6. Typescript biography of Mary E. Andrews in Sarah Boardman Goodrich papers, China Record Group, Yale Divinity School Library, ABCFM: North China Mission, Letter of Mary H. Porter, 24 February 1880.

7. Patricia Hill, *Their World Their Household: The American Woman's Foreign Mission Movement and Cultural Transformation, 1870–1920* (Ann Arbor, 1985), 46-54.

8. Adrian A. Bennett, "Doing More Than They Intended," in *Women in New Worlds: Historical Perspectives on the Wesleyan Tradition,* ed. Rosemary Skinner Keller, Louise L. Queen, and Hilah F. Thomas, 2 vols. (Nashville, 1982), 2:249-67; Charles W. Forman, "A Brief History of Foreign Mission Theory in America," in *American Missions in Bicentennial Perspective,* ed. R. Pierce Beaver (South Pasadena, 1977), 69-140.

FOR FURTHER READING

Beaver, R. Pierce. *American Protestant Women in World Mission: A History of the First Feminist Movement in North America,* Grand Rapids, MI, 1968.

Boydston, Jeanne, Mary Kelly, and Anne Margolis. *The Limits of Sisterhood: The Beecher Sisters on Women's Rights and Woman's Sphere,* Chapel Hill, NC, 1988.

Brumberg, Joan Jacobs. *Mission for Life: The Story of the Family of Adoniram Judson,* New York, 1980.

Carpenter, Joel A. *Earthen Vessels: American Evangelicals and Foreign Mission,* Grand Rapids, MI, 1990.

Douglas, Ann. *The Feminization of American Culture,* New York, 1977.

Hassey, Janette. *No Time for Silence: Evangelical Women in Public Ministry Around the Turn of the Century,* Grand Rapids, MI, 1986.

Hunter, Jane. *The Gospel of Gentility: American Women Missionaries in Turn-of-the-Century China,* New Haven, 1984.

Hutchison, William R. *Errand to the World: American Protestant Thought and Foreign Missions,* Chicago, 1987.

McDannell, Colleen. *The Christian Home in Victorian America, 1840–1900,* Bloomington, IN, 1986.

Philips, Clifton Jackson. *Protestant America and the Pagan World: The First Half Century of the American Board of Commissioners for Foreign Missions, 1810–1860*, Cambridge, MA, 1969.

Sweet, Leonard I. *The Minister's Wife: Her Role in Nineteenth-Century American Evangelicalism*, Philadelphia, 1983.

INTRODUCTION TO ESSAY 23

Although Methodists arrived on these shores late in the colonial period, they quickly grew to become one of America's largest denominations. Hatch describes Methodism as "the most dramatic social movement between the Revolution and the Civil War," and proceeds to use it as a gauge for studying all religions in this country. First, he makes some helpful observations about the study of religion as a respectable discipline, concluding ironically that Methodism is often neglected in such inquiries because the group is just too American to be noticed. He argues that as a denominationally loyal group, not given to intellectual rigor nor active in most social reforms, Methodists epitomize the average American and should not be ignored as simply part of the background which history often takes for granted.

In a rapid, compact summary we find here many of the factors that made Methodism successful during the past two centuries. Its use of lay preachers and itinerancy played a part; Arminian theology rather than Calvinism appealed to many; interracial congregations and elements of folk religion also enhanced church growth. In his chosen topic Hatch gives us four traits which he sees as characteristic of American religion in general: Methodists thrived on competition and voluntary support; they made religion part of popular culture; an emphasis on money and individualism corresponded to a mercantile frame of mind; and a malleability regarding cultural influences allowed the denomination to keep up with changing national trends. This practical, down-to-earth religious perspective illuminates a great deal about central traits in American life.

Original source - CH 63 (1994): 175-89.

23

The Puzzle of American Methodism

Nathan O. Hatch

Picture, if you will, the rich landscape of American religious history that has taken shape over the last half century. At least three features of this terrain stand out, the first being a richly textured panorama before us, a recognizable field of study that has come into existence in a relatively short span of time. This field has been shaped by a variety of forces, among them the vast expansion of religion departments since 1960, the recovery of the role of religion in the broader disciplines of history, literature, sociology, and political science, and the stubborn persistence of religion in modern American life which scholars struggle to explain.

A second feature of this terrain worth noting is the coherence of the background, the distinct set of towering peaks that frame the discussion on religion in America. Most historians linked the study of religion tightly to intellectual history, and most shared a basic story line of American religious development following a Puritan-turned-mainline-Protestant form of Christianity—in Winthrop Hudson's phrase, "the great tradition of the American churches."[1] They were also consensualists, believing in a common American character, and most held a positive, affirmative reading of the overall achievement of American culture and its religion. Until the mid-1960s, it is safe to say, the canon of American religious history was surprisingly uniform and coherent. Its primary institutional base remained divinity schools at elite universities, its institutional focus the intellectual history of American mainline Protestants.

Since the 1960s, a clash of convictions about the meaning of America has undermined the coherent and affirmative reading of the American religious experience. Instead of studying insiders, we have turned to study outsiders, subcultures, and the vast population of women, Native Americans, and African Americans that the consensus school overlooked or subordinated to the main story of American religion. Fresh studies have poured forth on

Pentecostalism, Holiness groups, and Fundamentalism, on Mormonism and Adventists and Shakers, on occultists and spiritualists, on Native American religion and nature religion, and on Roman Catholics of every ethnic stripe. This pluralistic enterprise has worked to redeem those on the margins and has shattered the dominant canon for American religious history. This scholarly ferment has been a creative, invigorating process, and it is far from complete.

Amidst all of this study of insiders and outsiders, of religion elite and popular, one glaring omission becomes apparent. It is the lack of attention given to American Methodism. More accurately, what I find surprising is the lack of interest in studying American Methodists, both among religious historians and the broader historical community. The result is that most American historians predictably treat Methodism blandly and uninspiringly as a component of the western phase of the Second Great Awakening. The subject never quite comes into focus and the Methodists, as historical actors, appear either as mere imitators or as faceless representatives of surging revivalism. In teaching a course covering the period from the Revolution to the Civil War, one would have trouble thinking of a single imaginative treatment that could be assigned, save Donald Mathews's book, *Methodism and Slavery*, or Timothy Smith's *Revivalism and Social Reform*.[2] There are few arresting biographies, compelling local studies, or renditions of Methodist ideology, no study of Methodists and the revolution in print communications, or overall treatments of the development of Methodism as an organization, or of its spirituality, and its music.

The theme of this essay is the puzzle of American Methodism—why and for what reasons the meteoric rise of Methodism in America has so little attraction for scholars. After exploring the significance of Methodism's explosive growth between the Revolution and the Civil War, the article will suggest why historians have been largely inoculated from interest in the subject. It will also argue that Methodism far more than Puritanism offers insight into the distinct character of religious life in the United States.

• • •

The explosive growth of the Methodist Episcopal Church was the most surprising development in a republic that turned its back on state-sponsored religion. The American followers of John Wesley, who could boast no more than four ministers and three hundred lay people in 1771, were threatened with extinction during the Revolution. All their leaders, save Francis Asbury, returned to England, leaving the Methodist faithful to struggle with the stigma of disloyalty throughout the war.

Under the tireless direction of Asbury, the Methodists advanced from Canada to Georgia emphasizing three themes that Americans found captivating: God's free grace, the liberty of people to accept or reject that grace, and the power and validity of popular religious expression—even among servants, women, and African Americans. Led by unlearned preachers committed to sacrifice and to travel, the Methodists organized local classes or cells and preaching circuits at a rate that alarmed more respectable denominations. When Asbury died in 1816, he could claim over two thousand ministers and two hundred thousand Methodist members.

Between 1776 and 1850 the Methodists in America achieved a virtual miracle of growth, rising from less than 3 percent of all church members in 1776 to more than 34 percent by 1850, making them far and away the largest religious body in the nation and the most extensive national institution other than the Federal government. Methodist growth terrified other more established denominations. By the middle of the nineteenth century, Methodists boasted four thousand itinerants, almost eight thousand local preachers, and over a million members. It was nearly one-half size larger than any other Protestant body and could muster more than ten times the preaching force of the Congregationalists, who in 1776 had double the number of clergy of any other church. By 1850, in a nation where only 25 to 30 percent of the people claimed any religious affiliation, almost one in fifteen Americans belonged to a Methodist church (1.5 million out of 23 million).[3]

The Methodists enjoyed great strategic advantage in the free-religious economy of a westward-moving nation which was increasingly suspicious of the pretensions of educated professionals—

lawyers, physicians, and clergymen. The Methodists could function anywhere. Boasting almost no college-educated clergy among their thousands of circuit riders and local preachers before 1840, the Methodists exploded in the American backcountry from Maine and the hill country of Vermont to Tennessee and Kentucky, Ohio and Indiana. Most Congregational ministers, educated at Yale, Harvard, and Dartmouth, simply chose to remain and serve congregations in "civilized" areas. While Methodism retained a stronghold in the seaports of the middle states, Asbury hammered its organization into one that had a distinct rural orientation, adept at expanding into thinly populated areas.

Methodism in America transcended class barriers and empowered common people to make religion their own. Unlike Calvinism, which emphasized human corruption, divine initiative, and the authority of educated clergymen and inherited ecclesiastical structures, the Methodists proclaimed the breathtaking message of individual freedom, autonomy, responsibility, and achievement. More African Americans became Christians in ten years of Methodist preaching than in a century of Anglican influence. Methodism did not suppress the impulses of popular religion, dreams and visions, ecstasy, unrestrained emotional release, preaching by blacks, by women, by anyone who felt the call. It was under Methodist auspices that religious folk music—white and black spirituals—prospered.

Methodism fostered social mobility. The movement appealed to petty bourgeoisie, people on the make. While Methodist hierarchy may have seemed out of step with the democratic stirrings of the times, the vital spring of Methodism under Francis Asbury was to make Christianity profoundly a faith of the people. From preachers like themselves, people received an invitation to join a movement promising dignity of choice and beckoning them to involvement as class leader, exhorter, local preacher, and circuit rider. Lay preaching, the hallmark of American Methodism, served as a powerful symbol that the wall between gentlemen and commoner had been shattered. Methodism had great appeal for upstarts who hungered for respect and opportunity.

As a movement, Methodism became a powerful symbol of social

mobility, a beacon of aspiring respectability. Leaders like Nathan Bangs and Wilbur Fisk, who began their ministry defiantly outside the religious establishment, later aspired to educational respectability, social standing, and genteel refinement—the former as an urbane New Yorker, the latter, as president of Wesleyan University.[4] Between 1840 and 1860, the Methodists founded at least thirty-five institutions of higher education. Between the Civil War and 1900, they founded more than one college or university per year. By 1852, eleven of thirteen congressmen from Indiana were Methodists, as well as the governor and one senator. By 1870, twenty-four of thirty-seven states, including ten of the original thirteen colonies, had been governed by a Methodist. In 1880, no denomination could claim the affiliation of more governors than the Methodists. The heirs of Wesley sealed their place as the nation's largest and wealthiest Protestant body in 1896 with the election of Methodist William McKinley, the presidential candidate clearly favored by the wealthy and powerful.

• • •

Why have scholars found this phenomenal mass movement so uninteresting, so unworthy of attention? Why do we know more about the dynamics of the growth of Fundamentalism and of Pentecostalism, even of Adventism, Mormonism, and the Shakers, than about what was the most dramatic social movement between the Revolution and the Civil War? Several other considerations multiply the force of this question. A problem of sources does not deflect interest in the subject. Methodists were inveterate record keepers and journal writers, and they pioneered the widespread use of the religious press. They were Puritan-like in their obsessive self-chronicling. Why has no one exploited Methodist newspapers, journals, and tracts to trace evolving ideologies within the movement?

The lack of attention to American Methodism is also hard to understand given the renewed interest of scholars in the early American Republic. Once neglected, this field currently may have become the most fertile and dynamic in American historical studies. Historians are currently probing the complicated dynamics of how the republican society of the founding fathers and of artisans and local farmers became the liberal, competitive, market-oriented democracy of the age of Jackson. The most burning questions in early American history concern the emergence of capitalism.[5] How does Methodism, the largest social movement of the period, bear upon these issues?

It is also curious that so few feminist scholars have found Methodist sources intriguing. Given the dynamic and entrepreneurial character of early Methodism, the movement provided far greater opportunities for women as active participants. Even if Methodists gave official recognition to very few women preachers, they actively encouraged female speaking and exhorting, even pausing in their sermons to allow inspired women to speak. As Catherine Brekus has pointed out in her recent study on female preaching, the Methodists valued inspiration over theological training and thus gave many more women public leadership roles in exhorting, praying, singing, and witnessing to their own dreams and visions.[6] The same is true if one wishes to study African Americans as central actors in the unfolding of American Christianity. The development of black preaching and of the African American spiritual took place in a largely Methodist context, as did the formation of African American churches in the North.

Given these indications of Methodist significance, why have historians not given the movement a more central place? The omission follows three patterns that have shaped the writing of American religious history. The first and most far reaching is the tradition of studying Christianity largely as intellectual history. Churches typically have interpreted their own history in terms of the evolution of dogma, the development of historical theology. In twentieth-century America, this tendency has been reinforced by the orientation of American religious history to New England sources. If intellectual profundity is the standard for religious history, as it is for most who have studied the Puritans and Jonathan Edwards, then the rise of the Methodists may represent a dark age for the American intellect.[7]

The one attempt in this century to establish a graduate center that took Methodism seriously was short-lived. William Warren

Sweet, who labored at the University of Chicago to bring Methodist sources to light and to train graduate students in this area, was succeeded by Sidney Mead, an equally formidable scholar. But Mead's views of the Methodist contribution could not have been more diametrically opposed to Sweet's. In his highly suggestive set of essays, *The Lively Experiment*, Mead argued that the Revolutionary era is the hinge upon which American Christianity turns and that the Second Great Awakening terminated the Puritan and inaugurated the pietist or Methodist age of American church history. Yet Sidney Mead did not welcome the Methodist onslaught, a "great tidal wave of revivalism." Instead, he saw it as the end of what had been noble about American religion: it "effectively scuttled much of the intellectual structure of Protestantism." Thereafter he lamented, America produced no theology or theologian of the first rank. In the same vein, a student of American politics might decry everything after the age of Jackson because the nation never produced another Thomas Jefferson or John Adams.[8]

A second reason for the lack of compelling Methodist histories is that Methodist historians have had reasons to sanitize their histories. Modern church historians have chosen to focus on those aspects of their own heritage linked to cultural enrichment, institutional cohesion, and intellectual respectability. Other mainstream Protestant church historians in the twentieth century have also emphasized themes of Protestant solidarity and the church's role in taming the frontier. An unswerving commitment to the unity of the church has made it virtually impossible for church historians to admit that God's ultimate plans could entail the splintering of churches. In this scheme, there is plenty of room for Baptists and Methodists, but only as they shed sectarian dogmatism, ecstatic display, and aggressive proselytizing. Modern church historians, in short, have had difficulty identifying with dimensions of their own ecclesiastical heritage that are diametrically opposed to the modern embrace of intellectual, liturgical, and ecumenical respectability.[9]

No interpretive vision of American religion has arisen organized around Wesleyanism because it so clearly represents that which we take for granted about American society. The Methodist story, replete with perfectionism and cultural accommodation, seems bereft of a prophetic voice, lacks profound insight into the human condition, and is unable to suggest alternatives to the main channels in which American culture has flowed. Perhaps historians ignore Methodists because Wesleyans are too quintessentially American.

• • •

Methodists certainly deserve study like any other American denomination. Yet the movement also provides a crucial vantage point from which one can assess the characteristic dynamics of American religion. American Methodism, both in its initial flowering and in its institutional growth, is a superb window to understand the characteristic styles, dispositions, and reflexes of the American religious experience. Let me support this argument in four ways.

First, American Methodists reconstructed the church along voluntary lines and welcomed a plural and competitive religious environment. Puritanism grew out of a context of state-sponsored religion whereas Methodism sprang from the collapse of the monopolistic relationship of religion with the state and with the local community. Methodism aroused the voluntary conscience, calling people to break with religious ties that were hereditary and organic. As a movement of self-conscious outsiders, Methodists embraced the virtues of pluralism, of competition, and of marketing religion in every sphere of life, far beyond the narrow confines of ecclesiastical space. The Methodists invented the American denomination, making obsolete the European reality of church at the cultural center and sect at the periphery.

Second, the Methodists injected vernacular Christianity into the bloodstream of America, faith incarnate in popular culture. In an emerging democratic society, it was the Methodists more than anyone else who were responsible for making Christianity a mass enterprise. Everyday folk rather than college-educated gentlemen scrambled to claim the office of minister. Rejecting the standard reformed sermon, a read discourse with a stiff theological spine, Methodists crafted sermons that were audience-centered, vernacular, and extemporaneous. The resulting religious culture made revivalism a fixture of American religious life.

Third, Methodism resonated with the logic of capitalism and liberal individualism. In the early Republic, American society became engrossed in commerce and evangelical religion at the same time. Alexis de Tocqueville took note of this striking intermingling of God and mammon within the nation's soul: "I know of no country, indeed, where the love of money has taken stronger hold on the affections of men. . . . [t]here is no country in the world where the Christian religion retains a greater influence over the souls of men than in America."[10] It is the meteoric rise of American Methodism that offers insight into a society that was awash in religion and in making money—and confident of divine favor upon both endeavors. American Methodism was the prototype of a religious organization taking on market form.

Fourth, the Methodists represent religion in an extremely pliable and adaptable cultural form. Most first-generation Methodists were staunch Jeffersonians. Their children were mostly Whigs, although Methodists were scattered across the political spectrum. Early Methodists stoutly opposed slavery, and the first African American churches took shape in a Methodist context. White Methodists, as a whole, quickly backtracked on the issue with the result that one finds Wesleyans both as leading abolitionists and as leaders in the pro-slavery defense. As the number of Methodists expanded, what it meant to be Methodist became far less clear. Some Methodists continued the plain-style worship and perfectionism of the early camp meeting. By the 1850s others were building Gothic churches and folding gentility and refinement into the very definition of being religious.

Puritanism provides a great paradigm for understanding America, if one thinks of transcending ourselves, of imagining what might have been, of finding an alternative vision and source of strength to confront the unpleasant realities of American life. It is like relishing the age of the founding fathers and wishing American political debate had retained the sophistication and wisdom of Thomas Jefferson, John Adams, and James Madison. The story of Methodism tells us much more about American religion as it actually unfolded: not great, not sophisticated, not awe inspiring, but what it is.

What would American religious history look like if Methodists were nudged closer to the center? From the point of view of theology and educational institutions, Methodists were imitators and followers. Yet they were pacesetters from the point of view of popular mobilization, effective communication systems, participation of women, and empowerment of African Americans. If Methodists were moved to the foreground, we would learn more about class, status, and social structure within religious institutions. We would more readily understand religion as experience and community rather than as abstract ideas. We would comprehend more about how religion has functioned as a powerful instrument of popular education and of vertical mobility. Most important, we would regain a sense of surprise at the ways in which America came to be Christianized between the Revolution and the Civil War. And, in the process, we would gain insight into how religion has so tenaciously gripped the soul of Americans—those on the margins as well as those who have tasted success. The American conviction of the paramount importance of religious belief, whatever the kind, has a distinct Methodist ring to it.

ENDNOTES

1. The epitome of this tradition is Sydney E. Ahlstrom's brilliant synthesis, *A Religious History of the American People* (New Haven, 1972).
2. Donald G. Mathews, *Slavery and Methodism: A Chapter in American Morality: 1780–1845* (Princeton, 1965); Timothy L. Smith, *Revivalism and Social Reform: American Protestantism on the Eve of the Civil War* (New York, 1957).
3. Richard J. Carwardine, *Evangelicals and Politics in Antebellum America* (New Haven, 1993), 114-15.
4. Abel Stevens, *The Life of Nathan Bangs, D.D.* (New York, 1863); George Prentice, *Wilbur Fisk* (Boston, 1890).
5. Robert H. Wiebe, *The Opening of American Society: From the Adoption of the Constitution to the Eve of Disunion* (New York, 1984); Sean Wilentz, *Chants Democratic: New York City and the Rise of the American Working Class, 1788–1850* (New York, 1986); Joyce Appleby, *Capitalism and a New Social Order: The Republican Vision of the 1790s* (New York, 1984).
6. Catherine Brekus, "'Let Your Women Keep Silence in the Churches':

Female Preaching and Evangelical Religion in America, 1740–1845" (Ph.D. diss., Yale University, 1993).

7. Richard Hofstadter, *Anti-Intellectualism in America* (New York, 1963); Ann Douglas, *The Feminization of American Culture* (New York, 1977).

8. James L. Ash, Jr., *Protestantism and the American University: An Intellectual Biography of William Warren Sweet* (Dallas, 1982). Sidney E. Mead, *The Lively Experiment: The Shaping of Christianity in America* (New York, 1963), 54.

9. R. Laurence Moore, *Religious Outsiders and the Making of Americans* (New York, 1986), 3-21.

10. Alexis de Tocqueville, *Democracy in America*, trans. Henry Reeve, 2 vols. (New York, 1945), 1:53, 314.

FOR FURTHER READING

Baker, Frank. *From Wesley to Asbury: Studies in Early American Methodism*, Durham, NC, 1976.

Hatch, Nathan O. *The Democratization of American Christianity*, New Haven, 1989.

Norwood, Frederick A. *The Story of American Methodism: A History of the United Methodists and their Relations*, Nashville, 1974.

Richey, Russell E. *Early American Methodism*, Bloomington, IN, 1991.

Richey, Russell E., Kenney E. Rowe, and Jean Miller Schmidt, *Perspectives on American Methodism: Interpretative Essays*, Nashville, 1993.

Rudolph, L. C. *Francis Asbury*, Nashville, 1966.

Schneider, A. Gregory. *The Way of the Cross Leads Home: The Domestication of American Methodism*, Bloomington, IN, 1993.

INTRODUCTION TO ESSAY 24

Millennialist expectations are not very strong or widespread in our own day. But the reverse was true at some points in the past, and Moorhead treats the demise of one such strong expectation. First he takes us through difficult terminology regarding eschatology and apocalypse, distinguishing pre- and then postmillennialism. With a sensitive feel for the interaction between culture and theological nuances, this author shows how the mid-nineteenth-century experiences of social instability made it easy to expect a cosmic end to everyday life. But the real focus of this essay is to account for why this supernatural perspective on society faded into oblivion, not losing out to alternative beliefs but rather to indifference.

Moorhead offers several explanations for the gradual collapse of postmillennial thinking, while also furnishing us with an excellent model for treating causation in intellectual history. On the one hand he notes that modern culture simply did not fulfill earlier expectations about progress. As the nineteenth century came to a close, fewer people used the Bible as an authority in their thinking; attitudes about heaven and hell did not cause as much widespread concern as they had before; the religious life had fewer contrasts between good and evil. Since many American churchgoers were influenced by this moderately liberal form of cultural Protestantism, their perceptions of Christ's Second Coming were put on a shelf where they have remained ever since.

Original source - CH 53 (1984): 61-77.

24

The Erosion of Postmillennialism in American Religious Thought, 1865–1925

James H. Moorhead

In 1859 an influential theological quarterly asserted without fear of contradiction that postmillennialism was the "commonly received doctrine" among American Protestants, but by the early twentieth century it had largely vanished. In part, this change resulted from the defection of conservatives, but the disappearance of postmillennialism outside of premillennial quarters has received scant attention.[1] There—especially among the moderate to liberal Protestants with whom this article is chiefly concerned—the once dominant eschatology appears not to have suffered outright rejection but to have ebbed away. Although its remnants endured as faith in progress, it gradually ceased to be a distinct biblically grounded eschatology.

To understand this erosion, one must begin by noting the complex character of postmillennialism. During its heyday in the mid-nineteenth century, this eschatology represented a compromise between an apocalyptic and an evolutionary view of time, between a history characterized by dramatic upheavals and supernatural events and one governed by natural laws of organic development. The theory postponed history's cataclysmic end until after the millennium and thereby allowed the temporal interval necessary for the gradual evangelical conquest of the world and the triumph of secular progress. Nevertheless, a hard residue of apocalypticism survived in postmillennial thought. Committed to the premise of an infallible Bible, Protestants could not discount predictions of an eventual supernatural Second Coming. Thus that end, though delayed to the far side of the thousand years, had to come. Moreover, in a time when most Protestants still believed that death was a moment of tragic confrontation between heaven and hell, the Last Judgment acquired a fearful imminence; and conversion, the center of evangelical piety, became an anticipation of the final battle of Christ and Antichrist. Postmillennialism was, as Professor George Cross of Rochester Seminary said in 1915, an "attempt to unite a modern spirituality with a primitive view."[2] As such, it was an inherently unstable compound: and during the years after the Civil War, it slowly decomposed.

• • •

Crucial to all millennial systems had been the notion that the Bible contains a unified system of accurate predictions. Without that conviction, debates about the timing of the Second Coming and the thousand years would have been meaningless. Although postmillennialists were more inclined than their premillennial counterparts to allow spiritual or metaphorical fulfillments, they, too, generally insisted that "every word and jot and tittle of prophecy" must transpire.

In the late nineteenth century that conviction became harder to sustain in light of new biblical studies. Emanating chiefly from German universities, this scholarship was not so much a specific set of conclusions as it was an often disturbing angle from which to view the Scriptures. Basic to that perspective was a commitment to analyze the Bible in the same fashion as secular documents, usually to the diminution of supernatural elements in the text. Applied to the prophetic and apocalyptic books, this method produced several revolutionary hypotheses. First, critics asserted that prediction occupied a relatively minor place in biblical thought. Second, the Bible yielded no single eschatology but rather multiple views which could not be assembled into a consistent scenario. Third, the apocalyptic books Daniel and Revelation—long the mainstays of millennial speculation—lost their uniqueness as scholars analyzed them as mere instances of a larger genre of literature, much of it noncanonical. Characterized by the faulty expectation that the present world would shortly end in a supernatural upheaval, apocalypticism had flourished because persons were suffering dire persecutions and craved drastic solutions. This highly dualistic eschatology, said many critics, was an aberration from the main direction of biblical thought.[3] A proper interpretation placed biblical forecasts in their own historical setting, admitted they often contained error, and then went on to look for the development of the prophets' moral vision in subsequent history.

The cloud darkening biblical prediction gathered with special fury over the apocalyptic writers. That genre, said British exegete Arthur Peake in a widely read commentary, seems "remote and bizarre, its imagery pretentious or grotesque." "We are even compelled," added an American colleague, "to explain away, or to offer apology for, the presence of such teachings in the New Testament." According to one author, the Revelation was a "queer bird" hatched from "visions of the impossible"—visions which the Christian community had fortunately dropped for "saner and more spiritual conceptions." Influential scholars at the University of Chicago carried this perspective to its logical culmination. Since the book of Revelation looked toward the imminent end of the world, observed Shirley Jackson Case, no modern reader could take it seriously on its own terms. Neither repristinating that eschatology (as premillennialists wished) nor trying to make it consistent with modern developmental ideas of progress (as postmillennialists desired) represented intellectual honesty. Rather, the twentieth-century Christian should recognize the apocalyptic hope for what it was—a "millennial mirage"—and then search for elements of abiding spiritual worth hidden within that illusion. Or, as the Chicago-based *Biblical World* declared, modern scholarship had brought about the "passing of apocalypticism." "A study of its origins," said the editor, "inevitably brings its validity under suspicion for us." At best it was "the shell of a great truth," but the shell could now be sloughed off.[4]

In place of the apocalyptic vision was a new understanding of the Kingdom of God. Along with Albrecht Ritschl (1822–1889), whose theology influenced many of them, liberals perceived this kingdom as a present ethical reality rather than a dominion to be introduced in the future, and they believed that it advanced according to organic laws of growth, requiring no dramatic intrusions. According to these liberals, apocalypticism had suffered a double discredit: not only had critical studies exposed its fallacious predictions, but modern science, particularly evolutionary theories, rendered it irrational and repugnant. God did not work by coups de main. "Is anything in the whole universe of God, when rightly understood, supernatural?" asked retired Congregational minister W. B. Brown of Newark, New Jersey, in 1900. He replied in the negative. "Laws and order are the agencies or instruments by means of which the creative and evolutionary processes of the universe are carried through." Throughout the cosmos, said Harris Rall, God's purpose was manifest in a seamless web of order. "As applied to the development of life upon the earth the scientist calls it evolution; as applied to the story of mankind we call it history; as applied to God's supreme purpose we call it the development of the kingdom of God."[5]

This mentality left little room for the great eschatological event Christians had long awaited, namely, the Second Coming. As early as the 1870s, Congregationalist Israel Warren of Maine wrote a major treatise contending that the Second Coming was not a single event but "a generic dispensation" in the form of Jesus' continued presence with his church. In the next several decades numerous voices were raised in support of that thesis. "No visible return of Christ to the earth is to be expected," said liberal Baptist William Newton Clarke in his influential *Outline of Christian Theology*, "but rather the long and steady advance of his spiritual kingdom." By 1916 such views, if far from universally accepted, were at least sufficiently acceptable to permit the Methodist denominational press to issue a book which labeled the New Testament belief in a literal Second Coming a "mistake."[6]

• • •

Millennialism, however, had been more than a view of history derived from biblical predictions. It had also described the destiny of individuals. The Reverend George P. Mains glimpsed this connection in 1920 when he noted that the book of Revelation suggested comparison with the *Pilgrim's Progress*. The point was well taken. Just as Christian in Bunyan's classic engaged in a relentless struggle against evil and endured suffering to escape hell and reach the Celestial City, so, too, in the Apocalypse the saints collectively participated in a sharply dualistic conflict of good against wickedness and passed through a series of woes culminating in the final victory of Christ. The pilgrimage of each soul, in other words, traced a course similar to that of history. Well into the nineteenth century, the congruence between apocalyptic views of history and conceptions of personal destiny persisted.

By the late nineteenth century this piety was waning, and the gradual deemphasis upon conversion symbolized its passing. Previously a rather clearly defined event marked by a period of deep anxiety for one's soul and followed by a dramatic release from that fear, conversion was subsiding into something less terror-ridden. The publication in 1847 of Horace Bushnell's *Christian Nurture* provided a premonitory signal of this transformation. In that classic, Bushnell emphasized that slow nurture of children in Christian homes could imperceptibly roll back the influence of sin so that the adult would never remember a time when he was not Christian. Although *Christian Nurture* aroused controversy when it first appeared, its ideas were so common by the late 1860s that the American Sunday School Union quietly shifted its focus from securing conversions to promoting gradual Christian growth. Nor was this change limited to the rearing of children. Even revivalistic literature, ostensibly committed to procuring conversions, increasingly described these rebirths in terms suggesting few wild swings of emotion, little of the fear that marked persons who felt the fires of hell already lapping at their feet. The procedure almost seemed routine in the Prayer Meeting Revival of 1857–1858 and in the subsequent evangelistic crusades of Dwight L. Moody after 1875.[7]

Perhaps the key word to describe the emerging attitude is "process." Distrustful of sharp discontinuities in the spiritual life, many Protestants preferred to speak of continuous maturation and of the natural unfolding of religious experience. Among late-nineteenth-century liberals, this notion became virtually canonical. In 1906 Professor William Adams Brown, professor of theology in Union Seminary in New York, explained, the "Christian life . . . is natural to man" and as such proceeds throughout an individual's experience. In this intellectual milieu, conversion's once dramatic passage from death to life had become passé. The spiritual life was now one of degrees.

Hell, the dread counterpoint to eternal felicity, had been in subtle decline throughout the nineteenth century, even among those who preached its terrors. Postmillennialism, as commonly interpreted since the post-Edwardsian theologians, contributed to this end by severely depopulating hell. Likewise, emphasis upon benevolence as God's chief attribute tended to put a greater burden of proof on defenders of damnation, and the softening of the doctrine of original sin made humans appear less deserving of such punishment. The change was particularly noteworthy in regard to children.

It would not be accurate, of course, to suggest that the majority of Protestants after 1880 directly assaulted the idea of hell; but evidence abounds of a new attitude which, though hard to measure in quantitative terms, was probably more significant than overt challenges to the doctrine. When they did speak, the clergy usually felt compelled to reduce the imagery of physical torment to metaphor, to stress the lightness of punishment suffered by some, and to emphasize that damnation derived from natural moral laws which did not require the direct intervention of a vindictive God. By this special pleading, many Protestants were groping for a way to mitigate a doctrine which had become an embarrassment.

Heaven, too, was assuming a new appearance, one of continuity with the present life. That outlook appeared most visibly in the mid- to late-nineteenth-century consolatory literature which promised celestial reunions with loved ones and extensions of earthly joys. Elizabeth Stuart Phelps's *Beyond the Gates* (1885), for example, provided a first-person account of a young woman who, through a near-death experience, briefly entered the afterlife to return with a detailed description. There she found a world where marriages persisted, a world of museums, universities, concerts, and pleasant cottages—a world, in short, like this one, only more beautiful. Perhaps the character of Phelps's heaven was most succinctly captured in the words of the narrator's father. "He [God] expects nothing of us but to be natural."[8] By the end of the century in the era of muscular Christianity, this domestic heaven often took on a more activistic character as the afterlife became the realm of eternal conquest and movement—a world where there would "ever be heights beyond the heights" for the redeemed to scale.

The new view of individual destiny implied an abhorrence of

dichotomies of any sort. Humans did not face the choice of two eternally opposed futures so much as they encountered a moral continuum with an almost infinite number of gradations. Accordingly, the passage from evil to good did not transpire as if by a sudden leap from one state to the other. Like all life, the religious existence proceeded by the slow organic law of growth. Similarly, this life and the next could not be set against one another too sharply. The deity was a God of continuity and thus would not arbitrarily work a miraculous transformation in persons at the moment of death. They would commence their spiritual pilgrimage on the other side precisely where they had left off here. As one opponent of the new eschatology had charged in 1886, Protestants were losing the sense that "the radiant cross [stood] over against the dark background of eternal night." It was a loss which removed elements of piety which once had sustained the apocalyptic outlook.

• • •

A central theme runs through late-nineteenth-century revisions in eschatology: the principle of natural continuity. The arbitrary or disconnected event was everywhere anathema. That perspective informed the dismissal of traditional "artificial" readings of prophecy; it motivated the rejection of apocalypticism and of the sharp dichotomies between the lost and the saved, heaven and hell, time and eternity; and it lay behind faith in a Kingdom of God advancing by rational planning. In a word, the erosion of postmillennialism was part of the waning of supernaturalism.

But Protestant ranks were splitting. Liberals warred with fundamentalists, many of the latter being premillennialists who, in Timothy Weber's words, "more than any others on the contemporary scene . . . maintained the supernaturalism of the past. . . . Their world view still had room for angels, demons, lakes of fire which burned forever, and a personal Son of Man who was coming soon on the clouds of heaven."[9] Yet relatively few critics of that persuasion responded with arguments for a traditional postmillennialism. Dismissing millennial categories of all sorts, they spoke instead of a natural and rational improvement, both in this world and the next. That this should occur is not surprising.

Postmillennialism, a tenuous amalgam of modern developmental views and older apocalyptic supernatural ideas, had been disintegrating slowly at least since the Civil War. Under the polarizing impact of the fundamentalist controversy in the 1920s, that process was virtually complete.

In that conflict, postmillennialism was hobbled by two disadvantages. First, as a mediating position, it satisfied neither of the contending parties. In the eyes of the militant conservatives, it appeared to concede too much to the modern temper; and from the liberal vantage point, it retained too much precritical biblicism and antiquated supernaturalism. Second, postmillennialism looked increasingly implausible because events had stubbornly refused to follow its scenario. The eschatology predicted that a pattern of improvement would be discernible in history and that evangelicalism would occupy a privileged place in this forward movement. Since the Civil War, much evidence had accumulated to the contrary. A tide of non-Protestant immigration made the nation more radically pluralistic. Labor unrest signified that the Protestant social ethic no longer meshed with the reality of burgeoning factories, corporations, and assembly lines. Unplanned growth created sprawling cities whose anonymity and disorder threatened the Protestant vision of stable community. Likewise, the new ethos of professionalism, efficiency, and scientific planning rendered evangelical values superfluous or at best vestigial in many areas. Then, amid these evidences of a dwindling role, Protestants aggravated their difficulties by turning on themselves and devouring one another over such issues as biblical criticism and evolution. In short, experience simply had not sustained postmillennialism. The product of an era when evangelicalism enjoyed cultural dominance, it could not survive when that ascendance waned. It became a relic of a lost world.

ENDNOTES

1. On the growth of premillennialism, see Ernest R. Sandeen, *The Roots of Fundamentalism: British and American Millenarianism, 1800–1930* (Chicago, 1970); Timothy P. Weber, *Living in the Shadow of the Second Coming: American Premillennialism, 1875–1925*, rev. ed. (Chicago, 1987);

and George M. Marsden, *Fundamentalism and American Culture: The Shaping of Twentieth-Century Evangelicalism, 1870–1925* (New York, 1980). Jean Quandt, "Religion and Social Thought: The Secularization of Postmillennialism," *American Quarterly* 25 (1973): 390-409, is one of the few explicit treatments of postmillennialism after 1865. William R. Hutchison, *The Modernist Impulse in American Protestantism* (Cambridge, MA, 1976), gives hints of the fate of postmillennialism among liberals.

2. George Cross, "Millenarianism in Christian History," *Biblical World* 46 (1915): 3-4.
3. J. Estlin Carpenter, *The Bible in the Nineteenth Century* (London, 1903); T. K. Cheyne, *Founders of Old Testament Criticism* (New York, 1893).
4. Shirley Jackson Case, *The Revelation of St. John* (Chicago, 1919), 407; *The Millennial Hope* (Chicago, 1918), 215-25; "The Passing of Apocalypticism," *Biblical World* 36 (1910): 147-51.
5. William B. Brown, *The Problem of Final Destiny* (New York, 1900), 298, 299; Harris F. Rall, *The Coming Kingdom* (New York, 1924), 26.
6. Israel Warren, *The Parousia* (Portland, 1879), 24; William N. Clarke, *An Outline of Christian Theology* (New York, 1909), 444; Metcalf, 65; James M. Campbell, *The Second Coming of Christ* (New York, 1919), 70.
7. Anne M. Boylan, "The Role of Conversion in Nineteenth-Century Sunday Schools," *American Studies* 20 (1979): 35-48; Sandra Sizer, *Gospel Hymns and Social Religion: The Rhetoric of Nineteenth-Century Revivalism* (Philadelphia, 1978), 111-37.
8. Elizabeth S. Phelps, *Beyond the Gates* (Boston, 1885), 47. See also William Branks, *Heaven Our Home*, 3d ed. (Boston, 1864); Adeline J. Bayard, *Views of Heaven* (Philadelphia, 1877); and H. Harbaugh, *The Heavenly Recognition* (Philadelphia, 1856).
9. Weber, *Living in the Shadow of the Second Coming*, 40.

FOR FURTHER READING

Barkum, Michael. *Crucible of the Millennium: The Burned-over District of New York in the 1840s*, Syracuse, 1986.

Bercovitch, Sacvan. *The American Jeremiad*, Madison, WI, 1972.

Bloch, Ruth H. *Visionary Republic: Millennial Themes in American Thought, 1756–1800*, New York, 1985.

Bozeman, Theodore Dwight. *To Live Ancient Lives: The Primitivist Dimension in Puritanism*, Chapel Hill, NC, 1988.

Cherry, Conrad, ed. *God's New Israel: Religious Interpretations of American Destiny*, Englewood Cliffs, NJ, 1971.

Davidson, James West. *The Logic of Millennial Thought: Eighteenth Century New England*, New Haven, 1977.

Hudson, Winthrop S., ed. *Nationalism and Religion in America: Concepts of American Identity and Mission*, New York, 1970.

Hughes, Richard T., ed. *The American Quest for the Primitive Church*, Urbana, IL, 1988.

Hughes, Richard T., and C. Leonard Allen. *Illusions of Innocence: Protestant Primitivism in America, 1630–1875*, Chicago, 1988.

Moorhead, James H. *American Apocalypse: Yankee Protestants and the Civil War, 1860–1869*, New Haven, 1978.

Taylor, Anne. *Visions of Harmony: A Study of Nineteenth-Century Millenarianism*, New York, 1987.

Tuveson, Ernest Lee. *Redeemer Nation: The Idea of America's Millennial Role*, Chicago, 1968.

INTRODUCTION TO ESSAY 25

The previous essay treated broad cultural trends and general patterns affecting most of this country's citizens. This one concentrates on a specific locality and identifies the religious influences at work in a microcosm: one city's early development. Urban studies is a relatively new field, and author Tweed here makes a significant contribution to its expansion. On the most basic level he shows the interaction between religious and social patterns. He is careful to base his observations on evidence from one city, then to expand his ideas to urban settings in southern states, and finally to make tentative comparisons with cities in the Northeast and on the Pacific Coast.

This study addresses both a tendency toward social dominance and the fact of pluralism, two contrary themes that recur in American life. Miami serves as a window for viewing how those who are socially powerful favor their religious preference and thus affect others around them. In this study white Anglo-Saxon Protestants dictated cultural standards in a setting that also included minorities of Catholics, Jews, African Americans, and a diminishing segment of Native Americans. As population became more complex within the growing metropolis, different religious orientations became more socially acceptable. Pluralism nurtured tolerance, and greater differentiation undermined the earlier inclination toward uniformity. Instead of the process taking a hundred years, it all happened in less than a decade.

Original source - CH 64 (1995): 412-37.

25

An Emerging Protestant Establishment
Religious Affiliation and Public Power on the Urban Frontier in Miami, 1896–1904

Thomas A. Tweed

A century after Miami's founding many observers celebrated (or condemned) the city as a symbol of America's diversity. Nonetheless, a mainline Protestant establishment persisted there alongside other "parallel establishments" into the 1990s, decades after migrants had transformed the cultural landscape. Informed by previous research on the national Protestant establishment and the American urban frontier, I brought two main questions to the city's founding: who had public power in early Miami and how did they get it? In other words, who had the ability to enact decisions by controlling individuals or mobilizing institutions in social sites outside the home? Here I take an initial step toward a fuller study by trying to determine who won elections, hired workers, controlled newspapers, shaped entertainment, led voluntary organizations, policed the streets, and influenced education.[1]

Power relations in pioneer Miami's cultural landscape resembled that of other cities in the region and that of other urban frontiers in America and elsewhere. First, despite its multiple regional influences, early Miami exhibited three characteristics that David R. Goldfield has associated with the urban South. Two of those—biracial society and northern colonialism—were especially important in Miami. Unlike most midwestern and western cities, Miami had a large black population from the start and economic dependence on the North was great. After all, a northern Protestant owned the hotel built in 1896 as well as the railroad that carried visitors and new residents to the town. More broadly, the social terrain of early Miami had much in common with other urban frontiers in the nineteenth century. Those urban frontiers, as the historian David Hamer has argued in a comparative study, shared four common characteristics: transience, speculation, boosterism, and "civilizing."[2]

Egalitarianism and harmony coexisted with hierarchy and conflict. A few members of marginalized groups gained some public power in the first four years of the city's history, but the egalitarianism of the urban frontier (and the company town) failed to reach many. Further, even during those early years, a local Protestant establishment had begun to form, and by 1900 it had solidified. I divide the essay into four sections. The first traces the emergence of a mainline Protestant establishment in Miami from 1896 to 1900. The next assesses the public power of Catholics, Jews, African Americans, and Native Americans during that period. Examining documents from 1904, eight years after the city's founding, the next section identifies changes in the composition of the leadership after the local Protestant establishment had solidified. I conclude by speculating about the significance of this case study.

• • •

Only 260 people lived in the Miami area when the first train, and the Protestant establishment, steamed into that fishing village on 15 April 1896. A northern Presbyterian, Henry Flagler (1830–1913), decided to expand his Florida railroad and hotel empire to Miami after the "Big Freezes" of December 1894 and February 1895 had made the area, which did not feel the effects of the frost, look especially attractive as a tourist destination and agricultural center. As news of the railroad extension traveled, the population swelled. It had multiplied to approximately 1500 when the city was incorporated in July 1896, less than four months after the railroad had arrived. Miami's population increased to 5,471 by 1910 and by more than 440 percent a decade later, when 29,571 people lived there.

One of the early ministers, E. V. Blackman, suggested that religion was, in Miami as elsewhere, "one of the foundations on which to build a city." Most of the Protestant churches had trouble constructing buildings for worship. Because they counted among their charter members one of the leading figures in early Miami, the Episcopalians managed to erect a small wooden church in the year of Miami's incorporation, but the other groups had to wait. The southern Methodists got their building in 1902; the northern

Methodists erected theirs two years later. Before that, Methodists had shared the Presbyterian tent, and later, its pavilion, a small temporary wooden structure. The Episcopalians had shared the Presbyterian tent in the first months, too, and the Baptists worshiped in the tent and pavilion until their first permanent structure was dedicated in 1901.

This, then, was a period of building—churches, houses, businesses, and government. Most residents in 1896 fought the mosquitoes and the heat in tents, thatched huts, or makeshift boarding houses. As the months and years passed, buildings rose and institutions, sacred and secular, emerged. Yet a traditionlessness reigned in this frontier town for about four years. The social fluidity was intensified by two other developments of this period. In 1898, the city was home to thousands of troops ready to fight in the Spanish-American war, and the next year a yellow fever epidemic struck. The city was quarantined from 22 October 1899 to 15 January 1900. Adjusting to the natural environment, flooded with temporary residents, and isolated by medical emergency, the city's leaders struggled to build a stable town.

Many of those early leaders were mainline Protestants. Among those with local influence, Henry Flagler stood out. Like other leaders of the establishment, this son of a Presbyterian minister and supporter of Sunday schools felt responsibility for the moral, social, and economic life of his fellow citizens. To fulfill his obligations to his "wards" in Miami, Flagler, for example, provided a waterworks system and power company and donated land for schools and churches.

Other mainline Protestants, many of them connected with Flagler's business empire, also exerted considerable local influence before 1900. Protestants controlled the newspaper, the schools, and the bank. They held most of the elected and appointed offices. One of the most influential Protestants was John Sewell (1867–1939). This physician's son from Georgia arrived a month before the railroad. He was an energetic and influential member of the local Baptist church. He helped to organize it and donated his time as its clerk for thirty years. In the fall of 1895 Flagler's builder asked him, in Sewell's words, "to go to Miami to start the city." Sewell found the area even more untamed than he had expected, but he promptly went to work. It was Sewell who oversaw the brush clearing, street paving, and hotel construction in the new city. He and his brother opened the first store in Miami proper—they sold men's furnishings—and he served on the board of directors of the Fort Dallas National Bank and the board of governors of the Miami Board of Trade. But even before then Sewell and several other white male Protestants shaped the local political culture.

• • •

At the same time, forces were at work that blunted the power of the Protestant establishment to some extent. The benevolent—and not so benevolent—arm of the Protestant establishment reached Miami during its first four years, but members of a few groups that were marginalized in Miami and elsewhere managed to slip in through the cracks in the emerging establishment. There were Catholics elsewhere in the South at this time, of course, but they wielded as much public influence only in a few other places in the region—for instance, cities in Texas, Maryland, and Louisiana. In the first election of 1896 Miami voters chose a Catholic mayor, and two of the seven aldermen were Catholics.[3]

Catholicism had been part of Florida's heritage since the Spanish arrived in the sixteenth century, and in 1567 Fr. Francisco Villareal had founded a mission for the Indians and Spanish at a site that is now in downtown Miami. Unlike in Los Angeles and Santa Fe, however, the Hispanic Catholic presence had disappeared long before the new city was incorporated. But a sizable Hispanic presence would reappear only six decades later when Cubans immigrated there in large numbers.

No Jew was elected to public office but Jewish merchants were visible in early Miami. As had happened in other cities in the South since the eighteenth century, Jews successfully fought subtle, and not so subtle, anti-Semitism to carve out a place in the business community in Miami. About twenty-five Jews, including children, lived in Miami when the railroad arrived in 1896. Almost all of the men were active in business. Russian and German Jews completely controlled the retail clothing and dry goods business, and twelve of the sixteen merchants in the city by the end of 1896 were Jewish. All but two of the original merchants would leave by 1900, as the establishment solidified, but a few new Jewish citizens would arrive as the years passed.

Isidor Cohen, one of the original Jewish merchants, managed to stay. Cohen had emigrated from Russia in 1883, arriving in Miami in 1896. He was a prominent member of the Miami business community and, almost from the start, the most influential Jew. He later served as president of the Merchants' Association, which represented fourteen stores; and he was an active member of the Miami Board of Trade, serving as treasurer of that group in 1907. His influence continued, even intensified, as the years passed. It was difficult for Cohen and the few other Jewish families—only ten families lived there as late as 1915—to preserve their religious heritage. Miami's first Jewish congregation, B'nai Zion, was not organized until 1913, and they had no temple until they purchased a church building from the Disciples of Christ in 1920. Yet they did their best. The original Jewish merchants had closed their stores and observed High Holy Days that first year, 1896, and they continued to do so every year thereafter.[4]

A few Catholics and Jews, then, had formal and informal access to public power in urban Miami between 1896 and 1900. How did it happen? Several cultural and social forces were at work. First, and least important, ecumenical impulses found among some Protestants, especially liberals in the mainline churches, had something to do with it. Between the 1880s and the 1920s, interdenominational rivalry flourished, nativist hostility raged, and racist attitudes persisted. Yet a number of leading Anglo-Saxon Protestants called for more inclusivist theology, ecumenical cooperation, and tolerant practice. Some of this was found in early Miami. As they did in other urban frontiers in nineteenth-century America, mainline Protestants shared the same tent, and sometimes even the same minister.

But we should not overestimate the significance of religious convictions—liberal Protestant ecumenism—in determining relations among ethnic, racial, and religious groups as they competed for power in early Miami. An egalitarianism born of necessity can be expected in frontier communities, and much of the interreligious cooperation noted above might be explained as a function of this leveling impulse. As in Miami, which grew proportionally as rapidly as Denver and San Francisco, new towns welcomed help however it arrived. Differences did not disappear, but they could be submerged temporarily. Migrants did not leave their prejudices behind, but in the discomfort and traditionlessness of the frontier, commonalities temporarily and partially obscured socially defined differences. At the start, all white settlers in Miami faced similar problems—no paved streets, too many mosquitoes, and too few turn-of-the-century conveniences. No one of European descent who stepped forward to build the city could be dismissed out of hand. So even those filled with an inherited anti-Semitism or anti-Catholicism might welcome —out of self-interest, if nothing else—energetic Jewish merchants or efficient Catholic businessmen. Once some Catholics and Jews got power, they kept it. Those who had squeezed through the cracks in the emerging establishment were not asked to leave as it solidified after the turn of the twentieth century. A bond seemed to form among some of the pioneers, and it endured.

Whatever the reasons for the wide-ranging influence of some Catholic men before 1900—and the social connections and economic stability of a few Jews—access to public power had its limits. Most women were constrained. Most Catholic and Jewish men could not enter the establishment; and company clout and frontier egalitarianism did not extend to African Americans and Native Americans.

The surviving evidence is scant, but one local historian has argued that frontier egalitarianism touched even African Americans to some extent in the first months and years of the new city and then decreased as racism became institutionalized in later years. Racism was intense in Miami before it became the most segregated city in America after World War II and even before the legal boundaries of "Colored Town" were drawn in the early years. It was pervasive even before state statutes in 1897 and 1901 allowed Democrats to exclude blacks from party membership and charge a poll tax that reduced dramatically the number of African American voters. The attitudes toward African Americans tended to be either condescending or hostile. The local press portrayed them as a violent menace to peaceful—that is, white—society.[5]

As expected, it also did not extend to Native Americans. The Tequesta Indians who were in Florida when the Spanish Catholics arrived either fled or were killed—in battle or by disease. The Creek Indians who had migrated to Florida from Georgia in the eighteenth and early nineteenth centuries, the Seminoles, fared only slightly better. The Seminole Wars of the early and mid-nineteenth century left many Seminoles dead. Others were transported against their will to reservations in other parts of the country. Those who remained in Florida hid in the almost impenetrable swamps of the Everglades. When the city of Miami was incorporated, Seminoles continued to live secluded in the South Florida area. Unlike the local blacks, however, the Seminoles lived and worked separately by choice. There was some intermittent interaction, but memories of earlier tragedies seemed to have been fresh enough to discourage most who felt tempted to enter white society or even maintain close ties.[6]

• • •

As in other cities, the limited egalitarianism of the urban frontier and the partial leveling of company affiliation faded in a few years; and a mainline Protestant establishment, increasingly southern as the years passed, solidified in Miami just after 1900. As historians would expect, access to public power remained elusive for blacks and Indians. It also became more difficult to find for Catholics and Jews. By 1904 white mainline Protestants, who were increasingly Baptist and Methodist as one would expect in the South, exerted significant, even disproportionate, public power. The mayor, John Sewell, was Protestant, as were four of the six aldermen with religious affiliations. Other government officials all were Protestant, including the city clerk, marshal, tax collector, and postmaster. The law enforcement system was dominated by Protestants. The county judge, county attorney, town sheriff, and bar association president affiliated with Protestant churches. As Catholics and Jews in many other parts of the United States complained, the public schools also were shaped wholly by Protestants. The school board, superintendent, principal, and teachers aligned themselves with Episcopal and Baptist churches. Other cultural institutions, such as the newspaper, also were led by Protestants. Members of the board of trade and leaders of the business community were overwhelmingly Protestant. Leaders among the skilled labor force also were Protestants: the presidents of the building trades council and the carpenter's union were Baptist and Southern Methodist, respectively.

In all, at least nineteen of these forty leaders were born in the South (47.5 percent). The overwhelming majority (92.5 percent) were from mainline Protestant denominations, even though they accounted for only 9.3 percent of local church members. Roman Catholics never were a majority in the power structures, but a few more Catholics had exerted public influence at the city's founding. Eight years later, only two of forty leaders affiliated with Catholicism. That meant Catholics were underrepresented since they constituted about 9.3 percent of South Florida church members, a higher percentage than in the state and a greater proportion than in all but four of the thirteen southern states. Cohen, who had achieved some prominence before the Protestant establishment had solidified, served as president of the thirty-one member Merchants Association in 1904; but no new Jewish residents managed to shape the public sphere for decades. Most of the Jewish merchants left town before the turn of the century, and it was not until the 1920s that there was a large enough Jewish presence to establish a permanent synagogue and not until the 1940s that they could wield local political power. At the same time, the exclusion of African Americans continued and intensified.

• • •

To return to the questions I posed at the opening of this essay, then—who had power and how did they get it?—I have argued that a few Irish Catholics, Russian Jews, and Protestant women gained some public influence in the transitional context of the first four years, as a consensus model might predict. On the other hand, as a conflict model would suggest, egalitarianism was limited and power contested. The "democracy" of the urban frontier and in this case also the company town—failed to reach many. Even during those first four years, a male Anglo-Protestant establishment had begun to form.

If this case study shows how egalitarianism and conflict coexisted in the urban frontier and, so, how both theoretical models provide insights, it also contributes to our understanding of how local Protestant establishments formed in the United States in the nineteenth and early twentieth century. First, there was a transitional period of varying duration in which a variety of residents cooperated to some extent and found some access to public power, even if hierarchy and conflict never disappeared. Second, the nature of the establishment and the rate at which it solidified varied from place to place, and that variation arose from a variety of factors, including the population profile, growth rate, and local economy. A final tentative conclusion to be drawn from a comparative analysis of these American cities is that despite differences in population, growth, and economy—and, so, differences in how and when a coalition solidified—an Anglo-Saxon Protestant establishment did form in each, which then wielded public power for decades afterward. That happened, I have suggested, even in Miami, which by the late twentieth century had become a symbol of America's ethnic and religious diversity.

ENDNOTES

1. The first scholar to talk about the "Protestant establishment" was E. Digby Baltzell in *The Protestant Establishment in America* (New Haven, 1964). Since then a number of other studies have appeared. Among the most useful is William R. Hutchison, ed., *Between the Times: The Travail of the Protestant Establishment in America, 1900–1960* (New York, 1989). On recent developments in Miami, including the rise of "parallel social structures," see Alejandro Portes and Alex Stepick, *City on the Edge: The Transformation of Miami* (Berkeley, 1993).
2. David R. Goldfield, "The Urban South: A Regional Framework," *Journal of American History* 86 (1981): 1009-34; David Hamer, *New Towns in the New World: Images and Perceptions of the Nineteenth-Century Urban Frontier* (New York, 1990).
3. On Southern Catholicism see *Catholics in the Old South*, ed. Randall M. Miller and Jon L. Wakelyn (Macon, GA, 1983). On Florida see Michael V. Gannon, *The Cross in the Sand* (Gainesville, 1983), and Michael J. McNally, *Catholicism in South Florida* (Gainesville, 1982).
4. Leonard Dinnerstein and Mary Dale Palsson, eds., *Jews in the South* (Baton Rouge, 1973); Louis Schmier, "Jews and Gentiles in a South

Georgia Town," in *Jews of the South,* ed. Samuel Proctor and Louis Schmier, with Malcolm Stern (Macon, GA, 1984), 1-16; Chariton W. Tebeau, *Synagogue in the Central City: Temple Israel of Greater Miami* (Coral Gables, 1972), 28-43; Deborah Dash Moore, *To the Golden Cities: Pursuing the American Jewish Dream in Miami and L.A.* (New York, 1994).

5. Paul S. George, "Colored Town: Miami's Black Community, 1896–1930," *Florida Historical Quarterly* 56 (1978): 432-47; Paul S. George, "Policing Miami's Black Community, 1896–1930," *Florida Historical Quarterly* 57 (1979): 431-50.

6. Charles Hudson, *The Southeastern Indians* (Knoxville, 1976); Harlan Trapp, *My Pioneer Reminiscences* (Miami, 1940), 2-3; Cora S. Maxwell, *Miami of Yesterday* (Miami, 1956), 12-13.

FOR FURTHER READING

Cristiano, Kevin J., *Religious Diversity and Social Change: American Cities, 1890–1906,* Cambridge, U.K., 1987.

Demerath, N. J., III, and Rhys H. Williams, *A Bridging of Faiths: Religion and Politics in a New England City,* Princeton, 1992.

Dolan, Jay P., ed. *The American Catholic Parish: A History from 1850 to the Present,* Volume 1, *The Northeast, Southeast and South Central States;* Volume 2, *The Pacific, Intermountain West and Midwest States,* Mahwah, NJ, 1987.

Engh, Michael E. *Frontier Faiths: Church, Temple, and Synagogue in Los Angeles, 1846–1888,* Albuquerque, 1992.

Hackett, David G. *The Rude Hand of Innovation: Religion and Social Order in Albany, New York, 1652–1836,* New York, 1991.

Haddad, Yvonne Yazbeck, ed. *The Muslims of America,* New York, 1991.

Haddad, Yvonne Yazbeck, and Jane I. Smith, eds. *Muslim Communities in North America,* Albany, 1994.

Maffly-Kipp, Laurie. *Religion and Society in Frontier California,* New Haven, 1994.

Singleton, Gregory H. *Religion in the City of Angels: American Protestant Culture and Urbanization, Los Angeles, 1850–1930,* Ann Arbor, 1979.

INTRODUCTION TO ESSAY 26

Another dominant theme in American religion is the proliferation of new churches. In this essay Leonard elaborates on the familiar process of dissidents separating from a parent body, developing in size and complexity, and harboring seeds for the next cycle of dissent and fragmentation when it enters the mainstream of large denominations. The author's focus on Baptists gives us further information about that denomination's historical emphases, and it also sheds light on recent liberal-fundamentalist antagonisms there. Looking primarily at the conservative side of that polarization, he proceeds to point out several ironies that confront these separatist congregations.

One of the tendencies among fundamentalists is their fear of being dictated to by secular culture. Leonard uses rhetoric that is familiar inside such groups to demonstrate this outsider mentality. At the same time, though, fundamentalists want to dominate culture through their own version of moral and spiritual renewal. These contrary impulses create identity crises within fledgling religious institutions. Some people in them embrace the primitivist theology of the "old time religion" that flourished in a bygone era. Others look to a future America made in their own image and achieved through the latest technology in mass communications. The old conundrum of wanting to maintain a position of prophetic distance while moving toward priestly control besets these groups as they ponder the options of their future.

Original source - CH 56 (1987): 504-17

26

Independent Baptists
From Sectarian Minority to "Moral Majority"

Bill J. Leonard

Raymond W. Barber, Baptist pastor and president of the Baptist World Fellowship, wrote in 1982, "Fundamentalists have moved out of the storefront buildings on back alleys into beautiful sanctuaries fronting the freeways and boulevards that dissect the nation's biggest cities. No longer do fundamentalists operate from the closet of inferiority, but from the parlor of influence, affecting the spiritual and cultural life of America." Fundamentalists, particularly independent Baptist Fundamentalists, have come of age in Ronald Reagan's America. Sectarian congregations and fellowships long ignored or dismissed as fringe elements by analysts of American religion are bringing their political and moral agenda to the public arena. Recent studies suggest that the "greatest support" for the so-called New Religious Political Right in America comes from "independent Baptist congregations."[1]

This study represents an effort to identify independent Baptists historically and theologically and to ask certain questions regarding their relationship to American culture. It suggests that independent Baptists have modified their earlier sectarian separatism to varying degrees in an effort to promote their particular moral and spiritual agendas within the broader and, in their view, increasingly humanistic culture. While continuing to use the rhetoric of separatism with their constituency, they have found it necessary to become more "civilized" (to use John Murray Cuddihy's motif) in their response to heretical and worldly outsiders. Their calling to bring moral and spiritual renewal to America sometimes has required them to join forces with individual groups they earlier had declared theologically and ethically corrupt. Given their strong emphasis on separatism, such new alignments may create serious identity crises for the independent Baptist constituency.

• • •

These questions provide direction for this article: (1) Who are the independent Baptists? (2) Where do they come from? (3) What do they believe? (4) What are the implications of their transition from sectarian, separatist minority to leadership of an American "moral majority"? The independent Baptist movement may be described as a collection of fiercely autonomous local congregations, Fundamentalist in theology, Baptist in polity, and separatist in their understanding of ecclesiastical relationships. Although most independent Baptist churches are small to moderate in size (100–500 members), the movement often is identified with certain "megachurches," characterized by huge memberships and presided over by a charismatic senior pastor (often founder) who is the primary authority figure within the community of faith. In 1982, for example, America's largest independent Baptist congregations ranged from the mammoth First Baptist Church, Hammond, Indiana (67,267 members), to the Anchorage Baptist Temple, Anchorage, Alaska (membership 4,800).

Many of these churches maintain a type of denominationalism in miniature, developing local programs and services which mirror those of national denominations. Such congregations frequently establish an extensive system of parochial schools, which may provide education from kindergarten through seminary. They send out their own missionaries and "church planters" for service at home and abroad. They often maintain media resources which may include a printing house, radio and television production, and a cassette-tape ministry.

Some congregations originally were related to other Baptist denominations, North and South, but "came out" in response to denominational liberalism, worldliness, compromise, and bureaucratic "hierarchy." Others originated as independent churches. In fact, one of the primary aims of the movement is "church-planting," the founding of new indigenous congregations throughout America in the independent Baptist tradition.[2]

Although most Baptist churches historically have reflected a high degree of congregational autonomy, the independent Baptist movement is a fairly recent phenomenon. It demonstrates a particular antidenominational, Fundamentalist interpretation of Baptist ecclesiology. Eschewing denominational structures as unbiblical, corrupt, and tainted by modernism, many of these churches maintain varying degrees of "fellowship" through groups and alliances of independent Baptists which share numerous similarities. Most were born in reaction to what one supporter called "worldliness, modernism, apostasy and compromise," often under the leadership of a charismatic pastor/authority figure. They generally maintain a loose confederation of local congregations, promoting and funding independent missionaries and "church-planters, periodicals and Bible schools."[3] Sociologist Nancy Ammerman observes that despite their independence, "there is remarkable uniformity among Fundamentalist churches" which makes cooperation, exchange of members, and "organizational networks" possible.[4]

What do independent Baptists believe? Frequently, their own self-descriptions typify their theology: "Independent, Fundamental, Premillennial and Baptistic."

Independent Baptists define their Fundamentalism in terms of the classic "five points": the infallibility and inerrancy of holy scripture; the virgin birth and full deity of Jesus Christ; the substitutionary atonement of Christ; the bodily resurrection of Christ; and the literal, premillennial, second advent of Christ.

By inerrancy they mean the plenary, verbal inspiration of the Scripture, "chapter by chapter, verse by verse, line by line, word by word, syllable by syllable, and letter by letter." The virgin birth, they believe, was a "supernatural union" resulting in a "supernatural conception that produced a supernatural Savior." Without it, "Christianity is only a myth that will succumb to its own deception." "Blood atonement" is necessary for human salvation since "apart from the saving efficacy of His blood there is no remission of sin." Likewise, they affirm that Jesus rose from the dead "bodily, physically, really, literally." The premillennial and, in most cases, pre-tribulational return of Christ remains an important and popular doctrine among independent Baptists. It involves a "rapture of the saints," who go immediately to be with Christ, and, following a period of intense tribulation, the establishing of Christ's kingdom on earth for a thousand years. These five doctrines provide a basis for fellowship and a means of identifying modernism and apostasy. The departure of independents from Baptist conventions North and South is a direct result of a perceived liberal drift in these denominations and the inability of Fundamentalists to impose the dogma of the five points on denominational confessions of faith. Thus defending Fundamentalist orthodoxy also means attacking modernist heresy.

These Fundamentalist Baptists also identify themselves as "independent." Independency involves several issues: the sovereignty of the local congregation as the basic source of ecclesiastical authority; the authority of the pastor as the "undershepherd" of the flock of God; a strong antidenominational polemic; and a doctrine of "biblical separatism," involving separation from all sin, worldliness, and compromise with modernism in both the church and the world. In their view of local church authority and independence, these Baptists reflect the Old Landmark interpretation of Baptist history. Landmark Baptists believe that Jesus Christ established the church as a succession of local congregations which extend from the New Testament era to the present. They reject any concept of a universal or invisible church, believing that only local congregations possess the "marks" of the true church of Christ. The failure of other Christian bodies to follow that New Testament program and their abiding compromise with modernism influenced one of the most prominent characteristics of independent Baptists, "biblical separatism." Any association with liberals, any tolerance for modernism in denominational life, was unacceptable for true believers.

This doctrine of separation provides the key for understanding independent Baptists and their relationship to American culture. It is this doctrine, not a hesitancy to speak out on questions of politics or morality, which until recently kept them out of the political mainstream. Separation kept them away from the denominationalizing pluralism of American religious life. It is also this doctrine which frequently turned independent Baptists against themselves, as one faction challenged the orthodoxy of another because of the violation of certain separatist norms.

These independents also claim the name Baptist and identify their heritage with that historical and ecclesiastical tradition. They reflect what might be called a type of Baptist scholasticism, born of certain legalistic, propositional segments of the diverse Baptist heritage. In many respects, twentieth-century independent Baptists are heirs of earlier eighteenth- and nineteenth-century landmark, successionist, antimission factions within Baptist life.[5]

Given these doctrinal attitudes, early independent Baptists occupied a paradoxical position in relation to American culture. On the one hand, they claimed the dissenting tradition of the Baptists, speaking out against those issues which they believed contrary to Scripture, conscience, and Christian morality. On the other hand, their concern for doctrinal order and authority made them sound like an establishment, protecting, enforcing, and maintaining the Fundamentalist status quo against various religious minorities (Catholics, Mormons) and against challenges to their concept of the American way of life. Their vision of world evangelism and Christian commonwealth created a tendency toward cultural domination, a call to subdue the land for Christ. But their separatist fear of being tainted by the world kept them from involvement in compromising political alliances. They gloried in their remnant status but longed for a day when they would evangelize the world into the image of Christ's kingdom. Premillennialism made them hesitant to change the world; evangelical conversionism compelled them to try. In this attitude they reflect George Marsden's contention that Fundamentalists show that "paradoxical tendency to identify sometimes with the 'establishment' and sometimes with the 'outsiders.'"[6]

Independent Baptist preachers have been outspoken in matters of politics and public morality since the beginning of their movement in the 1920s and 1930s. Their approach to politics and morality may be summarized as follows.

First, they insist that the primary mission of the church is not to reform the world, but to preach and teach the gospel of salvation to each individual soul. Political involvements are secondary, sometimes incidental, to evangelism. Second, they have not hesitated to address such issues of personal and public morality as alcohol, divorce, sexual immorality, card playing, gambling, smoking, and movies. In this area they freely assume the prophet's role in denouncing the sins of the age. Third, it is in the role of jeremiad that independent Baptist preachers have addressed political issues. They view America as a chosen nation, blessed by God, but, like ancient Israel, in constant danger of divine retribution because of immorality within and the forces of anti-Christ (Romanism, Communism, Liberalism) without.

The civil rights movement, integration, the Supreme Court rulings on prayer and abortion, rising divorce rates, and accompanying social upheavals set the stage for the increasing involvement of independent Baptists in the public arena. While they repudiated the participation of liberal churches in civil and political matters, they expressed increased concern for the decline of American morality. During the 1960s and 1970s independent Baptist periodicals were filled with editorials, sermons, and articles which responded to civil rights issues, civil disobedience, the expanding role of the federal government, and the assassinations of the Kennedys and Martin Luther King., Jr.

While deploring the murders, many preachers suggested that God "permitted" the Kennedys' assassinations due perhaps to judgment on their "liquor-selling" father, their socialistic tendencies, the sinfulness of a "communistic" assassin, and their efforts to build a political "dynasty." Rice wrote that if Martin Luther King, Jr. could promote violence among Negroes, why should not Arabs feel the same way? "Is it really any worse for an Arab to shoot at Senator Kennedy, than for a Negro in Chicago to shoot a policeman?" Most writers concluded that Martin Luther King, Jr. died, as one sermon title declared, "by the lawlessness he encouraged." Noel Smith, editor of the *Baptist Bible Tribune*, charged that King, though a Baptist pastor, was "not a Christian at all."[7]

Independent Baptists have not hesitated to speak out on political issues, usually reflecting sectarian, right-wing positions in American religio-political life. They willingly addressed such questions but, because of their strong separatism, were reluctant to become involved in the broader political context lest they compromise their distinctive witness. They also were pushed toward such rightist political alignments because they were courted by right-wing political action leaders and because they believed that American society was near total moral collapse, as evidenced by abortion, the public school system, criminal violence, sexual immorality, drinking, homosexuality, drugs, rock music, adultery, fornication, communism, and divorce. The right-wing Republican leaders moved to bring independent Baptists into the party as a new voting bloc through organizations such as Moral Majority and Religious Roundtable.

Independent Baptist leaders, long outspoken on the total depravity of American cultural life, became convinced that they could effect a revival of morality and were compelled to do so in order to save the Republic. Millennial expectations, while affirmed rhetorically, were no longer reason enough to withdraw from the arena of public morality and civil order. In a sense, Jesus may have tarried, but independent Baptists did not, in their efforts to influence social and political renewal in American life. In so doing, independent Baptists have maintained the rhetoric of sectarian separatism while increasing their involvement with certain groups (Catholics, Mormons, charismatics) whom they earlier repudiated as apostate.

• • •

Independent Baptists are facing a dilemma: how to work together to secure their social and political agenda while remaining true to their most distinctive traditions, fundamentalist doctrine and ecclesiastical separatism. At this time, conclusions regarding the outcome involve the following observations.

We might describe early independent Baptists as the "theological Amish" of the Baptist tradition. They, like other Fundamentalists, in Martin Marty's words, "encountered modernity, did not like what they saw and regrouped or refashioned their faith."[8] The early independents believed that fundamentalist faith could be preserved best by means of the ecclesiological and ethical separatism characteristic of nineteenth- and early twentieth-century Baptist sectarians. Much of the Baptist identity they seek to preserve is of relatively recent vintage. At the same time, they increasingly have reflected a technological modernism in their willingness to utilize numerous modern methods, particularly the media, for propagating their faith and organizing their churches.

While they may have modified their separatism, independent Baptists are by no means moderate in their theological, moral, or political agendas. They continue to affirm Fundamentalist ideology, rejecting apostasy and modernism wherever it may appear. Thus their dilemma. A people schooled in separatism may find it difficult to follow leaders who push them into too many uneasy alliances with apostasy. Compromise, even for political and moral ends, is difficult for those who have been taught that all compromise is equivocation from the truth. At present "moderates" like the Rev. Jerry Falwell must maintain a fragile contract with their own constituency. They must remain sectarian at home while eating and drinking with assorted Republicans and sinners in order to accomplish certain political and social goals.

Independent Baptists remain an important contemporary phenomenon in American life. Their continuing struggle with modernity makes them an important case study in American civil and "civilizing" religion.

ENDNOTES

1. Samuel S. Hill and Dennis E. Owen, *The New Religious Political Right in America* (Nashville, 1982), 15.
2. Robert C. Liebman, "Mobilizing the Moral Majority," in *The New Christian Right*, ed. Robert Liebman and Robert Wuthnow (New York, 1983), 63-66.
3. James O. Combs, ed., *Roots and Origins of Baptist Fundamentalism* (Springfield, MO, 1984), 62; and C. Allyn Russell, *Voices of American Fundamentalism* (Philadelphia, 1976), 37-40.
4. Nancy Ammerman, *Bible Believers: Fundamentalists in the Modern World* (New Brunswick, NJ, 1987), 21.
5. Robert A. Baker, *The Southern Baptist Convention and Its People, 1607–1972* (Nashville, 1974), 150-59.
6. George M. Marsden, *Fundamentalism and American Culture: The Shaping of Twentieth-Century Evangelicalism, 1870–1925* (New York, 1980), 6-7.
7. "Why Did God Allow Kennedy's Death?" *Sword of the Lord*, 24 January 1964; "What Was Back of Kennedy's Murder?" *Sword of the Lord*, 31 January 1964; Bob Spencer, "Dr. Martin Luther King Died by the

Lawlessness He Encouraged," *Sword of the Lord*, 14 June 1968; Noel Smith, *Baptist Bible Tribune*, 23 April 1965.
8. Martin E. Marty, "Modern Fundamentalism," *America*, 27 September 1986, 134.

FOR FURTHER READING

Ammerman, Nancy Tatom. *Baptist Battles: Social Change and Religious Conflict in the Southern Baptist Convention*, New Brunswick, NJ, 1990.

Hunter, James Davison. *American Evangelicalism: Conservative Religion and the Quandary of Modernity*, New Brunswick, NJ, 1983.

Leonard, Bill J. *God's Last and Only Hope: The Fragmentation of the Southern Baptist Convention*, Grand Rapids, MI, 1990.

Rosenberg, Ellen M. *The Southern Baptists: A Subculture in Transition*, Knoxville, 1989.

Wuthnow, Robert. *The Restructuring of American Religion: Society and Faith Since World War II*, Princeton, 1988.

PART V

Alternatives in Religion

INTRODUCTION TO ESSAY 27

When alternatives to religious norms emerge, they usually raise questions about belief or behavior. In this case the central figure is a woman, and that circumstance makes the problem even more complicated. There is great irony here because Westerkamp shows in yet another setting that women have been active and influential in American religion from its earliest days. Yet, through Hutchinson's experience, we see again that women have had to bear discriminatory assumptions about women's secondary place in the religious sphere. In a valuable survey of recent scholarship, Westerkamp also demonstrates that Hutchinson's historical significance has been distorted by later generations of male prejudice as well.

Unlike some accounts of Hutchinson's trial, this essay gives us a front row seat where we can see what really happened. We observe Hutchinson defending herself with formidable religious expressiveness and debating skill. But the struggle ultimately comes down to authority: who decides what is acceptable, individuals or social managers? Hutchinson favored personal choice, and for orthodox Puritans this threatened to undermine theological and social standards. Put another way, there was disagreement over whether one observed the spirit or the letter of God's law, one written in the heart and the other in a book. Because Hutchinson chose freedom over uniformity, because she challenged those in control, and because it was a woman who dared to do this, dominant social forces suppressed her without mercy or regret.

Original source - CH 59 (1990): 482-96.

27

Anne Hutchinson, Sectarian Mysticism, and the Puritan Order

Marilyn J. Westerkamp

Anne Hutchinson has been one of the few women to attain canonical status in the history of colonial New England. Her marvelous intellectual abilities (so unusual in a seventeenth-century woman), her popularity among Boston men as well as women, and the powerful political and theological implications of her challenge render Hutchinson a force that must be explored if colonial Massachusetts is to be understood. Not only are historians fascinated by this extraordinary woman herself, they are intrigued by the colony's response to her; for in that very response the founders may have revealed their essential character.

Three biographies published in 1930 all portray Hutchinson as a pioneer for civil and religious liberty, crusading against the strictures of Puritan society.[1] As a historical corrective, Edmund Morgan pointed out that while the modern scholar might sympathize with Hutchinson's plight, especially the arbitrary nature of her trial, the Puritan colony was fairly new and Hutchinson represented a real threat to its political stability.[2]

Intellectual historians have focused the debate upon theology, arguing, generally among themselves, as to whether the central issue was sanctification as evidence of salvation. These historians insist that Hutchinson was a heretic in a society that placed a premium upon orthodoxy. Since Massachusetts was a biblical commonwealth, heresy posed a serious threat to social unity and political stability.[3]

A final group comprises those interpretations that examine Hutchinson as a rebel. Legal scholars analyze the dynamics of Hutchinson's trial as the state trial of a disruptive dissenter. One social historian considers Hutchinson a latent feminist leading other women in protest against the rigid male hierarchy, while a sociologist emphasizes the state's response to her challenge as the means by which Winthrop solidified his power. These essays appear to offer different interpretations, yet beneath the surface lies a basic similarity revealed by the title of an essay collection on Hutchinson: "Troubler of the Puritan Zion."[4] Anne Hutchinson was a deviant, a disturber of an otherwise peaceful, stable Puritan society which, of course, identified itself with the promised land. Individual founders may have had clear plans for Massachusetts' government, but they did not share the same vision. In his first four years as governor, John Winthrop had problems controlling the colony as people criticized the lenity of his judgments and then voted him out of office in favor of his premier critic, Thomas Dudley. Because Winthrop triumphed, his history had identified his vision as the universal, unchanging Puritan way. In fact, Massachusetts Bay was still working out its salvation when Hutchinson became popular, and it might be argued that the defeat of Hutchinson marked the beginning of the stable, homogeneous society that has come to be known as New England Puritanism.[5]

Despite the complexity of the controversy, the facts can be recounted quite easily. Sometime in 1635 Hutchinson began holding small gatherings of women to discuss the weekly sermons. Her intelligence and learning made her the natural leader, and within a year sixty or more people, including many men, would attend her meetings. She soon began to preach her own opinions and theology, and, much to the dismay of the clerical establishment, she criticized all the ministers except John Cotton and John Wheelwright, her brother-in-law. At one point her followers tried to get John Wheelwright added to the ministry of the Boston church. At another, Wheelwright delivered an antiestablishment sermon with such vehemence that he was convicted of sedition and the Hutchinsonians responded with a petition criticizing the government. In the summer of 1637 her followers refused to serve in the regiments sent to fight the Pequots because the chaplain was the "unconverted" John Wilson.

In 1637 Winthrop returned to office, and the power balance shifted. The colony was in confusion, and Winthrop realized he must resolve the issues quickly to maintain his authority. Through that summer the ministers consulted with Hutchinson, to no avail. She seemed unwilling to change her views and, if the truth be known, they were unable to find serious flaws in her argument. Thus in November Winthrop gathered his political forces, and Hutchinson was tried by the General Court on charges brought by the political and clerical leaders. After one and a half days of theological wrangling, and at every point Hutchinson appeared in the lead, she admitted that she was guided by the Holy Spirit's voice. In claiming revelation she convicted herself of blasphemy, and she was banished from the colony. Through that winter she lived under a sort of house arrest in the homes of ministers who counseled her for the sake of her soul. The Boston congregation itself excommunicated her in March 1638. Throughout these months a few of her followers were banished, several more were disfranchised and disarmed, and the majority were convinced of their errors and returned to Winthrop's fold. When Hutchinson left the Boston congregation after the excommunication sentence had been read, she was accompanied by one lone woman.

Let us reconsider Anne Hutchinson's trial. For one and a half days she ran intellectual circles around her opponents. They quoted Scripture; she quoted back. They interpreted a verse against her; she responded with an alternative text and a valid exegesis. Winthrop moved on to the painful subject of the religious meetings held in her home. Once again the wrangling ended with Hutchinson agreeing that "if you have a rule for [restraining my meetings] from God's word you may." Winthrop's answer: "We are your judges, and not you ours and we must compel you to it."

She had forced them to charge her with heresy, but the only evidence supporting this charge was a private conference between herself and the clergy. The examination now revolved around questions of what she did or did not say, what she did or did not intend. Many ministerial speeches were delivered, with no satisfaction on either side. Then, in the midst of the intellectual jousting, came a most remarkable exchange. Addressing her own right to speak to her beliefs, Hutchinson warned,

Mrs. H.: Now if you condemn me for speaking what in my conscience I know to be the truth I must commit myself unto the Lord.

Mr. Nowell: How do you know that was the spirit?

Mrs. H.: How did Abraham know that it was God that bid him offer his son, being a breach of the sixth commandment?

Dep. Gov.: By an immediate voice.

Mrs. H.: So to me by an immediate revelation.

Dep. Gov.: How! an immediate revelation.

Mrs. H.: By the voice of his own spirit to my soul.

This woman, charged with holding subversive theological opinions, claimed that she was following the voice of the Holy Spirit. The New England clergy, as any student of Massachusetts can attest, did not believe in direct revelation. They affirmed the Bible as the revealed word of God and acknowledged the strange, symbolic language of divine providence, but the age of direct revelation had passed. Any person claiming direct revelation was either lying or experiencing delusion. As Winthrop concluded, almost gleefully, "now the mercy of God by a providence hath answered our desires and made her to lay open her self and the ground of all these disturbances to be by revelation." And again, "Pass by all that hath been said formerly and her own speeches have been ground enough for us to proceed upon."[6]

Why did she say it? She was an intelligent, knowledgeable woman. Her testimony at her examination, though published by hostile opponents, is evidence enough of that. She must have realized that such a statement would convict her. Perhaps she believed that what she said was true. Why have historians been so reluctant to consider this most obvious explanation? Recall her own phrases: an immediate revelation, the voice of his own spirit to her soul. A few moments later she referred to Daniel in the lions' den: "This place in Daniel [6:4-5] was brought unto me and did show me that though I should meet with affliction yet I am the same God that delivered Daniel out of the lion's den, I will also deliver thee." Her assertions were not desperate efforts at self-justification nor were they born amidst confusion and helplessness. They were warnings to those who would condemn her: proclamations of strength, strength founded in the power of the spirit dwelling within her, the power that was thought to come from gracious communion with God. The strength, power, and knowledge, in fact, of the mystic.[7]

In his *Short Story of the Rise, reign, and ruine of the Antinomians* John Winthrop reported a speech delivered by Hutchinson on the second day of her trial. Perhaps growing weary of arguments concerning what she did or did not say, perhaps exhausted by clerical efforts to defend their reputations, perhaps anxious to be understood, Hutchinson revealed some of her own spiritual history. As she traveled her spiritual journey with all its confusion, after she had wandered in the darkness for twelve months, Christ showed her that the primary obstacle to her salvation lay within herself: "the Atheism of my own heart." She had followed the covenant of works; she had opposed Christ. Not only did Hutchinson sink into a deep spiritual miasma, but, along with other mystics, her first progressive steps toward enlightenment involved the discovery that she, herself, had to be overcome.

This was the first of many revelations. Following upon her efforts to purge herself of evil, God began telling her whose words were good and who served evil. The glory of John Cotton's preaching, instructions to follow John Cotton to Massachusetts, and warnings of coming adversity were all shown to her. And as Hutchinson proclaimed the gradual illumination of God's truth in her soul she appeared to discover her own union with God. She warned her opponents to "take heed what yee goe about to doe unto me, for you have no power over my body, neither can you do me any harme, for I am in the hands of the eternall [sic] Jehovah my Saviour, I am at his appointment, the bounds of my habitation are cast in Heaven." Likening herself to Daniel and the three young men in the fiery furnace, Hutchinson looked forward to a day when her presence, her vision, already justified before God, would be vindicated in the eyes of men.[8]

Of course John Winthrop was frightened; of course he behaved as if he were fighting for his life. The battle between Winthrop and Hutchinson was not a battle between two different conceptions of church and society. A man committed to one model of religious social order struggled against a woman who professed commitment to no order but that order revealed directly by God and thus one beyond the control of any individual or community. In presenting an alternative to Winthrop's society, an alternative that was outside human control, she was offering the freedom from law and structure that revelation gave her. Since Winthrop did not believe in direct revelation at all, since he was firmly committed to a social vision that denied temporal equality and incorporated hierarchical privileges and responsibilities, and since he as the leader of one tradition had suffered personally at the hands of the Hutchinsonians, the violence of his response is understandable. As leader of the opposing party Hutchinson directly challenged Winthrop's own vision and control.

It is not enough to say that Winthrop was using any means available for discrediting Hutchinson's leadership nor that his comments merely reflected misogynist attitudes common to the seventeenth century. Winthrop was responding to a threat he had linked, consciously or not, to Hutchinson's gender. Whether or not he himself understood precisely the nature of that threat, there was a connection between Hutchinson's gender and her religiosity. In other words, I argue that in attacking Hutchinson's femaleness Winthrop was attacking her spirituality.

Anne Hutchinson in the end affirmed her belief in direct revelation from the Spirit. Although no original Hutchinson writings have survived, even within those words quoted by her enemies, one can see union with the Spirit, and anger in prophecy. She too invoked the experience and words of Daniel; she predicted the downfall of her enemies, clerical and political. Within Hutchinson's own description of her spiritual development one can recognize characteristics seen in the writings of other Civil War mystics: "great weariness with the ecclesiastical problem, the terrible discovery of the apostasy of the churches and clergy with their corruption of the Gospel into a covenant of works, and finally the conviction that such teachings as had been granted resulted from the direct communication of the divine Teacher." This very faith in her revelation compelled Hutchinson to speak publicly.

In this call to speech lies the true power of the mystic, the source of her or his ultimate challenge. Most Christian theologies hold that each soul is individual, but the structures of church institutions belie that assertion. In an established church order, only those who have access to priesthood, to sacred power, are perceived and treated as individuals; others are identified as a class and are expected to respond, if at all, passively, as in "wives submit yourselves to your husbands," or "the women should keep silence."[9] However, union with God is not silent, and in her speech Hutchinson realizes herself as a person, not a passive member of a class.

Reformist theologians began to underrate the mystical experience of free grace and emphasize the need for education to understand God. They attacked the more spiritual woman through images of the witch of Endor and the seductress Eve. In other words, although New England's Puritan men did agree that women were individual souls, they would not grant women the same, unmediated pathway to God. By affirming sexual distinctions and male godlikeness, men claimed an ordered society and affirmed their personhood, necessarily through the objectification of women.[10]

By her actions Anne Hutchinson challenged John Winthrop's authority over his people; in her mysticism she challenged his sense of order. The added quality of her femaleness challenged his relationship with God. Winthrop saw before him a woman who refused to accept passively the restrictions that patriarchal society had placed upon her, refused merely to play the roles of wife, housekeeper, mother. In proclaiming her right to teach others, in essence to speak, she was asserting her ability to relate to God without male mediation. She affirmed herself as a person of intrinsic value. And lest any doubt remained, at her trial she proclaimed explicitly that she heard the Spirit's voice in her soul. While her revelation denied Winthrop's vision, her very claim to revelation challenged his selfhood. In exploring a direct relationship with the Spirit Anne Hutchinson offered women an opportunity to recover, perhaps discover, the self. But the personhood of women undermined the integrity of John Winthrop and his clergy. For their sake women were disempowered; Anne Hutchinson had to be destroyed.

ENDNOTES

1. Winifred King Rugg, *Unafraid: A Life of Anne Hutchinson* (New York, 1930); Edith Curtis, *Anne Hutchinson: A Biography* (Cambridge, MA, 1930); Helen Augur, *An American Jezebel: The Life of Anne Hutchinson* (New York, 1930).
2. Edmund S. Morgan, "The Case Against Anne Hutchinson," *New England Quarterly* 10 (1937): 633-49.
3. Emery Battis, *Saints and Sectaries: Anne Hutchinson and the Antinomian Controversy in the Massachusetts Bay Colony* (Chapel Hill, NC, 1962); David D. Hall, ed., *The Antinomian Controversy, 1636–1638: A Documentary History* (Middletown, CT, 1968), 3-24.
4. Francis J. Bremer, ed., *Troubler of the Puritan Zion* (New York, 1981).
5. Kai T. Erikson, *Wayward Puritans: A Study in the Sociology of Deviance* (New York, 1966), 3-29.
6. "Examination of Hutchinson," in Hall, *Antinomian Controversy*, 314, 316, 337. The excerpts from the trial itself also come from this text, p. 337.
7. Most literature on English Protestant mysticism focuses upon the Quakers, although Rufus M. Jones in his *Spiritual Reformers in the Sixteenth and Seventeenth Centuries* (Boston, 1914) and his *Mysticism and Democracy in the English Commonwealth* (Cambridge, MA, 1932) explores other mystical sectarians. See also Nuttall, *Holy Spirit in Puritan Faith*. For an excellent precis of Puritan mysticism, see Jerald C. Brauer, "Types of Puritan Piety," *Church History* 56 (1987): 39-58.
8. One sees here touches of the prophet as well as the mystic. On Hutchinson as a prophet, see Elaine Huber, *Women and the Authority of Inspiration* (Lanham, MD, 1987), 65-122. For a general discussion of female prophecy, see Phyllis Mack, "Women as Prophets During the English Civil War,"*Feminist Studies* 8 (1982): 19-45.
9. Ephesians 2:5; 1 Corinthians 14:34.
10. Ben Barker-Benfield, "Anne Hutchinson and the Puritan Attitude Toward Women," *Feminist Studies* 1 (1972): 77, 83-84.

FOR FURTHER READING

Boyer, Paul, and Stephen Nissenbaum, *Salem Possessed: The Social Origins of Witchcraft*, Cambridge, MA, 1974.

Braude, Ann. *Radical Spirits: Spiritualism and Women's Rights in Nineteenth-Century America*, Boston, 1989.

Cohen, Charles Lloyd. *God's Caress: The Psychology of Puritan Religious Experience*, New York, 1986.

Hall, David D. *The Faithful Shepherd: A History of New England Ministry in the Seventeenth Century*, Chapel Hill, NC, 1972.

————. *Worlds of Wonder, Days of Judgment: Popular Religious Belief in Early New England*, Cambridge, MA, 1989.

Lang, Amy Shrager. *Prophetic Woman: Anne Hutchinson and the Problem of Dissent in the Literature of New England*, Berkeley, 1987.

Lovejoy, David S. *Religious Enthusiasm in the New World: Heresy to Revolution*, Cambridge, MA, 1985.

Porterfield, Amanda. *Female Piety in Puritan New England: The Emergence of Religious Humanism*, New York, 1992.

————. *Feminine Spirituality in America: From Sarah Edwards to Martha Graham*, Philadelphia, 1980.

Williams, Selma R. *Divine Rebel: The Life of Anne Marbury Hutchinson*, New York, 1981.

INTRODUCTION TO ESSAY 28

The Salvation Army is a good example of an alternative religious impulse, separating as it did in the mid-1800s from Methodism, which had previously left the Church of England, who in turn had departed from Catholicism several centuries earlier. The Army is also a good example of survivability, starting with a strong social conscience and building institutional strength through basic evangelical emphases. This important religious organization remains apart from mainstream denominationalism but has expanded to the point of having established affiliates around the world. Murdoch's essay focuses on the movement's cofounder, an influential woman who was able to introduce liberal measures in a setting that was unfettered by custom or church traditions.

To set the stage for Booth's innovations, Murdoch exhibits the way many used the Bible to keep women subordinate or in their place. He then shows how Booth and other reformers used Scripture to subvert chauvinist condescension. More to the point, this essay demonstrates the effect one individual can have on a movement, how Booth's preaching served as an example for others to follow, and how her influential position in the organization determined personnel changes. In her quiet way Booth made the Army a dynamic, forward-looking evangelical organization where women were able to participate more fully and equally in religious work.

Original source - CH 53 (1984): 348-62.

28

Female Ministry in the Thought and Work of Catherine Booth

Norman H. Murdoch

As with other professions, the ministry has a long record of excluding women from its ranks. Virtually all women, unlike all men, have been categorized as laity, although they have failed even to achieve that designation on occasion. George Bernard Shaw, in *The Doctor's Dilemma*, observed that "every profession is a conspiracy against the laity." Certainly this has been the case among lay women aspiring to become members of the clergy. But Shaw recognized in his play, *Major Barbara* (1905), a new kind of Christian minister, one who contested her business-tycoon father on a significant contemporary issue of how best to relieve poverty in Britain. Indirectly Shaw was paying tribute to the influence of Catherine Booth (1829–1890), co-founder of the Salvation Army, who recognized women's powers of intellect and innate equality and elevated them to clerical parity with men.

Although Catherine Booth did not break new hermeneutical ground in her discussion of scriptural support for the ministry of women, she did, through her public advocacy, force the introduction of thousands of working-class women into the ranks of ordained clergy. When the Salvation Army arrived in the United States in 1879, led by two women, the 1880 census recorded only 165 women clergy alongside 65,533 men. But by 1900 over 9 percent of all clergy, 11,027, were women, 108,537 were men. The Salvation Army, in the vanguard of this increase, had 1,854 officers in the United States in 1896, at least 1,000 of whom were women.[1] The Army's commitment to a female ministry began in the mind of Catherine Booth in the 1850s. It was amplified in the organization her husband founded in East London in 1865. By the time Catherine died of cancer in 1890, her influence for women's equality in the pulpit had been a principal attribute of the Army for over a decade.

• • •

Catherine Booth's ideas on the right of women to preach evolved gradually. In 1850, at age twenty-one, the year before she met William Booth, she wrote to a London Congregationalist clergyman after he demeaned woman as a moral being. Catherine was attending his church near her Brixton (London) home due to frustration with the "ordinary style" and "spirit of controversy" in her beloved Methodism. In a letter to Dr. David Thomas she presented her principal complaint concerning woman's long-standing inferior position. It was nurture, not nature, that crippled the female intellect. She argued that woman's "training from babyhood even in this highly favoured land, has hitherto been such as to cramp and paralyze rather than to develop and strengthen her energies, and calculated to crush and wither her aspirations after mental greatness rather than to excite and stimulate them. The day is only just dawning with reference to female education and therefore any verdict on woman as an intellectual being must be premature and unsatisfactory."[2] Not yet concerned with women in the pulpit, Catherine was joining the swelling crusade for equal opportunity to develop innate capacities, at a time when women's academies and seminaries were just starting.

Catherine Booth came to her final commitment to the idea of a female ministry in late 1859. American evangelists Dr. and Mrs. Walter Clark Palmer were holding meetings at Newcastle. Phoebe Palmer (1807–1874), the principal revivalist, preached the kind of Methodist holiness doctrine in which the Booths believed. The Booths had embraced the writings of William Bramwell, an English Wesleyan holiness preacher, and heard James Caughey, an American Methodist evangelist who had given them their sympathy for American revivalist methodology. Phoebe would step to the front of the chapel modestly after her husband had opened the service and the preacher had said a few words. Avoiding the pulpit for fear of causing offense, Phoebe spoke in the nave, giving her testimony.[3]

An attack on Mrs. Palmer's right to preach was made by the Reverend Arthur Augustus Rees, of Sunderland, who gave "Reasons for Not Cooperating in the Alleged Sunderland

Revivals." Catherine wrote to her mother concerning Rees: "Would you believe that a congregation half composed of ladies could sit and hear such self-depreciatory rubbish?" After reading Rees's pamphlet in December 1859, Catherine's ideas on female ministry matured and led, almost immediately, to her own preaching ministry which would extend over the last thirty years of her life. When other responses to Rees did not satisfy her, Catherine composed her 32-page pamphlet, *Female Ministry: Woman's Right to Preach the Gospel*, formulating her basic ideas on women in the clergy. She began with the "most common objection," namely, that women preachers are "unnatural and unfeminine." This, she wrote, confounded "nature with custom." Rather, woman's "graceful form and attitude, winning manners, persuasive speech, and above all, a finely-toned emotional nature" are ideal equipment for public speaking.

Her second, and most important, attack was against the allegation that "female ministry is *forbidden in the Word of God*." Paul, she alleged, actually supports female preaching. In 1 Corinthians 11:4-5, Paul saw women as prophesying with heads covered, and men without. Some held that women could speak only in assemblies of women, as Mrs. Finney did, but Catherine countered that since "two-thirds of the whole Church" is made up of women, it would be men who would be compelled to silence if this verse means speaking only to one's own sex. Like Mrs. Palmer, Mrs. Booth found great success in mixed congregations and was particularly popular with men. In Acts 2, she found, the early church fulfilled Joel's prophecy (2:28) that "your sons and your daughters shall prophesy," thereby confirming woman's right to preach.

But Catherine still had to tackle Paul's two admonitions against women "speaking" in church. First, just after having asserted woman's right to preach, he advised the Corinthians: "Let your women keep silence in the churches, for it is not permitted unto them to *speak*; but they are commanded to be under obedience, as also saith the law. And if they will learn anything, let them ask their husbands at home; for it is a shame for women to *speak* in the church" (1 Corinthians 14:34-35 KJV). Catherine took the Greek word, *lalein* (to speak), to mean "imprudent or ignorant talking," not to be confused with Paul's earlier recognition of woman's right to "prophesy." He was concerned with "attempts to usurp authority over men," an act of which "no woman would be guilty who is under the influence of the Spirit of God," according to Mrs. Booth.[4]

The second problematic passage is in Paul's first letter to Timothy: "Let the woman learn in silence with all subjection. But I suffer not a woman to teach, or to *usurp authority* over the man, but to be in silence. For Adam was first formed, then Eve" (1 Timothy 2:11-13). To relegate women to private ministries, "working for the temporalities of the Church," is "the supreme selfishness," allowing her "the hewing of wood and the drawing of water," while denying her the right to preach the gospel which Jesus himself did not deny the woman of Samaria (John 4:1-42). If a woman has the call from the Holy Spirit, there is no scripture which denies her right to preach. Catherine then recalled women of authority from the Old Testament to the present, regarding Paul's position in 1 Timothy to be out of step with the preponderance of his own teaching and the totality of scripture. To her, the "unjustifiable application of the passage, 'Let your women keep silence in the Churches,' has resulted in more loss to the Church, evil to the world, and dishonour to God, than any of the errors" she had previously discussed.

• • •

Catherine's own preaching began on Whit Sunday, 1860, following the publication of *Female Ministry*, at her husband's Methodist New Connexion Bethesda Chapel at Gateshead. Feeling "the Spirit come upon" her, she walked to the front where William was concluding his sermon and said, "I want to say a word." He introduced her and sat down. She gave her testimony concerning her struggle over a public ministry leading up to that moment. Many wept as she concluded, and William announced that his wife would preach that evening. This initiated thirty years of preaching in Britain which, many agree, no man of her era exceeded in popularity or spiritual results, including her husband.

After William founded his East London Mission in 1865, Catherine became the breadwinner for the family, preaching in West London and elsewhere and selling her writings, while her husband accepted no salary from his mission. When the mission began holding annual conferences in 1870, she insisted on the employment of women evangelists. As the mission grew into the Salvation Army in 1878, Catherine turned her energies to the recruitment and "mental culture" of thousands of young women who were trained and commissioned as Salvation Army officers under her daughters Emma, Eva, and Lucy to save "hundreds of the greatest roughs" in English slums.

As her children matured in the 1870s and 1880s, Catherine directed their thinking, marriages, and vocations; and they in turn led the Army in Britain, France, India, the United States, Australia, and Canada, with eldest son Bramwell serving as chief-of-staff to his father in London. The dynasty grew through advantageous marriages of Catherine's sons to women who shared their mother-in-law's zeal for a female ministry. The Booths' daughters who were active in the movement included Catherine Booth-Clibborn (1858–1955), Emma Booth-Tucker (1860–1903), Evangeline Booth (1865–1950), and Lucy Booth-Hellberg (1867–1953). They were all officer-administrators like their brothers until after Catherine's death. In 1904, the Booth-Clibborns resigned to follow Alexander Dowie, a Chicago-based cult leader. Emma died in a Missouri train accident in 1903. Two of the three sons, Ballington and Herbert, left "the work" in 1896 and 1902 respectively, to continue evangelistic careers separate from their father's. In 1896 Ballington founded the Volunteers of America, of which he was general. In addition to Catherine's daughters and daughters-in-law, other middle-class women were attracted to what some perceived to be a Protestant religious order. Little more than the names of some of these women of refinement is known, but their motivation was akin to that of middle-class women in settlement house, prohibitionist, purity, and woman's suffrage crusades.[5]

After recruitment these women entered the training home established by Mrs. Booth and her daughter Emma in London in 1880 to provide three to six months of intensive immersion in practical evangelism, basic management, and elementary literacy. Then as lieutenants they assisted several women captains prior to taking their own appointment as captain in a small town or section of a city. They preached nightly, indoors and out, visited from house to house, and raised enough money for their subsistence allowance through the sale of the *War Cry*, Booth's weekly. After three to six months they moved to another town, but continued the same routine, paired with another single woman. Married women bore the rank of their husbands and shared their work, although not as equally as William Booth.

• • •

In spite of the dilemma regarding hierarchical positioning, Catherine Booth's ideas, rooted in mid-nineteenth-century Anglo-American Wesleyanism, and released by Phoebe Palmer, produced three significant positive results. First, women officers receive and maintain an equal right to perform all "priestly" functions in the Salvation Army and continue to make up a majority of its 24,779 ordained officers. Compared to other communions, some still resisting female ministry and some experiencing recession from earlier equality, the Army's record is impressive, even though virtually no forward movement in status has taken place since Catherine's death in 1890. Married women still do not receive "equal pay" for "equal work," and "male dominance" is as apparent as ever in administrative and corps appointments.

Second, if it had not been for Catherine Booth's influence for female ministry, the Salvation Army would still be one of hundreds of insignificant inner-city missions. Its growth, begun under its new name in 1878, was more the result of the thousands of women recruited as officers than of its military structure and vernacular. The American branch of the movement, begun by two women in Philadelphia in 1879, impressed Francis E. Willard, who became a member of the auxiliary and a friend of Evangeline Booth and saw "General Booth in action" in 1893. It is likely that most local corps have been commenced by women.

Third, the Army as a social reform movement in the 1880s drew its concern for "fallen women." The Army's rescue homes and slum posts of 1883–1884, both commenced by women, antedated its food and shelter depots (1888) and William Booth's grandiose "Darkest England Scheme" (1890). The majority of single-woman officers have been attached to the Army's social institutions. Due to their selfless dedication, Beatrice Webb referred to them as a new class of "Samurai," a model for what Beatrice and Sidney Webb hoped to accomplish through government.

Catherine Booth's aggressive campaign for a female ministry produced the resource which gained worldwide recognition for the Army as a social reform and evangelizing agency. As her son-in-law wrote immediately after her death: "For what better argument could we find in favour of woman's ministry than the success achieved by the five thousand women officers and tens of thousands of women speakers whom Mrs. Booth left behind at her death."[6] All of this occurred during the formative period of the Salvation Army, 1870–1890, as a result of earlier Wesleyan examples and the influence of American evangelist Phoebe Palmer.

ENDNOTES

1. George Scott Railton, *Why Not? A Salvation Army Question* (London, 1896).
2. Catherine Booth, *Female Ministry: Woman's Right to Preach the Gospel* (1859; reprint ed., New York, 1975); Catherine Bramwell-Booth, *Catherine Booth: The Story of Her Loves* (London, 1970), 49-52; William T. Stead, *Catherine Booth* (London, 1900); Frederick St. George deLatour Booth-Tucker, *The Life of Catherine Booth, The Mother of the Salvation Army*, 2 vols. (London, 1893).
3. Richard Carwardine, *Transatlantic Revivalism: Popular Evangelicalism in Britain and America, 1790–1865* (London, 1978), 188.
4. C. Booth, *Female Ministry*, 5-7, 9-13.
5. Allen F. Davis, *American Heroine: The Life and Legend of Jane Addams* (New York, 1973); Flora Larsson, *My Best Men Are Women* (New York, 1974); Bernard Watson, *Soldier Saint* (London, 1970).
6. Booth-Tucker, *Catherine Booth*, 1:356.

FOR FURTHER READING

Batchelor, Mary. *Catherine Bramwell-Booth*, Tring, United Kingdom, 1986.
Boydston, Jeanne, Mary Kelly, and Anne Margolis. *The Limits of Sisterhood: The Beecher Sisters on Women's Rights and Woman's Sphere*, Chapel Hill, NC, 1988.
Green, Roger J. *Catherine Booth: A Biography of the Cofounder of the Salvation Army*, Grand Rapids, MI, 1996.

Hassey, Janeette. *No Time for Silence: Evangelical Women in Public Ministry Around the Turn of the Century*, Grand Rapids, MI, 1986.

McKinley, Edward H. *Marching to Glory: The History of the Salvation Army in the United States, 1880–1992*, 2d ed., Grand Rapids, MI, 1995.

Murdoch, Norman H. *Origins of the Salvation Army*, Knoxville, 1994.

Troutt, Margaret. *The General Was a Lady: The Story of Evangeline Booth*, Nashville, 1980.

White, Charles Edward. *The Beauty of Holiness: Phoebe Palmer as Theologian, Revivalist, Feminist, and Humanitarian*, Grand Rapids, MI, 1986.

INTRODUCTION TO ESSAY 29

Now we come to one of the largest, most distinctive groups in the wide array of American religions. While claiming ancient origins, Mormons emerged during the 1830s in this country, and they have been expanding ever since. In this essay the author is primarily concerned with accounting for Mormon growth in hopes of grasping what really makes this religious orientation attractive. We find here some details about the prophet Joseph Smith and the beginnings of his movement. But there is more emphasis on those who joined later, where they came from, and what environmental conditions affected their lives.

In an indirect way DePillis makes us grapple with the "frontier thesis" that was popularized by F. J. Turner in the early 1900s. This is good practice for us because it shows how difficult it is to define "frontier" and to measure its effect on American life. The author also adds to our knowledge of the Second Great Awakening, whose emphases Mormons perpetuated. In the last analysis we learn from DePillis that Mormonism developed from multiple social and intellectual sources. In canvassing early converts, we see no question of urban *versus* agrarian origins but rather a rich variety of origins. This demographic study offers no deterministic or exhaustive explanation of Mormon beginnings. It does, however, catch some of the dynamic spirit that helped it grow in strength and zeal.

Original source - CH 37 (1968): 50-79.

29

The Social Sources of Mormonism

Mario S. DePillis

Since the very beginnings of Mormon history, non-Mormon historians have traced the sources of the religion in one way or another to some conception of New England. The conceptions have been as varied as the writers themselves: New England has been the land of both enthusiasm and rational religion; of educated, enlightened Yankees and of credulous, anti-intellectual Yankees; of a culture east of the Hudson and of a culture extending across the northern half of the United States; a region of people with great civic and religious virtue but also a people noted for deception, cunning, and hypocrisy. The problem of the New England Mind has never been settled, but all writers have assumed that at one time or another western New York, the supposed birthplace of Mormonism, was a "frontier" of New England.

Western New York reached the apex of its fame in the first third of the nineteenth century, when it became the focal point of religious and social ferment. Surely it deserved its sobriquet of "Burned-over District." During the past twenty years historians have regarded the district as a phenomenon in American "social and intellectual" history, and the standard interpretation from this point of view is a monograph by Whitney R. Cross.[1]

Following Cross, some recent historians have maintained (1) that western New York was neither a frontier nor a cultural backwash in the 1820s; (2) that Mormonism arose in "the East" because most of its personnel was drawn from New England and from Europe; and (3) that Mormon polity and doctrine were eastern in origin. Cross himself conveniently summed up these three conclusions:

Neither the organization of the [Mormon] church, nor its personnel, nor its doctrines were frontier products. All belonged rather to that Yankee, rural, emotionalized, and rapidly maturing culture which characterized western New York so markedly in the second quarter of the nineteenth century.

By the word "rural" Cross meant long-settled, stable villages, like those of Europe. The key words are "Yankee" and "rapidly maturing."[2] One fine general study of Mormonism follows Cross's picture of an almost urbanized western New York quite closely and the author of a recent survey of the historiography of Mormonism simply stated: "Cross has convincingly demonstrated that neither the Saints nor their movement were products of the frontier."

One may best make some sense of the Mormon-New England relationship by subjecting Cross's logic and evidence to a detailed analysis. It will also be necessary to present additional and more representative evidence--though this must be limited by the scope of the article. The analysis will deal candidly with serious weaknesses in Cross's interpretation. But the mere fact that any genetic study of Mormonism must begin with Cross's brief one-chapter account is a tribute to his pioneering contribution to the contextual approach to Mormon religion and other "ultraisms" of the Jacksonian era.

• • •

From the very start Cross is careful to distinguish the ultraism of New England from the emotional revivalism associated with the famous Kentucky revival of 1801–1805. Immigrant Yankees like Joseph Smith, Sr., were "relatively staid" believers who were repelled by the violent, sensational "exercises" of the southern frontiersmen. Yankees had "calmer" revivalist experiences. Smith and his neighbors, put off by what Cross might have called the un-Yankee enthusiasm that seared the Palmyra area, sought a less orgiastic, true religion. Smith satisfied their "inbred desire to achieve an orderly, intellectual formulation of their beliefs." He provided authoritative answers which satisfied the needs of his excited, credulous, practical, intellectual, socially conscious Yankee followers. Converts were credulous, and were thus very receptive to the *Book of Mormon*: the story of an Indian (Hebrew) civilization torn by masonry, infant baptism, and similar issues.

Smith also appealed to Yankee practicality by combining "appeals to reason and self-interest with emotional attractions." While promising them physical comfort and early abundance, "his degree of communism resurrected the strong sense of social obligation that all should have for each and each for all, which had been long declining in the Puritan tradition of old New England." As much American as Yankee was the receptivity to the "democratic and flattering" Mormon doctrine that all lay men could participate in the special Mormon priesthood.

Though Cross does not define "Yankee" or "New England," this summary of his interpretation makes it evident that he unconsciously conceived of New England as a set of mental traits imported into western New York: credulous but desirous of rational formulations; practical, having a strong sense of social obligation. This rather ordinary conception of New England and its relation to Mormonism forms only part of Cross's overall interpretation. His major argument, more original and influential, is demographic. With maps of county population and a few details about the kind of "rapidly maturing culture" that allegedly formed the environment of Mormonism, he concludes that Mormonism was not a "frontier" religion. He asserts, with evidence that can be shown to be inconclusive, that (1) Mormonism arose in the "longest settled neighborhoods" of the rural but "rapidly maturing" culture which characterized western New York between 1825 and 1850; and (2) that it appealed not to midwestern frontiersmen but mainly to New Englanders born in New York and, after 1850, to Scandinavians and Englishmen.

The first part of Cross's analysis is ordinary intellectual history loosely tied to an impressionistic conception of the New England mind. The second and more important part is based on a somewhat unsophisticated demographic-cultural analysis. But because of his confused logic and his superficial grasp of the Mormon sources, Cross's account of the rise of Mormonism is quite inadequate.

We may, therefore, conclude that there is absolutely no evidence for Cross's statement that Joseph Smith consistently moved eastward, deterministically drawn by greater population density. So much for "peregrinations" toward the east. But what of Mormonism itself? Was there any such thing before 1830? Cross never defines early Mormonism; but one of its important elements—its communitarianism—arose after 1830 in Ohio. Cross attributes Mormon communitarianism to the Yankee sense of social obligation. Actually, this feature of Mormonism entered the as yet inchoate religion as a result of the Campbellite and Shaker influences Smith encountered when he fled westward to Kirtland, Ohio. These influences were not simply Yankee but middle-state and English. Alexander Campbell and Mother Ann Lee, the founders, respectively, of Campbellism and Shakerism, were both British immigrants. Indeed, religious communitarianism was a general Protestant phenomenon, one of the many reaffirmations in Christian history of the New Testament communism of Acts 2 and 4.

Not simply communitarianism but almost all of Mormonism developed after 1830 in the Midwest: its economics, theology, and social arrangements. Mormonism developed largely outside of the *Book of Mormon* in a series of over one hundred and thirty revelations, almost all of them issued by Smith between 1830 and his death in 1844. These revelations are collected in the *Doctrine and Covenants*, a volume which is far more important than the *Book of Mormon* for understanding the rise and historical development of Mormon institutions and doctrines.[3] Cross's "Mormonism" is a vague, nontheological, nondoctrinal movement that bears little relationship to the development that took place after 1830.

Cross's second major line of analysis was a demographic-cultural one. He stated that Smith's recruits were predominantly native-born Yankee New Yorkers who lived mainly in the more mature areas of western New York. His evidence for this generalization is so riddled by guesswork and virtual ignoring of basic Mormon sources that it is of practically no value. Cross asked: "How did the Church of Latter-day Saints select and emphasize from its Burned-over District milieu those principles of religion and society which would patently attract persons bred in the same environment?" His answers purport to prove that the new region was a product of the Burned-over District. This decades-old generalization, if applied to "Mormonism" as an unorganized movement (rather than the well-defined sect which took shape after 1830) can hardly be disputed. It is Cross's way of stating and supporting this truism that is so untenable; for in all four explanations of Mormonism he introduced oversimplifications and distortions which may be traced to his underlying antifrontier bias—more specifically, to his thesis that most of the Burned-over District was "not a frontier," but rather a "rapidly maturing" society.

Cross believed that the nonfrontier origins of Mormonism were proved by Joseph's alleged eastward "peregrinations." He thought to clinch this argument by trying to show that the Prophet found most of his recruits in the longer-settled regions of New York state, especially the Palmyra-Manchester area. Even if Cross were reliable or clear concerning the chronological and biographical facts of early Mormon history and the frontier, his account of the rise of Mormonism would still be weak because of the omission of the history of Mormonism in Ohio. The tiny sect would probably have disappeared along with the other isms of the day if it had not been transformed by a series of events in Kirtland, Ohio, in 1830–1831; namely, the conversion of over a hundred Campbellites, Rigdonites, and a few Shakers. The concomitant transformation of doctrine changed what was just another knot of typical, rural, New England "ultraists" into a solid and stable group—with new opportunities, great vitality, and better leadership.

• • •

Cross suggested four reasons for the appeal of Mormonism to the people of the Burned-over District: local Indian legends, Yankee traits, the ubiquity of *Book of Mormon* doctrines, and cultural-demographic factors (Smith's "eastward" peregrinations, the nonfrontier origins of converts, the nonfrontier nature of western New York). Not all of these can be analyzed in this essay, but two basic questions ought to be considered: first, whether the census report of 1860 lends any credence to the surmises of Cross; and, second, whether the biographical analysis of actual Mormons (as opposed to nameless census statistics) can reveal anything of Mormon social origins. Census statistics are useless unless illuminated by primary historical sources. Only a complete immersion in the history of Mormonism could have enabled Cross to use the census fruitfully. Depending on which variable is applied to the figures, Mormonism can be shown to have originated in Illinois or Iowa as much as New York.

In sum, Cross's seemingly scientific, quantified demographic argument is really quite speculative when not erroneous or misleading. Even if his speculations were useful, they would be limited by an ignorance of Mormon sources and by the construction of a strawman "frontier" defined sometimes as thinness of population, sometimes as "ripeness" of settlement. Cross must have been aware of the tenuousness of his argument: his tentative phraseology is qualified to the point of being almost meaningless.

It was perhaps this assiduous ingenuity as well as his East-West dichotomy that blinded Cross to important local evidence within particular states—political boundaries can encompass more than one social locality. American historians seem unable to accept the long-established sociological truth that the social dislocations giving rise to prophets can be either rural or urban—that the settlement of the woods of Wayne County, New York, could be as socially unsettling as the early nineteenth-century growth of Philadelphia, Pennsylvania; that both areas could provide Mormon converts. The roots of social discontent in these areas followed the classic rule of the sociology of religion: profound social or economic dislocation breeds sectarianism. In the Mormon locales of southeastern Pennsylvania (Chester and Delaware Counties), the change was neither "rural" nor "urban."

There is much more reliable evidence for the time and place of conversions to Mormonism than a fanciful reconstruction of demographic statistics. Because of the Prophet's injunction that elders keep journals and because of his conscientious gathering of materials for his own history, Mormon missionary activities and, indeed all Mormon history is probably more completely documented than any other comparable religion.

Using these rich Mormon materials on proselytizing at about the same time that Cross was consulting the census, S. George Ellsworth concluded from the geographical distribution of over two hundred Mormon congregations or locales in the 1830s and from the fact that the West and the South received less time and attention than the East, that during the 1830s "Mormon converts came chiefly (almost wholly) from those areas of the United States where the density of population varied from eighteen to ninety inhabitants per square mile. Mormon locales were in areas more rural than urban (even as the United States was then more rural than urban) and in neither frontier nor metropolitan areas."[4]

This is a fair conclusion from the evidence. But the antifrontier tone is there in the substitution of "almost wholly" for 71 percent and in the setting up of the old strawman "frontier" which Ellsworth explicitly defines as "that region of settlement where population density is from 2-6 inhabitants per square mile." More important, it is a static interpretation that does not do justice to the swift historical change that saw the total population of the United States nearly double between 1830 and 1850. Densities changed and Mormon centers of interest changed with them. No religion was ever established in the United States among coyotes and bears—the "frontier" of two to six persons per square mile. As Ellsworth himself points out, institutions presuppose people and missionaries "went where there were people to listen"; and there people had to have a compatible kind of evangelical or "seeker" religious background. Very few Calvinists, Lutherans, Anglicans, or Catholics were converted to Mormonism. It should also be noted that prospective converts almost always lived under unstable local social, economic, or religious conditions, usually in a newly settled, value-disoriented society. Converts were also found in the urbanized environs of the English Potteries. All early Mormon converts came from the lower, but not the lowest, classes, whether rural or urban in their origins.

Thus, any explanation of the genesis of Mormonism must be more complex than the "New England" traits of western New York in the 1820s. There is no doubt that as an inchoate movement consisting of Joseph Smith, his *Book of Mormon,* and about 30 to 180 followers (1827–1830), Mormonism was, in a very general sense, the product of the Burned-over District. But the "district" is merely a vague term for western New York. Within this large region one could find sizable areas that were nearly wilderness; only a few places became stable towns quickly. Smith was most successful in the newly settled and most rural localities.

But even this generalization fails to distinguish Mormonism from the movements of Smith's rival prophets and does not explain its unique social and historical significance in American history during its period of doctrinal formation (1830–1844). In other words, the psychosocial, environmental generalization must be extended to the very similar areas in the West: to the socially disoriented, rural, newly settled areas of Ohio, Missouri, Illinois; and also to the long-settled East, i.e., to a few eastern rural back-waters from Maine to West Virginia. The continuous association of Smith and his missionaries with such areas provided Mormonism with superb opportunities to elaborate both polity and doctrine between 1830 and 1844.

In Ohio and other parts of the Midwest, Smith continued to find the same kind of rural, evangelical, uneducated, receptive audience that had welcomed the *Book of Mormon* and the first few tentative revelations back in New York state. Most of Smith's direct, highly detailed revelations came after 1830, and the strong faith of the many new converts in these later teachings revealed a strong continuity of clientele. This continued appeal of a still incomplete "Mormonism" after 1830 in the Midwest is the key to any understanding of the genesis of Mormonism. Mormonism was not born in New York; it was simply announced there in connection with the translation of the *Book of Mormon*. Contrary to an almost universal misconception among non-Mormons (including scholars), the *Book of Mormon* was less important for doctrine and polity than the *Doctrine and Covenants*, a standard compilation of the Prophet's 134 revelations.[5]

The continuity of clientele enabled Smith to build a more substantial and lasting road to happiness than the less talented and less fortunately located prophets of his day. During this later period, he especially emphasized and institutionalized the Mormon form of millennialism; also the short-lived but deeply influential communitarianism above all the claim of Mormonism to exclusive and unerring religious authority. Such doctrines have always appealed to the socially disinherited, and converts in the mainly rural parts could be called disinherited despite their alleged Jacksonian optimism, happiness, and freedom. Such persons were socially disinherited in that they could no longer look to their former religious leaders and former ways of life for security and orientation—an almost universal experience among migrants.

Like almost all millennial sects in recent history, large-scale social and economic dislocations are the fundamental causes of such outbursts as took place during the Jacksonian "era of reform." The description of such fundamental dislocations is beyond the scope of an article. But certainly the furious economic growth and the extraordinary pace and fluidity of migration westward from the relatively stable eastern metropolis helped create the socially disoriented, rural environments of western New York, western Pennsylvania, Ohio, Missouri, and Illinois. By almost inescapable convention such areas are usually called "frontiers." But despite the equally inescapable modern suspicion of "frontier interpretations," no one can deny that a very special American social process of making new settlements did exist.

The continuous association of Mormonism during its formative years (1827–1844) with the "frontier"—and, as noted, with a few socially unstable areas in the East—kept Mormon missionaries in close contact with people who were predisposed to such a religion. When converted, such persons continually reinforced Mormon millennial teachings and sometimes even added to them. After 1837 Mormon missionaries discovered a rich field in parts of England, Wales, and Scandinavia, where a socially disoriented, evangelical population, very similar to that of the American "frontier," were quite ready to hear the new gospel. Almost everywhere during the first third of the nineteenth century, the backwoods environment provided the kind of fluid social milieu that resembled conditions in the first localities of Mormon success—in the Burned-over District.

The thesis of this article has been that the origin (1827–1844) of what can be called Mormonism was related to the disorientation of values associated with migration to and within the backwoods areas of the United States. Typically, these areas were newly settled, rural locales, and might be loosely called "frontier" areas—whether or not they contained more than six persons per square mile. Typically, the population was evangelical and sectarian in religion. If the "frontier" were defined as a social and economic process and a psychological milieu instead of an arbitrarily fixed arithmetical ratio or a vague "West," the social basis of religious discontent could be better described and perhaps understood.

ENDNOTES

1. Whitney R. Cross, *The Burned-over District: the Social and Intellectual History of Enthusiastic Religion in Western New York, 1880–1850* (Ithaca, 1950); David Brion Davis, "The New England Origins of Mormonism," *New England Quarterly* 27 (1953): 148-63.
2. Thomas F. O'Dea, *The Mormons* (Chicago, 1957), 7.
3. Brigham H. Roberts, *The Rise and Fall of Nauvoo* (Salt Lake City, 1900), 17, 165-215; Daryl Chase, *Joseph the Prophet* (Salt Lake City, 1944), 74-75. See also the *History of the Church*, 3:379-81, 386ff.
4. See the exhaustive study by S. George Ellsworth, "History of Mormon Missions in the United States and Canada, 1830–1860," (Ph.D. diss., University of California at Berkeley, 1951).
5. See Francis W. Kirkham, *A New Witness for Christ in America, the Book of Mormon*, 2 vols. (Salt Lake City, 1959–1960); Fawn M. Brodie, *No Man Knows My History: the Life of Joseph Smith, the Mormon Prophet* (New York, 1945); Norman F. Furniss, *The Mormon Conflict, 1850–1859* (New Haven, 1960).

FOR FURTHER READING

Arrington, Leonard J., and Davis Bitton, *The Mormon Experience: A History of the Latter-day Saints*, rev. ed., Urbana, IL, 1992.

Barlow, Philip L. *Mormons and the Bible: The Place of the Latter-day Saints in American Religion*, New York, 1991.

Bringhurst, Newell G. *Saints, Slaves, and Blacks: The Changing Place of Black People within Mormonism*, Westport, CT, 1981.

Brooke, John L. *The Refiner's Fire: The Making of Mormon Cosmology, 1644–1844*, Cambridge, United Kingdom, 1994.

Bushman, Richard L. *Joseph Smith and the Beginnings of Mormonism*, Urbana, IL, 1984.

Foster, Lawrence. *Religion and Sexuality: The Shakers, the Mormons, and the Oneida Community*, New York, 1981.

Hansen, Klaus J. *Mormonism and the American Experience*, Chicago, 1981.

Lyman, Edward Leo. *Political Deliverance: The Mormon Quest for Utah Statehood*, Urbana, IL, 1986.

Moore, R. Laurence. *Religious Outsiders and the Making of the Americans*, New York, 1986.

Shipps, Jan. *Mormonism: The Story of a New Religious Tradition*, Urbana, IL, 1985.

Underwood, Grant. *The Millenarian World of Early Mormonism*, Urbana, IL, 1993.

INTRODUCTION TO ESSAY 30

As Moorhead has already demonstrated, postmillennialism faded in the early 1900s. But premillennialism survives today and finds strong institutional support among the Seventh-day Adventists. In contemporary culture where almost everything is defined and judged by secular standards, Adventists persist in using the Bible as supreme authority for both thought and action. Butler tells us here of the group's origins in nineteenth-century revivals, expectations stirred up by William Miller, and the "great disappointment" of 1844. Further, we learn of Sabbatarian convictions as well as the visions and capacity for healing that were embodied in people like Ellen G. White. There are forces at work here that are potentially both volatile and cohesive at the same time.

Butler's treatment of Adventists explains how their concerns remain apart from mainstream ecclesiastical emphases. He also demonstrates ways in which this group has adjusted to modern trends in order to retain its special identity. The historical outline here shows a sect becoming a denomination, a radically other-worldly group coming to terms with this world through bureaucratic consolidation. Adventists remain apart from central religious and cultural strains in American life, but their alternative viewpoint has flourished due to a process of spiritual and institutional adaptation that is fascinating to observe.

Original source - CH 55 (1986): 50-64.

30

From Millerism to Seventh-Day Adventism
"Boundlessness to Consolidation"

Jonathan Butler

In his comparative analysis of various millennial movements, anthropologist Kenelm Burridge constructs a formula for cultural change, which he defines as "old rules" to "no rules" to "new rules." The first phase of these movements invariably involves a period of social unrest. Society deviates from the old rules as old formulas fail and institutions malfunction. People flout the political, religious, and social establishments with seemingly unpatriotic, blasphemous, and antisocial acts. In the next phase, society hangs between the old order and the new in an interim period in which neither the old standards nor the new hold sway. At that point, millennial movements often materialize in search of a new society. Burridge defines them as new cultures or social orders coming into being. Rather than "oddities" or "diseases in the body social," they involve "the adoption of new assumptions, a new redemptive process, a new political-economic framework, a new mode of measuring the man, a new integrity, a new community: in short, a new man."[1] In the third and final phase, the new rules solidify as the new culture takes shape, which in time may represent the old rules and old order for a future prophetic movement. Millenarians cannot last *as millenarians*. They endure only as they scuttle or transform their millenarian outlook.

American history may be interpreted as a series of cultural awakenings analogous to what the anthropologist describes. The Second Great Awakening, which ignited a series of religious conflagrations between the 1790s and 1860, was perhaps the pivotal event in shaping the American, the "new man." We suggest that the Federalist era represented the old rules, the era of Romantic revivalism and "freedom's ferment" marked the time of no rules, and post–Civil War corporate capitalism provided the new rules. In the evanescent, highly creative interim, the new religions of

Mormonism, Shakerism, and Oneida Perfectionism flowered, as did the social movements for temperance, abolition, feminism, peace, and dietary reform. Inevitably, however, the intensity of the era spent itself, and a move from no rules to new rules ensued. This was a transition from boundlessness to consolidation, and it happened in a single, critical decade, the 1850s.

The Millerite movement resulted from the preaching of William Miller, a farmer and Baptist layman of Low Hampton, New York, who concluded in 1818 that in about twenty-five years "all the affairs of our present state would be wound up." By the early 1830s he was circuit-riding through small-town New England with an illustrated series of lectures. By 1840, after receiving invitations to the cities, he had provoked as popular a millenarian movement as America has seen. Millerites met with a series of failed prophecies in the spring and fall of 1844; their "Great Disappointment" occurred at the passing of 22 October in that year. Like every other millenarian movement, Millerism met with obvious failure, and yet out of this failure eventually emerged another of the American sectarian success stories. The single-minded otherworldliness of Millerism in 1844 developed, by the 1860s, into the durable, complex, and established Seventh-day Adventist sect which held wide-ranging interests that included sabbatarianism, temperance, medicine, education, and religious liberty.

The colorful and spectacular boundlessness of millenarian beginnings generally has attracted more scholarly attention than the later quietistic and consolidated stage of these movements. This circumstance has left unexplored many of the more intriguing questions as to how millenarians transcend their origins. The purpose of this study, then, is not only to determine the ways in which Millerism imbibed of antebellum American boundlessness, freedom, movement, diversity, and spontaneity, but to document the means by which it successfully established itself, in Seventh-day Adventism, as an expression of late-nineteenth-century consolidation, control, stability, uniformity, and order.

• • •

Following the War of 1812 the new sense of national security; the vast widening of horizons geographically, technologically, and culturally; the emotional energy of evangelical Christianity; and the intellectual rationale of an imported Romanticism all proved conducive to an antebellum American assault on limits. Millerism, as much as any other social or religious movement of the time, reflected the boundlessness that resulted. When the boundaries of status eroded as a result of the egalitarian celebration of the common folk, the diffident Miller personified the self-made Jacksonian man. A theological rustic, proudly equipped with nothing more than the ordinary Bible and *Cruden's Concordance*, Miller attracted a diverse, popular movement of both the rabble and the respectable, much as Jackson had done for politics.[2] Millerism provides, then, as much a characterization of Jacksonian America as a caricature of it. The movement proved a child of its times, albeit a willful child, in regard to four prominent aspects of antebellum boundlessness.

Of the four impulses of antebellum America that prompted Millerism, millennialism proved obviously of primary importance. Belief in the millennium produced a sense of hope and progress in the new Republic which masked a deep anxiety and insecurity. The buoyant optimism and expansiveness knew a darker side. These two sides to millennialism yielded postmillennialists, marked by a gradualist, reformist vision of the world, and premillennialists, who held to an immediatist, revolutionist view of things. While Miller rejected the more human-achieved postmillennium for the more God-determined premillennium, historians now realize that too sharp a distinction can be drawn between the two orientations. Miller's projection of the world's end "about 1843" posed the "logical absolute" of contemporary millennialism, or a "sensational variant" of the views other Protestants then preached.[3] Moreover, both the Second Awakening's celebrated evangelist, Charles Finney, and the prophetic lecturer Miller looked eagerly for something of eschatological importance to happen in their immediate future. Following upon Finney's career, Miller sought only to reheat revival embers with the specificity of his prediction. While his efforts rekindled the revivals for a time, his ill-conceived tactic ultimately doused its flames, and Miller remains one of those tragic figures whose notoriety provoked precisely the opposite of the effect he had wanted.

Perfectionism resulted from the millennial desire to eradicate all evil in preparation for the world's end. Shunning social, political, and ecclesiastical means to the millennium, Millerites made whatever perfection might be attained in their wicked world purely an individual matter. They met long-standing financial and moral obligations. They cleansed body and soul. They prepared for the end. The weight of millennial expectation, however, proved crushingly burdensome to some of them, and their individualism turned idiosyncratic and neurotic.

Voluntaryism offered the practical means to millennial perfection. At the outset, Millerites might have been taken for one of the many voluntary associations of the day. Like the voluntary societies, they eschewed sectarianism for an interdenominationalism through which they remained, for the most part, Methodists, Baptists, Presbyterians, and Christians. And in this era of the multi-reformer, they recruited antislavery, temperance, and education advocates. Miller, who had been a radical abolitionist, viewed these benevolent reforms as forerunners of his own movement. But he proved to be the exception rather than the rule among the Millerites. The faltering enthusiasm for reform activity among evangelicals had become, for virtually all Millerites, a profound ennui. Accordingly, they looked to the second coming not to reward reform success but to erase its dismal failures.[4]

As revivalism flagged in the late 1830s, Millerites attempted to reawaken the awakening with evangelical techniques even more novel than Finney's "new measures." Primary among these was the prophetic chronology. Millerites defended the approximation of the world's end "about 1843" on scriptural grounds (the Lord had said only the day or the hour was in doubt, not the year) and on a sociological basis (preaching "the time" raised audiences and brought "results"). Another measure was the Millerite Great Tent, with a seating capacity of three to four thousand, which typified Millerism as a millenarian sensation both too popular to be contained in modest meetinghouses and too marginal to be tolerated there. The Millerite attempt to revive a dispirited Second Awakening met, in time, with its own disappointments. If in 1840 Millerites hoped to serve as the Second Awakening's avant-garde whose newest measures might invoke the millennium, their millenarian failures in the spring of 1844 escalated the novelty to eccentricity, the avant-gardism to affectation. Millerite time-setting charred this process.

Especially in 1843 and 1844 Millerites were scoffed, lampooned, ridiculed, and ostracized. Far from demoralizing them, however, the opprobrium and persecution only legitimated them as God's remnant. Flaunting their alienation from the old order, many threw themselves into an excitedly extravagant no-rules state. Status-labeling fashions were discarded, reportedly, for nudity. Acquisitive materialism gave way to a "no work" doctrine that left crops unharvested. Class-consciousness was abandoned for the bizarre practice of crawling on all fours through the streets in order to become as little children for the kingdom. The inhibition of Victorian society was relieved by "holy kissing" and "promiscuous" foot-washing. The limitations of bourgeois family life were exchanged for boundless sexual license, and gluttony was replaced by self-starvation. They sacrificed careers and all material goods to the cause, shared possessions among themselves in a primitive Christian communalism, lost family and friends in exchange for their warm, vital kinship, and occasionally suffered the heroic loss of life for their efforts. If the Millerites were to survive and transcend these times, they would do so by drawing upon the deeply satisfying spiritual resources of a community which had cost them so much of this world but had earned them so much of the "other world."[5]

• • •

Just as many aspects of antebellum American life became a permanent part of the national character and have surfaced in unsettling and stimulating ways throughout American history, Millerism contributed to the Seventh-day Adventist identity and has sustained an impact throughout Adventist history. For Adventism as a whole, as for the nation, the movement from diffusion to concentration, from spontaneity to order, has been less a steady, uninterrupted flow in one direction than an ebb and flow between boundlessness and consolidation. Nevertheless, the shift from Millerism to Seventh-day Adventism represents as marked a transformation as the change in American culture as a whole in the same period. Despite important continuity with Millerism, Adventism emphatically distanced itself from its millenarian origins. It remains for us to determine the nature of this development.

The key to converting an effervescent apocalypticism into an established, complex religious system includes, above all, an elongation of the eschatological timetable. As long as a group sustains short-term, specific predictions of the end, it remains volatile. With each passing of a prophetic date, conversions vaporize into apostasies, the promised harvest results in crop failure. The sooner the group can shed its short-term millenarianism, the sooner it can accommodate to the practical business of living life in the world. The product of Millerite boundlessness, Seventh-day Adventism achieved consolidation through the development of Adventist doctrine and structure. Doctrinally, formulating Adventist eschatology, seventh-day sabbatarianism, and the prophetic gift termed the "Spirit of prophecy" manifested this stabilizing process. Institutionally, organizing the church, professionalizing the ministry, and establishing educational and medical programs all contributed to this solidification.

Their moratorium on evangelism between 1844 and 1851 allowed Adventists a time to retrench and rebuild. However, with the further delay of the advent and with the unforeseen influx of converts who had not come by way of Millerism, the shut door creaked open as Adventists hesitantly embarked on missionary expansion. Prompted by revolutionism and conversionism, Adventists believed God, in his mercy, had delayed the advent to allow them more time to save souls for his coming. But the missionary expansion could not have occurred without the broadening and deepening of an institutional base, which, as we shall see shortly, further consolidated Adventism. At the same time, missionary outreach continued to expose Adventism to the boundlessness of the frontier—from western New York to southern Michigan, from the Midwest to the Far West to Australia, and then, much later, to the scene of perpetual instability, diversity, and diffusion, the Third World.

The doctrinal development which did the most to define

Seventh-day Adventism—to set the boundaries between it and other religious groups—was seventh-day sabbatarianism. In 1846 Joseph Bates, by then included with James and Ellen White in Adventism's leading triumvirate, urged the practice on Adventists. Though a legacy of Seventh-day Baptists, the belief found a somewhat new expression within the context of Adventism's eschatological system. For Adventists, sabbatarianism was imbued with pivotal significance: the Old Testament had been restored, and a symbol which looked backward to creation projected forward as well to the new creation. The sabbath evoked nothing less than the "new law" or the "new redemptive process" toward which these millenarians moved. By way of seventh-day sabbath observance, Adventists sought to attain that "new integrity," that "new mode of measuring the man," indeed that "new man" capable of standing without sin at the Last Day.

Late in 1844 Ellen Harmon began having visions which validated the sabbath doctrines. Her hometown of Portland, Maine, had been notorious for the "continual introduction of *visionary nonsense*," and nothing proved more spontaneous and boundless than charisma. In large camp-meeting crowds or in small meetings in houses or barns, the "gift of prophecy" poured itself out plentifully. Ellen might have faded into this inchoate charismatic background and entirely disappeared had not James White married her in August of 1846 and served not only as her husband and protector, but as her promoter and publisher. She as the visionary, exhorter, and counselor and he as the organizer and entrepreneur combined in the "first family" of Adventism both boundlessness and consolidation, as together they traversed the hazardous period of "no rules" and established "new rules."[6]

Turning from the doctrinal to the institutional transformation from boundlessness to consolidation, we find that Adventists, along with Americans in general after the turn of midcentury, struggled to impose social control on an undisciplined culture rampant with individualism. The 1850s were less the times for prophets and reformers than for planners and organizers. The millennial enthusiasm that sparked the reforms of the preceding era gave way to regulated, systematized, professional reformism. By

1859 sabbath-keeping Adventists had passed from the anticlerical-ism of Millerism to the ordination of clergy. The practical problems of providing for the ministry were met with a program of "sys-tematic benevolence" which would be replaced by the tithing of members. The Adventists grew from a "scattered flock" of two hundred members in 1850 to a membership of thirty-five hundred at their formal organization in 1863. By then there were twenty-two ordained ministers and one hundred twenty-five churches. The organization of the church resulted from the pragmatic need to incorporate the publishing enterprise. The free-spirited self-publishing of Millerite periodicals had centralized in Adventism in the single denominational press which began editing the *Second Advent Review* and *Sabbath Herald* in 1850. By the autumn of 1860 James White, the publisher, urged incorporation so that the church rather than a private party might own the press. This called for a legal organization of the church, which was done under the name "Seventh-day Adventist." The history of Adventism had been a matter of "publish or perish" since. Lofty spiritual vision led to the practical consideration of organization. As far as ecclesiastical bureaucracy was concerned, in the beginning was the word.

If publishing instigated organization, entry into medicine exerted as profound an impact on the nature of that organization as any-thing in Adventism. From the healings of Millerism, Adventism grew to establish a vast network of sanitariums and hospitals throughout the world. This development began in 1866, in the wake of an epidemic of illness among church leaders and Mrs. White's adoption of "water cure" and vegetarianism. Adventists built the Western Health Reform Institute in that year and began publishing the *Health Reformer*, a monthly magazine. Adventism would make still another leap, in the early twentieth century, from counter-establishment health reform to establishment medicine. This shift led, first, to a reorganized medical school, then to the accreditation of colleges to feed the medical school, then to profes-sional seminary education to keep the ministry apace with medi-cine. And this general upgrading of education and professionalism was accompanied by a social and economic upward mobility in Adventism at large. The blend of material and spiritual impulses which characterized mid-Victorianism played itself out in the movement as Adventists came a long way, rather quickly, from the sacrificial Millerites.

Sociologists inform us that nothing proves more inimical to sectarian fervor than bureaucracy. The new rules of one era become the old rules of the next, and millenarian transformation begins again. If Adventist developments are viewed as stages of life, Millerism provided a creative, if quixotic, adolescence that a more mature, stable sect outgrew but still recalled with nostalgia. In fact, Adventists periodically have precipitated a form of "mid-life crisis" by seeking, usually without lasting success, to recover their millenarian adolescence. Yet despite such wistfulness for a lost past, Adventist development has benefited both from periods of movement, spontaneity, and disorder and from those of stability and structure. Only through consolidation has Adventism continued to exist, but only the spirit of boundlessness has made that existence worthwhile.

ENDNOTES

1. Kenelm Burridge, *New Heaven, New Earth: A Study of Millenarian Activities* (New York, 1969), 13, 105-16, William G. McLoughlin, *Revivals, Awakenings, and Reform: An Essay on Religion and Social Change in America, 1607–1977* (Chicago, 1978).
2. For the best study of Millerism and its relation to popular culture, see David L. Rowe, *Thunder and Trumpets: Millerites and Dissenting Religion in Upstate New York, 1800–1850* (Chico, CA, 1985).
3. Whitney R. Cross, *The Burned-over District: The Social and Intellectual History of Enthusiastic Religion in Western New York, 1800–1850* (New York, 1956), 320; Timothy L. Smith, *Revivalism and Social Reform: American Protestantism on the Eve of the Civil War* (New York, 1965), 228; Marvin Meyers, *Jacksonian Persuasion: Politics and Belief* (Stanford, CA, 1957).
4. Francis D. Nichol, *The Midnight Cry: A Defense of the Character and Conduct of Miller and the Millerites, Who Mistakenly Believed That the Second Coming of Christ Would Take Place in the Year 1844* (Washington, D.C., 1944), 174-85.
5. P. Gerard Damsteegt, *Foundations of the Seventh-day Adventist Message and Mission* (Grand Rapids, 1977), 42; Edwin S. Gaustad, ed., *The Rise*

of Adventism: Religion and Society in Mid-Nineteenth Century America (New York, 1974).

6. Ronald L. Numbers, *Prophetess of Health: A Study of Ellen G. White* (New York, 1976); Richard Schwartz, *Light Bearers to the Remnant* (Mountain View, CA, 1979), 8-103; Schwartz, *John Harvey Kellogg, M.D.* (Nashville, 1970).

FOR FURTHER READING

Barkun, Michael. *Crucible of the Millennium: The Burned-over District of New York in the 1840s,* Syracuse, 1986.

Doan, Ruth Alden. *The Miller Heresy, Millennialism, and American Culture,* Philadelphia, 1987.

Land, Gary G., ed. *Adventism in America: A History,* Grand Rapids, MI, 1986.

Moore, R. Laurence. *Religious Outsiders and the Making of Americans,* New York, 1986.

Numbers, Ronald L., and Jonathan M. Butler, eds. *The Disappointed: Millerism and Millenarianism in the Nineteenth Century,* Knoxville, 1993.

Penton, M. James. *Apocalypse Delayed: The Story of Jehovah's Witnesses,* Toronto, 1985.

INTRODUCTION TO ESSAY 31

Pentecostalism has been another emphasis at work in twentieth-century American religious life outside of so-called mainstream churches. The following essay helps familiarize us with this many-sided movement in two ways. It furnishes basic information about central pentecostal concerns and gives details of early experiences that sparked so much interest across the country. The author also deals with major studies of this phenomenon and gives us a more balanced understanding of the literature. This is revisionist work at its best. Given a wide variety of voices, opinions, and priorities, Creech does well to warn against oversimplified accounts or interpretations that are too generalized.

Beginning with premillennialism, a concept now familiar to us, Creech also defines categories essential to this movement such as glossolalia and the "Latter Rain." He remains focused on pentecostals as a topic, but his findings instruct us further about tendencies toward perfectionism that have fascinated many religionists and about quests for physical healing that have intrigued others. While learning about people who seek fulfillment in these ways, we also gain deeper insight into some old standbys in historical studies: the role of racism and class discrimination as basic ingredients in groups that are variously called cults, sects, and denominations.

Original source - CH 65 (1996): 405-24.

31

Visions of Glory
The Place of the Azusa Street Revival in Pentecostal History

Joe Creech

As news of the great Welsh Revival of 1904 reached Southern California, Frank Bartleman, an itinerant evangelist and pastor living in Los Angeles, became convinced that God was preparing to revitalize his beloved holiness movement with a powerful, even apocalyptic, spiritual awakening. Certain that events in Wales would be duplicated in California, Bartleman reported in 1905 that "the Spirit is brooding over our land . . . Los Angeles, Southern California, and the whole continent shall surely find itself ere long in the throes of a mighty revival." Bartleman indeed witnessed such a revival, for in early April 1906, this "Latter Rain" outpouring had begun to fall on a small gathering of saints led by William J. Seymour, a black holiness preacher.[1] At a vacant AME mission at 312 Azusa Street, countless pentecostals received the baptism of the Holy Spirit evidenced by speaking in other tongues—a "second Pentecost" replicating the first recorded in Acts 2. Bartleman's accounts of the revival generated both short- and long-term effects. In the short run, they drew thousands from around the world to Azusa and sparked numerous subsequent revivals. In the long run, they gave rise to the central myth of origin for almost every pentecostal denomination. Briefly stated, this myth of origin, which has persisted until the present, has in one way or another identified the Azusa Street revival of 1906 to 1909 as the central point from which the worldwide penetecostal movement emerged.

In order to assess Azusa's place in the emergence of pentecostalism, I shall first clarify the substantive role Azusa played in the institutional, theological, and social development of early pentecostalism, fleshing out the limitations of considering Azusa the movement's sole historical point of origin, and correcting the misrepresentation of early pentecostalism as homogeneous. Historians of pentecostalism such as Donald Dayton, James Goff, Gary McGee, Grant Wacker, and Edith Blumhofer have shown that pentecostalism arose from multiple pockets of revival that retained their preexisting institutional structures, theological tendencies, and social dynamics. This fact demonstrates that Azusa played only a limited substantive role in the institutional, theological, and social development of early pentecostalism, and it underscores the diversity that has marked the movement from its start.

Second, I seek to understand why fledgling pentecostals considered the Azusa revival, despite its limited substantive role in the movement's early development, to be pentecostalism's central point of origin. The answer lies in the symbolic role Azusa has played in pentecostalism's expansion. Azusa became the central mythic event for early pentecostals because they perceived it to be the location where God initiated an eschatological plan for the restoration of the church. Bartleman and his colleagues cast Azusa as the point at which this restoration had begun. So Azusa came to symbolize early pentecostals' theological assumptions and especially their eschatological hopes. As a symbolic point of origin, Azusa offered theological and historical meaning for the pentecostal experience and the movement itself; consequently, Azusa assumed the central place in pentecostalism's emerging myth of origins. In time, Azusa was seen as the movement's historical point of origin by historians, theologians, and later generations of pentecostals who took Bartleman's accounts of the revival at face value without realizing they were appropriating theological perceptions of the events instead.

In order to understand the historical paradigm that developed around the Azusa revival, the historical consciousness of Azusa's journalistic boosters must be understood. Theirs was a world constantly visited by supernatural activity—they perceived even the most mundane events as divine intervention, judgment, or blessing. In addition, they expected that, at any time, God would instigate a worldwide revival signaling Christ's soon return. In their minds, Azusa was the epicenter of a worldwide pentecostal revival; the Holy Spirit flowed from Azusa to spark subsequent stirrings without human assistance. Since their reports intended to highlight the Holy Spirit's initiative and to confirm their eschatological presuppositions, the Azusa boosters never separated historical events from their theological interpretations of them. They felt confident that their perception of spiritual activity was as accurate as their perception of human activity; the Holy Spirit was as real an actor at Azusa as were the human participants. Their failure to make this distinction paved the way for future interpreters to see Azusa not as the symbolic but as the historical point of origin for the movement.

Despite revisions by recent pentecostal scholars who have corrected the theological biases of Bartleman and the other boosters by exposing pentecostalism's multiple points of origin, the centrality of Azusa persists in at least three ways. First, general historical works in American religion, because they have traditionally relied on older secondary sources for their sections on pentecostalism, identify Azusa as the movement's point of origin.[2] Those unfamiliar with more recent pentecostal historiography are left with the impression that Azusa was the sole point of origin for the movement. These historical syntheses lack a sense of pentecostalism's multiple points of origin, including, among others, Kansas, Chicago, and North Carolina. Second, many social scientists have characterized early pentecostalism as having had the same sociocultural ethos as Azusa. The application of "sect to church," "routinization of charisma," or other roughly Weberian or Troeltschian schemata has fabricated a supposed evolution in pentecostalism from the charisma, lack of structure, and racial and gender equality evident at Azusa to the ecclesial hierarchy, creeds, and routinized worship of the pentecostal denominations. Third, pentecostals and even nonpentecostals have considered Azusa's spiritual ethos the marrow of pentecostal theology and spirituality.

• • •

Most historians imagine early pentecostalism to have been a homogeneous movement marked by the social dynamics of Azusa that devolved into stale denominationalism. Such a generalization, however, simply does not conform to the early pentecostal record.

From the outset, pentecostals hotly divided over numerous theological and social issues. Even though early pentecostals adopted Charles Parham's doctrine of tongues as taught at Azusa, they did so in the context of their preexisting religious structures. The persistence of these structures gave these early pockets of pentecostal revival theological leanings, institutional structures, and a sociocultural ethos often quite different from Azusa's.

A detailed examination of some of the most important of these pockets demonstrates the diversity that marked early pentecostals in terms of theology, ecclesiology, and social ethos, revealing the paucity of their substantive connections to Azusa. As James R. Goff, Jr., and others have demonstrated, pentecostalism's theological raison d'être came not from Azusa but from Topeka, Kansas, by way of holiness teacher Charles Parham. Although Parham's three-step soteriology (salvation, sanctification, and pentecostal experience) was not altogether unique among holiness teachings, he innovated in two ways. First, he claimed that the "Gospel Evidence" for Spirit baptism was speaking in tongues. Second, he interpreted this restoration of tongues as the key indication that God was about to initiate the much anticipated revival (the "Latter Rain") that would replicate the first Pentecost and immediately precede the Second Coming. These two innovations constituted the foundation of early pentecostals' theological and historical self-awareness; while early pentecostals differed greatly among themselves on other soteriological points, they distinguished themselves from other evangelicals by embracing Parham's restorationist twist on the meaning of tongues.[3] The ethos of Parham's Apostolic Faith Movement reflected the rural areas and small towns of Kansas, Texas, Arkansas, Oklahoma, and Missouri, where the movement flourished. Parham not only believed in racial segregation but repeatedly made racist comments in his sermons and writings; in fact, Parham insisted that his student William Seymour sit outside the classroom door during lectures. Parham opposed ecstatic behavior during his services, stating that "by the Baptism with the Holy Spirit I do not mean all the chattering and jabbering, wind-sucking, holy-dancing-rollerism . . . which is the result of hypnotic, spiritualistic and fleshly controls, but a real sane reception."[4]

On 22 February 1906 Seymour, considering himself an emissary of Parham, arrived in Los Angeles to serve as pastor of a church affiliated with the Holiness Association of Southern California. By April he had become the leader of the Azusa revival and was promoting Parham's restorationist doctrines. The ethos at Azusa nevertheless diverged from that of Parham as it reflected the more cosmopolitan culture found in the holiness and evangelical churches around Los Angeles.

Between Parham and Azusa two different pentecostal subcultures were emerging—the egalitarian, ethical restorationism of Azusa and the conservatism of the Parham group. In time, the latter came to be known as the Old Apostolic Faith Movement (OAFM) and became the most important institutionalizing force among pentecostals in the Midwest and the Southwest. Between 1909 and 1912 the OAFM absorbed a number of smaller associations and established strong ties with midwestern pentecostals, especially those in Chicago. Thus the OAFM, arguably the most important institutional force in early pentecostalism, preceded Azusa chronologically, rejected its Wesleyan soteriology, bore little resemblance to the revival in terms of ethos, and maintained no institutional ties.

But what kind of relationship did other early pockets of revival have with Azusa? These early pentecostal revivals fall roughly into two categories: those with some historical relationship to Azusa—including pentecostals in the Southeast—and those without direct links to Azusa, namely, pentecostals in Chicago and the Christian and Missionary Alliance (CMA). Those "sent out" from Azusa to start subsequent revivals in the United States followed a fairly typical pattern. Usually, someone would hear about Azusa through a periodical, attend the revival, receive the pentecostal message, and then return to convert a church or denomination to the pentecostal theology; preexisting institutional structures, however, would remain the same. Moreover, the theological message of pentecostalism took hold among holiness and higher life devotees already familiar with its pneumatological and eschatological idioms; acceptance of Parham's innovations was often a natural and sometimes even anticipated development. Charles Mason, founder of the Memphis-based Church of God in Christ, the largest African American pentecostal denomination, exemplified this pattern. Sometimes free-floating revivals sprang up among family and friends of Azusa pilgrims, as under Rachel Sizelove in Springfield, Missouri, or within an isolated church, such as the Indianapolis CMA church converted to the pentecostal message by Glenn Cook. In each of these cases, however, the revivals flourished only as they were integrated into older institutional networks—in the case of Springfield, the OAFM, and for the Indianapolis church, the CMA. So while individual messengers had ties to Azusa, their revivals developed independently.

It would be difficult to overestimate the influence of the CMA on the development of early pentecostalism, since the hymnody, healing doctrine, ecclesiology, and organizational structures of both the OAFM and Assemblies of God were derived from this missionary and higher life organization based in Nyack, New York. Moreover, CMA founder and higher life patriarch A. B. Simpson influenced numerous early pentecostal leaders, including Bartleman and Parham. In 1914 Chicago, CMA, and OAFM pentecostal leaders converged in Hot Springs, Arkansas, to establish the Assemblies of God in order to provide needed ministerial oversight. By 1917 the Assemblies, now largely under the direction of leaders drawn from the CMA, was a centralized organization requiring creedal adherence and providing Bible schools to educate ministers and missionaries. This represented a stark contrast to Azusa. This contrast did not represent attrition or routinization; it did, however, represent the assertion of preexisting intellectual and social structures among three movements that had no direct institutional ties to Azusa. And yet, oddly, these pentecostals considered Azusa the point of origin for their fellowship. Why?

Frank Bartleman shared with other early pentecostals a holiness and premillennialist worldview established and maintained by countless summer conferences, books, Bible institutes, faith schools and, most important, an extensive international periodical network. Two theological clusters in this worldview proved to be most important for the spread of pentecostalism: Keswick or higher life spirituality, which provided the basis for pentecostal pneumatology, and premillennialism. Higher life spirituality was a religious outlook or set of theological emphases that swept through evangelical circles in the late nineteenth century. Its central teaching was that Christians should move through various stages of spiritual commitment or "emptying." Having achieved a state of utter human passivity ("death of self"), devotees were subsequently baptized by the Holy Spirit. With the Spirit now leading in all of life's ways, believers experienced the "Victorious Christian Life" and were empowered for missions. This "progressive" restorationist historiography provided the rationale for adopting doctrinal innovations such as premillennialism and tongues.[5]

By the start of the twentieth century, the premillennialism made popular by Moody and the Niagara and American Bible and Prophecy conferences was firmly established among evangelicals and especially among higher life adherents in the North Atlantic. Between 1890 and 1915 anticipation of the return of Christ was particularly acute. Although the apocalypse was near, premillennialists believed God was perfecting a holy remnant, a perfect bride, that would escape, through the "Rapture," the full extent of God's impending wrath. These "forward movements" would soon culminate in an end-time outpouring of the Holy Spirit that would induce one final worldwide revival just prior to the Rapture. The prophecies concerning the "former and latter rain of the Holy Spirit" in Joel 2, Zechariah 10, and Acts 2 contained the biblical precedent for this.

To pentecostals Azusa signaled, with all the telltale signs, the full outpouring of God's Latter Rain; it was the culmination of forward movements in a particular time and place that would precipitate world revival and the coming of Christ. Clearly, the presence of glossolalia at Azusa was paramount in convincing countless believers that it was the second Pentecost. Glossolalia not only duplicated a key feature of the first Pentecost but also, as an experience, itself bore visceral witness to this restoration. Glossolalia thus underscored the eschatological and historical meaning early pentecostals attached to Azusa. Those early participants understood the theological significance of the revival: its meaning, in terms of the way God acts in history, as the second

Pentecost; and this meaning eventually made Azusa the symbolic center of pentecostalism's myth of origins.

• • •

The way in which Bartleman and the other boosters cast the Azusa revival was critical for the spread of both the pentecostal message and experience. Most pentecostals never visited Azusa but heard of it either by word of mouth or more likely through a periodical. As they spread through the holiness periodical networks, these eyewitness reports inspired fledgling pentecostals to accept the pentecostal experience themselves. Within the world of Keswick, holiness, and premillennialist idioms Bartleman shared with his readers, Azusa's symbolism resonated deeply. Granted, the phenomenon of glossolalia brought Azusa's significance alive to anyone practicing it, but the theological and eschatological idioms symbolized in Azusa provided a blueprint for understanding the meaning of this new experience. Meaning and experience worked in a reciprocal manner; news of the Latter Rain's falling at Azusa created the anticipation of the experience and likewise provided the means to interpret the experience once it recurred. Parham's spiritual emphases and basic pneumatology present at Azusa resonated with the Keswick and holiness outlooks held by Bartleman's audience, making the doctrine of tongues an acceptable innovation. As a concrete symbol of eschatological hope, Azusa tapped early pentecostals' deepest religious yearnings and thus heightened their anticipation for the experience; it then provided meaning for the pentecostal experience by placing it within the providential designs of God.

Reports from Azusa convinced many that a new dispensation of the Spirit had begun. Bartleman synthesized in narrative form nearly fifty years of holiness piety, eschatological longing, and higher life pneumatology. God's dispensational act at Azusa stood at the center of his narrative. Azusa was the sign for which emerging pentecostals had hoped; it was the symbolic moment that provided the impetus to believe. Azusa has shaped academic literature because it so indelibly shaped the way early pentecostals understood themselves and their movement. They were participants in a worldwide revival—an eschatological act of God. If, in their minds, Azusa represented both the initial outpouring and the blueprint for interpreting similar stirrings, it is no wonder it would ultimately shape the way we tell the pentecostal story.

ENDNOTES

1. Quotations in Frank Bartleman, "How Pentecost Came to Los Angeles," in *Witness to Pentecost: The Life of Frank Bartleman*, ed. Donald Dayton (New York, 1985), 39, 53, 89.

2. Mark A. Noll, *History of Christianity in the United States and Canada* (Grand Rapids, MI, 1992), 387, 541; Sydney Ahlstrom, *A Religious History of the American People* (Garden City, NY, 1975), 2:292-93; Winthrop Hudson, *Religion in America*, 3d ed. (New York, 1981), 347; and Catherine Albanese, *America: Religions and Religion* (Belmont, CA, 1981), 105. Mitigating Azusa's centrality are Gary B. McGee, *This Gospel Shall Be Preached* (Springfield, MO, 1986), 48-53; Grant Wacker, "The Functions of Faith in Primitive Pentecostalism," *Harvard Theological Review* 77 (1984): 353-56; Edith Blumhofer, *Restoring the Faith: The Assemblies of God, Pentecostalism, and American Culture* (Urbana, IL, 1993), 43-87.

3. James R. Goff, *Fields White Unto Harvest* (Fayetteville, AR, 1988), 9-16; Wacker, "Functions," 359-70; and Blumhofer, *Restoring the Faith*, 55-56. For Parham's life and theology, see C. Parham, "A Voice Crying in the Wilderness," in *The Sermons of Charles F. Parham*, ed. Donald Dayton (New York, 1985), esp. chaps. 3-5, 15; C. Parham, "The Everlasting Gospel," in *Sermons*, 6-18, 31-32, 53-76, 92-95; and Goff, *Fields White*, 39-47, 69. On the relationship of early Pentecostals to other evangelicals, see Dayton, *Theological Roots of Pentecostalism* (Grand Rapids, MI, 1987).

4. C. Parham, "Everlasting Gospel," 55; "Voices," 22, 39, 62-63; and Goff, 106-33. Parham considered ecstasy a "negroism."

5. On Keswick and its Relationship to Pentecostalism, see George M. Marsden, *Fundamentalism and American Culture: The Shaping of Twentieth-Century Evangelicalism* (New York, 1980), 72-80; Reuben A. Torrey, *The Baptism with the Holy Spirit* (New York, 1895); Dayton, *Theological Roots*, chaps. 3-5. For historical consciousness, see A. B. Simpson, *The Coming One* (New York, 1912), 213-14; A. C. Dixon, *Evangelism Old and New* (New York, 1905), 34-40; A. T. Pierson, *Forward Movements of the Last Half Century* (New York, 1900), v-viii, 223-24; and A. J. Gordon, *The Ministry of the Spirit* (New York, 1894), x-xi.

FOR FURTHER READING

Anderson, Robert Mapes. *Vision of the Disinherited: The Making of American Pentecostalism*, New York, 1979.

Blumhofer, Edith L. *The Assemblies of God: A Chapter in the Story of American Pentecostalism*, Springfield, MO, 1989.

Harrell, David E., Jr. *All Things Are Possible: The Healing and Charismatic Revivals in Modern America*, Bloomington, IN, 1975.

Hollenweger, Walter J. *The Pentecostals*, London, 1972.

MacRobert, Iain. *The Black Roots and White Racism of Early Pentecostalism in the U.S.A.*, New York, 1992.

Moore, R. Laurence. *Religious Outsiders and the Making of Americans*, New York, 1986.

Synan, Winson, ed. *Aspects of Pentecostal-Charismatic Origins*, Plainfield, NJ, 1975.

INTRODUCTION TO ESSAY 32

Denominational affiliation has become relatively unimportant over the last 150 years. Even those who belong to mainstream churches agree that attitudes regarding biblical interpretation, ethical guidelines, and social welfare programs define a person's religious identity more than names over a sanctuary door. And among those who explore metaphysical worlds, one can see a similar preference for issues rather than labels. Albanese points out what may be a constant in American religious activity: people experiment with various options and often move from one affiliation to another. This is as true among members of churches with deep historical roots as it is among those who dabble in movements that hardly have traditions at all.

Probing for common features in nineteenth-century metaphysical theory, Albanese discerns several features. Spiritual harmony is a goal that has attracted many, though they might seek it in a great many ways related to the natural world around us. More immediate symptoms of this general objective are physical well-being and comfort. Albanese guides us through examples of such theologizing about health and wealth. While informing us of individuals along the way, she ultimately explains the background of Christian Science, the most influential contemporary form of this alternative approach to religious edification.

Original source - CH 55 (1986): 489-502.

32

Physic and Metaphysic in Nineteenth-Century America

Medical Sectarians and Religious Healing

Catherine L. Albanese

Writing in the first issue of *The Magnetic and Cold Water Guide* in 1846, an unnamed editor hailed the virtues of the cold-water cure: "Instead of the dosing and drugging of the old system of practice, it proposes to rely on the indwelling healing power of nature alone, to provoke and regulate which, it employs the widespread element of fresh unadulterated water." This charted the direction that a number of Americans would take as the century progressed. Together these Americans, many of them roughly middle class, would forge and express part of a popular mentality that deified nature and made it into religion. For them, nature became a symbolic and salvific center, encircled by a cluster of related therapeutic beliefs, behaviors, and values. Conformity to nature became a way of organizing both ordinary and nonordinary aspects of life and, especially, the recovery of *healthful* life. In a culture that was experiencing the rapid rise of industrialization and an urbanization that uprooted many from rural life, the healing virtues of nature seemed easy enough to long for. And in a culture that, in however bowdlerized a form, had inherited the republican Enlightenment, the invocation of nature was still surrounded with an aura of patriotism and religion.

In the unsophisticated world of popular mentality, the "nature" in this healing nature religion was never precisely defined. For some, it would signify, pure and simple, the physical world, the environment both without and within the body of elements not fashioned by human skill. For others, it would become an abstract principle in an environmentalism so far extruded into the starry skies that it lost the familiar touch of matter. For some, it would connote the truly real. For others, it would become the illusory outer garment of higher spirit, which often got in its (spirit's) way. Whatever its specific form, nature religion brought a persuasive theology, a way of viewing penultimates and ultimates that emerged from successful therapeutic experience and also shaped experience with metaphysical notions. Mixed ingredients of the popular mentality fostered ambiguity on issues ranging beyond the precise meaning of nature; conceptual inconsistency and confusion ran through the therapeutic world of nature religion. With the evangelical revival proclaiming the experiential power of the unseen, the joining of the forces of nature to the forces of mind was not a difficult step. And with mesmerism, Swedenborgianism, and (although less important here) Transcendentalism all conflating images of spirit and matter, the step became virtually effortless. Thus some Americans who hailed the curative powers of nature likewise were celebrating the healing properties of mind.

• • •

Rhetorical flourish was one thing. The theology of nature, for all its ambiguity, also could provide self-conscious apologetic something that water-cure journals delivered in abundance. A Christian physiology surely pervaded the analysis. But the logic of the theological language moved beyond the Christian legacy to another gospel. In the other gospel of the water-cure movement, nature and God (the divine mind that was source of law and truth) were congruent principles, mutual and intertwined in the living of life because they were very close to being identical. Beyond that, the experiential test of virtue was the healthy body, the body, as water curers would have it, in harmony with all of nature's laws. It followed that, by joining oneself to the working of these laws, a man or woman approached and, drinking tumbler after tumbler of cold water, incorporated God or truth. The everyday virtue of harmony was expressed ritually in the water-cure establishments that sprang up to accommodate a generation of refugees from the heroic medicine of the era. Here, in addition to the copious drinking of cold water, the sick underwent a series of hydropathic practices. They were packed or rubbed in wet sheets; they took head baths, leg baths, sitting (pelvic) baths, wash tub baths, half (body) baths, and plunge baths; and, in nineteenth-century style, they experienced douche, cataract, and hose baths that were variants on (also-offered) shower baths. Meanwhile, as they became used to the waters, they observed assiduously a regimen of diet and exercise to continue harmonizing their systems. With such a luxuriant ritual lexicon, individuals had little difficulty enacting, in focused form, a generalized theology of nature.[1]

Nor was the hydropathic the only enactment. In similar fashion, the theology of nature was focused and dramatized in a series of movements that, in many manifestations, understood nature and mind as primary principles and the healing act as the expression of virtue through ritual. A number of the followers of Thomsonian herbal healing and homeopathy and, later in the century, osteopathy and chiropractic articulated the pattern. Indeed, viewed from this patterned perspective, the inherent integrity of these curative procedures is highlighted, and their religious rationale becomes obvious. Thus, it is not enough to say that nineteenth-century religious healing meant overtly religious movements, as in the metaphysical systems of New Thought and Christian Science. Religious healing included representatives from a small army of medical sectarians as well as practitioners and patients whose healing expressed their theology of nature and their nature religion.

What had emerged in these writers was a reappropriation of the ancient doctrine of correspondence—of the axiomatic "as above, so below." The eighteenth-century visionary theologian Emanuel Swedenborg had revived and reinterpreted the doctrine in numerous writings, and the new-old teaching of the Swedish seer spread easily in the popular mentality that medical sectarians shared. The contagion of Swedenborg's model no doubt was augmented by its promulgation, in modified form, by the New England Transcendentalists. And the contagion was linked to Swedenborg's ideas, too, of a divine influx in the natural world—ideas which, as we shall see, resembled mesmeric teachings of magnetic tides and fluids. Most important here, the contagion made available the mingled, spirit-matter dimension of Swedenborg's thought. For in his copious reports of his visionary experience, Swedenborg had collapsed the distinction between spirit and matter in ways that could only encourage a similar indistinction in the popular mentality.[2]

By the end of the century, some representatives of osteopathy and chiropractic were echoing aspects of this earlier assessment as it had been absorbed into a therapeutic religion of nature. Late-century osteopaths hailed the machinery of nature and nature's God. From a related perspective, the *Journal of Osteopathy* saw "man as a microcosm, a miniature of the cosmic universe" and hailed the new osteopathic science for its "immovable basis in nature itself," with "operations . . . in harmonious accord with the ineradicable and irrepealable laws of nature." Meanwhile, Andrew Taylor Still, the founder of osteopathy—for a time a magnetic healer and perhaps also a spiritualist—wrote in his autobiography of the "principle of mind commonly known as God, which has the power to transpose and transform all substances." More explicitly than Still, one turn-of-the-century devotee could speculate that the "healing property" of nature might be "the working of a divine presiding mind set in closest vicinage to nature, by which the tides of life, as they ebb and flow within the body, are vivified and purified."[3]

From hydropathists to chiropractors, the litany of nature and mind repeated its affirmations through a series of sectarian healing movements. The affirmations embodied, in fact, as Palmer had said, a "New Theology" for the times.[4] And in keeping with its popular, do-it-yourself quality, the new theology bore the marks of its origins in the inconsistencies and confusions it mirrored. On the one hand, the theology of nature held to a view of matter as "really real," the vital embodiment of Spirit and God. On the other, the new theology implied that matter was illusion and unreality, ultimately a trap from which one needed to escape into the realms of mind. Nature, in other words, might be sacramental, an emblem of divine things that in some way actually *contained* the divinity to which it pointed. And it might therefore have a quality of absoluteness about it. Or, to follow the logic to a conclusion surely not willingly admitted by those medical sectarians who embraced nature religion, nature might be the subject of erroneous perception. It might need continual correction by mind if it were not paradoxically to become an obstacle on the path to natural and spiritual wholeness.

As this last assessment suggests, confused views of matter went hand in hand with ambivalent programs for action. If nature was, indeed, real and sacramental, then corresponding to it became paramount. Harmony with nature became the broad highway to virtuous living and, more, to union with divinity. One discovered what was permanent and lasting precisely by identifying with the regular tides of nature's flux. If, however, nature was at best a passing show, a foil to obscure the Absolute behind and beyond it, seeking the enduring truth of Mind became key. Mastery over nature through mental power became the avenue to a "salvation" that transcended, even as it managed, nature.

• • •

As some of the medical sectarians, in a series of alternative healing movements, were subtly or unsubtly marrying nature to mind, the birth of metaphysical religion in nineteenth-century America ought not to seem surprising. With an American culture that, even in the middle years of the nineteenth century, "stressed Mind—Mind raised to the level of divinity,"[5] the early mentalistic manifestations of what became New Thought almost suggest the commonplace. However, what may appear thoroughly surprising is that the New Thought movement (and, beside it, even in part Christian Science) from its side also expressed forms of the theology of nature.

To understand what this statement may mean, we need a longer look at American metaphysical religion. And there is no better way to gain a sense of its presence than to turn to its embryonic stages in the life and teachings of Phineas Parkhurst Quimby. A medical sectarian by his own accounting, Quimby gave the metaphysical movement an identifiable leader and, with his amateur theology, profoundly influenced a generation of disciples. Indeed, in Portland, Maine, before his death in 1866, he was doctor and teacher to metaphysical leaders ranging from New Thought's Warren Felt Evans and Julius and Annetta Dresser to Christian Science's Mary Baker Eddy.

Although Quimby had been engaged in the practice of spiritual healing for the twenty-five years prior to his death, he had begun as a clockmaker and then became a stage performer in a demonstration of clairvoyance in healing. He had moved from magnetism to mind. His homespun theology had provided a muddled link between matter and spirit, achieving through the metaphor of odor a cohesion that hid as much as it revealed. Like some medical sectarians who were celebrating nature but still exalting mind, Quimby was having things both ways and any way he liked. In fact, as he explained elsewhere, like Wisdom (or Truth) error was "an element or odor." And since, as he also said, "the minds of individuals mingle like atmospheres," it was clearly easy for error, like a noxious magnetic fluid, to spread.[6]

Not to be identified with the First Cause, mind was matter, and so was thought. Therefore, disease was "what follows the disturbance of the mind or spiritual matter." Or, in an inverted expression of the same view, disease came from the "spiritual body," while mind was "the spiritual earth which receives the seed of Wisdom, and also the seeds of the wisdom of this world of reason." "Disease is the fruit of the latter," he went on, explaining also that "the application of the wisdom of God or Science is the clearing away the foul rubbish that springs up in the soil or mind." These affirmations suggest that for Quimby there was something—First Cause, Wisdom, the Christ (in many of his references)—that lay beyond even spiritual matter. And so, as in the case of the other medical sectarians, matter shaded off into another realm, and the inexpressible took on the contours of idealism. If the mind was "spiritual matter," Quimby thought the body "nothing but a dense shadow, condensed into what is called matter, or ignorance of God or Wisdom."

Hence, there is no avoiding the equivocality of the teaching. And the equivocality dissolves into a total mixing of models when we confront the ethical practice that emerged from Quimby's thought. Put briefly, Quimby was advising, in clear and direct terms, the application of mind over matter. It was by destroying "error" in the "truth" that he would banish disease, by brushing away opinion and belief with true knowledge that healing would come. Leaning hard on the idealist side of the equation, Quimby had yet managed to turn in a decidedly physical reading of metaphysical reality; and he had managed a similar confusion, merging harmony with nature and control by mind, in his ethical model. Quimby's religion, like the religion of certain other medical sectarians, was caught in the crack: it was still a species of nature religion.

In time, of course, the ambiguousness, even panentheism, of Quimby's theology became less fashionable. New Thoughters cultivated idealism more consistently, as surely as they found ways to transform the material world with Truth. Still, something of Quimby's "vapor" remained consonant with the vapors of medical sectarians and New Thought continued to live, in some measure inconsistently, in the breach.

• • •

It remained for Mary Baker Eddy, former patient and student of Quimby, to achieve the greatest clarity regarding matter and mind, given the inconsistencies of the heritage. As the religion of Christian Science testifies, Eddy pushed the idealist cosmology as far as it would go. But even the founder of Christian Science could not escape totally the allure of nature. Even at the pinnacle of Eddy's authorial career, as she taught that matter was a false belief and the error of "mortal man," the final, authoritative edition of *Science and Health* separated nature from matter and found ways to speak admiringly of the former. "The legitimate and only possible action of Truth is the production of harmony," Eddy wrote, "Laws of nature are laws of Spirit."[7]

However inconclusively, Mary Baker Eddy had shown that the theology of nature could be inverted to coexist with the denial of matter. Idealism did not do away with nature: it simply killed nature's body. Matter had been outlawed, the passing show declared an error, but nature, even in its bodiless state, remained inescapably linked to mind. In sum, from hydropathists to mental healers, nineteenth-century physic and metaphysic showed striking points of connection and overlap. Healing language and ritual suggested considerably more in common than a mutual interest in curing disease.

ENDNOTES

1. James C. Whorton, *Crusaders for Fitness: The History of American Health Reformers* (Princeton, 1982), 38-61; Jane B. Donegan, *"Hydropathic Highway to Health": Women and Water-Cure in Antebellum America,*

Contributions in Medical Studies 17 (Westport, CT, 1986), xi-xx, 3-17, 185-201; George Rosen, *The Structure of American Medical Practice, 1875–1941*, ed. Charles E. Rosenberg (Philadelphia, 1983), 16.

2. See Sig Synnestvedt, ed., *The Essential Swedenborg: Basic Teachings of Emanuel Swedenborg, Scientist, Philosopher, and Theologian* (New York, 1970), and George Trobridge, *Swedenborg: Life and Teaching*, 4th ed. (1935; reprint, New York, 1962). For Swedenborg's conflation of matter and spirit, see the typical instances in Emanuel Swedenborg, *Heaven and Its Wonders and Hell, from Things Heard and Seen*, trans. J. G Ager (1852; reprint, New York, 1964), 6-7; *The True Christian Religion, Containing the Universal Theology of the New Church*, trans. John C. Ager (1853; reprint, New York, 1970), vol. 2:244-46, 100-101.

3. "The Scope and Spirit of Osteopathy," *Journal of Osteopathy* 4 (May 1897): 12; Andrew Taylor Still, "The Chemicals of Life" [Extracts from the autobiography of Andrew Taylor Still], *Journal of Osteopathy* 5 (July 1898): 63. See also Norman Gevitz, *The D.O.'s: Osteopathic Medicine in America* (Baltimore, 1982), 13-14; 156, n. 52.

4. I use the term "New Theology" advisedly, since the medical sectarians were, of course, simply rearticulating elements of the Western occult-metaphysical tradition. See, for example, Daniel P. Walker, *The Ancient Theology: Studies in Christian Platonism from the Fifteenth to the Eighteenth Century* (Ithaca, 1972).

5. Barbara Novak, *Nature and Culture: American Landscape and Painting, 1825–1875* (New York, 1980), 134.

6. Gail Thain Parker, *Mind Cure in New England: From the Civil War to World War I* (Hanover, NH, 1973), 42. The best study of the New Thought movement is still Charles S. Braden, *Spirits in Rebellion: The Rise and Development of New Thought* (Dallas, 1963).

7. Mary Baker Eddy, *Science and Health with Key to the Scriptures* (Boston, 1906), 183.

FOR FURTHER READING

Albanese, Catherine L. *Nature Religion in America: From the Algonkian Indians to the New Age*, Chicago, 1990.

Frankiel, Sandra Sizer. *Spiritual Frontiers: Religious Alternatives in Anglo-Protestantism, 1850–1910*, Berkeley, 1988.

Fuller, Robert C. *Alternative Medicine and American Religious Life*, New York, 1989.

———. *Mesmerism and the American Cure of Souls*, Philadelphia, 1982.

Gottschalk, Stephen. *The Emergence of Christian Science in American Religious Life*, Berkeley, 1973.

Judah, J. Stillson. *The History and Philosophy of the Metaphysical Movements in America*, Philadelphia, 1967.

Meyer, Donald. *The Positive Thinkers: Religion as Popular Psychology from Mary Baker Eddy to Norman Vincent Peale and Ronald Reagan*, Middleton, CT, 1988.

Moore, R. Laurence. *Religious Outsiders and the Making of Americans*, New York, 1986.

Thomas, Robert David. *"With Bleeding Footsteps": Mary Baker Eddy's Path to Religious Leadership*, New York, 1994.

INTRODUCTION TO ESSAY 33

It used to be commonplace in American religious history to say that fundamentalism had lost face and had lost all influence by the late 1920s. Carpenter's essay picks up the story at that critical point and shows in several particulars just where that overgeneralization was wrong. Writing from a perspective that understands commitment to conservative religious tenets as having been vital throughout the century, he gives us a more farsighted definition of fundamentalist theology and explains its survival under the rubric of Evangelical Protestantism.

When earlier observers proclaimed the demise of conservatives, they often referred to their loss of control over religious educational institutions. Carpenter shows that fundamentalists simply left the liberal oriented schools to build their own Bible institutes and liberal arts colleges. When the old study conferences faded, evangelicals responded with renewed emphases on religiously wholesome summer resorts and camp meetings. While left-wing preachers became disinterested in radio sermons, evangelicals have virtually captured radio and television for their own purposes. Missionary outreach to the American public is matched by similar efforts to people around the globe. In these and other areas Carpenter exhibits the resilience and vigor of conservative religious forces. We have seen in other areas that these expanding and consolidating structures could also be steps in the process of moving from outsider to insider, a process that eventuates becoming part of the mainstream itself.

Original source - CH 49 (1980): 62-75.

33

Fundamentalist Institutions and the Rise of Evangelical Protestantism, 1929–1942

Joel Carpenter

In April of 1952 an article in *Christian Life* magazine proclaimed Chicago "the evangelical capital of the U.S.A." To back this claim, editor Russell T. Hitt cited a host of evangelical agencies in greater Chicago: mission boards, denominational offices, colleges, Bible institutes, seminaries, publishing concerns (including *Christian Life* itself) and youth organizations. In total, the author mentioned over one hundred different agencies such as Youth For Christ International, the Slavic Gospel Association, Scripture Press, and the Swedish Covenant Hospital.[1] At first glance, the article appears to present a confusing list of unrelated organizations, but closer inspection reveals a coherent pattern. The agencies in the Chicago area represented the swiftly growing evangelical movement which observers have labelled the third force of American Christianity. Most institutions listed did not belong to the older, more prestigious denominations. The mission boards, such as Wycliffe Bible Translators, the Worldwide Evangelization Crusade, and the International Hebrew Christian Alliance were independents. The denominational headquarters, including those of the Conservative Baptist Association, the Evangelical Mission Covenant Church, the North American Baptist General Conference, and the General Association of Regular Baptist Churches, represented fundamentalists and other evangelicals. The schools—the Moody Bible Institute, North Park College, Trinity Seminary and Bible College, Wheaton College, the Mennonite Biblical Seminary, the Salvation Army Training College, and Emmaus Bible Institute—came from the same source.

Whether or not Chicago was the capital of evangelicalism is not as important as the image the article revealed. Chicago was a regional evangelical stronghold in the 1950s when the evangelicals were leading a revival of popular religious interest. This revival developed largely from the institutional base which evangelicals had established in the previous decades. The fundamentalists were especially prominent in the postwar evangelical revival. This fact might seem surprising to one who supposed that their movement had been crushed twenty years earlier. That was scarcely the case, as we shall see. Fundamentalism was not a defeated party in denominational politics, but a popular religious movement, which in the 1930s developed a separate existence from the older denominations as it strengthened its own institutions. By the 1950s, this building phase had paid off and Billy Graham, a fundamentalist favorite son, became the symbol of evangelicalism's new prominence.

As Hitt's article suggests, evangelicalism was not a monolithic fundamentalism but rather a broad mosaic that comprised clusters of denominations and institutions with different ethnic and doctrinal heritages. One of this mosaic's most visible segments is rightly called fundamentalism, a movement of conservative, millenarian evangelicals who came mostly from Presbyterian, Baptist, and independent denominations, such as the Evangelical Free Church. Other segments include the Holiness Wesleyans, such as the Church of the Nazarene; the pentecostals, including the Assemblies of God; the immigrant confessional churches, such as the Lutheran Church, Missouri Synod, and the Christian Reformed Church; southern-based conservatives, notable the Southern Baptists and the Churches of Christ; peace churches of Anabaptist, Quaker, or pietist backgrounds; and black evangelicals of Methodist, Baptist, Holiness, and pentecostal denominations.[2] As the twentieth century progressed, the evangelicals cut a progressively wider swath through the ranks of the American churches. By 1960 they comprised an estimated half of the nation's sixty million Protestants.

When the term fundamentalist is used to designate any or all of these churches, it becomes an ambiguous and derogatory term. But by precise and historical definition, fundamentalism is a distinct religious movement which arose in the early twentieth century to defend traditional evangelical orthodoxy and to extend its evangelistic thrust. The movement combined a biblicist, generally Calvinist orthodoxy, an evangelistic spirit, an emphasis on the higher Christian (Holy Spirit directed) life, and a millenarian eschatology. Because the urban centers were strongholds of Protestant liberalism and the most challenging home fields for evangelism, they became the principal centers of early fundamentalist activity. The movement drew its name from *The Fundamentals*, a twelve-volume series of articles published by conservative leaders between 1910 and 1915 to affirm and defend those doctrines which they considered essential to the Christian faith, such as the verbal inspiration and infallibility of the Bible and salvation only by faith in the atoning death of Jesus Christ. Fundamentalism was a popular movement, not merely a mentality; it had leaders, institutions, and a particular identity. Fundamentalists recognized one another as party members as it were, and distinguished themselves from the other evangelicals listed above.

As a complex aggregate entity, evangelical Protestantism in the twentieth century demands closer attention than it has received. Studies of the 1930s and early 1940s in particular have yielded little understanding of its development. The prevailing opinion among historians is that Protestantism suffered a depression during at least the first half in the 1930s, which was relieved only when neo-orthodox theology renewed the vision and vitality of the old-line denominations.[3] Evangelical Protestants fit into this scheme only tangentially. The institutional growth in the 1930s of the most vocal and visible evangelicals, the fundamentalists, challenges the widespread notion that popular Protestantism experienced a major decline during that decade. What really transpired was the beginning of a shift of the Protestant mainstream from the older denominations toward the evangelicals.

The older denominations did experience what Robert T. Handy called a "religious depression," beginning in the middle of the 1920s until the late 1930s, when their fortune revived somewhat. But in singular contrast to the plight of the major denominations, fundamentalists and other evangelicals prospered. During the 1920s, fundamentalists had grown more vocal and apparently more numerous, but the leaders had been publicly defeated in denominational battles, and had made themselves look foolish in the anti-evolution crusade. Adverse publicity from public contro- versy had discredited fundamentalists and established the Menckenesque image which had dogged them ever since.[4] Yet these defeats by no means destroyed the movement. Fundamentalism cannot be understood by studying only its role in headline-making conflicts. Rather, we must examine the growing network of institutions upon which fundamentalists increasingly relied as they became alienated from the old-line denominations.

• • •

One of the most important focal points of fundamentalist activ- ity in the thirties was the Bible institute, a relatively new type of institutional structure. The two pioneers of Bible institute educa- tion were A. B. Simpson, founder of the Christian and Missionary Alliance who in 1882 established the Missionary Training Institute in New York City, and Dwight L. Moody, who founded in 1886 what became the Moody Bible Institute of Chicago. The idea of a teaching center for lay Christian workers caught on quickly, and other schools sprang up across the country. By 1930 the funda- mentalist weekly *Sunday School Times* endorsed over fifty Bible schools, most of which were in major cities.

The Bible institutes became the major coordinating agencies of the movement by the 1930s, as popular fundamentalist alienation toward the old-line denominations reached new heights. While the nondenominational Bible institutes had been founded to train lay and paraministerial workers such as Sunday school superinten- dents and foreign missionaries, now they faced demands for edu- cating pastors and for other services that denominations formerly provided. Since the Bible institutes had already branched out into activities not directly connected with in-residence instruction, they were well equipped to meet such demands. Some of the schools had extension departments; many schools ran publishing and/or distributing ventures; as centers of religious enterprise, the Bible institutes soon saw the potential impact of radio broadcasting both as a religious service opportunity and a way to increase their con- stituency. With so many services to provide to fundamentalist indi- viduals and small Bible classes and congregations, the Bible schools became regional and national coordinating centers for the movement.

Fundamentalists who desired a Christian liberal arts education for their children in the 1930s sought it for the most part outside the movement proper. The fundamentalists themselves operated only a few such schools, notably Wheaton College near Chicago and Bob Jones College then located in Cleveland, Tennessee, while Gordon College of Missions and Theology in Boston was developing an arts and sciences division. Advertisements in fundamentalist periodicals show, however, that colleges sponsored by other evangelicals, including Taylor University in Upland, Indiana, and Grove City College in Pennsylvania, attracted students from fundamentalist congregations. These evangelical colleges prospered during the thirties. A survey of evangelical higher education in 1948 found that the total enrollment of seventy such schools in the United States doubled between 1929 and 1940.[5]

As millions of Americans motored each summer to popular resorts, a growing number of summer Bible conferences competed with tourist camps and resort hotels for the patronage of vacationing fundamentalists. From the Boardwalk Bible Conference in Atlantic City, and the Montrose Summer Gatherings in the Pennsylvania hills, at Winona Lake in Indiana, at Redfeather Lakes in the Colorado Rockies, and at Mount Hermon, California, Bible conferences offered a unique vacation: a blend of resort style recreation, the old-fashioned camp meeting, and biblical teaching from leading fundamentalist pulpiteers. The Bible Conference at Winona Lake, Indiana, in 1941 portrays the character of such meetings. Each summer, the whole Winona Lake community became a religious resort with thousands of fundamentalists renting cottages and streaming to the conference grounds. The meetings that capped off the 1941 summer schedule at Winona Lake attracted more than two thousand enrollees, including some four hundred ministers. They were joined by perhaps two thousand more daily visitors. Participants listened to as many as six sermons a day out of the thirteen to fourteen total sessions scheduled between seven in the morning and ten in the evening. Such events were a powerful force for cementing the bonds of commitment within the movement.

In the 1930s the rapidly rising commercial radio industry provided the fundamentalists with a new medium through which to send out their "old gospel" to the rest of the nation. The number of radio sets had doubled between 1930 and 1935 to over eighteen million. By 1938 a *Fortune* survey named radio listening the first preference for leisure time entertainment in America. Fundamentalist preachers quickly took to the airwaves. It became clear by the late thirties that paid programs drew the greater share of popular support. Charles E. Fuller's weekly "Old-Fashioned Revival Hour" became the most popular religious program in the country.[6]

From modest beginnings in 1925, Charles E. Fuller, fundamentalist pastor of Calvary Church in the Los Angeles suburb of Placentia, expanded the work in its early years to include three weekday broadcasts, two Sunday broadcasts from Calvary Church, and a Sunday broadcast over the CBS Pacific Coast network. Fuller left his church for full-time radio ministry in 1933 and soon was heard each Sunday on the Mutual Network. Six years later the "Old-Fashioned Revival Hour" was broadcast weekly coast to coast and overseas to an estimated fifteen to twenty million listeners. Fuller's coverage consisted of 152 stations in 1939 and 456 three years later, the largest single release of any prime time radio broadcast in America.

Of all the activities pursued by both fundamentalists and major Protestant denominations during the 1930s, their foreign missionary work portrayed most starkly their contrasting fortunes. The great missionary enterprise of the Protestant churches had entered the twentieth century with unbounded hope and zeal; but liberal disillusion with evangelism, inflation, and constituents' dislike of liberal programs depleted the denominational mission budgets and stifled enthusiastic young volunteers. Fundamentalists wanted missionaries who preached the old gospel of individual repentance and redemption. They recoiled from the denominational boards because of alleged theological liberalism, social gospel programs, and high overhead costs. But fundamentalist interest in missions did not flag. Fundamentalists supported independent, "faith" missions which were not denominationally connected and did not solicit funds directly. They also founded new denominational agencies. While the Laymen's Foreign Missions Inquiry reported in 1932 that evangelism in missions was passé, the fundamentalist-backed missions grew stronger, better financed, more evangelistically aggressive, and more successful in recruiting volunteers than ever before.

These missions worked in close association with Bible institutes which trained missionaries, housed mission offices, and helped raise funds. From the Moody Bible Institute alone came over 550 new missionaries from 1930 to 1941, while BIOLA housed both the Orinoco River Mission and the United Aborigines Mission offices. Unfortunately, we know little about this wave of missionary recruits from the Bible institutes and evangelical colleges. Likewise, we know next to nothing of the collective impact of the independent boards and those of conservative denominations since 1900. Yet this brief glimpse at activities during the 1930s shows that a movement of great proportions was underway. Evangelical fervor for missions generated by the Student Volunteer Movement had not died but rather had changed its institutional base. As a traditional indicator of religious vitality, missionary activity demonstrated the vigor of fundamentalism no less than the movement's other enterprises.

• • •

In these four areas of fundamentalist activity—education, summer Bible conferences, radio broadcasting, and foreign missions—the evidence shows a growing, dynamic movement. This brief survey demonstrates that the fundamentalist movement did not decline during the thirties. Rather, there was a shift of emphasis within the movement. Fundamentalist efforts to cleanse the denominations of liberal trends had seemed to fail. Rather than persisting along the 1920s lines of conflict, fundamentalists during the 1930s were developing their own institutional base from which to carry on their major purpose: the proclamation of the evangelical gospel.

Was there an "American Religious Depression" among Protestants during the 1930s? Not among fundamentalists and apparently not among other evangelicals either. Did the evangelicals provide the impetus for the post–World War II revivals? The fundamentalist community played a leading role. Billy Graham's crusades and other agents of revivalism such as Youth For Christ were not merely throwbacks to the Billy Sunday era. They were the postwar descendants of a continuing revival tradition preserved and transformed by the fundamentalist movement. For instance, Youth For Christ held its first nationwide convention at the Winona Lake Conference in the summer of 1944. Its first president, Torrey Johnson, was a Wheaton College graduate. Of course, Graham was a Wheaton graduate also. His evangelistic team included George Beverly Shea, a former soloist at WMBI, Moody Bible Institute's radio station, and song leader Cliff Barrows, a Bob Jones College graduate. Revivalism had not died during the depression. Rather, the fundamentalist movement nurtured that tradition, introduced innovations, and produced a new generation of revivalists.

The evidence of sustained growth is compelling; therefore, we need a reassessment of the nature and influence of fundamentalism. The revivalistic, millenarian movement that flourished in the urban centers of North America in the late nineteenth and early twentieth centuries continued under the banner of fundamentalism and left no break in the line of succession from Dwight L. Moody to Billy Graham. Once again, as had happened so many times in the past, part of Christianity had taken the form of a vigorous popular movement. Fundamentalists surged out of the bonds of older denominational structures to create flexible, dynamic institutions, such as independent mission agencies, radio programs, and Bible schools. Despite or perhaps in part because of opposition, the movement grew.

According to anthropologists Luther P. Gerlach and Virginia H. Hine, movements arise to implement changes, to pursue goals that people think the established order is unsuccessful in attaining. Thus, a movement often grows in opposition to the established order from which it came. Because movements are decentralized and based on popular support, they are virtually irrepressible.[7] So it has been with fundamentalism. This widely dispersed network of conservative evangelicals became increasingly at odds with the old-line Protestant establishment. Defeats in the denominational conflicts of the 1920s forced fundamentalists to strengthen their own institutional structures outside of old-line denominations. They responded creatively to the trends in contemporary popular culture and made a lasting place for themselves in American Protestantism. Fundamentalists and other evangelicals prospered. The outlines of a changed Protestant order began to emerge by 1950. However, the task of studying the growth of popular evangelical movements in the context of American cultural history remains. How these movements were involved in the larger process of cultural change has yet to be seen.

ENDNOTES

1. Russell T. Hitt, "Capital of Evangelicalism," *Christian Life* 5 (April 1952): 16-18, 46-48.
2. Hudson, *American Protestantism* (Chicago, 1961), 155-65; Ernest R. Sandeen, *The Roots of Fundamentalism, British and American Millenarianism, 1800–1930* (Chicago, 1970); Klaude Kendrick, *The Promise Fulfilled: A History of the Modern Pentecostal Movement* (Springfield, MO, 1961); James DeForest Murch, *Christians Only: A History of the Restoration Movement* (Cincinnati, 1962); William Wright Barnes, *History of the Southern Baptist Convention, 1845–1953* (Nashville, 1954); Milton L. Rudnick, *Fundamentalism and the Missouri Synod* (St. Louis, 1966); John Henry Kromminga, *The Christian Reformed Church: A Study in Orthodoxy* (Grand Rapids, 1949); Cornelius J. Dyck, ed., *An Introduction to Mennonite History* (Scottdale, PA, 1967).
3. Martin E. Marty, *Righteous Empire: The Protestant Experience in America* (New York, 1970), 233-43; Robert T. Handy, *A Christian America, Protestant Hopes and Historical Realities* (New York, 1971), 217-19; Paul A. Carter, *The Decline and Revival of the Social Gospel* (Ithaca, NY, 1954).
4. Norman F. Furniss, *The Fundamentalist Controversy, 1918–1931* (New Haven, 1954), 103-76; Stewart G. Cole, *The History of Fundamentalism* (New York, 1931), 250-64.
5. Harry J. Albus, "Christian Education Today," *Christian Life* 1 (September 1948): 26, 46; quoted in Louis Gasper, *The Fundamentalist Movement* (Hague, 1963), 104.
6. Daniel P. Fuller, *Give the Winds a Mighty Voice: The Story of Charles E. Fuller* (Waco, TX, 1972), 113-22, 140.
7. Luther P. Gerlach and Virginia H. Hine, *People, Power, Change: Movements of Social Transformation* (Indianapolis, 1970), xvi-xix.

FOR FURTHER READING

Brereton, Virginia Lieson. *Training God's Army: The American Bible School, 1880–1940*, Bloomington, IN, 1990.

Carpenter, Joel A. *Revive Us Again: The Reawakening of American Fundamentalism*, New York, 1997.

Dayton, Donald W., and Robert K. Johnston, eds. *The Variety of American Evangelicalism*, Knoxville, 1991.

Dollar, George W. *A History of Fundamentalism in America*, Greenville, SC, 1973.

Hart, D. G. *Defending the Faith: J. Gresham Machen and the Crisis of Conservative Protestantism in Modern America*, Baltimore, 1994.

Longfield, Bradley J. *The Presbyterian Controversy: Fundamentalists, Modernists, and Moderates*, New York, 1991.

Marsden, George M. *Fundamentalism and American Culture: The Shaping of Twentieth-Century Evangelicalism, 1870–1925*, New York, 1980.

———. *Reforming Fundamentalism: Fuller Seminary and the New Evangelicalism*, Grand Rapids, MI, 1987.

Moore, R. Laurence. *Religious Outsiders and the Making of Americans*, New York, 1986.

Russell, C. Allyn. *Voices of Fundamentalism: Seven Biographical Studies*, Philadelphia, 1976.

Sweet, Leonard I. *The Evangelical Tradition in America*, Macon, GA, 1984.

Weber, Timothy P. *Living in the Shadow of the Second Coming: American Premillennialism, 1875–1982*, rev. ed., Chicago, 1987.

INDEX